PROMOTING SOCIAL JUSTICE
THROUGH THE SCHOLARSHIP OF
TEACHING AND LEARNING

SCHOLARSHIP OF TEACHING AND LEARNING

Jennifer Meta Robinson,
Whitney M. Schlegel, and
Mary Taylor Huber, *editors*

PROMOTING SOCIAL JUSTICE THROUGH THE SCHOLARSHIP OF TEACHING AND LEARNING

Edited by Delores D. Liston and Regina Rahimi

Indiana University Press

This book is a publication of

Indiana University Press
Office of Scholarly Publishing
Herman B Wells Library 350
1320 East 10th Street
Bloomington, Indiana 47405 USA

iupress.indiana.edu

© 2017 by Indiana University Press

All rights reserved

No part of this book may be reproduced or utilized in any form or by any means, electronic or mechanical, including photocopying and recording, or by any information storage and retrieval system, without permission in writing from the publisher. The Association of American University Presses' Resolution on Permissions constitutes the only exception to this prohibition.

The paper used in this publication meets the minimum requirements of the American National Standard for Information Sciences—Permanence of Paper for Printed Library Materials, ANSI Z39.48-1992.

Manufactured in the United States of America

Library of Congress Cataloging-in-Publication Data

Names: Liston, Delores D., editor. | Rahimi, Regina, [date] editor.
Title: Promoting social justice through the scholarship of teaching and learning / edited by Delores D. Liston and Regina Rahimi.
Description: Bloomington, Indiana : Indiana University Press, 2017. | Series: Scholarship of teaching and learning | Includes bibliographical references and index. | Description based on print version record and CIP data provided by publisher; resource not viewed.
Identifiers: LCCN 2017027026 (print) | LCCN 2017001602 (ebook) | ISBN 9780253031327 (eb) | ISBN 9780253031310 (cl : alk. paper) | ISBN 9780253029645 (pb : alk. paper)
Subjects: LCSH: Social justice—Study and teaching. | Transformative learning.
Classification: LCC LC192.2 (print) | LCC LC192.2 .P76 2017 (ebook) | DDC 370.11/5—dc23
LC record available at https://lccn.loc.gov/2017027026

1 2 3 4 5 22 21 20 19 18 17

We would like to dedicate the volume to the memory of our colleague and friend, Lorraine Sophia Gilpin (1971–2014).

Also, Dr. Liston would like to acknowledge the support of Georgia Southern University and the College of Education for educational leave that was granted to her in the spring of 2015 to work on this edited volume and prepare the prospectus we submitted to Indiana University Press.

Contents

Introduction: Unlocking SoTL's Potential for
Transformative Education
Delores D. Liston and Regina Rahimi — xi

I. Examining Ethics toward Social Justice

1. Ethics and Social Justice: A Review of Theoretical Frameworks and Pedagogical Considerations
   Tiffany Chenneville — 3

2. Teaching the Ethics of Caring: Using Nursing History to Integrate Race Consciousness into Professional Values
   Melissa Garno and Carole Bennett — 15

II. Focusing on Marginalized Groups in SoTL

3. The Scholarship of Teaching and Learning and the Status of Women
   Maxine P. Atkinson and Scott T. Grether — 35

4. Teachers of Minorities as Agents of Change: A Global Model
   MaryJo Benton Lee and Diane Kayongo-Male — 50

III. Community Service, Activism, and Civic Consciousness

5. Learning as We Go: Risk Taking and Relationship Building through Service Learning in Belize
   Mary R. Moeller, Lonell Moeller, and Susan L. Filler — 77

6. Champions for Health in the Community: Critical Service Learning, Transformative Education, and Community Empowerment
   Karen Meaney, Jo An M. Zimmermann, Yongmei Lu, Gloria Martinez-Ramos, and Jacquelyn McDonald — 98

Contents

7   Teacher Candidates' Dispositions for Civic Engagement and Social Responsibility: Discernment and Action
    Patricia Calderwood, Stephanie Burrell Storms, Thomas Grund, Nicole Battaglia, and Emma Sheeran 117

8   Transforming Student Ideas about Community Using Asset-Based Community Development Techniques
    Lisa Garoutte 143

9   Transforming Awareness into Activism: Teaching Systems and Social Justice in an Interdisciplinary Water Course
    Cathy Willermet, Anja Mueller, and David Alm 162

IV. Classroom Practices of Reflection and Counternarratives

10 Swinging with a Double-Edged Sword: Using Counterstories to Fight for Social Justice in the Classroom
    Scott D. Farver and Alyssa Hadley Dunn 177

11 When Walking the Walk Changes the Talk: Using Critical Reflection to Inform Practices of Social Justice Research and Social Justice
    Sabrina Ross and Alma Stevenson 189

12 Consciousness Raising for Twenty-First-Century Faculty: Using Lessons from Diversity Flashpoints
    Alejandro Leguizamo and Jennifer Campbell 209

13 "The Way I View the World Has Changed": Student and Teacher Reflections on Transformative Social Justice Education
    Annemarie Vaccaro, Athina Chartelain, Sarah D. Croft, Brooke D'Aloisio, Tiffany Hoyt, and Brian Stevens 228

14 Using Attitude Measures and Student Narratives about Diversity to Enhance Multicultural Teaching Effectiveness
    Robert Lake and Kent Rittschof 241

15 Building Student Self-Awareness of Learning to Enhance Diversity in the Sciences
    Erin Peters-Burton and Giuseppina Kysar Mattietti 270

V. Applied Classroom Practices and Social Justice

16 Reimagining the Student Evaluation: Using Democratic Frameworks in College Teaching and Learning
   Phillis George *297*

17 Minding the Brain: Three Dimensions of Cognition in Social Justice Curriculum
   Dan Glisczinski *309*

18 Using Applied Learning to Engage with Social Justice: Lessons Learned from an Online Graduate Course in Social Justice
   James M. DeVita *318*

SoTL: Next Steps toward Social Justice
Delores D. Liston and Regina Rahimi *328*

Index *333*

Introduction: Unlocking SoTL's Potential for Transformative Education

Delores D. Liston and Regina Rahimi

The Scholarship of Teaching and Learning (SoTL) represents a movement in higher education to revolutionize scholarship in relationship to teaching.

Many scholars enter academia because they want to conduct cutting-edge research in their fields. So they become experts in their particular fields, and then, once they've obtained the coveted terminal degree and landed a tenure-track position at a college or university, they discover that in addition to researching and writing about their area of expertise, they must teach undergraduate or graduate students or both. For these faculty members, research is primary and teaching is secondary. Teaching is often viewed as a hindrance to their *real* work as scholars, which involves presenting and publishing their research findings.

For others, obtaining the terminal degree is a means to the ends of entering a teaching profession at the collegiate level. Members of this group might have started as K-12 teachers, but their goal is to teach in higher education (generally for less pay than they earned in public schools, but that is a story for another day). For these faculty members, teaching is primary and research is secondary. Researching becomes a task they *must* do in order to remain in their teaching post at the college or university.

At this point, I'm sure there are some readers wondering about the "third leg" of the academic stool: service. For most college and university faculty, the service component (service to the profession and service to the institution) remains tertiary. Although I'm sure there are *some* who enter the realm of college teaching in order to serve on various institutional, departmental, and even professional committees, this cadre is fewer in number. Further, this cadre also moves quickly into administrative positions within the university, places where teaching *and* scholarship become secondary to the business of managing the institution. Therefore, for the most part, the service component of academic life is outside the scope of this volume. Activities of teaching and learning, on the other hand, are central to the discourse of this text and form the basis of SoTL.

Whether teaching or research is primary for an individual faculty member, a tension between these two aspects of being a college professor undoubtedly exists. For the former group, teaching is an activity that pulls the researcher away from the primary task at hand and interrupts the flow of the research and scholarship process. For the latter group, researching and scholarship are drudgery, activities that must be completed to justify their continuation in the academy.

SoTL has emerged as a vehicle with the potential to resolve, or perhaps better stated *dissolve*, the tension between research and teaching that has plagued academia. Seemingly simple, the idea behind SoTL is that teaching *is* a scholarly activity (Boyer, 1990; Menges & Weimer, 1996). Therefore, scholars ought to recognize that their teaching and their research need not be at odds with one another, but rather scholarship should support teaching and teaching should support scholarship.

The Scholarship of Teaching and Learning has great potential as a vehicle to elevate the work of teaching, improve classroom engagement practices, and enable us to learn more about pedagogy, classroom management, and most importantly our students. This opportunity to explore our personal interactions with our students, the sociology behind teaching, and the diverse perspectives explored through a teaching and learning relationship is perhaps the most powerful promise of SoTL. Examination of social justice and opportunity for equity in the work of SoTL is what the contributions of this text hope to provide.

What Is SoTL?

As noted earlier, SoTL is a movement within higher education that seeks to revolutionize scholarship in relation to teaching. As Gilpin and Liston (2009) noted in an earlier publication,

> SoTL seeks a transformation in the academy through its threefold agenda: 1) recognizing teaching as inquiry relevant to research; 2) recognizing the act of teaching as a public rather than private endeavor, and thus related to the formation of community or commons; and 3) recognizing teaching as a scholarly endeavor, and thus subject to peer review and evaluation (McKinney, 2007; Huber & Hutchings, 2005; Huber & Morreale, 2002; Shulman, 2002; Bender & Gray, 1999; and Bass, 1999). We see this transformative aspect of SoTL as potentially manifesting in two significant ways: 1) turning teaching into scholarship to be used for tenure and promotion in order to increase the emphasis and importance of pedagogy throughout the university community; and 2) establishing commons whereby learning communities grow in their understanding of one another and our roles in society in order to

transform those roles. Of these two, our focus in this research specifically addressed the second of these manifestations of transformation. Indeed, we believe that the expression of threefold agenda of SoTL as manifested through establishment of the commons holds potential to go beyond technical machinations of our pedagogical practices. We believe that the commons can move us into a reconceptualization of teaching and learning as a shared endeavor that transforms not only teaching and learning but our relationship of one to another and of ourselves to our world. (p. 2)

The implications of SoTL's agenda for dissolving the tension between research and teaching are clear. Teaching and learning become part and parcel of research and scholarship. Conventional lines between when one is teaching and when one is conducting research are erased; teaching is research and research is teaching. Additionally, reconceptualizing teaching in this way, as a scholarly activity, heightens awareness that teaching is public and open to peer review and evaluation. Further, in community, distinctions between when one is a learner and when one is a teacher are also blurred. Not only does teaching become a feature of academic life worthy of scrutiny as an aspect of one's research agenda, but one's research agenda also shifts to ensure timely relevance and accountability to the *community of learners* (Huber & Morreale, 2002; Gilpin & Liston, 2009).

In this way, SoTL reminds us, we are *always already* (Heidegger, 1926, 1962) learners, teachers, and researchers. SoTL's existence brings this truth to the forefront and insists that we remain ever cognizant that embodying this triad of learner, teacher, and researcher constitutes the heart of being a scholar. Further, recognizing the diverse positionality that each brings to the teaching-researching-learning praxis is at the heart of the potential for a transformative experience and efforts toward social justice.

Guiding Question

Simply put, the guiding question for this edited volume is "How can SoTL be used to make education a transformative experience for *all* learners and teachers?" As noted above, SoTL directs a change in the conceptualization of teaching, learning, and scholarship to better match an integrated understanding of scholarship in a community of learners. But, as stated by Gilpin and Liston (2009), "Will the transformation of the academy promised by SoTL shift priorities from research in the disciplines to research in pedagogy? Or will SoTL pursue more in-depth transformation of the conception of teaching and learning?" (p. 1).

Our hope and desire was that SoTL offer more than a mere shift from discipline-based research to pedagogical-based research, which means the learner, teacher, and scholar are always fully considered. We hoped that SoTL could offer a strong platform from which to use the transformation authorized through SoTL to promote a more socially just society. In our view, descriptions of the essence of SoTL align with this agenda. Braiding together the value base and essential characteristics of SoTL, critical pedagogy, and transformational or transgressive education (hooks, 1994) provides a path to more in-depth transformation of teaching and learning.

Therefore, the purpose of this introduction is to explore the foundations of SoTL in order to excavate its potential to support transformative education and critical pedagogy, forwarding a social justice agenda through SoTL. The conceptualization of the commons (supportive communities of teacher-learner-researchers), and reconceptualization of the classroom as a space for scholarly praxis, establishes moral and pedagogical imperatives for SoTL to participate in the promotion of social justice (Huber & Hutchings, 2005; Hutchings, 2002; Shulman, 2002; and Huber & Morreale, 2002). Thus, clearly, SoTL promotes concepts of social justice, inclusion of diverse perspectives, and critical dimensions of pedagogy. For this reason, SoTL may be (or become) a vehicle for "transformative education" (hooks, 1994), forwarding social justice. This edited volume provides examples of SoTL scholarship built on this foundation. Each chapter of this edited volume contributes to a richer picture of the potential of SOTL as transformative education.

Through exploration of the unique perspective offered through development of pedagogical innovations supported through the commons, this edited volume seeks to unlock SoTL's potential for transformative education (Gilpin & Liston, 2009). This introduction will establish the context through which the ensuing chapters address the question "How can SoTL be used to make education a transformative experience for *all* learners and teachers?" To establish this context, we will explicate the characteristics and value base common to SoTL, transformative education, and critical pedagogy, focusing on the ways in which these three threads can be braided together to support social justice through the commons, supporting learning and teaching and resulting in scholarship that supports and furthers equality, before providing a brief description of the subsequent chapters.

Value Base and Essential Characteristics of SoTL

The primary impetus of SoTL is to give us pause regarding the relationship between teaching and learning and scholarship. That is, SoTL makes us think again or reconsider (Boyer, 1990) our intentions and outcomes relevant to teaching and learning and scholarship. This rethinking is meant to reignite our love of learning as scholars share their passion about their areas of expertise with novices and apprentices.

Second, SoTL seeks to combine teaching and learning with scholarship, resulting in publications. In turn, these publications make our endeavor public, promote discussion, and elevate the discourse on pedagogy. As Huber and Hutchings (2005) have written, SoTL contributes to "viewing the work of the classroom as the site for inquiry, asking and answering questions about student learning in ways that can improve one's classroom and also advance the larger profession of teaching" (p. 1). This is certainly true when this work enters the public domain of scholarship and publication. Such attention to the scholarly work of publication and presentation enlivens the teaching and learning experience and provides evidence of the effectiveness and significance of teaching and learning. This results in a win-win for faculty and for teaching and learning as a whole. The win for faculty is peer-reviewed publications, the gold standard by which scholars are judged. The win for teaching and learning is the promotion of better teaching through the attention these publications draw to pedagogy and the long-term outcomes of teaching and learning.

A third and closely related purpose of SoTL is the improvement of pedagogy. As noted earlier, many scholars enter the professoriate with the aim of generating cutting-edge research, and teaching is an afterthought with which they are confronted after entering the field. Others may enter the field wanting to teach but lacking knowledge of the methods and foundations of good teaching. SoTL helps raise awareness of the methods and foundations of good teaching across disciplines. Generating discussion across the academy of the importance of teaching has therefore been a primary purpose of SoTL (Hutchings, 2002). Indeed, over the past twenty years, many colleges and universities have opened (or transformed) centers to support faculty development in teaching and learning. Previously, these centers were aimed at remediation of faculty deficits and therefore were often expressly avoided by most faculty. But the transformation generated through SoTL has changed these centers into enlivening spaces where faculty share ideas, concerns, and enthusiasm for teaching and learning as scholarship on their campuses and in their respective fields. This transformation has resulted in improving how we teach as well as how (and sometimes how often) we publish.

Finally, the spirit of SoTL is best captured through the concept of the learning commons—a community of learners producing knowledge together. "The commons" is a conceptual space for the exchange of ideas (Huber & Hutchings, 2005). As we pause to reconsider the intentions and outcomes of our teaching and learning practices, we rediscover the communal dimension of teaching and learning. Our love of learning is not only an individualized experience but also something shared with others. This sharing may take place through a community of scholars—through peer-reviewed publications—or through faculty development seminars, presentations at conferences, or even informal groups of faculty who gather to share insights about their teaching and learning. This activity, at the heart of transformative practice, requires a level of engagement with "others." It requires that we examine the learner, the teacher, and the researcher, perhaps in ways we have not done before in higher education. As we search for exemplary practices and innovative pedagogies within the academy, we also necessarily must account for the experiences of members of the community of learners. Every learner must be counted while teachers strive for the improvement of learning. Conversations of diversity, differentiation, experience, epistemology, approaches to learning, and modalities of teaching and learning have to be explored. It is through this exploration that social justice and equality can emerge.

The discerning reader will no doubt have picked up on the interwoven relationships between each of these purposes of SoTL. This weaving together of purposes creates a very strong thread, characterizing SoTL as supportive of "good teaching" through publishing and sharing knowledge, which in turn ignites and reignites our passion for the teaching and learning scholarship continuum. This keeps us ever mindful that teaching and scholarship do not have to be opposing forces vying for our limited time and attention. Rather, teaching and scholarship are recognized through SoTL as a mutually supporting dynamic continually renewing those passions that brought us into our respective academic disciplines in the first place.

Thus the concept of the commons cuts across the previously noted purposes of SoTL and paves the path we (the authors of this edited volume and others who contribute chapters or otherwise join us on this journey) take toward a social justice agenda through the Scholarship of Teaching and Learning. Just as SoTL in general redirects our attention toward integration of scholarship and teaching, the commons redirects our passions toward the deeper meaning and purpose of scholarship and teaching: they can help us live better lives. We learn to value how we, and others, view the world and construct meaning. We can challenge our own notions of teaching and learning to develop more reciprocity within our relationships in this process.

Several aspects of the commons explicitly and implicitly support moves toward social justice. Although many of these aspects are difficult to discuss individually, they all warrant being clearly identified. Engaging in community requires accountability, such as peer review and public evaluation. Our work must hold up to the scrutiny of others in our community. This accountability also comes with responsibility, including being responsive to the needs of others as well as relevant and timely to the context. These contexts are simultaneously local and global or international. SoTL scholar Lee Shulman (2002) notes that engagement in scholarly teaching supports "moral action aimed at cultural change" (p. vii). Engaging in the commons also brings to the forefront our commonality as we seek similar means and ends in a community of like-minded others. Raising this specter also highlights the opposing and equally powerful dynamic of diversity. We need more than interactions solely with those who look like us, think like us, and agree with us. To remain vibrant, a commons, a community of scholars, also needs fresh ideas, diverse perspectives, various theoretical frameworks, and even *arguments*. And last, engagement in the commons highlights the idea that commitment in SoTL carries moral and pedagogical imperatives. As Shulman (2002) states, we have an "obligation to inquire into the consequences of one's work with students" (p. vii). In this way, the concept of the commons paves the pathway for SoTL's social justice agenda.

Value Base and Essential Characteristics of Critical Pedagogy: Theoretical Foundations for Social Justice

Until now, we have avoided defining what we mean by "social justice." We have skirted over differences of opinion and conflict as well as the grim reality that justice for one may be injustice for another. Although these differences of perspective are important—indeed, they are key to establishing social justice—they can become a distraction to the pursuit of social justice. That is, although one must know what constitutes social justice in order to realize it, if one gets bogged down in the theoretical morass trying to determine how to meet *all* the needs of *all* the people *all* the time, or hierarchizing (Lorde, 1984) whose issues are more important, making the changes needed to bring about greater social justice can get lost.

We are not saying that theory is unimportant or that philosophizing about social justice is a waste of time. In fact, we believe quite the opposite. Theory and philosophy are fundamental. Proceeding without a theoretical base leaves one open to meandering aimlessly and ultimately accomplishing little to nothing.

This text, however, is not about establishing exacting criteria regarding what constitutes social justice. Rather, this text is about how SoTL, while enlivening passions of teaching, learning, and scholarship, may also enliven passions about advancing social justice. In this pursuit, providing a narrow definition that limits this passion to only perspectives that advance economic, racial, or gender equalities (or even all of the above) places an unwarranted damper on this passion. Therefore, this edited volume seeks to make space for exploring the broadest avenue upon which SoTL may advance social justice.

In constructing this avenue, we have somewhat arbitrarily created two subheadings for establishing foundations of social justice: The first we have labeled "critical pedagogy" and aligned with the theoretical foundations for social justice. The second we have labeled "transformative education" and aligned with perspectives that highlight theory-informed practice, also termed "praxis." We have deliberately used the term "pedagogy" for our theoretical base because this term highlights our conviction that theory is imminently practical, and practice without theory is malpractice.

Now that we have established that separating theory from practice is more for the purpose of explanation than a reflection of real differences, we may proceed to discuss the value base for critical pedagogy.

We are using "critical pedagogy" as an umbrella term to encompass a variety of theoretical perspectives that encourage learners (both students and teachers are learners in the context of SoTL) to think critically. These include perspectives such as multiculturalism (Banks & McGee Banks, 2013), postmodernism (Peters, 2010), deconstructionism (Biesta, 2010), constructivism (Jones & Brader-Araje, 2002), critical theory (Apple, 2001), feminism (Mayo & Stengel, 2010), black feminist thought (Collins, 1990), critical race theory (Lynn & Dixson, 2013), and critical race feminism (Wing, 2003). These are only a few of the major perspectives that establish the general parameters of what is meant by "critical."

These perspectives differ vastly in philosophical and theoretical underpinnings. Some postulate truth as discoverable, or at least socially constructed from empirical evidence (e.g., constructionism), while others deconstruct conceptions of truth and are vehemently opposed to any and all "master narratives" (e.g., postmodernism and deconstructionism). Still others hold positions somewhere in between, postulating that social locations (positions of privilege and oppression in society, feminisms, and critical race theories) yield differing understandings of truth. These views maintain that with oppression comes an epistemic privilege that yields a more complete picture on which we can base our actions (Moya & Hames-Garcia, 2000; Harding, 2004).

Acknowledging that these perspectives conflict with one another, our purpose in this volume is to explore points of relative agreement in order to pave that broad avenue mentioned earlier. In spite of their differences, all of these theoretical perspectives share significant insights that are relevant to advancing social justice.

First, they all concur that we do not already live in a world that is socially just. Rather, there is injustice in the world, and we need to change this. All critical pedagogy perspectives agree there *is* oppression, inequity, and injustice. There is a power imbalance by which some are oppressed. The results of this oppression privilege some over others. Thus, *all* critical pedagogy perspectives seek to raise awareness and generate conversations about imbalances of power and how to take action to generate social justice and equity. This is the primary component linking these various perspectives under the umbrella of critical pedagogy.

A second and related link between critical pedagogy perspectives is that investigations of power are central to improving the well-being of those who are oppressed. Questions such as "Who benefits?" "Who are the oppressed?" "Who is privileged?" and "How is power obtained, maintained, and wielded?" are all fundamental to this aspect of critical theory.

Another significant component of critical theory is an investigation into what is meant by "who" in the above questions. For example, during the 1960s, black women were active in two simultaneous civil rights movements—one of which addressed their race—but the "who" of oppression was characterized as male. The other movement addressed their sex, but the "who" of oppression was characterized as white. Ultimately, these women found that neither movement accurately addressed them as the "who" in oppression. Through black feminist thought and similar theoretical perspectives, the intersections between race and gender (and eventually other aspects of one's being) became highlighted, adding concepts such as intersectionality (Collins, 1990) and essentializing (Spelman, 1988) to the vernacular of critical pedagogy.

As the perspectives of critical theory have matured, it has become commonplace to recognize diversity as one of its complex and multifaceted components. Further, concepts of commonality and similarity, essential qualities defining who "belongs" in which category and why, have all come under closer scrutiny and interrogation.

Nonetheless, and we would argue because of this interrogation, the critical pedagogies underneath this umbrella supporting social justice press on toward enacting the moral imperatives Shulman (2002) identifies as necessary for SoTL to create a better, more equitable and socially just world.

Thus, although differing in epistemology, and sometimes even ethics, we maintain that these varied theoretical perspectives all share lanes on the avenue toward enhancing social justice. In sum, critical pedagogies, as we have delineated the category here, all share the following beliefs: (a) there is injustice in the world; (b) some are oppressed and others are privileged; (c) investigations of power are central to change; (c) tensions of diversity and commonality are multifaceted; (d) we must avoid essentializing and move toward intersectionality; and (e) the way forward requires engaging in these challenging and conflict-laden conversations.

Value Base and Essential Characteristics of Transformative Education: Praxis

Having explored the assumptions of the theoretical perspectives related to critical pedagogy, we move now to the ways these theories have been put into praxis (Freire, 1970/2006), theory-informed practice.

Transformative education, also called "transgressive education" by bell hooks (1994), uses critical pedagogy to engage students in "the practice of freedom" (p. 13). Alternatively, Parker Palmer (2004) advocates for social justice through a focus on democracy, renewal, and wholeness. Rather than viewing teaching as merely instilling (or as my undergraduates perhaps more accurately misspell, "installing") curriculum into the minds of students, hooks (1994) encourages us to recognize teaching as a "sacred calling" (p. 13) and "pedagogy of hope" (2003). Similarly, Freire (1970/2006) describes traditional conceptions of teaching as a "banking method" whereby ideas are "deposited" into students for later "withdrawal" in a test and opposes it to his preferred method of teaching, which he terms "a pedagogy of the oppressed" (1970/2006) or a "pedagogy of freedom" (1998). Whichever nomenclature is employed, transformative education seeks to ignite a passion for learning connected to changing the world for the betterment of humanity.

As Freire's text makes abundantly clear, "the oppressed" (1970/2006) know their own social locations intimately and, when given tools of expression, can and will enact their own salvation and path to freedom and justice. This thread of thought links clearly to the concept of epistemic privilege (Harding, 2004; Moya & Hames-Garcia, 2000) mentioned earlier. The role of the teacher is not to deposit bits and bytes of knowledge into students. Rather, teachers must recognize their role as one of mentor, and even peer, on the journey toward greater justice in society.

On this journey and toward this end, theories of praxis have generated a broad lexicon of terms to help draw the map. Among these are terms such as "culturally relevant pedagogy" (Ladson-Billings, 1995), "culturally responsive pedagogy" (Gay, 2000), "conscientization" (Freire, 1970/2006), "transgressive pedagogy" (hooks, 1994), "revolutionizing pedagogy" (McLaren, Macrine, & Hill, 2010), "curriculum for renewal and wholeness" (Palmer, 2004), and "critical pedagogy" (Darder, Baltodano, & Torres, 2009).

Hooks's term, "transgressive pedagogy" (1994), emphasizes the critical and often conflicting dynamic of seeking social justice and freedom. While the term "transformative" emphasizes "feel-good" aspects of change, "transgressive pedagogy" reminds us that rectifying the imbalance of power is often met with resistance.

The terms "culturally relevant pedagogy" (Ladson-Billings, 1995) and "culturally responsive pedagogy" (Gay, 2000) emphasize two other paths toward more inclusive pedagogy and curriculum. The primary focus of culturally relevant pedagogy (Ladson-Billings, 1995) is to ensure that what is being taught, and how it is being taught, are in sync with the people who are being taught. The primary focus of culturally responsive pedagogy (Gay, 2000) is enhancing awareness of who is being taught in order to be more sensitive and responsive to the culture of the learners. Much of the educational preparation of K-12 teachers focuses on the context of student learning: the experiences, differences/diversity, abilities, interests, and assets that students bring to a classroom. Classroom teachers are very immersed in course work and research that highlights differentiating classrooms and addressing the needs of students. The focus on student-centric classroom experiences has not been readily embraced by academe. However, through the commons and SoTL, conversations logically emerge that place learning as central to the classroom experience and thus the recognition that learning is both personal and specific as well as public and global. The teacher and the learner bring their perspectives and experience to the learning process.

Thus, the value base of transformative education is focused on empowerment and recognition that the oppressed have epistemic privilege (Moya & Hames-Garcia, 2000; Harding, 2004), a greater understanding of their social location and needs than those who are privileged. Further, engaging students in "changing the world" is not just about engaging them while we are doing something else. Praxis draws attention to the fact that learners and teachers are peers on the journey toward greater social justice.

Shared Values and Essential Characteristics of SoTL and Transformative Learning

At this point, the intersections we perceive between SoTL and transformative learning are clear. First, both SoTL and transformative education recognize that there is no line dividing learning from teaching. Teachers ought to be learning, and likewise learners ought to be teaching. Both are scholars en route to greater understanding of the world. Learners are not to be acted on but are the critical and active element to the work of teaching and learning.

Second, both SoTL and transformative education agree that teaching and learning is a public enterprise and not a private venture of individual gain. Indeed, critical pedagogy goes one step further in clearly claiming that education is also political in nature. That political nature requires examination of social injustice.

Also, this greater understanding gained through exploration of teachers and learners as peers has consequences. Shulman (2002) states, SoTL brings our attention to the "consequences of one's work with students" and is linked to "moral action aimed at cultural change" (p. vii). Thus, the goal of learning goes beyond accumulation of knowledge to forwarding cultural change advancing social justice. Therefore, the development of critical consciousness is fundamental.

For SoTL, the commons is the primary vehicle for learning. As noted earlier, the concept of the commons emphasizes key terms relative to the progression of social justice, critical pedagogy, and transformative education. Concepts of commonality and diversity; accountability and responsibility; arguments, conflict, and "transgression"; and commitment are all expressly part of SoTL. Meanwhile, related concepts, such as intersectionality, cultural sensitivity, and cultural responsiveness, are implicit in learning to work together in establishing and maintaining the commons. Therefore, we maintain that coupling SoTL with critical pedagogy and transformative education is compatible to forwarding a social justice agenda.

SoTL and Transformative Education: A Review of the Literature

Having established the compatibility of SOTL with forwarding a social justice agenda, the next question is "To what extent has a social justice agenda been forwarded through SoTL?" To address this question, two literature reviews have been conducted. The results of the first literature review were published in the *International Journal of the Scholarship of Teaching and Learning (IJSoTL)* (Gilpin & Liston, 2009). The second was completed in preparation for this edited volume.

The initial literature review investigated 252 journal articles (from the *International Journal of the Scholarship of Teaching and Learning*, the *Journal of the Scholarship of Teaching and Learning [JoSoTL]*, and *MountainRise*), 8 books, and 63 conference presentations (Liston & Gilpin, 2009). Our findings supported SoTL's claim to be an international movement addressing the integration of scholarship, teaching, and learning across a wide range of disciplines, ranging from the hard sciences to the humanities to education and to health-related disciplines. The books we reviewed were useful for establishing the parameters of the SoTL movement and the expectations set forth for this undertaking in higher education. The conference presentations were used to provide a more "up-to-the-minute" glimpse of the contemporary discourse, possibly providing a glimpse of future publications. And the journal articles provided the data on which our conclusions were grounded. Of the 252 articles we reviewed, 34 were identified as contributing toward a transformative view of education through SoTL. These are discussed in detail in the *IJSoTL* article.

The more recent review of literature investigated 431 journal articles from two major SoTL outlets: *IJSoTL* and *JoSoTL* (*MountainRise* is now out of print). The first, and most obvious, finding is that the sheer volume of articles has significantly increased. In a seven-year period (the first review covered ten years) nearly twice as many articles have been published in these two SoTL journals. However, the number of articles specifically addressing SoTL as transformative education has not increased at the same rate. Only thirty-two articles were identified as addressing SoTL as transformative education over this seven-year period.

Service learning and interdisciplinary projects stood out as most likely to lend themselves to a transformative educational agenda highlighting social justice. For example, "Water as life, death and power: Building an integrated interdisciplinary course combining perspectives from anthropology, biology and chemistry" by Willermet, Mueller, Juris, Drake, Upadhaya, and Chhetri (2013) encourages social activism through involvement of faculty and students in exploration of the timely issues raised by water scarcity, both locally and globally. Throughout this course, students were encouraged to develop "real-world solutions," which they presented at a "student research showcase" (p. 106).

Transformative education was present in articles from a diverse range of disciplines, including law (Miretsky, 2013), climate change (McCright, 2012), neuroscience (Glisczinski, 2011), counseling (Johnson & Lambie, 2012), and psychology (Chenneville, Toler, & Gaskin-Butler, 2012) as well as education (White & Nitkin, 2014). Because teaching and learning is so closely connected with the field of education, several subfields within education were distinguishable as supporting a social justice agenda. These varied from faculty development initiatives (Considine, 2014) to English as a second language (Teemant, 2010) to physical education (Meaney, Housman, Cavazos, & Wilcox, 2012), music education (Levy & Byrd, 2011), and higher education focusing on graduate (Oh & Nussli, 2014) and undergraduate (Lake & Rittschof, 2012) students.

Other shifts in the discourse were noted in the course of completing this two-phased literature review. Most obvious is the fact that fewer articles in the second phase of the literature review justify or legitimize SoTL as worthy of the designation "scholarship," since that now seems to be a given within the discourse. Further, more articles press further into explorations of pedagogy and the influences of technology on classroom practice. The wide breadth of disciplinary representation is evident in both literature reviews, as is the international scope of the movement. The majority of publications address SoTL in the United States, but the United Kingdom and Canada are close behind. Other articles address learning and teaching in Asia, the South Pacific, and Latin America.

This review of literature supports the need for this edited volume to solidify the place of social justice in SoTL literature. Clearly, several articles highlighting social justice have been published in these outlets, but the quantity of articles has, so far, remained limited. An edited volume explicating the importance of transformative education and social justice to the international and interdisciplinary field of SoTL, and demonstrating ways this agenda has resulted in praxis of social justice, is warranted at this time. This volume seeks to explicate and highlight the interlocking frameworks of SoTL and transformative education such that each position supports the other, allowing each to advance. The purpose of this volume is to solidify the place of a transformative agenda within the Scholarship of Teaching and Learning.

Promoting Social Justice through SoTL

The aims and purposes of this book are clear. The primary purpose is to solidify the foundation of social justice as fundamental to SoTL. Frameworks of transformative education vary from postmodernism to critical theory to feminism and multiculturalism, as noted above, but the overarching agenda of generating a more just society resonates throughout these various views. This book does not seek to limit the range of social action but rather to open up venues for explorations that broaden the potential for growth of social justice. For that reason, the editors of this volume deliberately sought out contributing authors whose work uses different definitions of social justice. The thread that connects these chapters is SoTL and the impulse to continue to investigate ways to improve our conditions as learners, teachers, and researchers. We have organized the chapters around the themes they explore.

This collection begins with chapters 1 and 2, in which "ethics" as a means of forwarding social justice within classroom settings is explored. "Ethics and Social Justice: A Review of Theoretical Frameworks and Pedagogical Considerations" by Tiffany Chenneville provides a review of outcomes-based research and best practices for classroom pedagogy for teaching ethics and promoting social justice. In chapter 2, Melissa Garno and Carole Bennett explore civic engagement and learning to care in the pursuit of developing professional identity among nursing students. "Teaching the Ethics of Caring: Using Nursing History to Integrate Race Consciousness into Professional Values" focuses on a dark chapter in nursing history (c. 1912–1969), Jim Crow to civil rights, to highlight nursing's struggle with inequality and the conflict with caring dispositions generated by inequalities.

The next set of chapters (3 and 4) focus on work explicitly with marginalized populations. In chapter 3, Maxine Atkinson and Scott T. Grether explore implications for SoTL in raising the status of women in the academy. Their work, titled "The Scholarship of Teaching and Learning and the Status of Women," focuses on the gendered expectations of classroom teaching and ways SoTL validates relationship building in the classroom. Moving from the local back to a global perspective, in chapter 4, "Teachers of Minorities as Agents of Change: A Global Model," MaryJo Benton Lee and Diane Kayongo-Male present a standard to allow teachers and teacher educators to reflect more deliberately on various aspects of change agency and on the important role teachers can play in bringing about a more just society.

In chapters 5 to 9, the works focus on community service projects and community activism as a means of inspiring social justice. Chapter 5, "Learning as We Go: Risk Taking and Relationship Building through Service Learning in Belize" by Mary R. Moeller, Lonell Moeller, and Susan L. Filler develops pedagogical praxis aimed at enhancing preservice teachers' sensitivity to multicultural differences. They chronicle the transformations of their students as they take risks and negotiate intercultural relationships during their study abroad experience in Belize. Karen S. Meaney, xxiv | Introduction

Jo An M. Zimmermann, Gloria Martinez-Ramos, Yongmei Lu, and Jackie McDonald present a more local service-learning initiative in chapter 6, "Champions for Health in the Community: Critical Service Learning, Transformative Education, and Community Empowerment." This chapter explores the transformation of one low-income neighborhood in San Marcos, Texas, over a three-year period as students at the university engaged in service learning with local communities. Chapter 7, "Teacher Candidates' Dispositions for Civic Engagement and Social Responsibility: Discernment and Action" by Patricia Calderwood, Stephanie Burrell Storms, Thomas Grund, Nicole Battaglia, and Emma Sheeran is another collaboration focusing on the importance of community membership and civic engagement. This chapter demonstrates how preservice teachers grow toward validation of appropriate dispositions for emerging teachers. Although dispositions are difficult to determine, the words and deeds of teacher candidates provide evidence of their disposition toward becoming change agents for equity and social justice. In chapter 8, Lisa Garoutte presents "Transforming Student Ideas about Community Using Asset-Based Community Development Techniques." This chapter demonstrates that students are changed in two significant ways when they engage in asset-based community development techniques: First, they are more likely to become invested in their own communities, and second, they are less likely to employ individualistic ways of understanding the world around them. This chapter thus bridges the gaps between theory and practice and between classroom and community, highlighting ways SoTL can enhance civic engagement. In the final chapter in this section, chapter 9, "Transforming Awareness into Activism: Teaching Systems and Social Justice in an Interdisciplinary Course," Cathy Willermet, Anja Mueller, and David Alm collaborate in teaching an interdisciplinary course using water as the focus, bringing together perspectives from anthropology, biology, and chemistry to help students understand the political and power dynamics that surge around the use of scarce resources. They document student focus shifting from "Third World" problems to political control and human rights.

Chapters 10 to 15 of this collection feature examples of the use of classroom practices of reflection and counternarratives to develop personal voice and responsibility on the path toward social justice. In chapter 10, Scott D. Farver and Alyssa Hadley Dunn use the concept of counternarratives (Delgado & Stefancic, 2001) to advance a social justice agenda in SoTL. Their chapter, titled "Swinging with a Double-Edged Sword: Using Counterstories to Fight for Social Justice in the Classroom," draws on their teaching experiences to highlight pitfalls and offer readers innovative ways to think about counternarratives as a means to make education a transformative experience for all learners and teachers. Sabrina Ross and Alma Stevenson explore their own transformations over the course of teaching a group of African American boys (first- and second-graders). Chapter 11, "When Walking the Walk Changes the Talk: Using Critical Reflection to Inform Practices of Social Justice Research and Social Justice Education," uses the phrase "walking the walk and talking the talk" to illustrate the ways that putting our commitment to social justice into practice requires subsequent changes in how we articulate these commitments and then carries forward into new practices and new articulations of our commitments. Chapter 12 carries forward the theme of teacher transformation in "Consciousness Raising for Twenty-First-Century Faculty: Using Lessons from Diversity Flashpoints." Through exploration of a faculty development initiative exploring "diversity flashpoints" identified through student vignettes, Alejandro Leguizamo and Jennifer Campbell use SoTL to enhance faculty awareness of and sensitivity to diversity concerns across campus. Chapter 13 presents a faculty-student collaboration, "'The Way I View the World Has Changed': Student and Teacher Reflections on Transformative Social Justice Education" by Annemarie Vaccaro, Athina Chartelain, Sarah Croft, Brooke D'Aloisio, Tiffany Hoyt, and Brian Stevens. This chapter explores social justice teaching and SoTL in action through reflections from the professor and her master's- and doctoral-level students engaged in conversation about moving from discussion to reflection to action aimed at social justice. Chapter 14, "Using Attitude Measures and Student Narratives about Diversity to Enhance Multicultural Teaching Effectiveness" by Robert Lake and Kent Rittschof, uses the Rasch model of measurement to ascertain the efficacy of models for teaching multiculturalism in an undergraduate setting. Their work also uses student narratives to flesh out the data to gain greater understanding from the students' perspective. Enhancing preservice teachers' ability to work with diverse students is imperative in our multicultural and global society and makes this work especially timely and relevant for enhancing transformative education. Chapter 15 of this volume addresses student self-awareness as a means to encourage diversity within the sciences. Erin E. Peters-Burton and Giuseppina Kysar Mattietti urge students to develop a greater understanding of themselves as learners in order to increase their probability of entering science fields. This process of making science more approachable from diverse perspectives, and supporting students as they come to view themselves as generators of knowledge, leads to more open and enriched scientific inquiries.

Finally, the last group of chapters in this book focuses on applied classroom practices that have proven successful in addressing social justice issues. In chapter 16, Phillis L. George investigates the ubiquitous student evaluation process, suggesting new ways to make this process more authentic and democratic in her chapter, "Reimagining the Student Evaluation: Using Democratic Frameworks in College Teaching and Learning." Rather than delivering Likert scale evaluation forms at the end of the semester, George provides a detailed and systematic method for integrating ongoing evaluation into the fabric of the course and at the same time enhancing student investment in course content. She uses the "strengths, weaknesses, opportunities, and threats" framework to support this system of student evaluation. Daniel J. Glisczinski draws on recent findings in neuroscience to strengthen the impact of classroom practices on student learning in chapter 17, "Minding the Brain: Three Dimensions of Cognition in Social Justice Curriculum." As he points out, the "stand and deliver" lecture method of education (Freire's banking method) results in about a 10 to 15 percent retention rate among learners. Recent findings in neuroscience can help educators draw on the brain's natural resources of "motion, emotion, and elaborative encoding" to enable more "robust cognition." This chapter ties together neuroscience with transformative education aimed at advancing learning and social justice. Applying social justice principles to an online course in a higher education graduate program is James M. DeVita's focus in chapter 18. He explains a two-pronged philosophy of teaching for social justice that addresses both learning about and engaging with marginalized populations. In this online graduate course, students identify a "marginalized population" and then design a project to enhance social justice related to the identified group. Students share their projects and engage in online discussions to broaden their understanding of the role of school leaders in advancing social justice initiatives.

The final chapter in this volume provides an afterword highlighting the interconnections between the preceding chapters and pointing to next steps in advancing social justice initiatives through the Scholarship of Teaching and Learning.

In this way, each chapter in this edited volume provides a different thread, woven together to strengthen the fiber of social justice work through SoTL. From service learning to history, and from theory and models to neuroscience, each chapter in this volume contributes to the brilliant diversity SoTL brings to transformative education.

DELORES D. LISTON is Professor of Curriculum and Foundations at Georgia Southern University. Her research and teaching interests focus on the application of philosophical, ethical, and feminist understandings to education. She is author of *Joy as a Metaphor of Convergence: A Phenomenological and Aesthetic Investigation of Social and Educational Change, Learning to Teach: Critical Approaches to the Field Experience* (with Natalie Adams, Christine Shea, and Bryan Deever), and *Pervasive Vulnerabilities: Sexual Harassment in School* (with Regina Rahimi).

REGINA RAHIMI is Associate Professor and Interim Department Head of Secondary, Adult, and Physical Education at Armstrong State University. Her research and publications have focused on issues related to race and gender as well as educational practices and instructional methods in secondary classrooms. She is author (with Delores D. Liston) of *Pervasive Vulnerabilities: Sexual Harassment in School.*

References

Apple, M. (2001). *Educating the right way: Markets, standards, God and inequality.* New York, NY: Falmer.
Atkinson, M. (2001). The scholarship of teaching and learning: Reconceptualizing scholarship and transforming the academy. *Social Forces, 79*(4), 1217–1230.
Banks, J. A., & McGee Banks, C. A. (2013). *Multicultural education: Issues and perspectives* (8th ed.). Hoboken, NJ: Wiley & Sons.

Bass, R. (1999). The scholarship of teaching: What's the problem? *Inventio: Creative Thinking about Teaching and Learning, 1*(1), 1–9. Retrieved from https://my.vanderbilt.edu/sotl/files/2013/08/Bass-Problem1.pdf.

Bender, E., & Gray, D. (1999). The scholarship of teaching. Research & creative activity, 22(1). Retrieved from http://www.indiana.edu/~rcapub/v22n1/p03.html.

Biesta, G. (2010). "This is my truth, tell me yours": Deconstructive pragmatism as a philosophy for education. *Educational Philosophy and Theory, 42*(7), 710–727.

Boyer, E. L. (1990). *Scholarship reconsidered: Priorities of the professoriate.* New York, NY: Carnegie Foundation for the Advancement of Teaching.

Chenneville, T., Toler, S., & Gaskin-Butler, V. T. (2012). Civic engagement in the field of psychology. *Journal of the Scholarship of Teaching and Learning, 12*(4), 58–75.

Collins, P. H. (1990). *Black feminist thought: Knowledge, consciousness and the politics of empowerment.* Boston, MA: Unwin Hyman.

Considine, J. R. (2014). "Who am I to bring diversity into the classroom?" Learning communities wrestle with creating inclusive college classrooms. *Journal of the Scholarship of Teaching and Learning, 14*(4), 18–30.

Darder, A., Baltodano, M. P., & Torres, R. D. (2009). *The critical pedagogy reader.* New York, NY: Routledge.

Delgado, R., & Stefanic, J. (2001). *Critical race theory: An introduction.* New York: New York University Press.

Freire, P. (2006). *Pedagogy of the oppressed.* New York, NY: Continuum Press. (Original work published 1970.)

Freire, P. (1998). *Pedagogy of freedom: Ethics, democracy and civic courage.* Lanham, MD: Rowman & Littlefield.

Gay, G. (2000). *Culturally responsive teaching: Theory, research, & practice.* New York, NY: Teachers College Press.

Gilpin, L. S., & Liston, D. (2009). Transformative education in the scholarship of teaching and learning: An analysis of SoTL literature. *International Journal for the Scholarship of Teaching and Learning, 3*(2). Retrieved from http://academics.georgiasouthern.edu/ijsotl/index.htm.

Glisczinski, D. J. (2011). Lighting up the mind: Transforming learning through the applied scholarship of cognitive neuroscience. *International Journal of the Scholarship of Teaching and Learning, 5*(1). Retrieved from http://digitalcommons.georgiasouthern.edu/cgi/viewcontent.cgi?article=1274&context=ij-sotl.

Harding, S. (2004). *The feminist standpoint theory reader: Intellectual and political controversies.* New York, NY: Routledge. Retrieved from http://cscs.res.in/courses_folder/dataarchive/textfiles/textfile.2012-02-24.1205832218/file.

Heidegger, M. (1962). *Being and time.* (J. Macquarrie & E. Robinson, Trans.). New York, NY: Harper & Row. (Original work published 1926.)

hooks, b. (1994). *Teaching to transgress: Education as the practice of freedom.* New York, NY: Routledge.

hooks, b. (2003). *Teaching community: A pedagogy of hope.* New York, NY: Routledge.

Huber, M. T., & Hutchings, P. (2005). Surveying the scholarship of teaching and learning. *The advancement of learning: Building the teaching commons.* San Francisco, CA: Jossey-Bass.

Huber, M. T., & Morreale, S. M. (2002). *Situating the scholarship of teaching and learning: A cross-disciplinary conversation. Introduction to disciplinary styles in the scholarship of teaching and learning: Exploring common ground.* Retrieved from http://www.carnegiefoundation.org/publications/pub.asp.

Hutchings, P. (Ed.). (2002). *Ethics of inquiry: Issues in the scholarship of teaching and learning*. Menlo Park, CA: Carnegie Foundation for the Advancement of Teaching.

Johnson, J. M., & Lambie, G. W. (2012). A multicultural personal growth group as a pedagogical strategy with graduate counseling students. *Journal of the Scholarship of Teaching and Learning, 12*(3), 125–141.

Jones, M. G., & Brader-Araje, L. (2002). The impact of constructivism on education: Language, discourse and meaning. *American Communication Journal, 5*(3). Retrieved from http://ac-journal.org/journal/vol5/iss3/special/jones.pdf.

Ladson-Billings, G. (1995). Toward a theory of culturally relevant pedagogy. *American Educational Research Journal, 32*(3), 465–491.

Lake, R., & Rittschof, K. (2012). Looking deeper than the gradebook: Assessing cultural diversity attitudes among undergraduates. *Journal for the Scholarship of Teaching and Learning, 12*(3), 142–164.

Levy, D. L., & Byrd, D. C. (2011). "Why can't we be friends?": Using music to teach social justice. *Journal for the Scholarship of Teaching and Learning, 11*(2), 64–75. Retrieved from http://josotl.indiana.edu/article/view/1818/1815.

Lorde, A. (1984). *Sister outsider: Essays and speeches*. Trumansburg, NY: Crossing Press.

Lynn, M., & Dixson, A. D. (2013). *Handbook of critical race theory in education*. New York, NY: Routledge.

Mayo, C., & Stengel, B. (2010). Feminism and education. In R. Bailey, R. Barrow, D. Carr, & C. McCarthy (Eds.), *The SAGE handbook of philosophy of education* (pp. 151–166). London, England: SAGE.

McCright, A. M. (2012). Enhancing students' scientific and quantitative literacies through an inquiry-based learning project on climate change. *Journal of the Scholarship of Teaching and Learning, 12*(4), 86–102. Retrieved from http://josotl.indiana.edu/article/view/2050/2994.

McKinney, K. (2007). *Enhancing learning through the scholarship of teaching and learning: The challenges and joys of juggling*. San Francisco, CA: Jossey-Bass.

McLaren, P., Macrine, S., and Hill, D. (Eds.). (2010). *Revolutionizing pedagogy: Educating for social justice within and beyond global neo-liberalism*. London, England: Palgrave Macmillan.

Meaney, K. S., Housman, J. M., Cavazos, A., & Wilcox, M. L. (2012). Examining service learning in a graduate physical education teacher education course. *Journal of the Scholarship of Teaching and Learning, 12*(3), 108–124. Retrieved from http://josotl.indiana.edu/article/view/2148/2062.

Menges, R. J., & Weimer, M. (1996). *Teaching on solid ground: Using scholarship to improve practice*. San Francisco, CA: Jossey-Bass.

Miretsky, D. (2013). From rationalization to reflection: One teacher education law class. *Journal of the Scholarship of Teaching and Learning, 13*(5), 61–76. Retrieved from http://josotl.indiana.edu/article/view/3452/3867.

Moya, P. M., & Hames-Garcia, M. R. (2000). *Reclaiming identity: Realist theory and the predicament of postmodernism*. Berkeley: University of California Press.

Oh, K., & Nussli, N. (2014). Challenging, eye-opening and changing: U.S. teacher training in Korea: Creating experiences that will enhance global perspectives. *Journal of the Scholarship of Teaching and Learning, 14*(4), 67–87. doi:10.14434/josotl.v14i4.12764.

Palmer, P. J. (2004). *A hidden wholeness: The journey toward an undivided life*. San Francisco, CA: Jossey-Bass.

Peters, M. A. (2010). *The last book of postmodernism: Apocalyptic thinking, philosophy and education in the twenty-first century*. New York, NY: Peter Lang.

Shulman, L. S. (2002). "Forward." In P. Hutchings (Ed.), *Ethics of inquiry: Issues in the scholarship of teaching and learning* (pp. v–vii). Menlo Park, CA: Carnegie Foundation for the Advancement of Teaching and Learning.

Spelman, E. V. (1988). *Inessential woman: Problems of exclusion in feminist thought.* Boston, MA: Beacon Press.

Teemant, A. (2010). ESL student perspectives on university classroom testing practices. *Journal of the Scholarship of Teaching and Learning, 10*(3), 89–105. Retrieved from http://josotl.indiana.edu/article/view/1797/1794.

White, S. K., & Nitkin, M. R. (2014). Creating a transformational learning experience: Immersing students in an intensive interdisciplinary learning environment. *International Journal of the Scholarship of Teaching and Learning, 8*(2). Retrieved from http://digitalcommons.georgiasouthern.edu/cgi/viewcontent.cgi?article=1471&context=ij-sotl.

Willermet, C., Mueller, A., Juris, S. J., Drake, E., Upadhaya, S., & Chhetri, P. (2013). Water as life, death, and power: Building an integrated interdisciplinary course combining perspectives from anthropology, biology, and chemistry. *Journal of the Scholarship of Teaching and Learning, 13*(5), 106–124. Retrieved from http://josotl.indiana.edu/article/view/3875/3870.

Wing, A. (2003). *Critical race feminism: A reader* (2nd ed.). New York: New York University Press.

I.
Examining Ethics toward Social Justice

1 Ethics and Social Justice: A Review of Theoretical Frameworks and Pedagogical Considerations

Tiffany Chenneville

Eᴛʜɪᴄs ʜᴇʟᴘ ᴜs to distinguish between what is right and what is wrong. Because values influence these distinctions, ethics vary by culture and by discipline despite the fact that morality is considered to be universal (Haidt, 2007). Definitions of social justice also vary. Aristotle described two different types of social justice—equal justice and distributive/proportional justice (Walster & Walster, 1975). Meanwhile, Adams, Bell, and Griffin (2007) describe social justice as both a process and a goal. Variations notwithstanding, there is a clear link between social justice and ethics. In fact, Novak (2000) argues that any definition of social justice that does not include a focus on virtue should be dismissed. According to Haidt (2007), "people are selfish, yet morally motivated" (p. 998), suggesting that despite competing self-interests, we all are oriented toward social justice to at least some degree.

There is also a relationship between ethics and the Scholarship of Teaching and Learning (SoTL). However, most discussions in this context are centered on the ethical issues surrounding the scholarly activities around teaching and learning (Hutchings, 2003), not necessarily the importance of teaching ethics. For example, Hutchings (2003) describes issues related to sharing student work and research design as ethical considerations when researching teaching. Nonetheless, SoTL is inexplicably linked to both ethics and social justice. Recognizing the important relationship between social justice, ethics, and the Scholarship of Teaching and Learning, the purpose of this chapter is to explore theoretical frameworks and approaches for teaching ethics as part of larger social justice initiatives in the college setting.

Ethical Frameworks and Social Justice

Ethical frameworks help guide moral decision-making and, therefore, are important when thinking about SoTL related to social justice. Because of their popularity and the likelihood of student familiarity, the following theories are highlighted as a place to launch college classroom discussions about the importance of social justice: virtue ethics, deontology, utilitarianism, and principle-based ethics. These theories can be categorized as either ethics of conduct or ethics of character. A cursory overview of each theory is provided below along with a discussion of how each applies to the Scholarship of Teaching and Learning about social justice.

Virtue Ethics

Aristotle is the name most commonly associated with virtue ethics, a normative moral theory that focuses on the importance of possessing certain virtues (Willows, 2013). Normative moral theories are theories that describe how people should behave based on standards or norms. Aristotle's virtue ethics assumes that virtues are stable character traits, and the focus is on individual character. Aristotle distinguished between intellectual virtues and moral virtues and was concerned primarily with the latter with the exception of prudence, or "practical wisdom" (Willows, 2013, p. 9), which allows us to act on our virtuous dispositions. Other virtues include justice, courage, generosity (Willows, 2013), integrity, benevolence, and respectfulness (Knapp & VandeCreek, 2012). Virtue ethics assumes an ethical person will have the right mix of motivation, knowledge, and character. Whereas some ethical theories stress the enforcement of rules, virtue ethics stresses character building. Virtue ethics lends itself nicely to discussions about social justice. After all, justice is among the important virtues a person should possess, according to Aristotle. By stressing justice as a virtue worth possessing, students are forced to ponder what justice really means in a societal context. In its broadest definition, social justice is concerned with the fair distribution of wealth, privilege, and opportunities. Those who embody justice as a virtue are likely motivated to better understand how to ensure the fair distribution of wealth, privilege, and opportunities among individuals in a society.

Deontology

Kant is the name most commonly associated with deontology, also known as duty-based ethics, which relies on compliance with rules (Knapp & VandeCreek, 2012). The imperative is to do the right thing for the right reason. Intentions matter but consequences do not. Others can be used as a means, but not *only* as a means, to an end. In deontology, a distinction is made between hypothetical and categorical imperatives. Adherence to hypothetical imperatives, which involve if-then reasoning (e.g., If I want to earn a good participation grade, then I have to go to class), is prudent. Adherence to categorical imperatives, on the other hand, is a duty. Categorical imperatives command people to act in certain ways at all times, regardless of the "if" (e.g., you should always tell the truth). Within the context of teaching about social justice, students can be encouraged to think about, and even brainstorm, what societal rules are important for ensuring justice for all and whether or not the golden rule differs when thinking about social justice definitions that focus on equality versus those that focus on distribution and proportionality.

Utilitarianism

Mill is the name most commonly associated with utilitarianism, in which morality is defined by the consequences of one's actions, not necessarily the actions themselves (Knapp & VandeCreek, 2012). This theory focuses on the sum of happiness and unhappiness for everyone involved or affected by an action. The concern is always with maximizing the benefits for all or, at least, most people. There are three features of utilitarianism: consequentialism, hedonism, and universalism. Consequentialism refers to the fact that consequences matter, hedonism to the fact that happiness matters, and universalism to the fact that happiness matters for everyone. In fact, with regard to the latter, the happiness of others is just as important as the happiness of the individual. Utilitarianism is ultimately concerned about the greatest good for the greatest number. On the surface, utilitarianism is consistent with definitions of social justice that focus on equality and equal opportunity for all citizens within a society. The concept of the greatest good for the greatest number seems to strive for equality. Indeed, Blackorby, Bossert, and Donaldson (2002) provide a review of utilitarian theories of justice, and Mill himself described utilitarianism as an "anthropomorphic approach to social justice" (Mill in Zajda, Majhanovich, & Rust, 2007, p. 9). However, upon further reflection, this framework might actually support oppression, which is, in essence, the antithesis of social justice in situations where the greatest good for the greatest number reinforces significant disparities in the distribution of goods, resources, and opportunities between majority and minority groups (Reisch, 2002). To address concerns, Rawls (1971) offered a theory of fairness as an alternative to utilitarianism in his landmark text. Nonetheless, the extent to which utilitarianism supports or opposes notions of social justice is a discussion worth having with students, especially given the prevalence of utilitarian views in our society.

Principle-Based Ethics

Ross is the name most commonly associated with principle-based ethics, a theory designed to address the problems inherent to both utilitarianism and deontology (Knapp & VandeCreek, 2012). Within this framework there are prima facie duties, including, for example, fidelity, gratitude, justice, beneficence, self-improvement, and nonmaleficence. Principle-based ethics dictates that an obligation holds unless a superior obligation overrides it. What this framework gains in flexibility it loses in consistency (Fryer, 2011). The advantages and disadvantages of this framework are a worthy debate to encourage among students within the context of lessons about what duties are most important for creating and maintaining socially just environments.

Social Justice: An Ethics of Justice or an Ethics of Care?

Kohlberg's theory of moral development is consistent with an ethics of justice. According to Kohlberg, there are three stages of moral development: preconventional, conventional, and postconventional (Kail & Cavanaugh, 2012). At the preconventional level, moral reasoning is based on external forces. Within this level, an obedience orientation whereby authorities are thought to know the difference between right and wrong precedes an instrumental orientation whereby one's own needs factor into reasoning about moral issues. At the conventional level, moral guidance is sought by societal norms. Within this level, there is an interpersonal norms stage wherein one is guided by a desire to win the approval of others followed by a social systems morality stage that is marked by the belief that social expectations, roles, and laws are for the good of all people. At the postconventional level, considered to be the highest level of moral reasoning, one develops one's own moral code. This level includes a social contracts stage, which is marked by the belief that social expectations, roles, and laws are good *only* if they benefit all people, and a universal ethical principles stage, wherein individuals choose the ethical principle of most importance to them. Research provides some evidence of a relationship between moral reasoning and moral action. Nonetheless, Kohlberg's theory has been criticized. One of the strongest criticisms is regarding Kohlberg's overemphasis on justice to the exclusion of care, compassion, and other feelings that may play a pivotal role in moral reasoning. This is particularly problematic given that justice is considered to be more characteristic of males while caring and compassion tend to be more characteristic of females, thus creating ill-founded gender differences, which favor men, in levels of moral reasoning. A student of Kohlberg's, Gilligan (1982) proposed an ethics of care to combat the shortcomings of Kohlberg's theory, particularly its gender inequities. Gilligan's ethics of care is widely touted as a feminist ethic. The relationship between justice, care, and gender has been widely debated (Flanagan & Jackson, 1987; Botes, 2000; Jaffee & Hyde, 2000). When trying to reconcile the differences between an ethics of justice and an ethics of care, there is debate about whether justice or care should be the primary consideration when there is a conflict between the two. Some argue that justice is necessary for care, and others argue that care is necessary for justice (Flanagan & Jackson, 1987). Still others argue that reliance on an ethics of justice versus an ethics of care depends on culture (French & Weis, 2000). Clearly, ethics of justice and care are both important frameworks when thinking about social justice.

Ethics and Social Justice: Pedagogical Considerations

A leader in the field of moral psychology, Haidt (2007) describes the following four principles as critical to our thinking about morality: (1) "intuitive primacy, but not dictatorship," which refers to the idea that moral reasoning is secondary to initial, intuitive, emotional reactions; (2) "moral thinking is for social doing," which refers to the idea that moral reasoning is used to justify our position and our actions, not for seeking truth; (3) "morality binds and builds," which refers to the existence of moral communities that dictate the behavior of their members; and (4) "morality is about more than harm and fairness," which refers to the idea that loyalty, authority, and spiritual purity are also important tenants. Haidt (2007) proposes a social intuitionist model that addresses these principles and illustrates the new synthesis for moral psychology. Within this model, Haidt suggests there are three ways to override our initial, intuitive, emotional reactions. First, we can consciously employee verbal reasoning skills, for example, by conducting a cost-benefit analysis. Second, we can attempt to reframe the situation, which may elicit an intuitive response that competes with the first. Third, and most relevant to discussions about teaching ethics for social justice, we can trigger new intuitive responses by discussing moral issues with others who raise arguments different from our own, which is then followed by moral reasoning. Essentially, within this model, classroom discussions and activities can trigger formal moral reasoning skills, which is important given that "moral reasoning can correct and override moral intuition" (Haidt, 2007, p. 1001).

The importance of ethics and social responsibility in education has been demonstrated across disciplines, including, to name a few, science (Schultz, 2014), nursing (Fahrenwald, 2003), teaching (Guojonsdottir, Cacciattolo, Dakich, Davies, Kelly, & Dalman, 2008), law and medicine (Tyler, 2010), and counselor education (Pack-Brown, Thomas, & Seymour, 2008). Helping students to understand the social and political oppression experienced by people around the world and the ethical implications of such oppression is a critical aspect of encouraging global citizenship (Martin, Smolen, Oswald, & Milam, 2012). Below is a description, not meant to be exhaustive, of pedagogical considerations and strategies related to the incorporation of social justice into ethics education.

A Systems Approach

Creating an educational environment that effectively fosters ethical behavior and encourages students to be socially conscious, concepts that go hand in hand, requires a systems approach. Institutions must commit to socially just pedagogies, which will require the integration of social justice into the mission that drives institutional practices and policies. In this type of learning environment, there is a commitment to encouraging students to be change agents not only within their own lives but also in the lives of others. Kraft (2007) proposes a schoolwide model of teaching social justice comprised of three primary elements: (1) the assimilation of social justice issues within and across the curriculum, (2) the adoption of socially just teaching pedagogies and practices, and (3) the establishment of a socially just school community. Within this model, there is an emphasis not only on what is taught but also on how and where social justice is taught. Commitment, skill, and self-reflection among faculty, administrators, and students are necessary. A democratically run administration is also important. The values and virtues of the school community must be identified and reinforced throughout the institution. For example, Kraft (2007) describes one school that developed a strong sense of identity around the virtues of justice, propriety, harmony, truth, balance, community, respect, and perseverance. Schoolwide exploration of ethical frameworks and their relationship to social justice will help facilitate the identification of values and virtues within an institution.

Ethical Leadership

Given the relationship between ethics and social justice, ethical leadership is a worthy pedagogical consideration. The emerging construct of ethical leadership is also important within the systems approach to creating socially just learning environments described above. The role and impact of ethical leaders on the creation of school environments that promote social justice has been documented in the literature (e.g., Christian & Pacino, 2013). Shapiro (2006) describes an ethical movement called the New Democratic Ethical Educational Leadership (New DEEL), which has important ethical and social justice implications. Of particular importance to this discussion, Shapiro describes some of the important values an ethical educational leader must embody in order to guide an organization or institution in the area of social justice. Specifically, ethical leaders must not only know and understand ethical philosophies and frameworks and professional ethics codes but also value the importance of ethical decision-making that is focused on an ethics of care. Also described by Shapiro is the paradox between control and democracy and the fact that social justice is, in fact, at the core of this paradox. Shapiro describes the need for experiences that engage and empower young people across genders, races, ethnicities, social classes, and other defining categories. Clearly, to expect students to become ethical leaders in their communities requires that the leaders in higher education model ethical decision-making with social justice in mind.

Pedagogy of Discomfort

The pedagogy of discomfort, first described by Boler (1999), describes a tool for teaching and learning about difficult issues of relevance to social justice (e.g., racism, classism, gender inequities). Specifically, the pedagogy of discomfort is a teaching practice that challenges students to question long-held beliefs and assumptions, thus pushing them outside of their comfort zones in order to make the individual and social transformations necessary to disrupt social inequities. Since Boler's initial writing on this topic, there has been a considerable amount of discussion in the literature about both the benefits and the ethical implications of pedagogies of discomfort, which promote pain and suffering among students for the purpose of understanding inequity (Boler & Zembylas, 2003; Butler, 2005; Leibowitz, Bozalek, Rohleder, Carolissen, & Swartz, 2010; Zembylas, 2015). Research suggests that the impact of activities grounded in such pedagogies varies, and there are concerns about the effect of power differential and inequality in the classroom on the extent to which such pedagogies can be transformational for students (Zembylas & McGlynn, 2012; Leibowitz et al., 2010). For example, Zembylas and McGlynn (2012) describe some of the risks associated with teaching activities grounded in the pedagogy of discomfort, namely the differences in power and privilege that can exist between teachers and students and the ethical issues surrounding the placement of students in a position of disadvantage, even if temporarily. While the research their description is based on was focused on elementary-age children, the risks described certainly should be cautioned against in higher education settings. Zembylas (2015) describes the relationship between a pedagogy of discomfort and an ethic of discomfort, which is defined as "an economy of affect that uses discomfort as a point of departure for individual and social transformation" for the purpose of challenging oppression (Zembylas, 2010, p. 703). Clearly, pedagogies of discomfort can be powerful when teaching issues of relevance to social justice. However, educators using activities to create discomfort are encouraged to do so within the context of a safe classroom space. After all, discomforting spaces and safe spaces need not be mutually exclusive (Zembylas, 2015).

Ethical Decision-Making

Ethical decision-making that results in priorities that support socially just actions is critical. The influence of personal values on the ethical dimension of decision-making has been documented (Fritzsche & Oz, 2007), which reinforces the importance of exploring values that are consistent with social justice initiatives. Of course, there are many ethical decision-making models published in the literature, and educators are encouraged to explore these models with students (e.g., Ford & Richardson, 1994; Cottone & Claus, 2000; Levitt, 2013). As just one example, the worst-case scenario model encourages decision-makers to consider the worst possible outcome of their decision even if the probability of that outcome is low (Nagy, 2011). Subsequently, decision-makers are encouraged to balance the risk of an adverse outcome with the likelihood of a beneficial outcome. For decisions concerning socially just behavior, adverse outcomes would include those that support or sustain oppression.

Despite the prevalence and popularity of ethical decision-making models, there is emerging evidence that people consistently rely on only one or a few pieces of information and ignore the rest when making decisions, including those of an ethical nature. Gigerenzer and Gaissmaier (2011) describe this process as heuristic decision-making. Heuristics are defined as "efficient cognitive processes, conscious or unconscious, that ignore part of the information" (Gigerenzer & Gaissmaier, 2011, p. 451). Historically, the belief was that the use of heuristics would lead to more errors than methodical decision-making processes. However, research suggests that heuristics can be used in adaptive ways and that ignoring some of the available information when making decisions can actually result in more accurate judgments. With regard to teaching social justice, the trick becomes understanding which pieces of information may be most salient for socially just outcomes.

Case Studies

Case studies are commonly used to teach ethics and social responsibility. For example, Schultz (2014) argues in favor of case studies that result in deep engagement among students around ethics and social justice. Discussion and debate when assessing case studies are also encouraged. Not only are case studies typically interesting to students, they also allow students to make connections between ethical issues and the experiences they encounter in everyday life (Chamany, 2006). The use of case studies can also promote collaborative and interdisciplinary techniques. For example, Tyler (2010) describes the value of using case studies in a course designed to blend professionalism, ethics, and problem-solving to understand the important intersection of law, health, and poverty. Combining case studies with practice using ethical decision-making (see discussion above) may be particularly useful. Because the hypothetical nature of case studies may pose problems, one strategy is to have students create their own cases based on lived experiences or real-life observations of social inequities.

Service Learning and Civic Engagement

Broadly speaking, civic engagement refers to the actions of individuals or groups of people for the purpose of addressing issues of concern to the public. As described by Chenneville, Toler, and Gaskin-Butler (2012), the terms "civic engagement" and "service learning" are often used interchangeably despite distinct and important differences in meaning. While service learning typically refers to credit-bearing activities primarily designed to benefit the student, civic engagement has a broader purpose. Nonetheless, service-learning activities can and often do support civic engagement. The importance of service-learning activities for teaching ethics with the goal of social justice cannot be overstated and is supported in the literature (Opazo, Aramburuzabala, & García-Peinado, 2014). As one example, Redman and Clark (2002) describe the use of service learning to incorporate social justice into the teaching curriculum for nurses. In this context, social justice areas were prioritized to include minority health, environmental health, poverty, and the medically underserved. Students were required to participate in fifteen to twenty hours of service learning designed to advocate for an underserved population. Self-reflection and classroom discussion were included as components of the service-learning activity. Similar approaches can be used across disciplines. Ultimately, the goal is to provide students with a lived experience that demonstrates the importance of ethics when attempting to address issues of social concern.

Life Histories

Life histories can be an effective educational tool for increasing awareness about social issues and for promoting social engagement. Life histories can be individual or collective and are typically completed through direct interviews, although other methods are also possible (e.g., group discussions, biographies). They have great potential for increasing self-reflection, compassion, and empathy. Describing an ethics of access, Johnson (2007) used life history methods to trace ethical development related to social justice. Meanwhile, Osler and Zhu (2011) used life history narratives to encourage students to consider the idea of being responsible to others in a society within the context of human rights as dominant ethical demands. These are but a few examples of the potential utility of life history methods to explore social justice as an ethical issue.

Research Directions for the Scholarship of Teaching and Learning Related to Ethics and Social Justice

Further research is needed to explore SoTL as it relates to ethics and social justice. For example, more research using measurable outcomes is needed to assess the utility of school change models for creating ethical and socially just learning environments. In addition, given that ethical leadership is an important construct for SoTL related to social justice, more research is needed in the area of ethical leadership. Brown and Treviño (2006) provided a review of the ethical leadership literature and suggested directions for future research in this area. They offer formal propositions designed to advance research that is grounded in social learning theory and that takes into account the individual and contextual factors that influence ethical leadership and outcomes. Pedagogies of discomfort as they relate to promoting social justice are also in need of further examination, primarily with regard to the ethical concerns associated with these strategies. This is not to suggest that such pedagogies should not be used but rather that ethical risks should be minimized. The burgeoning field of heuristics is also worthy of study within the context of teaching ethics to promote social engagement. Specifically, research is needed on the impact of using decision-making models to produce socially just outcomes and whether or not, and how, heuristic decision-making can be valuable. Finally, research on specific pedagogical strategies (e.g., case studies, service learning, life histories) that can promote best practices related to ethics education and social justice initiatives is needed.

Conclusion

Ethics education is important for raising awareness and deepening empathy for the social injustices that are common in our society. Ethical theories and frameworks can structure discussions about social justice, and multiple pedagogies exist for teaching ethics in ways that promote social equality and discourage oppression. While research is needed to further explore the Scholarship of Teaching and Learning as it relates to ethics education and social justice, the available literature supports the notion that ethics is at the heart of creating socially just environments.

Equally, there is a relationship between ethics and the Scholarship of Teaching and Learning itself. First, there are the ethical issues surrounding scholarly activities related to teaching and learning (e.g., ethical concerns about sharing student work as part of research on teaching). Second, and as important, is the need to include ethics across the curriculum as a part of a best-practices approach to teaching. Although there is debate about whether or not ethics can be taught and whether or not ethical decision-making models are effective given emerging knowledge about heuristics, there is evidence to suggest that discussions and activities can trigger formal moral reasoning skills, which can override intuitive emotional and moral reactions. For these reasons, ethics should permeate scholarly activities related to teaching and learning.

TIFFANY CHENNEVILLE is Associate Professor and Graduate Program Director in the Psychology Department at the University of South Florida, St. Petersburg, with a Joint Appointment in the Department of Pediatrics. She is also a licensed psychologist in the state of Florida and a nationally certified school psychologist. Her longstanding interest in social justice stems, in large part, from her research in the area of HIV.

References

Adams, M., Bell, L. A., & Griffin, P. (Eds.). (2007). *Teaching for diversity and social justice* New York, NY: Routledge.

Blackorby, C., Bossert, W., & Donaldson, D. (2002). Utilitarianism and the theory of justice. *Handbook of Social Choice and Welfare, 1*, 543–596.

Boler, M. (1999). *Feeling power: Emotions and education.* New York, NY: Routledge.

Boler, M., & Zembylas, M. (2003). Discomforting truths: The emotional terrain of understanding difference. In P. Trifonas (Ed.), *Pedagogies of difference: Rethinking education for social justice* (pp. 110–136). New York, NY: Routledge.

Botes, A. (2000). A comparison between the ethics of justice and the ethics of care. *Journal of Advanced Nursing, 32*(5), 1071–1075.

Brown, M. E., & Treviño, L. K. (2006). Ethical leadership: A review and future directions. *The Leadership Quarterly, 17*(6), 595–616.

Butler, J. (2005). *Giving an account of oneself.* New York, NY: Fordham University Press.
Chamany, K. (2006). Science and social justice: Making the case for case studies. *Journal of College Science Teaching, 36*(2), 54–59.
Chenneville, T., Toler, S., & Gaskin-Butler, V. T. (2012). Civic engagement in the field of psychology. *Journal of the Scholarship of Teaching and Learning, 12*(4), 58–75.
Christian, P., & Pacino, M. A. (2013). An ethics course for K-12 educators. *International Journal of Religion & Spirituality in Society, 2*(2), 113–120.
Cottone, R. R., & Claus, R. E. (2000). Ethical decision-making models: A review of the literature. *Journal of Counseling and Development, 78*(3), 275–283.
Fahrenwald, N. L. (2003). Teaching social justice. *Nurse Educator, 28*(5), 222–226.
Flanagan, O., & Jackson, K. (1987). Justice, care, and gender: The Kohlberg-Gilligan debate revisited. *Ethics, 97*(3), 622–637.
Ford, R. C., & Richardson, W. D. (1994). Ethical decision making: A review of the empirical literature. *Journal of Business Ethics, 13*(3), 205–221.
French, W., & Weis, A. (2000). An ethics of care or an ethics of justice. *Journal of Business Ethics, 27*(1–2), 125–136.
Fritzsche, D., & Oz, E. (2007). Personal values' influence on the ethical dimension of decision making. *Journal of Business Ethics, 75*(4), 335–343.
Fryer, M. (2011). *Ethics and organizational leadership: Developing a normative model.* Oxford, England: Oxford University Press.
Gigerenzer, G., & Gaissmaier, W. (2011). Heuristic decision making. *Annual Review of Psychology, 62,* 451–482.
Gilligan, C. (1982). *In a different voice: Psychological theory and women's development.* Cambridge, MA: Harvard University Press.
Guojonsdottir, H., Cacciattolo, M., Dakich, E., Davies, A., Kelly, C., & Dalmau, M. C. (2008). Transformative pathways: Inclusive pedagogies in teacher education. *Journal of Research on Technology in Education, 40*(2), 165–182.
Haidt, J. (2007). The new synthesis and moral psychology. *Science, 316*(5827), 998–1002. doi:10.1126/science.1137651
Hutchings, P. (2003). Competing goods: Ethical issues in the scholarship of teaching and learning. *Change: The Magazine of Higher Learning, 35*(5), 26–33. doi:10.1080/00091380309604116
Jaffee, S., & Hyde, J. S. (2000). Gender differences in moral orientation: A meta-analysis. *Psychological Bulletin, 126*(5), 703–726.
Johnson, A. S. (2007). An ethics of access: Using life history to trace preservice teachers' initial viewpoints on teaching for equity. *Journal of Teacher Education, 58*(4), 299–314.
Kail, R. V., & Cavanaugh, J. C. (2012). *Human development: A life-span view* (6th ed.). Belmont, CA: Thomson Wadsworth.
Knapp, S. J., & VandeCreek, L. D. (2012). *Practical ethics for psychologists: A positive approach* (2nd ed.). Washington, DC: American Psychological Association.
Kraft, M. (2007). Toward a school-wide model of teaching for social justice: An examination of the best practices of two small public schools. *Equity & Excellence in Education, 40*(1), 77–86.
Leibowitz, B., Bozalek, V., Rohleder, P., Carolissen, R., & Swartz, L. (2010). "Ah, but the whiteys love to talk about themselves": Discomfort as a pedagogy for change. *Race Ethnicity and Education, 13*(1), 83–100.
Levitt, D. H. (2013). Ethical decision-making models. In D. H. Levitt & H. J. H. Moorhead (Eds.), *Values and ethics in counseling: Real-life ethical decision making* (pp. 213–218). New York, NY: Routledge.

Martin, L. A., Smolen, L. A., Oswald, R. A., & Milam, J. L. (2012). Preparing students for global citizenship in the twenty-first century: Integrating social justice through global literature. *The Social Studies, 103*(4), 158–164.

Nagy, T. F. (2011). *Essential ethics for psychologists: A primer for understanding and mastering core issues.* Washington, DC: American Psychological Association.

Novak, M. (2000). Defining social justice. *First Things, 108,* 11–12.

Opazo, H., Aramburuzabala, P., & García-Peinado, R. (2014). Service-learning methodology as a tool of ethical development: Reflections from the university experience. *AISHE-J: The All Ireland Journal of Teaching & Learning in Higher Education, 6*(1), 1531.

Osler, A., & Zhu, J. (2011). Narratives in teaching and research for justice and human rights. *Education, Citizenship and Social Justice, 6*(3), 223–235.

Pack-Brown, S. P., Thomas, T. L., & Seymour, J. M. (2008). Infusing professional ethics into counselor education programs: A multicultural/social justice perspective. *Journal of Counseling & Development, 86*(3), 296–302.

Rawls, J. (1971). *A theory of justice.* Cambridge, MA: Harvard University Press.

Redman, R., & Clark, L. (2002). Service-learning as a model for integrating social justice in the nursing curriculum. *Journal of Nursing Education, 41*(10), 446.

Reisch, M. (2002). Defining social justice in a socially unjust world. *Families in Society: The Journal of Contemporary Social Services, 83*(4), 343–354.

Schultz, M. (2014). Teaching and assessing ethics and social responsibility in undergraduate science: A position paper. *Journal of Learning Design, 7*(2), 137.

Shapiro, J. (2006). Ethics and social justice within the New DEEL: Addressing the paradox of control/democracy. *International Electronic Journal for Leadership in Learning, 10*(32). Retrieved from http://iejll.journalhosting.ucalgary.ca/index.php/ijll/article/view/633/295.

Tyler, E. T. (2010). Teaching social justice and health: Professionalism, ethics, and problem-solving in the medical-legal classroom. *Journal of Law, Medicine & Ethics, 38*(3), 701–707.

Walster, E., & Walster, G. W. (1975). Equity and social justice. *Journal of Social Issues, 31*(3), 21–43.

Willows, A. (2013). Aristotle's virtue theory. *Challenging Religious Issues, 3,* 7–12.

Zajda, J., Majhanovich, S., & Rust, V. (2007). Introduction: Education and social justice. *International Review of Education, 52*(1), 9–22.

Zembylas, M. (2010). Teachers' emotional experiences of growing diversity and multiculturalism in schools and the prospects of an ethic of discomfort. *Teachers and Teaching: Theory and Practice, 16*(6), 703–716.

Zembylas, M. (2015). "Pedagogy of discomfort" and its ethical implications: The tensions of ethical violence in social justice education. *Ethics and Education, 10*(2), 163–174. doi:10.1080/17449642.2015.1039274

Zembylas, M., & McGlynn, C. (2012). Discomforting pedagogies: Emotional tensions, ethical dilemmas and transformative possibilities. *British Educational Research Journal, 38*(1), 41–59.

2 Teaching the Ethics of Caring: Using Nursing History to Integrate Race Consciousness into Professional Values

Melissa Garno and Carole Bennett

On a university campus, a nursing professor is leading a discussion of professional ethics with a class of undergraduate nursing students. In another town, a similar nursing class is exploring nursing history in relation to the evolution of professional ethical standards in place today. The learning outcome for both educational activities is the same: to promote student integration of nursing's ethical standards into their professional identity and value system. However, the two strategies being used to achieve that outcome are vastly different. The class exploring nursing history is using professional narrative and critical analysis of past events to make connections to the present and future. This critical study of history helps students internalize their learning and further develop their professional identity.

Nursing is universally defined as a caring profession. Nursing programs include the development of caring professional values within their learning outcomes. Using nursing history to help students achieve these outcomes is a purposeful and effective teaching and learning strategy. Through exploring nursing's past, especially in relation to race and social injustice, students begin to define their beliefs toward patient care and develop an identity of who they are going to be as future nurses. The social injustices of the past illustrate how nurses have been pioneers in caring for patients from all walks of life, even in the era of the segregated South. Studying the path of nursing education in the southern United States over the last two centuries provides a foundation for students to understand the social climate and events that have shaped the profession.

This chapter provides support for the study of history, or historiography, as a scholarly teaching method. Presented here are three stories from regional nursing history that have been used in the classroom, along with student reactions and outcomes of the teaching strategy as recorded by the authors. The chapter illustrates how historiography helps students gain awareness of their own beliefs, critically challenge the stories they have heard, and explore how they can integrate this learning into their roles as professional nurses.

Why Study History in Nursing?

Some educators have questioned the merit of performing historical scholarship. The relative scarcity of professional organizations, publications, and courses devoted to nursing history suggests that scholars do not place a high priority on history in professional education (Holme, 2015). But history does matter. For nearly a century, professional organizations and educators have endorsed including history in nursing curricula for two compelling reasons: to develop critical thinking skills and to provide students with a sense of identity (Holme, 2015; Madsen, 2008; Lewenson, 2004; American Association for the History of Nursing [AAHN], 2001; Lait, 2000; American Association of Colleges of Nursing [AACN], 1999; Woolley, 1997; Lynaugh, 1996; Kalisch & Kalisch, 1976; Committee on Education of the National League of Nursing Education [NLN], 1917). The American Association for the History of Nursing explains that history not only promotes the development of critical thinking skills but also contributes to professional identity. As students uncover the roots of their professional past and question historical events, they develop a socially "contextual perspective" and "enlightenment" (AAHN, 2001, p. 1). Students develop a sense of pride in nursing as they learn about its history, and they develop an appreciation of the past through scholarly inquiry. As students engage with the stories through scholarly activities, history becomes more understood, more meaningful, and more foundational in developing one's professional values.

From a broad perspective, the study of history is grounded in the fact that we have a historical consciousness and a concept of past, present, and future. If we lose our history, we "suffer the loss of our memories, we lose our past and a part of ourselves" (Woolley, 1997, p. 4). Including history in professional education provides an avenue to develop essential critical thinking skills that nurses are expected to use in their practice. An academic study of history does not provide answers as much as it raises more questions. As Fairman and D'Antonio (2013) note, a study of the past "exposes historical tensions reflected in modern policy debates" (p. 346). Exploring the history of their chosen profession helps students understand how the past has shaped the present.

It can be further argued that the study of history is relevant in the health professions in a sociopolitical context. Health care is as much influenced by politics and economics as it is the biological and social sciences. To further understand the evolution of health care over time, one must grapple with the histories of geographic regions, social classes, political pressures, prevailing and competing cultural values, economic forces, and the known body of scientific knowledge among countless other factors. Nurse educators have supported bringing these discussions into the classroom to prepare students for the "social reality confronting the nursing profession" (Sullivan, 1996, p. 4). Scholarly inquiry into these and other influences on health care broadens students' understanding of the compounding social forces influencing the ethics of patient care.

Students gain insight into where nursing has been, what it is, and what it can be as a seamless context. To carry this further, understanding the past not only situates the present but also informs best practices for the future. In 2015, in the wake of the tragic racially motivated shooting during a Bible study in Charleston, South Carolina, President Barack Obama delivered perhaps his most pointed reflection on race when he eulogized the Rev. Clementa C. Pinckney, the pastor of Emanuel A. M. E. Church, where the shootings occurred: "For too long we've been blind to the way past injustices continue to shape the present" (Obama, 2015). When we forget the trials and tribulations of the past, and ignore the lessons learned, the possibility of repeating them in the future is confounded. History provides multidimensional lessons with the aim of raising our consciousness of "social, moral, and cultural complexities" (Holme, 2015, p. 636).

Historical research provides a source of professional understanding often displaced by the vast body of theoretical and clinical research and the marvel of technological developments. As Lynaugh (1996) states, history is "our source of identity, our cultural DNA" (p. 1). It is not enough to study historical facts, dates, and figures. More important than the *what* of the past is studying the *how* and the *why* (Smith, Brown, & Crookes, 2015). By asking these questions, history becomes scholarly in teaching students to critically reflect, analyze, problem-solve, and consider the competing forces impacting a bygone era and link that awareness to current and future practice. Designing learning activities such as presentations, debates, or research papers gives students an opportunity to delve further into the complexities surrounding any historical figure or event. Deeper understanding of all the factors influencing another's experience translates into more ethical nursing practice.

Is History Really Scholarship?

A discussion of history as scholarship would be remiss without acknowledging the expanded concept of scholarly work introduced in Ernest Boyer's seminal work *Scholarship Reconsidered: Priorities of the Professoriate* (1990). Boyer broadened the definition of scholarship to include activities related to discovery, teaching, application, and integration. In 1999, the American Association of Colleges of Nursing (AACN) released a position statement supporting an expanded concept of scholarship based on Boyer's model. Historical scholarship, or historiography, clearly falls under the category of the scholarship of discovery, according to the AACN (1999): "Historical research includes original investigations using manuscripts, documents, oral narrative, and other printed materials" (p. 373). Historical scholarship can broaden the way nurses think about clinical care and can provide direction for clinical practice and policy making (Fairman & D'Antonio, 2013). Consequently, many nurse educators have expanded their intellectual endeavors to include not only science but economics, policy, culture, education, and history, among others.

When studying history, should data simply be reported as factually as possible, or should the data be situated in a theoretical framework? The mere suggestion that history consists only of facts overlooks the understanding that the reporting, recording, and interpreting of historical events is filtered through the lenses of those involved. There is no single version of history or one formula for explaining complicated problems across societies (D'Antonio, Connolly, Wall, Whelan, & Fairman, 2010). Each person interprets current events through a personal subjectivity. As they are recorded for historical preservation, those authoring the accounts cannot avoid writing from a subjective standpoint. As time passes, those studying the historical accounts contribute another layer of subjectivity. Scholarly interpretation of history therefore requires continual reflection on one's self and professional practice. One must ask, "What is my subjective lens? How does my experience influence the lessons I learn from the past? How are these lessons important to me?" Historiography is an effective way to help students uncover the hidden biases that we all bring and to better understand the challenges that others face. How can nurses provide ethical care if their education does not involve developing self-awareness? How can nurses provide equal care to all if hidden biases toward others are not recognized?

This chapter not only supports the foundation of historical research as important to professional nursing education but further provides a collection of historical narratives to contextualize and explore the issues of gender, race, politics, and economics in professional nursing in the southern United States. Madsen (2008) delineated several benefits to studying nursing history as related to social consciousness. History can debunk romanticized myths, such as "Florence Nightingale single-handedly turning nursing around" (Madsen, 2008, p. 526) and place nursing in a larger social context. The assumption that nursing is founded on naturally feminine traits such as caring and subservience should also be challenged. For example, historically, more men than women have been employed in nursing in Australia's health care system (Cushing, 1997). Neither has nursing always been relegated to primarily hospital-based care. Significant roles that nurses have played in the community need to be highlighted for students to understand the scope of nursing's impact on health care. Lastly, by studying nursing's expectations and the hierarchy of health care in the past, future professionals can gain an understanding of some of the unwritten rules that still exist today.

The following historical essays on race and nursing in Charleston, South Carolina, have provided opportunities for students to critically analyze a dark era of professional history, understand how nursing in the United States came to be what it is today, especially in regards to racial consciousness, and integrate where we have come from into where we are going as a profession. We explore nursing history with a central theme of race in nursing and nursing education in the South, as racism continues to impact nursing education and nursing practice today. Recent data indicate implied racism in nursing. While over one-third of the United States' population belongs to racial and ethnic minority groups, nearly 75 percent of nurses are white (United States Department of Health and Human Services [USDHHS], 2013). The disproportionately low representation of minorities in nursing is contrary to the recommendation of the Institute of Medicine (2010) that the health workforce mirror the diversity of the greater population served.

Studies indicate that most racism in nursing is either implicit or unconscious. A recent study of unconscious race and class biases by Haider, Swoboda, Haut, Freischlag, and MacKenzie (2015) revealed the subtle nature of most biases, implying the vast degree to which stigma can influence nursing care. Of the nurses surveyed, 71 percent reported no conscious race or class preferences for a specific social group. Yet the study instrument revealed that only 14.7 percent *actually* demonstrated no racial preference and 6.53 percent had no class preference. Clearly, gaining an awareness of one's own biases coupled with a dedicated study of the social complexities of minority populations is indicated to develop caring health professionals.

An essential element of professional growth is the development of race consciousness, which includes exploring the historical journey of minority populations (Watts, 2003). Educators have not adequately addressed implied racism in nursing curricula through open dialogue, historical awareness, and research (Hall & Fields, 2013). Therefore, it seems imperative that conversations regarding racial biases be threaded throughout the curriculum for nurses to develop an inclusive, just, and caring professional identity. For nurses to care for all, regardless of race, ethnicity, gender, religion, sexual orientation, or socioeconomic status, their own biases have to be illuminated and confronted. Without deliberate efforts to gain awareness of unconscious racism and develop cultural competence, nurses will perpetuate the social injustices that have existed throughout history. Scholarship of Teaching and Learning (SoTL) activities that promote analysis of and reflection on racial and other social biases encourage a level of engagement that promotes professional development.

A Case Study

As part of our undergraduate nursing curriculum, we have brought stories from regional nursing history into the classroom as a tool to help students gain awareness of their own beliefs, critically challenge the stories they have heard, and explore how they can integrate this learning into their roles as professional nurses. Student demographics are relevant in that their reactions while studying history are situated in their cultural context and past experiences. It should be noted that the typical student profile reflected in these discussions consists of undergraduate nursing majors, mostly in their early to midtwenties, with a vast majority having been raised in the southeastern United States. About 40 percent come from middle-class urban backgrounds; another 60 percent have grown up in rural and underserved areas. While the ratio of white to black students averages four to one, there are cultural intersections with generational and regional similarities. Throughout the stories from nursing history that follow, student reactions to the social and professional issues raised offer insights into the development of professional values congruent with the ethical standards of any helping profession.

The following historical case study addresses nodal events in Charleston, South Carolina, from the advent of nursing education in 1883 in a deeply segregated society to 1972, when the first African American student graduated from a previously all-white nursing school. These nodal events each herald a change regarding race in nursing education and practice. The unfolding of events raises questions about the role of nurses in social justice, not only for patients but also for colleagues and the profession. The case study begs the question, "What is our role in issues of social justice, and what do these events mean in the development of our nursing practice?" Through the critical study of nursing history, educators and students together have explored driving forces in nursing's history, critically analyzed the impact of social injustices, questioned the subjectivity of historical scholarship, uncovered ongoing hidden racism and other inequities, and integrated personal lessons gained into their current identity as members of the profession.

Nineteenth-Century Nursing Education in Charleston, South Carolina

Early Nursing Education for White Women

Working in the homes of the sick poor since it was founded in 1813, the Ladies Benevolent Society (LBS) was an organization of 250 white women from Charleston who each paid five dollars a year for their membership and who accepted donations from all local churches and synagogues and individual bequests (Buhler-Wilkerson, 2001). Members of this organization made rounds in each ward of the city, seeking citizens who were in need of care. They cared for all sick poor, free blacks and whites, regardless of race, by hiring "granny nurses," or elderly women who needed employment and who provided basic in-home nursing care for these poor sick citizens under the LBS's supervision. Tragically, at that time, widowed or abandoned women in Charleston begged openly in the street in order to support themselves and feed their children as there were few opportunities for employment for women other than fostering orphaned children or providing nursing care for the LBS.

In addition to nursing care, the LBS provided tents and beds for the sick and homeless and food vouchers for all in their care. Patients were taken to a free clinic run by the city and examined by a physician. This physician would diagnose and certify their illness and prescribe the care that was needed. The nurse would then be paid by the LBS to provide care as long as the illness persisted. The LBS also provided pensions for some elderly women, such as three free women of color with leprosy who lived together on Pinckney Street. Each received a small pension, and a nurse was hired to care for them (Bellows, 1993).

In Charleston in 1883, the hospital commissioners for the city hospital sent an envoy to New York to hire a nurse from Bellevue Hospital to become supervisor of the new school of nursing that they wished to open. The school, which became known as the South Carolina School for Training Nurses, accepted white women of good moral character who were recommended by physicians from small rural communities throughout South Carolina (City Hospital Commissioners, 1882). Prior to the opening of this school, nursing care had only been provided by the Ladies Benevolent Society.

Unfortunately, the South Carolina Hospital for Training Nurses, after its well-intended opening and under constant strain from lack of funding, closed after only three years of operation when the earthquake of 1886 destroyed the city hospital; however, years later, the nursing school reopened, this time affiliated with Roper Hospital. Opened in Charleston in 1859, Roper Hospital was funded by a generous bequest of Thomas Roper "for the purpose of erecting and maintaining a hospital for the reception and treatment of such sick, maimed and diseased paupers as need medical aid, without regard to religion, complexion, or national origin" (Roper St. Francis, 2015) and, at that time, provided white physicians with a place to practice medicine. The faculty of the Medical School of the State of South Carolina provided lectures to the medical students. After the opening of the nursing school, medical faculty also gave lectures to the nursing students on asepsis, anatomy, and other topics.

After the reopening, nursing students, upon completion of the required number of hours "on duty" at the hospital caring for patients and assisting on surgical cases, were given an exam and received a diploma. The school graduated its first class in 1897. Most nurses who graduated from a nursing school at that time provided private care to an individual or a family in the patient's home.

Early Nursing Education for Black Women

In 1897, Alonzo McClennan (Hoffius, 2012), a black physician who had graduated from Howard University, opened a pharmacy called the Peoples' Pharmacy on King Street in Charleston but could not gain admitting privileges to practice medicine at Roper Hospital because of his race. Therefore, he purchased a three-story brick building on Cannon Street, where he opened a twenty-four-bed hospital for black people and poor whites of his community. Needing a nursing workforce to provide bedside care to his patients, he opened a school of nursing for black women—The Hospital and Training

School for Nurses. In addition to caring for patients, the student nurses at Cannon Street Hospital were required to raise chickens, collect their eggs daily, and tend the garden on the hospital grounds where the food was grown to feed the students, staff, and patients (Johnson, 2008).

Relationship to Teaching and Learning

When discussing early nursing education for whites versus blacks in Charleston, South Carolina, with today's nursing students in the same region, the reaction is somewhat uniform. The era studied is generationally so far removed from contemporary culture that regardless of race, gender, or age, students tend to respond as though they are studying disconnected facts from historical documents rather than the path that has led to the present. For instance, the fact that any nursing student, white or black, had to grow food and care for the hospital grounds is considered nearly unbelievable and somewhat humorous.

Many students today have little concept of legal segregation in education. Faculty often has to bring similar issues surrounding racism into awareness through discussing racial tensions apparent in current news events. One example is the public racial slurring of African American students on the University of Missouri campus that prompted a major student protest in the fall of 2015. This came in the aftermath of the racially motivated protests surrounding the death of a black crime suspect in Ferguson, Missouri, that garnered national attention the same year.

Using SoTL provides an avenue to engage students in complex questioning of racism as it existed at the foundations of nursing education and practice. Although racial segregation has been legally restricted since the Civil Rights Act of 1964, racism obviously remains an issue in our university communities. Addressing these larger social issues in nursing curricula is especially relevant in developing a professional value system that is inclusive of people of all walks of life. Higher education provides an opportunity for young adults to question the dogma of their parents, cultures, and educational systems and develop a personal value system that they will take into their professional nursing practice. Teaching values with history using SoTL shifts learning from a teacher-centered, content-driven classroom to a student-centered contextually situated classroom.

Many strategies can be used to integrate nursing history into a SoTL classroom, such as preparing papers or presentations tracing the origin and evolution of the Nightingale pledge, including the larger corresponding social issues, or tracing the American Nurses Association's policies on minority membership over the course of the organization's existence (Lewenson, 2004). These types of scholarly activities allow students to engage with the stories, explore multiple social determinants of the time, challenge the ethical issues, and begin to establish a personally meaningful value system. Exploring the historical path of social injustices allows students to translate former questions of racism into the current social context of nursing practice and patient care. This level of engagement is rarely achieved when studying the facts and faces of nursing history. More importantly, SoTL delves into the *how* and *why* of the past that provides so much insight into how nurses have become some of the biggest advocates for quality patient care.

Issues of social justice in current nursing practice and education become more evident as the timeline of nursing history turns to the twentieth century. The early roots of contemporary culture and the current health care system begin to emerge in the stories of these rapidly changing times. The following sections begin to trace the emergence of movements that fought for issues such as equal employment, fair compensation, and racial integration. Nursing begins to emerge as a profession that greatly impacts health policy and health care services.

The Twentieth Century: Early Integration of the Nursing Profession

White LBS Hires Black Professional Nurse

In Charleston in 1905, under the leadership of Katherine Ravenel, superintendent of the Ladies Benevolent Society, the organization was persuaded to hire a professional nurse to provide care to the society's patients in the city. Although the membership was not convinced of the necessity of a professional nurse, Ravenel gave interviews to newspaper reporters extoling the benefits and value of professional education for nurses. Through her lobbying in the community, people became more accepting of this type of professional nurse to replace the lay "granny" nurse. After several attempts to hire a white nurse, all of whom quit after no more than two weeks of employment, the LBS hired Anna DeCosta Banks, beginning their thirty-year continuous professional relationship (McGahan & Bustos-Nelson, 2013). Ms. Banks, a woman of color and a Charleston native, had previously graduated from the Dixie Institute in Hampton, Virginia, as a professional nurse and returned to Charleston as the nursing supervisor at Cannon Street Hospital. She used her new role as visiting community nurse for the LBS to employ her students during times of great need, such as yellow fever epidemics, offering them valuable clinical experience outside of the hospital. The Cannon Street Hospital and School of Nursing was paid by the LBS for the employment of these students, who were credited with saving lives during times of dreaded epidemics in the city.

In 1909, for instance, Banks and presumably her students made 1,800 visits for the LBS to 147 patients in the city of Charleston (McGahan & Bustos-Nelson, 2013). The physicians who were members of Charleston's South Carolina Medical Society had referred many of these patients. At this time, the South Carolina Medical Society also served as the State Board of Medical Examiners, who administered tests to graduate nurses in order for them to become registered nurses. Anna DeCosta Banks was examined in the state of South Carolina, becoming a registered nurse in 1910 (Johnson, 2008), undoubtedly because of her close affiliation with the LBS and her demonstration of competence to the members of the Medical Society. Her work was revered by medical professionals and community members, both black and white. However, there can be no doubt that she was paid less than white nurses, which was the custom of the time (Buhler-Wilkerson, 2001).

Federal PWA Funds, the Duke Endowment, and Racial Collaboration in Nursing

In 1920, Roper Hospital had 224 beds. Money was allocated in the county budget to provide funds for indigent patients, presumably to include black people, to be admitted to "Old Roper." In 1933, the Roosevelt administration provided money for 668 hospital building improvement projects nationally, which added eight thousand new beds in segregated wards of biracial hospitals. Roper Hospital used Public Works Administration funds to make improvements to the "Old Roper" section of the hospital, where indigent patients were admitted (City Hospital Commissioners, 1882). Unfortunately, these federal funds did not reach Cannon Street Hospital, and Dr. McClennan's hospital continued to struggle with a lack of funds and too few paying patients.

In 1948, Cannon Street Hospital lost its license and the students had to find other hospitals to complete their clinical requirements and classroom training. Melvina Gadsden, director of the Cannon Street Hospital School of Nursing, made an appeal for assistance to Ruth Chamberlain, the director of the school now named Nursing School of the Medical College (previously called the Roper Hospital School of Nursing and the South Carolina Training School for Nurses). While Ms. Chamberlain said the students could not be admitted to the school because of laws at the time, they could complete their clinical training at Roper Hospital, and the faculty would assist them to prepare for the nursing board exams (Johnson, 2008). The Cannon Street Hospital Nursing School officially closed.

WWII and New Horizons for Black Nurses

By World War II, the military and veterans' administration hospitals provided leadership for integrated health care services. This federal effort toward integration of health care facilities offered employment opportunities for black nurses at locations such as Fort Jackson in Columbia, South Carolina, and actively sought to recruit young black women into nursing. The federal government funded the 1943 Bolton Nurse Training Act, which produced one hundred and twenty-four thousand nurses nationally by offering funding to twenty-one all-black nursing schools and thirty-eight integrated nursing schools, which ultimately educated three thousand black nurses (Thomas, 2011).

Relationship to Teaching and Learning

When critiquing the previous case, students recognize the injustice inherent in hiring Anna DeCosta Banks "by default" only when the administration was unable to retain white nurses. But students today report that when gaining employment, race is less important than the ability to do the job, which might reveal implied racial bias. No matter how slight, the consideration of race as a qualifier of a nurse's competence is evidence that social equality for blacks and whites is not yet a reality.

Another revelation students have reported in the classroom is that even in the era of legal segregation, nursing was a profession that provided care for all. Students express pride when relating to the stories of the pioneers that demonstrated working for equality in health care. Nurses have been pioneers of equality through their care for their patients, even when being oppressed themselves. This signifies the humanistic values that are foundational to nursing. Today's nursing students display a predominant ethic of caring for all people regardless of social determinants, especially in their clinical education. Never have the students questioned a patient assignment based on race or social class. Today's nursing students self-report entering the field for the love of people. This is evident in their caregiving.

Regarding the issue of unequal pay, students today recognize the inequality of pay based on gender and understand the historical basis for the lingering inequity. They recognize that nursing remains a primarily female profession, and members of the profession earn less than members of the historically male-dominated medical profession. While history reveals that nursing is female dominated in many cultures, the profession has gained much salary momentum in recent years. Simultaneously, medicine is becoming more gender balanced. With medicine becoming more gender neutral, the future of pay equity is uncertain. With the current shortage of physicians, especially primary care physicians in rural areas such as the southern United States, advanced practice nurses are afforded roles and salaries more equitable to their medical counterparts. This salary equity is attracting more males into the profession. Whether the push is driven by more males in the profession or increased demand for nurses, the profession is experiencing tremendous growth.

Regardless of race, many students prefer engaging in scholarship surrounding more recent periods of history, especially the postwar era of the twentieth century. History comes to life when interviewing staff nurses, faculty, or patients who have lived some of the issues students are studying. Students are able to connect the past to the present more seamlessly and with more relevance. They have seen films and read stories depicting twentieth-century events and find them more relatable. Some of the twentieth-century issues surrounding race and gender inequality linger in their families and everyday lives, especially for students of color. They have heard their parents' firsthand stories and may have personally experienced social injustices.

The Postwar Era: A National Push for Racial Integration

Federal Intervention through the Hill-Burton Act

In 1946, the federal government provided funds for building hospitals through the Hill-Burton Act. The act required that racial integration be practiced by all hospitals accepting federal building funds. Roper Hospital and the South Carolina State Medical Society, suspect of outside interference regarding race in the running of their hospital, did not take advantage of this legislated federal funding. However, the Medical College of South Carolina took this opportunity to build its own hospital facility with Hill-Burton financing. The Medical College Hospital was a biracial but segregated hospital with an H-shaped configuration with one wing on each floor for blacks and the other wing for whites. The staff provided services across wings to all patients. This was thought to be the most efficient method to serve people of both races. The Hill-Burton Act is still considered to be the most important legislation in history for bringing modern health care to blacks in the South.

In June 1968, the federal government brought a lawsuit against the Medical Society of South Carolina and the administration of Roper Hospital (*United States v. Medical Society of South Carolina*, 1969) for managing the hospital on a segregated basis and discriminating against black employees and applicants for employment because of race. The lawsuit required that Roper Hospital treat all patients equally without race as a consideration for admission, treatments offered, and placement or room assignments. It further required equal employment opportunities regardless of race, including job opportunities, hiring, advancement, and pay.

Black Hospital Workers Organize against Discriminatory Employment Practices

At the Medical College Hospital in December of 1967, there was evidence of racial tension in the nursing department among black nonprofessional nursing workers. The hospital fired five workers who reportedly refused to carry out the head nurses' instructions. The workers were soon reinstated at the request of the local Office of Health, Education, and Welfare (HEW), which was the government agency mandated with carrying out civil rights regulations. In 1968, the disgruntled workers began meeting with union leaders of 1199 Hospital and Nursing Home Workers, forming a local chapter (Case study: The Charleston Hospital Strike, 1971). Mary Moultrie, the president of the local Union 1199B, made a formal statement regarding her employment at the Medical College Hospital, outlining the inequity of wages between black and white nurse technicians (Moultrie, 1969).

A meeting was planned with the hospital administration. However, the meeting became disorderly and resulted in police intervention. As a result, the hospital fired twelve workers from the ICU for "abandoning their patients." Later that evening, the union hospital workers voted to strike.

At dawn, two hundred workers formed a ring around the hospital, starting a 121-day strike that would gain the support of the Southern Christian Leadership Conference (SCLC) and garner national media attention. Public unrest led the governor of South Carolina to declare a state of emergency in the city. The National Guard was called out to maintain order, and curfews were imposed. The SCLC picketed the White House to gain the support of President Nixon for the hospital workers' plight. The president sent "observers" to the scene of the strike, resulting in the issue receiving national attention.

Following these events, the local department of HEW recommended the Medical College Hospital reinstate the twelve hospital workers and pay them from time of discharge. However, upon the request of US senator Strom Thurman, and under further examination by secretary of HEW Robert Finch, it was determined that the hospital had not violated the workers' civil rights, and the hospital withdrew its offer for rehire after twenty-four physicians threatened to resign if the workers were reinstated. The American Federation of Labor and Congress of Industrial Organizations union director became involved and provided support by threatening to close the Charleston seaport facilities and stop all trade if the workers were not rehired. In response, two federal dispute mediators were sent to Charleston and a settlement was reached. The workers from Charleston County Hospital and Medical College Hospital were either rehired or other employment places were found for them.

First African American Graduates from Medical College School of Nursing

At the same time, a significant change was taking place in nursing education. That same year, 1969, Rosslee Douglas enrolled in the Medical College of Nursing, later becoming their first African American graduate (Fox, 2010). Upon graduation, she became the administrator of the Franklin C. Fetter Clinic, which cared for inner-city black indigent residents of Charleston from the very same neighborhoods where Anna DeCosta Banks had made hundreds of home visits for the Ladies Benevolent Society. Douglas established regulations to license home health agencies in South Carolina. Later she was appointed by Nixon to increase the participation of historically black colleges and universities in government programs. She helped to establish a minority bank development program and provided financial aid to black colleges and universities. In 1985, she was awarded a doctorate of humane letters from the Medical University of South Carolina in recognition of her national achievements. In spite of these changes, recruiting minority students and maintaining their graduation rates remains a struggle today.

Relationship to Teaching and Learning

When students critique the discrimination experienced by health care providers at the Medical College Hospital in the postwar era, they understand the social climate but cannot relate it to the bases of unequal pay in today's professional environment. Current nursing salaries are largely based on shift differentials or positions and are accepted as equitable. The postwar era of nursing history illuminated the power of collective bargaining for salary equity, advancement of the profession, and the overall quality of health care.

Many students today do not engage in the political climate that our predecessors used to influence our health care system. A constant emphasis for nursing faculty is to promote the personal and collective benefits of involvement in professional organizations. Nurse educators must ask the questions, "What is the role of collective bargaining in health care?" "Do nurses have a voice in hospitals of today?" and "What are the current concerns regarding social justice and nursing?"

Conclusion

The history documented in this chapter provides a means for educators in health professions to help students develop their professional identity, values, and critical thinking skills, just as the authors have shared. It gives students a window to explore how the health professions have developed within the system we have today and the role that system plays in the larger social context. Educators can design any number of methodologies to engage students in dialogue with nursing's history. Teacher scholars have offered specific instructional methods in the literature, such as essays, journals, presentations, and posters to name a few.

Regardless of the topic discussed, it is interesting to note that when using stories from nursing history to develop professional values toward social injustices, minority students are often more aware of lingering segregation that exists today than are white students. While white students are more "colorblind," believing that all students in the same institution have the same opportunities for success, black students often report having personally felt like victims of racism for most of their lives. White students believe that all citizens have a right to a public education and often do not consider the multiple barriers to equal education. Essentially, white students do not understand white privilege (Case, 2012). Black students more readily relate to a culture where minorities are less likely to get the same quality education for reasons such as lack of value for education, poor socioeconomic resources, lack of educated role models, and limited access to high-quality schools. While black students are able to illuminate implicit racism, they are very hesitant to discuss it openly in classrooms where they themselves are the minority.

The reluctance to openly and directly discuss experiences of social injustice in varied classrooms further supports the use of SoTL in nursing education. White students are often unaware of the impact of race, and black students are often unwilling to share racial issues in integrated classrooms. Granted, whites cannot express what they do not know, and blacks may be guarded as a coping strategy. The question for educators in this situation is "How can students develop inclusive professional values if we cannot talk to each other?" There is a distinct possibility that the unsaid is as relevant to the development of professional identity as that which is shared. Scholarly inquiry of nursing's history provides a "neutral" field in which to explore issues of race and social justice in a nonthreatening context and exchange dialogue to bring future nurses together through an inclusive narrative.

The sociopolitical influences that affected oppression and empowerment in the eras presented provide a complex canvas from which to teach nursing's professional lessons. The challenge for educators is to avoid a boring reporting of facts and dates. Instead, effective use of historical scholarship in teaching, facilitated through SoTL, is needed to complicate the vast amount of information found in historical documents. Historical research needs to be studied critically, reflected on subjectively, and discussed genuinely. Including history in the curriculum requires a thorough reading beneath the events and questioning the why and how, not just the what.

Why were things the way they were? How were injustices perpetuated? What were the power structures? How did the powers shift during the era of study? What change strategies were used, and how were they successful? What were the failures? How can these strategies be employed in today's health care system? What sociopolitical factors exist today, and how can nurses advocate for betterment? A greater contextualization of current practice arises from studying history. Decades ago, Adelaide Nutting (1931) herself incorporated one of nursing's most iconic historical images associated with Florence Nightingale when she declared, "I have but one lamp by which my feet are guided and that is the lamp of experience. I know of no way of judging the future but by the past" (p. 1389). Nursing professionals, or any discipline with a documented history, can learn where they came from, who they are, and how they might move forward to a better future through engaging in challenging historiographic study. Using our histories to understand ourselves and our social context is both an obligation and a privilege.

MELISSA GARNO is BSN Program Director at Georgia Southern University. Her expertise is in psychiatric/mental health nursing practice and educational program development, management, and assessment of program/learning outcomes.

CAROLE BENNETT is a psychiatric/mental health advanced practice nurse. She has worked with children, adolescents, and adults who have mental illness or addiction.

References

American Association for the History of Nursing. (2001). *Nursing history in the curriculum: Preparing nurses for the 21st century*. Retrieved from http://aahn.org/position.html.

American Association of Colleges of Nursing. (1999). Defining scholarship for the discipline of nursing. *Journal of Professional Nursing, 15*(6), 372–376. doi:10.1016/s8755-7223(99)80068-4

Bellows, B. (1993). *Benevolence among slaveholders: Assisting the poor in Charleston 1670–1960*. Baton Rouge: Louisiana State University Press.

Boyer, E. L. (1990). *Scholarship reconsidered: Priorities of the professoriate*. New York, NY: Carnegie Foundation for the Advancement of Teaching.

Buhler-Wilkerson, K. (2001). *No place like home: A history of nursing and home care in the United States*. Baltimore, MD: Johns Hopkins University Press.

Case, K. A. (2012). Discovering the privilege of whiteness: White women's reflections on anti-racist identity and ally behavior. *Journal of Social Issues, 68*(1), 78–96. doi:10.1111/j.1540-4560.2011.01737.x

Case study: The Charleston Hospital Strike. (1971). *Southern Hospitals, 39*(3), 10–39. Charlotte, NC: Clark.

City Hospital Commissioners. (1882). *Minutes*. Charleston, SC: Charleston County Library Special Collections.

Cushing, A. (1997). Convicts and care giving in colonial Australia. In A. M. Rafferty, J. Robinson, & R. Elkan (Eds.), *Nursing history and the politics of welfare* (pp. 1788–1868). London, England: Routledge.

D'Antonio, P., Connolly, C., Wall, B. M., Whelan, J. C., & Fairman, J. (2010). Histories of nursing: The power and the possibilities. *Nursing Outlook, 58*(4), 207–213. doi:10.1016/j.outlook.2010.04.005

Fairman, J., & D'Antonio, P. (2013). History counts: How history can shape our understanding of health policy. *Nursing Outlook, 61*(5), 346–352. doi:10.1016/j.outlook.2013.07.001

Fox, E. B. (2010). *Opening doors: Women at the Medical University of South Carolina: Rosslee Thenetha Green Douglas*. Charleston, SC: Waring Historical Library, Medical University of South Carolina Library. Retrieved from http://waring.library.musc.edu/exhibits/MUSCwomen/Douglas.php.

Haider, A. H., Swoboda, S. M., Haut, E. R., Freischlag, J. A., & MacKenzie, E. J. (2015). Unconscious race and class biases among registered nurses: Vignette-based study using implicit association testing. *Journal of the American College of Surgeons, 220*(6), 1077–1086. doi:http://dx.doi.org/10.1016/j.jamcollsurg.2015.01.065

Hall, J. M., & Fields, B. (2013). Continuing the conversation in nursing on race and racism. *Nursing Outlook, 61*(3), 164–173. doi:10.1016/j.outlook.2012.11.006

Hoffius, S. (2012). *McClennan Banks Hospital & Training School for Nurses*. Charleston, SC: Waring Historical Library, Medical University of South Carolina Library. Retrieved from http://waring.library.musc.edu/exhibits/mcclennanbanks/McClennan.php.

Holme, A. (2015). Why history matters to nursing. *Nurse Education Today, 35*(5), 635–637. doi:10.1016/j.nedt.2015.02.007

Institute of Medicine, Committee on the Robert Wood Johnson Foundation Initiative on the Future of Nursing. (2010). *The future of nursing: Leading change, advancing health*. Washington, DC: National Academies Press.

Johnson, S. A. (2008). *Healing in silence: Black nurses in Charleston, South Carolina, 1896–1917* (Doctoral dissertation, The Medical University of South Carolina). Retrieved from https://www.musc.edu/nursing.

Kalisch, B. J., & Kalisch, P. A. (1976). Is history of nursing alive and well? *Nursing Outlook, 24*(6), 362–366.

Lait, M. E. (2000). The place of nursing history in an undergraduate curriculum. *Nurse Education Today, 20*(5), 395–400. doi:10.1054/nedt.2000.0477

Lewenson, S. B. (2004). Integrating nursing history into the curriculum. *Journal of Professional Nursing, 20*(6), 374–380. doi:10.1016/j.profnurs.2004.08.003

Lynaugh, J. E. (1996). Editorial. *Nursing History Review, 4,* 1.

Madsen, W. (2008). Teaching history to nurses: Will this make me a better nurse? *Nurse Education Today, 28*(5), 524–529. doi:10.1016/j.nedt.2007.09.008

McGahan, E. M., & Bustos-Nelson, J. (2013). *The Ladies Benevolent Society of Charleston: Two hundred years of service.* Charleston, SC: Ladies Benevolent Society.

Moultrie, M. (1969). *Statement following termination regarding employment at the Medical College of South Carolina.* Charleston, SC: Waring Historical Library, Medical University of South Carolina Library.

Nutting, M. A. (1931). The past, present, and future of nursing. *American Journal of Nursing, 31,* 1389–1391.

Obama, B. (2015). *Remarks by the president in eulogy for the honorable reverend Clementa Pinckney.* Charleston, SC: The White House Office of the Press Secretary. Retrieved from https://obamawhitehouse.archives.gov/the-press-office/2015/06/26/remarks-president-eulogy-honorable-reverend-clementa-pinckney.

Roper St. Francis. (2015). History. Retrieved from http://www.rsfh.com/about/history/.

Smith, K. M., Brown, A., & Crookes, P. A. (2015). History as reflective practice: A model for integrating historical studies into nurse education. *Collegian, 22*(3), 341–347. doi:10.1016/j.colegn.2014.04.005

Sullivan, E. J. (1996). Expanding the definition of scholarship. *Journal of Professional Nursing, 12*(1), 4. doi:10.1016/s8755-7223(96)80066-4

The Committee on Education of the National League of Nursing Education. (1917). *Standard curriculum for schools of nursing.* Baltimore, MD: The Waverly Press.

Thomas, K. K. (2011). *Deluxe Jim Crow: Civil rights and American health policy, 1935–1954.* Athens: University of Georgia Press.

United States Department of Health and Human Services & Health Resources and Services Administration. (2013). *The U. S. nursing workforce: Trends in supply and education.* Retrieved from http://bhpr.hrsa.gov/healthworkforce/reports/nursingworkforce/nursingworkforcefullreport.pdf.

United States v. Medical Society of South Carolina, 298 F. Supp. 145 (D.S.C. 1969).

Watts, R. (2003). Race consciousness and the health of African Americans. *Online Journal of Issues in Nursing, 8*(1), 3. Retrieved from www.nursingworld.org//MainMenuCategories/ANAMarketplace/ANAPeriodicals/OJIN/TableofContents/Volume82003/No1Jan2003/RaceandHealth.aspx.

Woolley, A. S. (1997). Doing history. *Journal of Professional Nursing, 13*(1), 5. doi:8755-7223/97/1301-0004$09.00/0

II.
Focusing on Marginalized Groups in SoTL

3 The Scholarship of Teaching and Learning and the Status of Women

Maxine P. Atkinson and Scott T. Grether

We BEGIN THIS chapter with brief biographies focused on how we became teacher scholars and how we see the Scholarship of Teaching and Learning (SoTL) strongly linked with issues of social justice. We focus on the status of women but are acutely aware that SoTL should, and hopefully does, serve the interests of other disadvantaged groups. We believe that reflection is an important part of SoTL and that thinking about thinking is fundamental to the work we do. SoTL inspires us to be better teachers and to work toward a more just society. We are both sociologists; Atkinson is a full professor and Grether is a senior-level graduate student.

> GRETHER: I am twenty-seven years old, white, heterosexual, American, and male. Along with my brother, I was reared in a two-parent, middle-class household. My social location has afforded me many unearned privileges and continues to do so. One of the biggest challenges I have to becoming a sociologist is to recognize these unearned privileges, one of which is being ascribed authority, competence, and respect in the classroom.
>
> My experiences in the classroom have been fairly straightforward. My learning objectives and lesson plans are designed around active learning, and, for the most part, students are compliant. Rarely do I get pushback on my classroom management or pedagogical practices. My evaluations indicate that students enjoy how they are learning and how classes are structured. Furthermore, I consistently score above the department mean in almost all measures of teacher effectiveness.
>
> When talking with my colleagues, the majority of whom are women, their experiences are quite different. They have harsh student evaluations and encounter instances of sexual harassment, unruliness in the classroom, and

consistent challenges to their authority. Like me, they have an intermediate level of teaching experience, attend teaching workshops, actively participate in teaching communities, and read in the Scholarship of Teaching and Learning.

I like to think that I am better at teaching than my colleagues. But I know better. Something seemed odd because my training and level of enthusiasm were matched by many of my colleagues. As embarrassing as it is to say, I was not thinking like a sociologist about what happens in the classroom and how to account for the differences between my colleagues and myself.

Not until I started to actively read and research in SoTL did I become aware of inequalities in the classroom. This body of research forced me to confront how my assessment strategies, interactions with students, assigned readings, classroom activities, facilitation of class discussions, and so on catered to students from a similar social location as myself. Not only were there discrepancies between what I said and what I did, but I was unintentionally contributing to institutional forms of inequality by catering my class to students like me!

Being involved in SoTL helps me recognize how I am advantaged, both culturally and structurally, to succeed as a teacher and offers strategies to address issues of social injustice. For example, I have begun to incorporate material from sociologists who are women and nonwhite. An evaluation on a lecture of mine discussing government and the economy suggested that including research from sociologists who are women and nonwhite would demonstrate to students that sociologists are not just white and male. I have started to implement a variety of assessment techniques after researching the difficulties associated with "deep learning" (Roberts & Roberts, 2008) and how traditional forms of assessments, such as exams, contribute to forms of institutional bias against nonwhite students (Steele, 1997). I also create learning objectives and active-learning techniques that demonstrate the (re)production of inequality because such activities engage students with the material and enable them to apply what they learn in the classroom to the world in which they live (Van Auken, 2013; McKinney, 2005).

ATKINSON: I am an older white woman who grew up in poverty; issues of social justice have been a driving force in my life. The teaching and learning movement that produces the Scholarship of Teaching and Learning was transformational for my career. To say that it changed my life is not an exaggeration. By the late 1990s on my campus, there was a move toward a learning (versus teaching) paradigm (Barr & Tagg, 1995) and the recognition of SoTL as a legitimate form of scholarship worthy of tenure and promotion. This came at a time when I was struggling with the weakness of the trickle-down system of science. I was questioning the value of writing yet one more article that only a handful of sociologists would read. Counting the lines on my vita felt hollow and inauthentic. I was struggling with how to get beyond being the sage on the stage, experiencing deep dissatisfaction with my work, questioning the value of higher education as I saw it being enacted, and yearning to do more for my students. Discovering SoTL (although we did not yet have consensus on that term) was a light at the end of a tunnel, and the community of teacher scholars who practiced SoTL became my reference group, colleagues who shared my values and with whom I struggled to move toward a learning paradigm rather than being stuck in the teaching paradigm (Barr & Tagg, 1995).

In 2000, I presented my presidential address to the Southern Sociological Society, titled "The Scholarship of Teaching: Conceptualizations and Implications for Sociologists." That was the beginning of my public announcement of what some of my departmental colleagues called my "downfall." I stopped teaching in our graduate concentration in sociology of the family, stopped my family sociology research agenda, and began to focus exclusively on teaching graduate students to teach, learning all I could about how to practice more student-centered pedagogies for my undergraduates, and creating the SoTL.

SoTL takes us to work that matters, to addressing issues of social justice and experiencing the true joy of seeing learning happen around issues of social justice. It takes us to that magical place where a student sees the world in a different light, asks questions, and truly wants to know and to make a difference. As Hutchings (2000) contends, SoTL has a "transformational agenda." That is, SoTL is produced to generate change. That change is not just a difference in the way we teach, although that is certainly a large part of it. SoTL can create community among scholars and between current and future scholars. SoTL opens our eyes to the possibility of a world where knowledge is created, valued, shared, and used to create a more just world (Atkinson & Lowney, 2015).

Becoming an SoTL scholar felt like a new life, and it has been. SoTL allows me to be my authentic self, to do the work I want to do, to have the relationship with my undergraduates that I find rewarding, and to help other teacher scholars develop their skills. But there were prices to pay both as an individual and as a feminist. My promotion to full professor did not come nearly as quickly as it would have if I had stayed with my original research agenda. SoTL does not earn one the prestige that more traditional scholarships do. I also realized that I was placing myself into another marginalized status and perhaps reinforcing the stereotype of women as teachers, and on a research-intensive campus, being a researcher is by far the more valued status.

Being a SoTL scholar creates a contradiction for female faculty especially. We are already marginalized, seen as less intelligent, less committed to work, less professional, and more keepers of the kin than creators of knowledge. Yet, in this paper, we will argue that SoTL is one of the keys to raising the status of women on campus.

Examining the potential that SoTL has for both addressing and raising the status of women requires that we explore the contexts within which women do their work in the academy. These contexts include the cultural milieu of values and beliefs that create gendered expectations and the structures of higher education.

The Culture of Higher Education, Teaching, and SoTL

The most well-developed literature that connects the culture of higher education and SoTL is the work on student evaluations. While this is certainly not the only literature that addresses cultural issues and SoTL, it is certainly one of the most contentious and perhaps one of the most impactful for female teachers. What students say about us has different effects on our careers in different types of colleges and universities, but their evaluations create a vital context within which we do our work. For example, in research-intensive universities, you might only need to be perceived as adequate by your students in order to formally succeed, while in small, private liberal arts colleges, student evaluations may play a greater role in our success. Regardless of the part student evaluations play in the formal advancement of our careers, it would be hard for most of us to ignore what our students say about us and our teaching. Regardless of how important teaching is for our career advancement, teaching is personal. We are in the spotlight, and how our students respond to us can have a powerful impact on the way we see ourselves as teachers, and student evaluations can affect our job satisfaction.

Studying student evaluations is a form of SoTL, and we argue that the literature that has developed on student evaluations is vital to female faculty's careers. Without careful attention to this literature, the expectations and evaluations of female faculty's performance in the classroom can easily be biased and unjust. If you asked most higher education administrators if there was a gender difference in student evaluations, they would probably tell you "no." That is the case perhaps because of the most well-known work related to gender and student evaluations—Feldman's meta-analyses (Feldman, 1992; Feldman, 1993). Feldman concludes essentially there are no gender differences in student evaluations of instructors. That quick and concise answer lets us off the hook. If there are no differences, then we need not worry about gender and student evaluations. However, to conclude there are no gender differences in student evaluations conceals more than it reveals.

The Feldman studies may say more about the methods by which the data were gathered than the realities women and men face in the classroom. If you read the work closely, you see there is quite a bit of variation from study to study, across disciplines, and across campuses; but often only the global results are reported and remembered. The unintended consequences of the Feldman studies are a disservice to both women and men. Perhaps the most significant positive contribution of this research is that it spurred more nuanced work.

To be fair, Feldman's work is certainly not the only research that has failed to find gender differences in student evaluations. Other studies have reported contradictory findings. Some research suggests that men have higher student ratings (Basow & Silberg, 1987), some finds that women have higher evaluations (Bachen, McLoughlin, & Garcia, 1999), and some finds no differences (Centra & Gaubatz, 2000). We focus our work here on reviewing literature that we believe helps untangle the research.

Here is a challenge for you. Go to http://benschmidt.org/profGender/#. This site lets you see how often students use which adjectives to describe their instructors in twenty-five different disciplines on RateMyProfessor.com. According to RateMyProfessor.com, these data come from about fourteen million reviews (Schmidt, 2015). Choose any characteristic that interests you and see if it is gendered.

We entered words such as "caring," "understanding," and "helpful." There is a gender difference. Women are more likely to be seen as having these characteristics. We also entered words like "intelligent" and "interesting." Men were more likely to be perceived as having these characteristics. Then we entered more negative characteristics, like "mean," "unfair," "rigid," "cold," "arrogant," and "boring." Would you like to guess which of these words were used to describe men versus women? If you thought that women would be more likely to be seen as mean, unfair, rigid, and cold, you would be right. Men are the professors who were more likely to be seen as arrogant and boring. Obviously there are different expectations for women as compared to men. If women are good, they are caring, understanding, and helpful. If men are good, they are intelligent and interesting.

We chose these particular phrases based on research by Sprague and Massoni (2005). These researchers asked about three hundred students from a university on the East Coast and one in the Midwest to provide up to four adjectives to describe the best and worst teachers they had ever had. We chose the same adjectives Sprague and Massoni found to be gendered. RateMyProfessor.com is not a site many of us are likely to use for research purposes, but when the results are the same as those of a study published in *Sex Roles*, it gives the findings much greater validity.

And so what if good female teachers are seen as caring, understanding, and helpful while good male professors are seen as intelligent and interesting? Most of us would like to be seen as having any of those characteristics. However, this research, confirmed by the data from RateMyProfessor.com, allows us to see the standards on which women and men will be judged to be good professors. Women have to live up to being caring, understanding, and helpful while men need to live up to being intelligent and interesting. What behaviors are required to be caring, understanding, and helpful? Students may expect the instructor to spend time with them going over material, to allow them to make up work, to allow more time on a task, to allow them to hand in late work; in short, female professors are expected to be nurturing, to do a lot of emotion work. How about male professors? Male professors are expected to be good entertainers. Think about the effort required for both of these performances. Nurturing requires the most time and emotion work. If women get the same student evaluation as men, it may very well be because they had to spend a lot more time and effort to achieve the same result. Sprague and Massoni (2005) call this the "Ginger Rogers effect." Ann Richards, the former governor of Texas, coined this phrase, arguing that Ginger Rogers did the same thing Fred Astaire did, but she had to do it backwards and in high heels!

MacNell, Driscoll, and Hunt (2015) provide us with a unique examination of the effect of gender on student evaluations. Specifically, they enlighten how gender differences may be difficult to tease apart from other influences on student evaluations, such as the skill of the instructor and the course taught. To hold other possible explanations constant, they examined data from an online course where the gender of the instructor could be masked. They constructed four groups of students. One group believed that they had a female instructor, and their instructor was in fact female. The second group believed they had a female instructor, but their instructor was actually male. The third group believed that their instructor was male, but the instructor was actually female; and the fourth group believed their instructor was male, and indeed he was. Combining the groups that were taught by a woman, the researchers compared student evaluations across the actual gender of the instructor. They did the same for the two groups that had a male instructor. Then they compared the groups who perceived they had a woman instructor to those who perceived they had a male instructor. The results are instructive. There are no differences between the student ratings of the actual male and female instructors; however, when students perceived that they had a male instructor, they rated "him" more highly than when they perceived that they had a female instructor.

Miller and Chamberlin (2000) report similar findings when they study students' perceptions of their instructor's educational attainment. Men are much more likely to have a PhD attributed to them than are women, regardless of their actual educational attainment. In short, women are seen as teachers, and men are seen as professors. These perceptions come with a cost for women—they are marginalized and stereotyped as not being as well qualified as their male counterparts.

We also need to consider that gender may interact with other factors. Women who are not white, or heterosexual, may face even more negative attributions. Anderson and Smith (2005) add evidence to the idea that the preconceived notions students bring to the classroom have an effect on their perception of faculty. Anderson and Smith's study includes a large sample of 633 students who were 44 percent Latino, 34 percent African American, and 22 percent Anglo. Students were provided with a syllabus that included the professor's name, which was indicative of gender and ethnicity. Syllabi were also constructed in a way such that the researchers believed the students would see the professors as lenient or strict in their teaching styles. The importance of Anderson and Smith's work for this paper is their finding that gender interacted with ethnicity to predict students' evaluations. For example, Latino professors with a strict teaching style were ranked lower than Anglos with the same style, and favorable reviews for Latina professors came from a more lenient teaching style, but not for Anglo women. Much work remains to be done on the effect of ethnicity and teaching evaluations.

We also need to think about the influence of sexuality on student evaluations. Do students perceive gay men and lesbian women differently than their heterosexual counterparts? While we know less about the impact of sexuality on student perceptions, recent research suggests that students do bring their world views of sexuality into the classroom just as they do their perceptions of gender and ethnicity. Anderson and Kanner (2011) find that gay and lesbian professors are seen as more politically biased than heterosexual professors and that professors' sexuality influences whether or not students are interested in taking a course from them.

Students' perceptions are important whether we are considering gender, ethnicity, or sexualities. Students do not leave their world views outside the classroom, and it would be surprising if they did. Yet, universities continue to compare male and female professors as though this is the one area of life where everything we know about devalued groups does not matter. Our culture's gendered expectations leave women at a distinct disadvantage. Even in wrestling we have weight classes because it would be inherently unfair to force a 125-pound bantamweight to compete against someone weighing over 225 pounds. There would be no sport in that. That is easy for us to see. Our gendered expectations are no less real; we are often simply less willing to take them seriously. To expect female professors to be Ginger Rogers while men get to be Fred Astaire is inherently unjust.

SoTL has a vital role to play in achieving justice for female faculty. This literature on student evaluations clearly indicates that regardless of whether or not there are absolute differences in student evaluations of women's and men's teaching, we need to pay attention to the expectations students bring with them to the classroom. First, we need to be careful to remember the lessons intersectionality literature has taught us (Anderson & Kanner, 2011; Anderson & Smith, 2005). White women and black women, lesbians and heterosexual women, and young women and older women do not teach under the same conditions. To simply compare women versus men is to see only a small part of the complex situation that is our teaching. Second, to ignore the gendered expectations that influence every other arena of our lives and assume that our teaching is not gendered is simplistic in the extreme. SoTL literature on teaching evaluations has a vital role to play in achieving justice for women in the academy.

The Structures of Higher Education

Women live and work in both cultural and structural contexts. These contexts are powerful determinants of their opportunities and life experiences. It is not possible to understand the status of women in the academy without examining both. We turn now to the structures of higher education.

In 1999, the Massachusetts Institute of Technology (MIT) released a report on female faculty in six science departments at this university. This report brought to light many ways in which MIT was discriminating against female faculty members on an institutional level and spurred even more interest in gender equity in higher education. Specifically, this report found that as female faculty advanced in their careers, they increasingly felt marginalized and excluded from their departments, which largely stemmed from the inequitable distributions of space, nine-month salaries paid from individual research grants, teaching assignments, awards and distinctions, inclusion on important committees, and assignments within the department between men and women. Not only did this report clearly, and unequivocally, unearth MIT's gender discrimination, it also illustrated that institutions of higher learning are not impervious to institutional discrimination against women.

Since this time, numerous studies have further examined the intersection of gender and higher education. What follows here is a brief review of some of the structural-level constraints that place women in subordinate positions while unfairly placing men in advantageous positions within the academy. Specifically, we highlight previous literature demonstrating how gender differences in the types of jobs, pay, and experiences of working within the academy facilitate the career advancement of men over women.

Jobs

Women now earn more than 50 percent of all doctoral degrees awarded in the United States (National Center for Education Statistics [NCES], 2012a) and about 50 percent of science and engineering doctoral degrees (National Center for Science and Engineering Statistics [NCSE], 2015). However, when women are employed in the academy, it is more likely to be in lower-ranking positions. Women are more likely to work as adjunct faculty than men (Wolfinger, Mason, & Goulden, 2009) and to be part-time faculty members rather than full-time members (Toutkoushian & Bellas, 2003). There has been some improvement in women's ability to get a full-time job in community colleges. During the 1980s and 1990s, more men than women worked at community colleges, but they now work at community colleges in about equal numbers (Eagan, 2007). The National Center for Education Statistics (2012b) supplies us with recent data on types of jobs occupied by women and men in academe. The NCES gathered data on full-time instructional faculty in degree-granting institutions and found that in 2009, men outnumbered women at the highest ranks in academia. Seventy-two percent of all full professors, 59 percent of all associate professors, and 52 percent of all assistant professors were men, whereas 28 percent of all full professors, 41 percent of all associate professors, and 48 percent of all assistant professors were women. Women outnumbered men only at the rank of instructor, where 55 percent of all instructors were women and 45 percent were men, and lecturer, where 53 percent were women and 47 percent were men. These differences persisted through 2011, where more men were employed at the highest ranks of academia than women. Other scholars have noted similar gender disparities, such as the low representations of women and minorities as being tenured or in tenure-track positions (Perna, 2001) and the underrepresentation of women faculty in STEM (science, technology, engineering, and mathematics) fields (Xu, 2008).

Data from the NCES also show some evidence of advancement for female faculty between 2009 and 2011. During this time, women's employment increased by 6.9 percent, 6.5 percent, 7.3 percent, 3.5 percent, and 5.5 percent for full, associate, and assistant professor, instructor, and lecturer, respectively. These gains were larger than the gains made to men's employment, and, in fact, there was a slight decrease to the percentage of men working at the ranks of assistant professor and lecturer (a 0.6 and 0.2

percent drop, respectively). On the other hand, an American Association of University Professors (AAUP) report puts the data in historical perspective (Curtis, 2011). Over four decades of data indicates that women still comprise only 42 percent of full-time faculty in American colleges and universities. Still, the percentage of full-time faculty who are women has increased from 23 percent to 42 percent since the 1970s. Progress can be slow.

Pay Equity

Despite the encouraging numbers of women entering the academy, pay equity at every level is still an important issue. Women in the United States earn about 79 percent of what men earn, and this is true for those with doctoral degrees as well (American Association of University Women [AAUW], 2015). Curtis (2011) reports on what he terms the "persistent inequity" in gender and academic employment. Women working full time as faculty members earn less than men at every rank, assistant to full professor, and in every type of institution from doctoral universities to community colleges. In the AAUP salary study in 1975–1976, women faculty earned 81 percent of men's salaries, and the same was true in their salary study in 2009–2010.

Experiences in Jobs

Women and men differ greatly in the experiences they have while working in academe. For example, Buckley, Sanders, Shih, Kallar, and Hampton (2000) address how women view their career progress, the resources they have available for career development, and the values they have related to academic success and recognition. In conjunction with Virginia Commonwealth University's survey research laboratory, they devised a questionnaire assessing how faculty valued specific accomplishments as indicators of their success. This questionnaire was administered to all full- and part-time faculty at the VCU School of Medicine and the associated Veterans Affairs Medical Center. They find that not only do women progress in their careers more slowly than men, but this progression largely stems from more women being employed part time (which precludes the possibility of seeking tenure), working in clinical rather than research positions (which limits the chances for scholarly work and publication), and having fewer discussions with their department heads about promotion than their male colleagues (which means they have less formal instruction on the criteria needed for promotion).

These findings are limited because they are derived from a survey administered to only one academic institution. They are illustrative, however, of other findings on the structural constraints of academe. For example, because more white men are hired into tenure-track positions and hold higher-ranking positions within academics—and because mentors tend to find mentees like themselves—women and faculty members of color report difficulties finding a mentor (Bova, 2000). Additionally, women often report that mentoring relationships with male colleagues are difficult because their male mentors are not empathetic to challenges women face in the academy (Bernas & Major, 2000), they are unable to provide suggestions for these challenges (Quinlan, 1999), or they might be subject to departmental gossip if seen outside of the department with their mentors (Blake-Beard, 2001; Kalbfleisch, 2000).

Another important dimension in which men and women differ in their academic employment experiences is balancing time between work and family. For example, Wolfinger, Mason, and Goulden (2009) report that being married and having children largely accounted for why recently minted female doctorates left the labor force rather than seek a tenure-track position. Indeed, wives are more likely than husbands to take time off from their careers to care for family members (Parker, 2015) and perform the majority of child-rearing tasks (Bianchi, Robinson, & Milkie, 2006) and household tasks (Bianchi, Robinson, & Sayer, 2001). This is true even among academics, where women in the academy report more work–family conflicts than their male counterparts (Wolfinger et al., 2009). While some women working in the academy might have been able to surmount workplace-related structural barriers, they are still being held accountable for "doing gender" within the institution of family. This means they are spending more time meeting familial obligations than their male colleagues, which reduces the amount of time they have available for working toward career advancement. Indeed, this is one of the findings from the aforementioned MIT report (1999) where women junior faculty members expressed concerns on finding a balance between family and work.

What about women who already have families before seeking employment? Other studies exploring the "competing devotions" between family and work find that forming families during or after graduate school significantly contributes to lower rates of women obtaining tenure than men (Mason & Goulden, 2004; Wolfinger et al., 2009). When considering the average age at which women receive their doctorates is 35.5, some scholars raise the concern that women wanting families are forced to consider the timing of having a family and their current age because of the potential health risks associated with having children after thirty (Jacobs & Winslow, 2010). Even further, women must also take into account the often-stringent deadline of making tenure within six or seven years after completing graduate school.

Conclusion

SoTL is important to the status of women in both direct and indirect ways. The literature on student evaluations of faculty provides a direct example of how SoTL can help women in their academic careers. When we are conversant with this literature, we understand that even if there are no quantitative differences in student evaluations of women and men, teaching requires qualitatively different skills. Women are expected to be nurturing and to do a lot of emotion work in order to be successful. This is time-consuming and energy-sapping work. Men are expected to be interesting and entertaining. While this does require expertise and work, our fields provide us with many ways to engage students with the fundamentals of our disciplines and fields. Few of us find our topics of study uninteresting and, thus, it is less time-consuming to engage than to constantly nurture. And if we fail to be entertaining, our colleagues are very supportive because they understand that to be thought of as "boring" is a complaint that anyone could get. We are, after all, not professional entertainers. But when women fail to be nurturing, they are seen as "mean" and "cold," much more negative characteristics.

The structural conditions under which female faculty work put them at a disadvantage compared to their male counterparts. Women work in lower-status jobs in the academy, earn less money than their male counterparts, report fewer positive working experiences, and live with the challenges of demanding family expectations more than do their male counterparts. They indeed have to be "Ginger Rogers," doing the same jobs as men but with fewer rewards and resources and more hurdles.

SoTL can be directly and indirectly helpful to advancing the position of women who work in less-advantageous positions compared to their male counterparts. Doing SoTL work allows you to integrate the numerous demands of faculty life in an effective way. You can assess your own teaching and publish the results. This gives you the opportunity to combine teaching with research. We must all evaluate our students, and we can publish our evaluations of teaching strategies in any number of venues. There are journals about teaching in every major field and discipline, and there are more generic journals as well. For example, a chemist could publish in *Chemistry Education Research and Practice*, a sociologist can publish in *Teaching Sociology*, and an English professor can publish in *Research in Teaching of English*. Or anyone, for any field, can publish in journals such as *Academic Exchange Quarterly*, *College Teaching*, *Effective Education*, or the *International Journal of the Scholarship of Teaching and Learning*. In addition to formal publishing, one can present SoTL research at regional and national meetings.

Because of the kinds of positions women hold, SoTL is more likely to be valued on the campuses where they teach. Women are overrepresented in positions that require more teaching and thus have less time for research. Combining teaching with research is an effective way to practice scholarship.

SoTL also allows one to combine skills and knowledge about teaching effectiveness and service commitments. Those of us who understand assessment are highly valued on today's campuses. If you know SoTL literature, you can also be a more effective member of curriculum committees. Our national organizations associated with our fields and disciplines usually have committees and that are organized around teaching that field. Sociology, for example, has as one of its major groupings a "section" titled "Teaching and Learning." National leadership roles are available that need those of us who know SoTL literature.

Of course, knowing SoTL makes teaching easier and more fulfilling. It is much more rewarding to be good at a job than to flounder. When you understand what an effective class is, it is easier to create one. Your students are likely to be much more intrigued by engaging activities than by yet another talking head.

Teaching awards are often defined in such a manner that knowledge of SoTL is recognized. When you know this literature, colleagues often identify this expertise and reward it in the form of teaching awards. Many of us are popular with students, but to also be knowledgeable in the academy, a place where expertise is highly valued, is a tremendous advantage. Whether you work at a community college or a research-intensive university, a string of teaching awards is likely to be valued and acknowledged.

We also argue that colleagues in SoTL are very likely to be accepting of women in the academy. SoTL scholars are more likely to read the literature about higher education and effective teaching. They are therefore more likely to be aware of the challenges women continue to face in the academy. SoTL is also a new field. The field was "born" in 1990, when Ernest Boyer published *Scholarship Reconsidered*. New fields are always easier to break into than fields with old traditions that have been created by men. Women have been a part of the SoTL movement from the beginning, most notably Pat Hutchings and Mary Taylor Huber. Pat Hutchings is the former vice-president of the Carnegie Foundation for the Advancement of Teaching and continues to work part time as a senior associate. Mary Taylor Huber continues to work with the Carnegie Foundation as a senior scholar emerita and consulting scholar. While both have been prolific scholars, they are perhaps most well known for their monograph, *The Advancement of Learning: Building the Teaching Commons*.

SoTL can play an important role in elevating the status of women in the academy. Knowledge of the SoTL literature that addresses student evaluations is directly helpful to women because it puts teaching in context. It allows us to more accurately see, and hopefully reward, the work women do in their classrooms. SoTL provides numerous opportunities for women to perform their duties in more efficient ways, combining teaching and research and teaching and service and providing opportunities for local, regional, and national recognition. SoTL is an important tool for social justice for women.

MAXINE P. ATKINSON is Professor of Sociology at North Carolina State University. She was the first woman to win the North Carolina college and university system's Board of Governors' Award for Excellence in Teaching (BOG) at NC State and is the only woman to have served as head of the Department of Sociology and Anthropology at NC State.

SCOTT T. GRETHER is a PhD candidate in the Department of Sociology and Anthropology at North Carolina State University. He specializes in the sociology of marriage and family, the Scholarship of Teaching and Learning, race and ethnicity, and qualitative methods.

References

American Association of University Women. (2015). *The simple truth about the gender pay gap (fall 2015)*. Retrieved from http://www.aauw.org/research/the-simple-truth-about-the-gender-pay-gap/

Anderson, K. J., & Kanner, M. (2011). Inventing a gay agenda: Students' perceptions of lesbian and gay professors. *Journal of Applied Social Psychology, 41*(6), 1538–1564. doi:10.1111/j.1559-1816.2011.00757.x

Anderson, K. J., & Smith, G. (2005). Students' preconceptions of professors: Benefits and barriers according to ethnicity and gender. *Hispanic Journal of Behavioral Sciences, 27*(2), 184-201. doi:10.1177/0739986304273707

Atkinson, M. & Lowney, K. S. (2015). *In the trenches: teaching and learning sociology*. New York, NY: W. W. Norton & Company.

Bachen, C. M., McLoughlin, M. M., & Garcia, S. S. (1999). Assessing the role of gender in college students' evaluations of faculty. *Communication Education, 48*(3), 193–210. doi:10.1080/03634529909379169

Barr, R. B., & Tagg, J. (1995). From teaching to learning—A new paradigm for undergraduate education. *Change: The Magazine of Higher Learning, 27*(6), 12–26. doi:10.1080/00091383.1995.10544672

Basow, S. A., & Silberg, N. T. (1987). Student evaluations of college professors: Are female and male professors rated differently? *Journal of Educational Psychology, 79*(3), 308–314. doi:10.1037/0022-0663.79.3.308

Bernas, K. H., & Major, D. A. (2000). Contributors to stress resistance: Testing a model of women's work-family conflict. *Psychology of Women Quarterly, 24*(2), 170–178. doi:10.1111/j.1471-6402.2000.tb00198.x

Bianchi, S. M., Robinson, J. P., & Milkie, M. A. (2006). *The changing rhythms of American family life*. New York, NY: Russell Sage Foundation.

Bianchi, S. M., Robinson, J. P., & Sayer, L. C. (2001, September). *Family interaction, social capital, and trends in time use study*. Retrieved from http://web.stanford.edu/group/ssds/dewidocs/icpsr3191/cb3191.all.pdf.

Blake-Beard, S. D. (2001). Taking a hard look at formal mentoring programs: A consideration of potential challenges facing women. *Journal of Management Development, 20*(4), 331–345. doi:10.1108/02621710110388983

Bova, B. (2000). Mentoring revisited: The black woman's experience. *Mentoring and Tutoring, 8*(1), 5–16. doi:10.1080/713685511

Buckley, L. M., Sanders, K., Shih, M., Kallar, S., & Hampton, C. (2000). Obstacles to promotion? Values of women faculty about career success and recognition. *Academic Medicine, 75*(3), 283–288.

Centra, J. A., & Gaubatz, N. B. (2000). Is there gender bias in student evaluations of teaching? *Journal of Higher Education, 71*(1), 17–33. doi:10.2307/2649280

Curtis, J. W. (2011, April 11). *Persistent inequality: Gender and academic employment*. Retrieved from http://www.aaup.org/NR/rdonlyres/08E023AB-E6D8-4DBD-99A0-24E5EB73A760/0/persistent_inequity.pdf.

Eagan, K. (2007). A national picture of part-time community college faculty: Changing trends in demographics and employment characteristics. *New Directions for Community Colleges, 140*, 5–14. doi:10.1002/cc.299

Feldman, K. A. (1992). College students' views of male and female college teachers: Part I. Evidence from the social laboratory and experiments. *Research in Higher Education, 33*(3), 317–375. doi:10.1007/BF00992265

Feldman, K. A. (1993). College students' views of male and female college teachers: Part II. Evidence from students' evaluations of their classroom teachers. *Research in Higher Education, 34*(2), 151–211. doi:10.1007/BF00992161

Huber, M. T., & Hutchings, P. (2005). *The advancement of learning: Building the teaching commons*. Menlo Park, CA: Carnegie Foundation for the Advancement of Teaching.

Hutchings, P. (2000). *Opening lines: Approaches to the scholarship of teaching and learning*. Menlo Park, CA: Carnegie Foundation for the Advancement of Teaching.

Jacobs, J. A., & Winslow, S. E. (2010). The academic life course: Time pressures and gender inequality. *Community, Work & Family, 7*(2), 143–161. doi:10.1080/1366880042000245443

Kalbfleisch, P. J. (2000). Similarity and attraction in business and academic environments: Same and cross-sex mentoring relationships. *Review of Business, 21*(1/2), 58–61.

MacNell, L., Driscoll, A., & Hunt, A. N. (2015). What's in a name: Exposing gender bias in student ratings of teaching. *Innovative Higher Education, 40*(4), 291–303. doi:10.1007/s10755-014-9313-4

Mason, M. A., & Goulden, M. (2004). Marriage and baby blues: Redefining gender equity in the academy. *Annals of the American Academy of Political and Social Science, 596*, 86–103. doi:10.1177/0002716204268744

Massachusetts Institute of Technology Faculty Newsletter. (1999). A study on the status of women faculty in science at MIT. *The MIT Faculty Newsletter, 11*(4), 2–15.

McKinney, K. (2005). Sociology senior majors' perceptions on learning sociology: A research note. *Teaching Sociology, 33*(4), 371–379. doi:10.1177/0092055X0503300403

Miller, J., & Chamberlin, M. (2000). Women are teachers, men are professors: A study of student perceptions. *Teaching Sociology, 28*(4), 283–298.

National Center for Education Statistics. (2012a, May). *The condition of education 2012*. Retrieved from http://nces.ed.gov/pubs2012/2012045.pdf.

National Center for Education Statistics. (2012b, July). *Digest of education statistics*. Retrieved from https://nces.ed.gov/programs/digest/d12/tables/dt12_291.asp.

National Center for Science and Engineering Statistics. (2015, January). *Women, minorities, and persons with disabilities in science and engineering*. Retrieved from http://www.nsf.gov/statistics/2015/nsf15311/tables/pdf/tab72.pdf.

Parker, K. (2015, March 10). *Despite progress, women still bear heavier loads than men in balancing work and family*. Retrieved from http://www.pewresearch.org/fact-tank/2015/03/10/women-still-bear-heavier-load-than-men-balancing-work-family/.

Perna, L. W. (2001). Sex and race differences in faculty tenure and promotion. *Research in Higher Education, 42*(5), 541–567. doi:10.1023/A:1011050226672

Quinlan, K. M. (1999). Enhancing mentoring and networking of junior academic women: What, why, and how? *Journal of Higher Education Policy and Management, 21*(1), 31–42. doi:10.1080/1360080990210103

Roberts, J. C., & Roberts, K. A. (2008). Deep reading, cost/benefit, and the construction of meaning: Enhancing reading comprehension and deep learning in sociology courses. *Teaching Sociology, 36*(2), 125–140. doi:10.1177/0092055X0803600203

Schmidt, B. (2015, February). *Gendered language in teacher reviews*. Retrieved from http://benschmidt.org/profGender/#.

Sprague, J., & Massoni, K. (2005). Student evaluations and gendered expectations: What we can't count can hurt us. *Sex Roles, 53*(11–12), 779–793. doi:10.1007/s11199-005-8292-4

Steele, C. M. (1997). A threat in the air: How stereotypes shape intellectual identity and performance. *American Psychologist, 52*(6), 613–629. doi:10.1037/0003-066X.52.6.613

Toutkoushian, R. K., & Bellas, M. L. (2003). The effects of part-time employment and gender on faculty earnings and satisfaction: Evidence from the NSOPF: 93. *The Journal of Higher Education, 74*(2), 172–195. doi:10.1353/jhe.2003.0018

Van Auken, P. (2013). Maybe it's both of us: Engagement and learning. *Teaching Sociology, 41*(2), 207–215. doi:10.1177/0092055X12457959

Wolfinger, N. H., Mason, M. A., & Goulden, M. (2009). Stay in the game: Gender, family formation and alternative trajectories in the academic life course. *Social Forces, 87*(3), 1591–1621. doi:10.1353/sof.0.0182

Xu, Y. J. (2008). Gender disparity in STEM disciplines: A study of faculty attrition and turnover intentions. *Research in Higher Education, 49*(7), 607–624. doi:10.1007/s11162-008-9097-4

4 Teachers of Minorities as Agents of Change: A Global Model

MaryJo Benton Lee and Diane Kayongo-Male

TRANSFORMATIVE EDUCATION SEEKS to ignite a passion for learning connected to the betterment of humanity. Teachers must recognize their roles as mentors and peers to students on the journey toward greater justice in society. So write the editors of this text in the introduction to this volume. In this chapter, we present a model that allows teachers of minorities to reflect deliberately on their role as change agents and on their responsibility to bring about a more equitable world.

Besides teachers, the audience for our chapter also includes administrators, policy makers, parents, and teacher educators. As the literature suggests, the best teacher education programs are those that prepare students to be "educational change agents in their respective milieus" (Ashraf, Khaki, Shamatov, Tajik, & Vazir, 2005, p. 275). Dilshad Ashraf, Jan-e-Alam Khaki, Duishon Alievich Shamatov, Mir Afzal Tajik, and Nilofar Vazir (2005), writing about the Aga Khan University Institute for Educational Development in Pakistan, say this is particularly important when working with "multicultural, multiethnic, and multifaith" (p. 275) teachers who will return home to serve in diverse classrooms.

Preservice teachers in the twenty-first century must be trained to enter "changed classrooms" (Dyson, 2010, p. 11), significantly different from those in which they themselves were educated. The "extensive poverty and inequality," described by Michael Dyson (2010, p. 11) in his work on Australian schools, are now endemic in classrooms worldwide. Both teachers and students must learn how to change their frameworks rather than simply change within their frameworks, Dyson (2010, p. 15) says.

This chapter will examine both minority teachers and teachers of minorities acting as change agents in diverse countries, including the United States but also ranging from Bolivia (Canessa, 2004), Great Britain (Robinson & Heyes, 1996), and Israel (Kass & Miller, 2011) to Mexico (Malekzadeh, 2005), Canada (Lund, 2006), and the People's Republic of China (PRC) (Lam, 2007). The PRC holds particular interest for the chapter's authors because they have been studying minority teachers in China's Yunnan Province, an area of great ethnic diversity, for the past fifteen years.

Research for this chapter began with a review of forty-five of the most significant books and articles on the topics of teachers, minorities, and change agents, works drawn largely from the sociology of education. Few attempts have been made to weave the disparate ideas from this literature together in a coherent way. This chapter is a beginning attempt to do so. We will develop a tentative theoretical model for examining teachers of minorities as agents of change, using a global perspective.

Theoretical Background

It should be noted at the start that much of the social change pedagogy is rooted in the foundational work of Brazilian educator Paulo Freire (1990). Applying Freirean pedagogy in contexts different from its origins, however, is problematic (Choules, 2007, p. 161). Diverse theoretical perspectives deliberately chosen for inclusion in this chapter are those of American Henry A. Giroux (1997) on teachers as activists, of Canadian Jim Cummins (1993) on teaching and empowerment, and of Italian Antonio Gramsci (1917) on personal accountability.

Theoretical Cumulation

Early work on what is now called "change agent theory" (Travis, 2008, p. 20) was done by Everett M. Rogers (1971), who wrote about how change is adopted and diffused. Raymond Caldwell (2003), writing in the business management field, later developed a model that outlined four types of change agency: leadership, management, consultancy, and team. Change agency was first applied in school settings in the early 1970s (Jarrett, 1973).

In developing our model, we build on these earlier contributions in a modest attempt at what Jonathan H. Turner (1989, p. 9) calls "theoretical cumulation." This is best described by Sir Isaac Newton's much-quoted phrase "If I have seen further it is by standing on the shoulders of giants." We gather evidence and draw conclusions using an idiographic approach. We examine literature dealing with a wide range of situations in which teachers of minorities function as agents of change. We then generate categories that describe how teachers assume change agent roles, how they develop strategies to realize change, and the outcomes of their change agency. As we will discuss later, the "strategies" section of the model is the weakest, but it does suggest fruitful ground for future research. What we are attempting to develop is a "nested" model. This means that each subsequent part assumes and builds on the previous one (Kerckhoff, 1991, p. 155).

Two theoretical concerns—micro-macro linkages and agency-structure relationships—emerged from our literature review on minority teachers and change agency. Since these concerns informed our model-building work, they will be addressed briefly in the following sections.

Micro-Macro Linkages

Our model incorporates change agency behaviors on the micro level, such as those described by Kmt G. Shockley and Joy Banks (2011, p. 223). During a two-year master's degree program, teachers were exposed to curriculum "designed to foster *personal transformation* (emphasis added) on issues related to language and culture, deconstructing assumptions, creating democratic spaces in classrooms for young students, teacher reflection, and moral professionalism" (Shockley & Banks, 2011, p. 223).

Our model also incorporates change agency behaviors on the macro level, such as those described by Bree Picower (2013). She discusses a teacher residency program operating in culturally diverse city schools, where more than 90 percent of those enrolled are students of color and more than 80 percent of those enrolled qualify for free or reduced-cost lunch. Teachers in the program are specifically trained to challenge, when possible, *large-scale policies* that reproduce patterns of inequality. These policies include "neoliberal forces pillaging public education funds, implementing ethnocentric mandated curricular programs and using high-stakes testing to justify increased privatization" (Picower, 2013, p. 187).

Such policies, and those who attempt to implement them, regularly call into question the legitimacy of teachers' knowledge. "It is not always easy to bring teachers to the point where they view their experiences as important and themselves as active agents of change," Judith T. Lysaker and Shelly Furuness (2011, p. 184) write in the *Journal of Transformative Education*.

Agency-Structure Relationships

It is important to note that there is also considerable tension between agency and structure as reported throughout the writings on teachers and change. The literature in some cases depicts teachers as agents relatively free to spearhead change. Such was the situation at Maya Lin High School, located near San Francisco (Sather, 1999, p. 522). One teacher there said, "Administrators come and go here. A constant is the faculty, the real strength of the school." Another added, "We the teachers run the school, and that is a good thing."

In other cases, teachers find themselves in what ethnographer Angela Valenzuela (1999) calls "culturally subtractive" schools where overwhelming structural barriers prevent them from being the agents of change they would rather be. Valenzuela (1999) describes her study site, the predominantly Mexican Juan Seguin High School in Houston, Texas, as "large, overcrowded, and underfunded" (p. 3). "Committed teachers

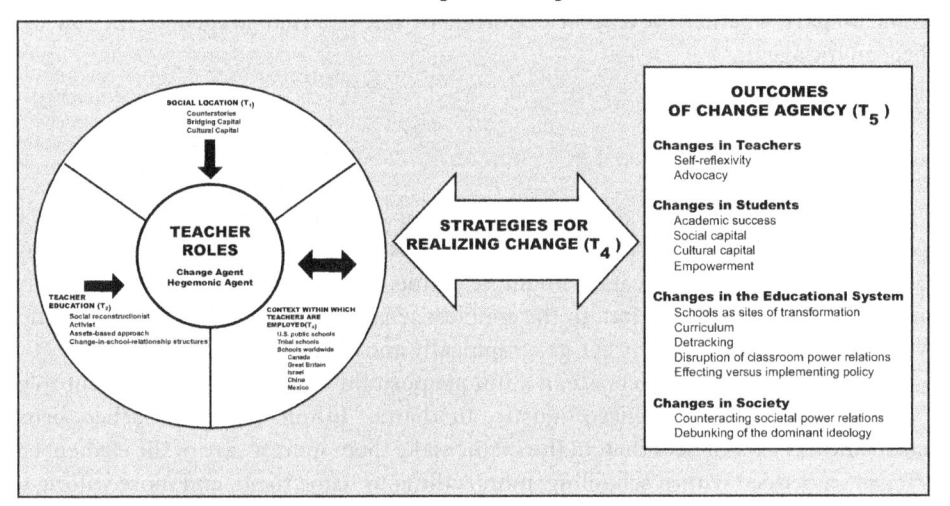

Teachers of Minorities as Change Agents | 53

Teachers of Minorities as Agents of Change: A Tentative Model

FIGURE 4.1. Teachers of minorities as agents of change: A tentative model.

who invest their time in students are chided for their efforts, with the reminder that working hard is not worth the effort 'since these kids aren't going anywhere anyway,'" Valenzuela (1999, p. 64) writes.

The Model: Teachers of Minorities as Agents of Change

Overview

The model developed here (figure 4.1), like most others, is tentative and limited, subject to modification as more data become available. We intend for the model to be used as a guide for future research, by others and ourselves. The remainder of the chapter will describe this model in further detail:

- The first section will discuss teachers' roles as either change agents or hegemonic agents. Factors such as social location, teacher education, and context within which teachers are employed all affect teachers' roles.
- The second section will cover teachers' strategies for realizing change.
- The third section will address outcomes of change agency, including changes in teachers, changes in students, changes in the educational system, and changes in society.

In this model, time is illustrated along a continuum indicated by T_1, T_2, T_3, T_4, and T_5. One-way arrows indicate the direction of change. For example, a teacher's social location, education, and the context within which that teacher is employed each determine, in part, whether the teacher performs the role of a change agent or the role of a hegemonic agent.

Teacher Roles

SOCIAL LOCATION

"Social location" has been defined as "the groups people belong to because of their place or position in history and society" (University of Victoria School of Nursing, 2015). A teacher's social location might be defined by gender, race, class, age, ability, religion, or sexual orientation. In the simplest sense, social location is "from whence you came" (Baldwin, 1963, p. 22), geographically and chronologically.

Ethnic minority teachers are in a unique position to perform change agent roles because most have experienced injustice firsthand. "Ethnic minority teachers bring sociocultural experiences that, in the main, make them more aware of the elements of racism embedded within schooling, more willing to name them, and more willing to enact a socially just agenda for society (generally) and schooling (specifically)," explain Alice Quiocho and Francisco Rios (2000, p. 487).

Writing specifically about African American teachers, Tamara Beauboeuf-Lafontant (1999) describes them as having "political clarity" (p. 702). They can use their knowledge of society's inequities to empower marginalized students.

Zhixin Su (1997) surveyed fifty-six teacher education candidates (African American, Asian American, Hispanic, and white) about their feelings toward teaching as a profession. She found significant differences between the students, with those in the first three groups expressing much more frequently a desire to teach in urban schools and to make a difference in the lives of low-income youth of color. Many more students of color than white students said they recognized that educational inequalities exist and that they were "important players in restructuring schools and society" (Su, 1997, p. 337).

COUNTERSTORIES

"Counterstories," a term that grows out of critical race theory, are narratives of people whose experiences often go untold. Students of color who choose to become teachers bring to the educational table counterstories that would otherwise remain unheard. Daniel G. Solorzano and Tara J. Yosso (2002) see the counterstory as "a tool for exposing, analyzing, and challenging the majoritarian stories of racial privilege" (p. 32). The counterstories that teachers of color bring with them into schools and classrooms can challenge the dominant ideology and ultimately promote social justice.

One such counterstory is that of Isabella Aians Abbot, a Chinese/Hawaiian woman who became a renowned science educator in the mid-twentieth century despite high social barriers (Chinn, 1999). In an article in the journal *Teaching Education*, Abbot makes clear that "her life could only be understood in the context of the racist, colonial, plantation society into which she was born" (Chinn, 1999, p. 157).

What can be learned from Abbot's story relative to minority teachers, change agency, and student success today? Abbot's biographer, Pauline W. U. Chinn (1999) says, "Minority teachers, occupying multiple networks and functioning as institutional agents, might be more successful in helping minority students acquire middle class cultural capital without alienating them from their familiar worlds" (p. 165). The next two sections, on bridging capital and cultural capital, explore these ideas in more detail.

BRIDGING CAPITAL

Academic failure by minority children is often attributed to a discontinuity between the culture of the home and the culture of the school (Trueba, 1988). Minority children may perform poorly in school because schooling promotes middle-class, majority-culture values. Put another way, failure is due to culturally incongruent exchanges between minority students and the schools they attend.

"Bridging capital," as first defined by Robert Putnam (2000), refers to social networks that bring together people of different sorts. Minority teachers can play a critical role for minority students by acting as bridges linking the different social worlds of family, peers, community, and school.

CULTURAL CAPITAL

For Isabella Aians Abbot, acquiring "middle class cultural capital" meant learning to speak standard English rather than the pidgin English that was used by most native Hawaiians at the time. "Cultural capital," as first defined by Pierre Bourdieu (1977), is the informal interpersonal skills and abilities that legitimate the maintenance of status and power. Cultural capital is a resource inherited by children of high-status families and passed on via the system of formal schooling. Bourdieu's notions of capital constitute a fundamentally pessimistic and fatalistic view of society and education. He maintains that the dominant classes are able to reproduce and perpetuate their culture to ensure their continued dominance. His ideas have held sway for more than a quarter of a century.

Some of the more current educational literature, however, looks at Bourdieu's ideas in a new light. Hugh Mehan, Irene Villanueva, Lea Hubbard, and Angela Lintz (1996, p. 216) say that students from low-income families can gain cultural capital, if not from their families, then directly from "state-sponsored" sources such as schools. Some contemporary examples of "middle class cultural capital," shared by minority teachers with minority students, might be the values of timeliness, orderliness, and neatness (Mehan et al., 1996, p. 216).

Su (1997) provides a good summation for this section on teachers and their social location: "Many minority candidates have clear and strong visions for social justice and for their own roles as change agents in the schools and society. . . . It is argued that the minority candidates should be considered as the most important resource in restructuring teacher education programs" (p. 325). Teacher education, as another factor contributing to the change agent roles that individuals ultimately assume, will be discussed next.

Teacher Education

From our review of literature, four models emerged for educating teachers prepared to be change agents:

- A social reconstructionist model (Hill-Brisbane & Easley-Mosby, 2006)
- An activist model (Cochran-Smith, 2004)
- An assets-based model (Villegas & Lucas, 2002)
- A change in school relationship structures model (Nel, 1992)

The social reconstructionist model is the only one that specifically addresses teacher education for students of color. It is this approach that will be discussed first.

Social Reconstructionist Model

"Students who need the best prepared, most experienced, and most committed teachers are being taught by the least prepared teachers," write Djanna Hill-Brisbane and Kenya Easley-Mosby (2006). While this article is about urban schools in Paterson, New Jersey, the authors' comment resonates in schools throughout the country that serve black, Hispanic, and Indian students.

The authors examine strategies for training teachers "who are committed to remain in those schools and do the difficult, long-term work of reform and renewal." (Hill-Brisbane & Easley-Mosby, 2006, p. 53). The project described is known by the acronym PT4T (Paterson Teachers for Tomorrow). It was begun to increase the number of high school students of color enrolling in teacher education programs and becoming teachers in urban schools. The program aims to nurture "community teachers," that is, students who complete college and then return as teachers to the same (or similar) school districts from which they came. These teachers are invested in the community and in the education of urban students because they can identify with many of these students' experiences.

PT4T is rooted in social reconstructionist theory. The theory posits that the purpose of schools is to develop individuals who are skillful critical thinkers, willing to use their talents to reconstruct society to be more equitable (Freire, 1990). Educational theory clearly informed practice in the case of PT4T. "The basic assumption in the design of PT4T is that those who understand a system by virtue of having lived in the system and learned to deconstruct that system (insiders) are in the best position to utilize their knowledge, skills, and dispositions to improve that system," Hill-Brisbane and Easley-Mosby (2006, p. 55) explain. "Prospective teachers need to be empowered with the tools to become resilient change agents and school leaders" (Hill-Brisbane & Easley-Mosby, 2006, p. 55).

Activist Model

Prospective teachers must learn to be both educators and activists, Marilyn Cochran-Smith (2004) argues in her book, *Walking the Road: Race, Diversity, and Social Justice in Teacher Education*. They must be taught "to think of themselves as agents for change and understand reform as an integral part of teaching," Cochran-Smith (2004, p. xxii) says.

Cochran-Smith uses as her springboard an essay by Antonio Gramsci (1917), "I Hate the Indifferent." Gramsci, writing in prewar Italy, claimed that political action was everyone's responsibility, no matter how powerless individuals might feel themselves to be. Similarly, Cochran-Smith (2004) says teachers who are change agents must be willing to "teach against the grain" (p. 24).

Preparing students to teach against the grain requires teacher educators to create "critical dissonance" and "collaborative resonance," Cochran-Smith (2004, p. 25) writes. "Critical dissonance" means focusing on the incongruity of what students learn about teaching at the university and what they already know (and continue to learn) about teaching in the schools. "Collaborative resonance" means deliberately linking student teachers' university-based experiences with their school-based experiences. Cochran-Smith illustrates her points with qualitative data collected at four urban Philadelphia schools.

Assets-Based Model

Ana Maria Villegas and Tamara Lucas (2002) propose a curriculum for educating "culturally responsive teachers." The curriculum has six "strands," and one of these strands is "developing the commitment and skills to act as agents of change" (Villegas & Lucas, 2002, p. 53).

Villegas and Lucas (2002) view teaching as a "political and ethical activity" (p. 198). Their mission is to prepare prospective teachers to be "agents of change who are skilled at identifying inequitable school practices and challenging them" (Villegas & Lucas, 2002, p. 198). The goal is to make schooling more responsive to students from diverse backgrounds. This starts with the realization that differences among students are resources and not problems (Villegas & Lucas, 2002, p. 53).

Miguel A. Guajardo and Francisco J. Guajardo (2002) call this an "assets-based approach" to education (p. 286). In their work with low-income Mexican American students in the Rio Grande Valley, they find that students who speak two languages and live in two cultures are amazingly resilient in overcoming obstacles and achieving academically. More than sixty of their Edcouch-Elsa (Texas) High School students have gained acceptance into Ivy League universities in the past twenty years (Guajardo & Guajardo, 2002, p. 287).

Tara Yosso (2005) explains this same idea another way. She defines "community cultural wealth" as "an array of knowledge, skills, abilities and contacts possessed and utilized by Communities of Color to survive and resist macro and micro-forms of oppression" (p. 77). Clearly to Yosso and to Guajardo and Guajardo, the differences from mainstream culture that students of color bring with them into the classroom are seen as resources and not as problems.

Change in School Relationship Structures Model

Canadian Jim Cummins (1993) developed a widely accepted theoretical framework explaining why minority students fail at school. At issue, Cummins says, are the relationships teachers have with minority students and with the communities from which these students come. Students from "dominated" groups are either "empowered" or "disabled" as a direct result of their interactions with teachers.

Johanna Nel (1992) redesigned a multicultural teacher education course so that students could acquire the skills necessary to change "school relationship structures" (p. 3). Skills taught in the course include the following:

- Incorporating minority students' languages and cultures into classroom and school programs
- Increasing active minority community participation
- Using teaching techniques that encourage students to construct their own knowledge
- Becoming advocates for minority students when involved in assessment procedures

Context within which Teachers Are Employed

This section of the chapter addresses the questions of "where teachers go" and of "the nature of schooling contexts" (Achinstein & Ogawa, 2011, p. 67). Clearly a teacher's ability to effect change is determined to a great extent by what is possible in the particular classroom, school, and district where that teacher works. In attempting to perform change agent roles, teachers are engaged in constant negotiation, maneuvering among the structural supports and constraints present in the contexts in which they are employed.

US Public Schools

The literature on change agency is filled with references to constraints imposed by context. Betty Achinstein and Rodney T. Ogawa (2011) write that there are two related sets of conditions in schools that limit the ability of many teachers of color to act as agents of change:

- Teachers of color often work in schools that are "culturally subtractive" (Valenzuela, 1999). While this term was discussed previously, Achinstein and Ogawa (2011) provide a more detailed explanation: "Subtractive schooling may . . . inhibit teachers of color by silencing a dialogue about issues of race in schools, limiting their access to supportive colleagues, constricting their roles and access to learning, making them adhere to restrictive curricula and pedagogical practices, and thus inhibiting their ability to enact the cultural/professional roles that may have drawn them into the profession" (p. 7).
- Teachers of color often work in schools where there is great pressure to meet state and federal accountability standards. They must use standardized instructional materials rather than materials that draw on their own and students' cultural and linguistic backgrounds. Accountability pressures also force some teachers to unwillingly leave certain students behind.

The result is that standards designed to promote educational equity actually prevent committed teachers from redressing inequitable access for minority students.

Also writing about context, Tamara Lucas and Ana Maria Villegas (2002) outline these factors that work against classroom teachers becoming change agents:

- The hierarchical and bureaucratic nature of the educational system
- Time pressures
- Insufficient opportunities for collaboration with others
- Resistance by those in power to equity-oriented change

Tribal Contract or Grant Schools

These are run by American Indian tribes with operating funds received under a contract or grant from the federal Bureau of Indian Education. The Rough Rock Community School, described in Teresa L. McCarty's book, *A Place to be Navajo* (2002), is one such school. McCarty's chapter 11 discusses "indigenous teachers as change agents" (McCarty, 2002, p. 147). The Rough Rock English-Navajo Language Arts Program (RRENLAP), begun there in 1987, has increased tremendously students' biliteracy development, self-efficacy, and school achievement.

McCarty spends considerable time in her book discussing the context in which indigenous teachers were able to be change agents. "The changes effected by RRENLAP teachers occurred within a site of possibility and hope," McCarty (2002, p. 160) writes. "We have described this as a zone of safety—a socially constructed space within which teachers moved from a deficit view of their teaching and learners, to a stance focused on their and students' agency and strengths" (McCarty, 2002, p. 160).

Changes at Rough Rock were also aided by an infusion of long-term financial assistance, by administrative support from the building principal, and by a fundamental democratization of the teacher-principal relationship. Teachers learned that they were able to achieve more through collaboration than they were alone. "These were the very conditions teachers strove to create with and for their students," (McCarty, 2002, p. 161) adds.

CANADA

Canada and Great Britain are the two national contexts closest to that of the United States among those reviewed for this chapter. Darren E. Lund (2006), in writing about Canadian teacher activists, points out that much of the research in this area has been informed by American conceptions of "multicultural education" and British formulations of "antiracist education." Lund (2006) says that Canada is unique because it is "the only nation with its multicultural ideals entrenched into its constitution and a range of national government policies" (p. 257). Canadian teachers acting as change agents are described as being involved in "social justice education." Multicultural, antiracist, and social justice education are each framed very differently, one from another. As competing narratives, they profoundly influence how teachers in the United States, Great Britain, and Canada perform change agent roles.

GREAT BRITAIN

John Robinson and Irene Heyes (1996) discuss a change in teacher education policy in Great Britain and how this might affect teachers' ability to perform change agent roles in their classrooms. At the time the article was written, some right-wing groups were proposing that teacher education shift from a "professional model," in which most of the training occurs in higher education institutions, to an "apprenticeship model," in which most of the training occurs in schools (Robinson & Heyes, 1996, p. 127). In the former model, equal treatment of ethnic minorities is emphasized; in the latter model, classroom management and subject knowledge are emphasized. Here the "context" being discussed is that in which teachers are educated in Great Britain. Robinson and Heyes (1996) argue that "a further shift towards exclusively school-based teacher education will not be conducive to more equal treatment of ethnic minorities" (p. 120). By extension, the authors suggest that such a shift also will not be conducive to preparing prospective teachers to be change agents.

ISRAEL

In research involving Bedouin Arab teachers in southern Israel, many said they chose special education as their field of study in order to become "agents of social change." Researchers Efrat Kass and Erez C. Miller (2011, p. 788) found that the "social change" to which the teachers aspired occurred in three spheres. The first was the external sphere: Teachers expressed a desire for more Bedouin Arabs like themselves to be involved in special education so there would be less dependence on non-Bedouin Arabs. The second was the internal sphere: Teachers wanted to change the negative attitude toward special education of people within their own culture. The third was the personal sphere: Teachers wished to upgrade their professional qualifications in order to better cope with the challenges they faced in special education.

People's Republic of China

Educators are among the many "agents" who determine in China whether an individual student will embrace the chance to learn the standard official language (Putonghua), a foreign language (such as English), or, in some cases, a minority language. Agnes S. L. Lam (2007) says that whether China achieves its goals for national language planning depends on whether students abide by choices made by the state and whether intermediary agents such as teachers cooperate. The "social change" being considered here is the learning of a second language, or, as in the case of China's minorities, the learning of a third language. The Chinese context, as it is explained in this article, is far different from those of the countries discussed previously. China is a Communist country, where decision making is highly centralized. Consequently, language policy has been guided by three principles important to advancing the interests of the state. These principles are the standardization of Chinese (to enhance literacy and educational opportunity), the propagation of foreign languages (to further China's ties with the West), and the development of minority languages (to integrate ethnic groups without antagonizing them).

Mexico

In contrast to Lam's focus on national planning, Shervin Malekzadeh (2005) argues that the best level of analysis for understanding change agency is the classroom. He has studied in depth the role that teachers played in creating hegemony and consolidating identity in postrevolutionary Mexico. With an emphasis on the context for change, Malekzadeh (2005) writes, "Revolutions are negotiated in the classrooms" (p. 2). He says that scholars have had a tendency to focus on the politics surrounding the adoption of particular textbooks or curricula rather than on their implementation. "The assumption seems to be that if a certain lesson is placed in a textbook, then surely that same lesson will be delivered whole and unmediated to the student. The teacher serves, without compunction, as the state's agent," Malekzadeh (2005, p. 33) says. "This is not the case. Who the teacher is and his or her place in the community plays a tremendous if not decisive role in how educational policy is implemented. If social science is to better understand how national identities are formed and sustained, greater attention must be paid to these agents of change" (p. 33).

This concludes our sampling of contexts, in the United States and abroad, in which teachers of minorities can function as agents of change. These contexts are varied, some containing supports and others obstacles to change agency.

Teacher Roles as Change Agents or Hegemonic Agents

Before proceeding, let us review the main headings of the model discussed so far. "Social location," "teacher education," and "context within which teachers are employed"—the inward-facing arrows indicate that each of these three factors influences teacher roles. Put another way, the three factors just discussed determine, in part, whether a teacher is likely to assume the role of a change agent or of a hegemonic agent. It is to this topic that we next turn our attention.

Change Agent

Our understanding of change agent roles comes primarily from the foundational work of sociologist Everett M. Rogers. In his book *Communication of Innovations*, Rogers (1971, pp. 229–230) discusses the seven steps a change agent follows when introducing an innovation to others:

1. Develops need for change
2. Establishes a change relationship
3. Diagnoses the problem
4. Creates intent to change in the client
5. Translates intent into action
6. Stabilizes change and prevents discontinuance
7. Achieves a terminal relationship

Despite some criticism, Rogers's work on the diffusion of innovation and on agents of change has proved to be surprisingly enduring. Some of the criticisms that run throughout the literature center on issues of equality and the socioeconomic gap that more often than not separates change agents and their clients. Rogers's model addresses only top-down diffusion from "experts" to "locals." There is definitely a "pro-innovation" bias in his model. Little consideration is given to questions such as "Who gets to decide which innovation to diffuse?" "Why should a particular innovation be adopted by all members of a social system?" and "Why could an innovation not be reinvented or rejected?"

As mentioned earlier, change agency was used to explain educational reform as early as the 1970s (Jarrett, 1973). Rogers's definition of what it means to be a change agent still resonates throughout the literature today (Travis, 2008).

Hegemonic Agent

The notion that underrepresented students benefit academically from exposure to teachers from their own racial or ethnic groups has been a theme running throughout this chapter. Because minority teachers are often deeply committed to improving educational opportunities for students from nondominant backgrounds, they may willingly assume change agent roles in their schools.

Andrew Canessa, however, presents an example in which social location, teacher education, and school context bring about the opposite effect. In his study of an indigenous school in highland Bolivia, Canessa (2004) finds that "teachers who themselves come from Indian communities ... are principal agents in reproducing hegemonic racism in Indian communities" (p. 185). Rural schoolteachers with Indian backgrounds have successfully separated themselves from peasant lifestyles. They are products of a state education system that promotes a particular vision of civilization and hierarchy of knowledge. Teachers trained in this system do not advocate for Indian cultural values. As teachers, they reject traditional life and indigenous knowledge. The themes of civilization and progress run through all kinds of lessons in the school that Canessa observed, with mainstream Bolivian culture promoted as being far superior. "White people are better because they are clever and live in cities and are wealthy," one student interviewee told Canessa (2004, p. 192). "We indians (indios) are poor and stupid" (p. 192).

This concludes our discussion of teachers as agents of change or agents of hegemony. We move next to the topic of strategies teachers use to realize change.

Strategies for Realizing Change

This part of the model has the potential to be the most theoretically interesting because it addresses the mechanisms by which the process of change occurs. The dialectical (or two-way) arrow between "strategies" and "context" denotes that the context in which change occurs determines to a degree the strategies teachers employ, and the strategies teachers employ also affect the context in which they operate.

That said, at present, the weakest link in our tentative model is the strategies element. Little of the literature reviewed addresses specifically how teachers of minorities go about acting as agents of change. We intend to apply the model in our future research, on teachers of minorities as agents of change in the People's Republic of China. In proposing this as an exploratory model, we feel it could be usefully applied in other settings as well, both within and outside of the United States.

Raymond Caldwell (2003), writing in the field of business management, has developed a typology titled "Models of Change Agency." While not directly applicable to minorities and teachers, it may provide the scaffolding for future work by sociologists of education. For that reason, we present a brief overview of Caldwell's model here. Caldwell (2003, p. 140) classifies change agents as being leaders, managers, consultants, or teams.

Leaders are change agents at the top of an organization who envision, initiate, or sponsor change that is of a transformational nature. These individuals fit the old mold of Rogers's "innovators" (Rogers, 1962).

Managers are change agents who are middle-level personnel or functional specialists. They adapt, carry forward, or build support for strategic change within an organization.

Consultants are change agents working inside of or outside of an organization who provide advice, expertise, management, coordination, or process skills to facilitate change. To use a perspective developed by Anselm Strauss (1978), consultants "negotiate order" to complete tasks in complex organizations.

Teams include managers, functional specialists, employees, internal consultants, and external consultants who are able to effect change at any level within an organization. They employ the "bridging capital" (Putnam, 2000) described earlier in this chapter.

To repeat, the strategies that teachers and others use for realizing change are context specific. More empirical research is needed to determine, in a variety of places and times, exactly what these strategies are. The tentative model we present is fruitful in that it can lead to more explanations of teacher behavior in multiple contexts.

Outcomes of Change Agency

The model's final section addresses an important substantive question: What are teachers of minorities trying to change? Put another way, what are the results of teachers acting as agents of change? What purposes drive their actions?

The outcomes of change agency are grouped under four headings: Changes in Teachers, Changes in Students, Changes in the Educational System, and Changes in Society. Each of these will be discussed in some detail in the following pages.

CHANGES IN TEACHERS

We begin with changes in teachers.

Self-reflexivity. Patricia Ruggiano Schmidt (2002) describes a year filled with cultural conflicts in a kindergarten classroom as these were experienced by two Asian children and by their teacher. The final chapter of Schmidt's book is titled "Epilogue: Teacher as Change Agent." It tells the story of the teacher's efforts during the following year to enact multicultural literacy learning in her own classroom and to engage other teachers in a similar process. After reading Schmidt's (2002) ethnographic account of year one and the struggles that "Peley" and "Raji" experienced in her class, the teacher, "Mrs. Starr," said, "I have to learn how to work effectively with children from other cultures" (Schmidt, 2002, p. 123). Mrs. Starr's reflections, as recorded in a journal and reported in Schmidt's (2002) book, give us insight into "how individual teachers think as they are involved in a change process in their own classrooms and schools" (p. 124).

Advocacy. Lilia I. Bartolome (2002) looks at four exemplary educators at a large southern California high school. The school serves primarily students of color from low-income families. The educators interviewed all performed change agent roles in that they worked aggressively to equalize what they perceived to be an unequal playing field for their students. Now about 70 percent of the school's students attend college and receive millions of dollars in scholarship money. A common characteristic of the exemplary teachers is their willingness "to act as advocates and cultural brokers for their students" (Bartolome, 2002, p. 182).

The teachers define the "success" they are helping their students achieve as including self-confidence and life skills to navigate their current lives, social integration into high school culture, and academic success.

CHANGES IN STUDENTS

Changes in students, such as those just listed, will be discussed next.

Academic success. Academic success is typically thought of as passing courses, graduating from high school, and going on to college. Throughout the review of literature for this chapter, however, another theme has emerged: For many teachers of minorities, helping their students become academically successful means helping them learn English. Audrey Friedman (2002) describes the process by which she and another teacher became "agents of literacy change" while working with Somali students in a large urban middle school. The teachers' goal was to improve the students' ability to use English for reading, writing, listening, and speaking. "An important piece of the work involves identifying and using various change agents in our classrooms and throughout the school and beyond," Friedman (2002, pp. 143–144) writes. She also suggests implementing strategies for change that have proven effective elsewhere and encouraging students themselves to act as agents of change.

Social capital. Bartolome (2002), in her study of exemplary teachers, writes, "It is interesting that they did not focus solely on academic definitions of success in their discussions, but also recognized the significance of the social and cultural dimensions of effective schooling" (p. 170). The change agent teachers she interviewed wanted to give their culturally and linguistically diverse students "a sense of belonging and comfort in school" (Bartolome, 2002, p. 170). Certainly "social integration in the high school culture" (Bartolome, 2002, p. 170) is one kind of social capital, but there are others as well.

For many years researchers have used the notions of capital developed by Pierre Bourdieu (1977) to frame discussions about how social class shapes educational achievement. Social capital is understood to be positions and relations in social networks. The social capital that change agent teachers provide for minority students is access to social networks. An example is provided by Mehan et al. (1996) in their description of the Advancement Via Individual Determination program: "AVID coordinators lead their students through the murky maze of the college application and financial aid process. They play the role usually played by parents of elite students—intervening on their behalf with administrators or teachers who resist their academic plans or desires" (pp. 216–217).

Cultural capital. "Minority teachers, occupying multiple networks and functioning as institutional agents, might be more successful in helping minority students acquire middle class cultural capital without alienating them from their familiar worlds," writes Chinn (1999, p. 165). This particular outcome of change agency was discussed in detail earlier in the chapter. As well, Yosso's concept of "community cultural wealth," as it contrasts with Bourdieu's traditional notion of "cultural capital," has already been mentioned (Yosso, 2005, p. 77). The example cited earlier in this chapter was the work of Guajardo and Guajardo (2002, p. 286) with Mexican American students at Edcouch-Elsa High School.

Empowerment. African American teachers "use their knowledge of society's inequities and their influence to empower their marginalized students" (Beauboeuf-LaFontant, 1999, p. 702). Remarks such as this one about teachers and empowerment appear frequently throughout the change agency literature. Exactly what is meant by empowering minority students is unclear. Examples of attempts to empower students, such as the following one involving a Chicana teacher named Alejandra, are few and far between (Achinstein & Ogawa, 2011): "She also discussed institutional racism and local instances of oppression. In one discussion, students challenged Alejandra's distinction between individual and institutional racism, arguing that 'White people run the system.' Alejandra's response reflected her purpose in raising the issue: to engage students in changing society. She explained, 'The system has a lot of problems, but you can't just write it off, because then you're never going to change it'" (p. 97).

In Freirean terms, what was happening in Alejandra's classroom was "learning based on genuine dialogue between students and teachers, who work as partners in a united quest for 'critical consciousness' leading to a humane transformation of, rather than a passive accommodation to, one's world" (McLaren, 2003, p. 251).

Teachers can *change students* by supplying them with the academic tools, social capital, and cultural capital they need to achieve in society as it currently exists. Empowerment, however, suggests that teachers are preparing students to *change society*.

CHANGES IN THE EDUCATIONAL SYSTEM

"Schools can be vehicles for social change, community building, and access to the mainstream" (Beauboeuf-LaFontant, 1999, p. 718), and teachers must be "agents of transformation and hope" (McLaren, 2003, p. 258). The literature on teachers of minorities as agents of change is laced with such remarks. Some concrete examples of what is meant by this will be discussed next.

Schools as sites of transformation. One such example is found in Susan E. Sather's report on the Leading for Diversity Research Project (Sather, 1999). Sather studied twenty-one schools, focusing on how administrators, teachers, and students served as change agents. One of her study sites was Maya Lin High School, which Sather (1999) describes as "a place where teachers spearhead change":

> The first site-visit to Maya Lin High School (MLHS) began at 6:30 a.m. as two members of the research team met the entire staff—administrators, teachers, and classified staff including custodians—and loaded into charter buses for a visit to the Simon Wiesenthal Museum of Tolerance in Los Angeles. This event symbolized the deep concern for social justice held by an important cadre of teachers at the school, who took a year to plan this event. . . . This trip was one of many teacher-led efforts that focused on creating respect and harmonious relations among diverse groups at MLHS. (p. 519)

Curriculum. "Teachers at all levels of schooling represent a potentially powerful force for social change," writes Giroux (1997, p. 28), who together with Freire is considered a father of critical pedagogy. In Giroux's view, the problem with curriculum, especially social studies curriculum, is that it totally ignores "ethical and normative dimensions" (Giroux, 1997, p. 3). Material is presented in atheoretical, ahistorical, and unproblematic ways. "Commonsense" assumptions go unchallenged by both teachers and students, masking the fact that all forms of knowledge are socially constructed. "What classroom teachers can and must do is work in their respective roles to develop pedagogical theories and methods that link self-reflection and understanding with a commitment to change the nature of the larger society," Giroux (1997, p. 28) says.

Detracking. When Ruth Wright Hayre was named Philadelphia's first black high school teacher and then first black principal in the mid-twentieth century, she became "all too aware of how high school officials tracked low-income students, students of color, and young women into courses that reproduced socio-economic stratification and limited their prospects for future employment or higher education" (Delmont, 2010, p. 205). Hayre and the faculty at the William Penn High School, which served primarily black students, started a program called Project WINGS. Its goals were offering a college preparatory option, an enriched curriculum and tutoring to bring students up to grade level. WINGS was an effort to help *all* of the school's students. "This is not another program for the gifted child," Hayre said. "It is for the average youngster from underprivileged areas whose potentiality has not been recognized" (Delmont, 2010, p. 212).

Disruption of classroom power relations. "Students from 'dominated' societal groups are 'empowered' or 'disabled' as a direct result of their interactions with educators in the schools," Cummins (1993, p. 104) writes. Cummins's ideas were introduced earlier in the chapter. Here it is important to add that he offers a number of explicit suggestions for consciously disrupting the power relations that exist in classrooms. These include incorporating minority students' languages and cultures into the school program and encouraging minority community participation as an integral part of children's education. Cummins also advises that second language learners be taught via talking and writing with teachers, rather than by using more passive instructional techniques. Finally, Cummins urges teachers to become advocates for minority students in the assessment process. In conclusion, Cummins (1993) adds that teachers "must redefine their roles within the classroom, the community, and the broader society so that these role definitions result in interactions that empower rather than disable students" (p. 117).

Effecting versus implementing policy. Many teachers of color feel that they can effect policy, rather than just implement it, only by leaving the profession. One of these teachers, "Alicia," explained her decision to switch from teaching to administration this way (Achinstein & Ogawa, 2011): "I really felt like I had much more to contribute than what I was doing in the classroom to education, to reform. . . . Specifically as a teacher of color, I would have liked to have more administrative support and colleague support for developing new programs to address the needs of students of color. . . . I feel like as a teacher of color . . . I may have a better understanding of what these students are going through and what some of their needs might be. I never really felt supported in the sense of developing my ideas and implementing my ideas" (p. 73).

One way to ensure that more teachers of color are effecting policy instead of just implementing it is through efforts such as the Cary Leadership Fellows Program. Funded by the Mary Flager Cary Trust, the five-year project was designed to train a selected group of experienced teachers of children—especially minority group teachers from inner-city schools—"to become educational leaders and effective agents of change in improving public education" (Rosen & Palmer, 1973,p. 1). All the students involved in the program were working toward a master's degree in supervision and administration. By the second year of their two-year program, the fellows were challenged with taking over the total responsibility for some aspect of an educational program as salaried professionals in schools. "Just before their graduation, the fellows universally stated that they felt well prepared for positions as educational leaders," Jacqueline Rosen and Mary B. Palmer (1973, p. 35) explain. The program was later incorporated as a permanent component of the Bank Street College of Education, a small independent school in New York City.

CHANGES IN SOCIETY

Literature on this final outcome of teacher change agency was scarce.

Counteracting societal power relations. Teachers can play an important role in counteracting power relations that exist in the larger society outside their classrooms, Villegas and Lucas (2002) argue in their book, *Educating Culturally Responsive Teachers*:

> Those who view teachers as agents of change see schools and society as interconnected. They believe that, while education has the potential to challenge and transform inequities in society, without intervention, schools tend to reproduce those inequities by giving greater status to the ways of thinking, talking, and behaving of the dominant cultural group. Those with this perspective recognize that teaching is a complex activity that is inherently political and ethical. They are aware that institutional structures and practices do not exist in a vacuum, but that people build and sustain them, whether consciously or unconsciously. They therefore believe that teachers must have a clear vision of their own roles as teachers and of the goals of education. They view teachers as participants in a larger struggle for social justice whose actions either support or challenge current inequalities. (p. 55)

Debunking of the dominant ideology. "Dominant ideology" is a term that has grown out of Marxism. Critical race theory (CRT) challenges the dominant ideology, which suggests that "the educational system offers objectivity, meritocracy, color-blindness, race neutrality, and equal opportunity" (Yosso, 2006, p. 7). CRT questions approaches to schooling that pretend to be neutral but in fact privilege white, United States–born, monolingual, English-speaking students.

Prospective teachers frequently resent having to take courses that challenge the dominant-culture ideologies they hold. Bartolome (2002, p. 169) explains that even when prospective teachers acknowledge that certain minority groups have historically been poorer, have underachieved academically, and have had higher mortality rates than whites, they cannot offer any explanation for such inequalities. "Unfortunately, this reproduction of the dominant ideology and lack of political clarity often translates into uncritical acceptance of the status quo as natural, and of assimilationist and deficit-based views of non-White and language minority students," Bartolome (2002, p. 169) writes. Educators who do not "interrogate their negative, racist and classist ideological orientations" (Bartolome, 2002, p. 169) will in the end reproduce the existing social order.

Conclusion

In reviewing a substantial body of literature on schools, teachers, and change agency, we feel some synthesis is needed. In this chapter we have developed a tentative model attempting to explain how teachers of minorities may act as agents of change.

The model assumes that change agency is influenced by a wide range of macro- and micro-level factors. In addition, we acknowledge that there is considerable tension between agency and structure operating, as teachers are either enabled to or constrained from assuming change agent roles. Teachers' social location, education, and the context in which they work are all variables that influence in part either change agent or hegemonic agent behavior.

Future work, in national and international contexts, is clearly needed to better understand strategies for realizing change as well as outcomes of change agency. One of the chapter's authors will apply the model in work with ethnic minority teachers in Southwestern China. Fieldwork is planned for the 2016–2017 academic year. This will be a follow-up study of thirty ethnic minority teachers who she first interviewed fifteen years ago as they were about to graduate from Yunnan Normal (Teachers) University in Kunming, PRC. The study will explore whether the teachers have managed to generate the changes they aspired to create and what supported or hindered these changes.

We offer this exploratory model as a beginning attempt to explain the important role that teachers of minorities can play in enacting change in schools and society. We hope that others will find the model useful for their future research and that they will contribute to efforts aimed at redressing educational inequality. If so, the goal of transformative education—to bring about greater justice throughout society—will be realized.

MARYJO BENTON LEE is an adjunct assistant professor in the Department of Sociology and Rural Studies at South Dakota State University. She is a 2016–2017 Fulbright US Scholar to China, teaching at Yunnan University. She is the author of *Success Academy: How Native American Students Prepare for College (and How Colleges Can Prepare for Them)*.

DIANE KAYONGO-MALE is a professor in the Department of Sociology and Rural Studies, South Dakota State University. She has specialized in evaluation research, including assessment of higher education initiatives dealing with diversity and inclusiveness of campus environments.

References

Achinstein, B., & Ogawa, R. T. (2011). *Change(d) agents: New teachers of color in urban schools*. New York, NY: Teachers College Press.

Ashraf, D., Khaki, J., Shamatov, D. A., Tajik, M. A., & Vazir, N. (2005). Reconceptualization of teacher education: Experiences from the context of a multicultural developing country. *Journal of Transformative Education, 3*(3), 271–288.

Baldwin, J. (1963). *The fire next time*. New York, NY: The Dial Press.

Bartolome, L. I. (2002). Creating an equal playing field: Teachers as advocates, border crossers, and cultural brokers. In Z. F. Beykont (Ed.), *The power of culture: Teaching across language difference* (pp. 167–191). Cambridge, MA: Harvard Education.

Beauboeuf-LaFontant, T. (1999). A movement against and beyond boundaries: "Politically relevant teaching" among African American teachers. *Teachers College Record, 100*(4), 702–723.

Bourdieu, P. (1977). Cultural reproduction and social reproduction. In J. Karabel & A. H. Halsey (Eds.), *Power and ideology in education* (pp. 487–511). New York, NY: Oxford University Press.

Caldwell, R. (2003). Models of change agency: A fourfold classification. *British Journal of Management, 14*, 131–142.

Canessa, A. (2004). Reproducing racism: Schooling and race in highland Bolivia. *Race Ethnicity and Education, 7*(2), 185–204.

Chinn, P. W. U. (1999). A scientific success: Isabella Aians Abbot and the education of minorities and females. *Teaching Education*, 10(2), 155–168.

Choules, K. (2007). Social change education: Context matters. *Adult Education Quarterly*, 57(2), 159–176.

Cochran-Smith, M. (2004). *Walking the road: Race, diversity, and social justice in teacher education*. New York, NY: Teachers College Press.

Cummins, J. (1993). Empowering minority students: A framework for intervention. In L. Weis & M. Fine (Eds.), *Beyond silenced voices: Class, race, and gender in United States schools* (pp. 101–117). Albany: State University of New York Press.

Delmont, M. (2010). The plight of the "able student": Ruth Wright Hayre and the struggle for equality in Philadelphia's black high schools, 1955–1965. *History of Education Quarterly*, 50(2), 204–230.

Dyson, M. (2010). What might a person-centred model of teacher education look like in the 21st century? The transformation model of teacher education. *Journal of Transformative Education*, 8(1), 3–21.

Freire, P. (1990). *Pedagogy of the oppressed*. New York, NY: Continuum.

Friedman, A. A. (2002). Agents of literacy change: Working with Somali students in an urban middle school. In Z. F. Beykont (Ed.), *The power of culture: Teaching across language difference* (pp. 121–145). Cambridge, MA: Harvard Education.

Giroux, H. A. (1997). *Pedagogy and the politics of hope: Theory, culture, and schooling*. Cumnor, England: Westview Press.

Gramsci, A. (1917, February 11). The indifferent. *La Citta Futura (The Future City)*. Retrieved from https://overland.org.au/2013/03/i-hate-the-indifferent/.

Guajardo, M. A., & Guajardo, F. J. (2002). Critical ethnography and community change. In Y. Zou & H. T. Trueba (Eds.), *Ethnography and schools: Qualitative approaches to the study of education* (pp. 281–304). Lanham, MD: Rowman & Littlefield.

Hill-Brisbane, D., & Easley-Mosby, K. (2006). Exploring issues of support and leadership in the experiences of prospective teachers of color: Retaining minority students and producing change agents for urban schools. In *E-yearbook of urban learning, teaching, and research*. Retrieved from http://files.eric.ed.gov/fulltext/EJ843792.pdf.

Jarrett, H. H., Jr. (1973). Change agent qualities and situation feasibility in higher education. *Liberal Education*, 59(4), 442–448.

Kass, E., & Miller, E. C. (2011). Bedouin special-education teachers as agents of social change. *Teaching and Teacher Education*, 27, 788–796.

Kerckhoff, A. C. (1991). Creating inequality in the schools: A structural perspective. In J. Huber (Ed.), *Macro-micro linkages in sociology* (pp. 153–169). Newbury Park, CA: SAGE.

Lam, A. S. L. (2007). The multi-agent model of language choice: National planning and individual volition in China. *Cambridge Journal of Education*, 37(1), 67–87.

Lucas, T., & Villegas, A. M. (2002). Preparing culturally responsive teachers: Rethinking the curriculum. *Journal of Teacher Education*, 53(1). Retrieved from http://www.sagepub.com/eis/Villegas.pdf.

Lund, D. E. (2006). Addressing multicultural and antiracist theory and practice with Canadian teacher activists. In D. E. Armstrong & B. J. McMahon (Eds.), *Inclusion in urban educational environments: Addressing issues of diversity, equity, and social justice* (pp. 255–274). Greenwich, CT: Information Age.

Lysaker, J. T., & Furuness, S. (2011). Space for transformation: Relational, dialogic pedagogy. *Journal of Transformative Education*, 9(3), 183–197.

Malekzadeh, S. (2005, September). *Agents of change: The role of teachers and schools in creating hegemony and consolidating identity in postrevolutionary Mexico and Iran*. Paper presented at the meeting of the American Political Science Association, Washington, DC.

McCarty, T. L. (2002). *A place to be Navajo: Rough Rock and the struggle for self-determination in indigenous schooling*. Mahwah, NJ: Erlbaum.

McLaren, P. (2003). *Life in schools: An introduction to critical pedagogy in the foundations of education.* Boston, MA: Allyn & Bacon.

Mehan, H., Villanueva, I., Hubbard, L., & Lintz, A. (1996). *Constructing school success: The consequences of untracking low-achieving students.* New York, NY: Cambridge University Press.

Nel, J. (1992, April). *Teacher preparation: Implications of Cummins' theoretical framework for analyzing minority students' school failure.* Paper presented at the meeting of the American Educational Research Association, San Francisco, CA.

Picower, B. (2013). You can't change what you don't see: Developing new teachers' political understanding of education. *Journal of Transformative Education, 11*(3), 170–189.

Putnam, R. D. (2000). *Bowling alone: The collapse and revival of American community.* New York, NY: Simon & Schuster.

Quiocho, A., & Rios, F. (2000). The power of their presence: Minority group teachers and schooling. *Review of Educational Research, 70*(4), 485–528.

Robinson, J., & Heyes, I. (1996). Conflicting models of teacher training in multi-ethnic classrooms: Journal of a mentor. *Language, Culture and Curriculum, 9*(2), 120–132.

Rogers, E. M. (1962). *Diffusion of innovations.* New York, NY: The Free Press of Glencoe.

Rogers, E. M. (1971). *Communication of innovations: A cross-cultural approach.* New York, NY: The Free Press.

Rosen, J., & Palmer, M. B. (1973). *A descriptive analysis of the Cary Leadership Fellows Program: An experiment in training for educational leadership.* Unpublished manuscript, Bank Street College of Education, New York, NY.

Sather, S. E. (1999). Leading, lauding, and learning: Leadership in secondary schools serving diverse populations. *The Journal of Negro Education, 68*(4), 511–528.

Schmidt, P. R. (2002). *Cultural conflict and struggle: Literacy learning in a kindergarten program.* New York, NY: Peter Lang.

Shockley, K. G., & Banks, J. (2011). Perceptions of teacher transformation on issues of racial and cultural bias. *Journal of Transformative Education, 9*(4), 222–241.

Solorzano, D. G., & Yosso, T. J. (2002). Critical race methodology: Counter-storytelling as an analytical framework for education research. *Qualitative Inquiry, 8*(1), 23–44.

Strauss, A. L. (1978). *Negotiations: Varieties, contexts, processes, and social order.* San Francisco, CA: Jossey-Bass.

Su, Z. (1997). Teaching as a profession and as a career: Minority candidates' perspectives. *Teaching & Teacher Education, 13*(3), 325–340.

Travis, T. A. (2008). Librarians as agents of change: Working with curriculum committees using change agency theory. *New Directions for Teaching and Learning, 114,* 17–33.

Trueba, H. T. (1988). Culturally based explanations of minority students' academic achievement. *Anthropology & Education Quarterly, 19,* 270–287.

Turner, J. H. (1989). Introduction: Can sociology be a cumulative science? In J. H. Turner (Ed.), *Theory building in sociology: Assessing theoretical cumulation* (pp. 8–18). Newbury Park, CA: SAGE.

University of Victoria School of Nursing. (2015). *Cultural safety module two: Peoples' experiences of oppression.* Retrieved from http://web2.uvcs.uvic.ca/courses/csafety/mod2/glossary.htm.

Valenzuela, A. (1999). *Subtractive schooling: U.S.-Mexican youth and the politics of caring.* New York: State University of New York Press.

Villegas, A. M., & Lucas, T. (2002). *Educating culturally responsive teachers: A coherent approach.* Albany: State University of New York Press.

Yosso, T. J. (2005). Whose culture has capital? A critical race theory discussion of community cultural wealth. *Race Ethnicity and Education, 8*, 69–91.

Yosso, T. J. (2006). *Critical race counterstories along the Chicana/Chicano educational pipeline.* New York, NY: Routledge.

Acknowledgment:

The authors are grateful to Cynthia Strande for her invaluable assistance with the model.

III.
Community Service, Activism, and Civic Consciousness

5 Learning as We Go: Risk Taking and Relationship Building through Service Learning in Belize

Mary R. Moeller, Lonell Moeller, and Susan L. Filler

During the past three years of conducting a study abroad service-learning program for preservice teachers in a primary and high school in Belize, Central America, we, as US teacher educators, have learned along with our students about working in a diverse setting to become agents of change. Through the lens of our students' perspectives, ourselves as participant observers (Spradley, 1980), and the frameworks of Villegas and Lucas (2002, 2007) and Ludlow, Enterline, and Cochran-Smith (2008), we will describe our new understandings about the requisite skills and dispositions to become culturally responsive teachers working in a multicultural setting toward social justice goals. Specifically, we will consider our experiences as both teacher educators and preservice teachers creating relationships across borders within a complex, multi-institution study abroad service-learning program and to taking the necessary risks to do so. Using a narrative inquiry approach (Savin-Baden & Van Niekerk, 2007), we will use informal coding to analyze data from reflections, program evaluations, and focused interviews from program participants. As an important outcome, we will provide suggestions for best practices for teacher educators as they seek to improve their praxis related to culturally responsive teaching and social justice.

The Need for Culturally Responsive Teachers

"It's a dangerous business, Frodo, going out your door.... You step into the road, and if you don't keep your feet, there's no knowing where you might be swept off to." This warning from Tolkien's *Lord of the Rings* (1954/1994, p. 84) about leaving the security of home resonates with many of us. We prefer the comfortable feeling of knowing the rules of the road, and we find friends by surrounding ourselves with like-minded people. In our schools, we, as teachers, often prefer working with students who look like us and speak as we do (Kea, Campbell-Whatley, & Richards, 2006; Marbley, Bonner, Malik, Henfield, & Watts, 2007; Villegas & Lucas, 2002), perhaps because we recognize the limits of our culturally bound communication skills and teaching effectiveness. Similarly, in our communities, we tend to associate with and live near those whose income level and lifestyle match ours.

And yet, the demographic shift in our society and in US schools wherein minority groups have become the majority requires us all to be culturally responsive citizens and practitioners (Holsapple, 2012). Our democratic ideals require us to recognize and respect diverse voices; the professional standards in education require us to develop future teachers with dispositions and skills to effectively educate all students. As such, we intend to graduate culturally responsive students who critically examine their own assumptions and beliefs about the social order, who seek positive changes in their schools and communities to support the needs of all, and who see diversity as a positive attribute (Cochran-Smith, 1991; Villegas & Lucas, 2002, 2007). Further, we as faculty intend to become agents of change and reform on a larger scale than our classrooms. We recognize the need to create communities that are responsive to the needs of diverse neighbors at home as well as abroad. How is it possible to effect these daunting transformations? Doing so requires us as teacher educators and faculty to keep learning through experiences along with our students (Kolb, 1984). Service learning has been identified as a way for participants to "challenge their assumptions . . . of cultural diversity and poverty" and to augment "understanding of and appreciation for the complexities of others' lives" (Villegas & Lucas, 2002, p. 140). Through service learning, faculty create authentic course experiences to engage directly with people in communities, such as schools, and to meet the community's self-identified goals. Within that problem-solving context, students learn course content and meet course goals, and significantly, in this process, transformation happens. As we see people in a new light, stereotypes dissolve; as we identify previously unrecognized strengths, we become more hopeful about individual and community development. The Scholarship of Teaching and Learning agenda envisions teaching as a public activity and "thus related to the formation of community" (Gilpin & Liston, 2009, p. 2). In pursuit of community and in looking for transformative methods, how might educators continue to develop service learning as a method for promoting civic responsibility, interest in social change, and advocacy for justice (Bolk, 2010; Bringle & Hatcher, 2011; Mitchell, 2008)? Our students are with us for only a few short semesters, and we have limited opportunities in our largely homogenous university and community setting to engage with diverse populations. Going out of our doors, stepping onto the road: these are incremental steps on a lifelong professional journey. Yet, even these relatively small steps involve taking risks to create relationships, to challenge our own assumptions, and to learn as we go. As Lyday, Winecoff, and Hiott (2001) explain, "Effective service learning programs require practitioners who are . . . good change agents . . . not afraid of uncertainty, risk taking, or thinking big while starting small" (p. 1).

In this chapter we, as teacher educators and researchers, will describe how a study abroad service-learning course has impacted our own development as culturally responsive educators. We also identify our students' new understandings related to social justice as they explain them. Within the broader scholarship of teaching commons, we consider how the course design and the service-learning immersion in Belize has created a community of practice focused on making a positive difference.

Context of Course

Course Design

As an International Service Learning (ISL) course, the pedagogical structure shows potential to enrich the experiences and thus the outcomes for participants, including the students and the leaders (Bringle & Hatcher, 2011). Key elements of an ISL include having a planned service project that meets local needs, engaging directly by interacting with others in an international setting, and learning from the experience through reflection. Through service-learning projects, the program participants have the opportunity to develop an understanding of global citizenship (Anderson, Swick, & Yff, 2001; Bringle & Hatcher, 2011; Holsapple, 2012; Ibrahim, 2012; Plater, 2011). This elective course is titled Educational Leadership in Service-Learning: Study Abroad Belize, and students can enroll for one or two credits at the undergraduate or graduate level. Although we primarily market this course to preservice teachers, students from other majors are welcome, and about half of the students who have enrolled over the past three years major in areas other than teacher education.

A unique element in this course model capitalizes on a community resource not commonly recognized as such by in-state institutions of public higher education—the faith-based organizations in our community. As such, the program planning and course design challenges the concepts of traditional associations related to partnership and power (Sandmann, Kiely, & Grenier, 2009). By breaking down the walls between institutions, specifically faith-based and state-supported organizations, the course design explores their boundaries and thus expands the possibility of collaboration across community. The old "town and gown" stereotype generates constricted thinking, "reinforcing a false dichotomy" that "such boundaries are problematic" (Sandmann, Moore, & Quinn, 2012, p. 36). As faculty we appreciate the willingness of leaders in both institutions to take the inherent risk in developing a relationship between the public university and a local resource, a church in town. Recognizing and respecting the roles and responsibilities of these institutions has required negotiation to ensure that expectations for service do not infringe on students' rights, as we will explain later. In addition, by collaborating with a faith-based institution in our town and with local community members, we have stretched the definition of an academic community of practice in a way that "reconceptualiz[es] . . . teaching and learning as a shared endeavor that transforms not only teaching and learning but our relationship of one to another and of ourselves to our world" (Gilpin & Liston, 2009, p. 2).

We have travelled to Belize for the past three years as a cross-generational group from the university and the community who comprise one team with a common purpose: serving others by completing a variety of projects, all related to social justice, by expanding and extending equitable opportunities to others. In addition, the service-learning course offers the opportunity for all participants, meaning students who have enrolled in the course as well as community members who travel with us, to develop an understanding of global citizenship. We do this collectively as we engage with culturally diverse schoolchildren, teachers, administrators, and community members in Belize.

Course delivery happens over spring break for several reasons: school is in session in Belize, so our students can work in the classrooms; university students can use their spring break time to add a study abroad experience to otherwise full schedules; and university instructors have time to focus free from classroom obligations. We typically have eight days available with five days for classroom contact and other service-learning projects in Belize and two days to add other cultural experiences. We spend the last two days in country debriefing and visiting sites such as the rainforest and archeological ruins, which has helped us gain a broader perspective on the country.

How We Organize: Multiple Groups, the Leaders, and Their Roles

In the Belize program, multiple leaders from two distinctly separate institutions, the university and local churches, work together in an unusual collaboration to make this experiential course feasible and, in fact, possible. In the following paragraphs, we describe the roles played by faculty from the university and community leaders from the church. The collaboration itself has significance in terms of social justice values: we dialogue extensively to develop relationships of mutual respect and reciprocity. Yet with multiple leaders come various risks in terms of negotiating priorities, communicating clearly, accepting responsibilities, and respecting roles.

University Leadership

Faculty leadership from the university comes from the teacher education program. Mary Moeller had previous experience in service learning and developed the course. Moeller also taught a diversity course and recognized the potential for service learning to promote social justice classroom goals. She approached the department head and the university study abroad office with a proposal to deliver a new type of study abroad opportunity over spring break. She knew of another group from the community, centered out of a local church, who would be traveling to Belize at that time, and since they were already connected and working with a school, it seemed feasible to join forces in a collaborative experience. At this time, Moeller was not yet tenured; she took a risk in moving toward gaining expertise in a new area of scholarship and in attempting a new leadership role in developing a study abroad course. There was risk with an experimental course model, considering the separation of church and state. After receiving support from university administrators, the course planning and student recruitment began.

In considering this collaboration, the study abroad office staff were cautious and thoughtful. They assessed the potential and advised the instructor on policies and practices to ensure a proper separation of church and state interests. For example, university students are able to choose their level of participation in any activity with a religious purpose (e.g., attending a school chapel service in Belize). We further determined that, for a nominal provider fee, local church leaders could efficiently organize the logistical support for travel, room, and board. Although this organizational structure used an untried design, university administrators believed it had potential to be an effective and innovative approach to program delivery.

As study abroad faculty, we rely on the university's international education office for teaching students about cultural perspectives, health and safety concerns, managing the paperwork and budget, recruiting students through flyers and posters, providing funds from tuition and training for faculty, and managing risk for the group. This office also supports us with an essential safety net and secure link to home and family while we are abroad by providing access to twenty-four-hour communication. Their reliable services minimize the inherent risk for traveling, especially to international locations where cell phone and internet services might not be readily available. As faculty leaders, we place a priority on the health and well-being of the students, and the university's support in this area gives us the assurance necessary for us to travel abroad.

As the course instructor of record, Moeller recruits enrollees and promotes the course through multiple presentations, interviews and accepts students into the course, and communicates course goals and logistical information. In Belize, the university faculty plan and monitor the teaching service-learning projects in the classrooms, including helping to develop the lesson plans and materials our students use. Faculty also gather materials for the requested in-service workshops and deliver that instruction to the teachers in Belize.

Community Leadership

By collaborating in appropriate ways, we have added capacity to our study abroad program as we draw on the resources and expertise in the community. The main community group leader, also a local pastor, grew up in Africa and has studied extensively in Europe. She had an established relationship with the Belizean pastor and an invitation to return to his community. We have used her expertise and connections in Belize to make travel arrangements to and within the country, to plan the week's itinerary, and to arrange for room and board. In her role as community group leader, she adds a cross-cultural understanding and the perspectives of a global citizen to our group. A second community leader with multiple volunteering experiences abroad brings a contagious spirit of service to meet the needs of others. This leader coordinates much of the fundraising efforts, organizes supplies required for projects, and supports the Belizean community sewing group. In working with those women, she has goals to empower them by developing their craftsmanship, product line, and marketing skills.

Benefits and Risks of Multiple Leaders and Partnerships

As leaders working together to define program priorities and parameters, we self-monitor to accomplish specific duties and responsibilities within our partnerships. We have needed to recognize where our leadership roles leave a gap or overlap in ways that compromise relationships and trust, both within our larger team and with the leaders in Belize (Sandmann & Kliewer, 2012). Any challenges that arise are largely through miscommunication, misunderstanding expectations, and differences in priorities. For example, our stateside team debates about what fundraisers to pursue, which projects to prioritize, and how to allocate our resources, time, and talents. At times our capacity to fundraise feels stretched, and we have questioned how much financial support we can provide. We also consider how much project support money should be sent to Belize ahead of time and how much money to reserve to meet needs identified after we arrive. We dialogue among our leadership team and with the one in Belize to establish the "equitable partnerships characterized by mutuality and reciprocity" that Boyer advocates (as cited in Sandmann & Kliewer, 2012, para. 7). Keeping a focus on the end goals of serving the community in Belize, according to *their* self-identified needs, helps us to work through differences of opinion and management styles. Over the years, our leadership team has intentionally worked to cultivate and maintain a high level of trust among all stakeholders. By committing ourselves to respectful communication styles and planning protocols in our praxis, we identify with the relational model of service learning (Sandmann et al., 2009) characterized by ongoing dialogue and reflection. These are hallmarks of social justice within service learning (Mitchell, 2008).

With multiple people comprising a leadership team of university and community members, we have developed a communication style that spreads decision making and power across the program. Sharing authority is a social justice value that we model within our team during predeparture planning. For example, one student's mother volunteered to purchase a list of items for us to transport. In response, we deferred to our project leaders for advice, and we consulted directly with our Belizean partners for their suggestions on availability of goods; we prefer to purchase materials in the Belizean markets if possible. Buying in country supports social justice values by providing economic support to their local stores, and we can eliminate fees to transport goods. In addition, we consult with each other before making decisions on the travel schedule, food preparation, and our itinerary in Belize. Although the process is time-consuming, the practice of consensus building and listening carefully helps us align our work with core principles of social justice. This intragroup communication style models how we intend to interact in Belize with the school/church leadership team and how we will avoid paternalistic attitudes in service-learning partnerships.

University Students and Community Members as Collaborators

STUDENT PARTICIPANTS

Our land-grant university draws from a largely rural population. Many are first-generation college students. They tend to be conservative in philosophy and hard-working by nature. In our region of the country, work ethic is a point of pride; we as leaders promote quality work, timeliness, and project accomplishment. To cover their tuition costs, students often take out loans and have a part-time, or even full-time, job. Some participants have traveled abroad before, some have participated in mission trips, but some have never even traveled on an airplane before. Most participants have been upperclassmen with the majority being female. Over the past three years, twenty-seven university students have traveled with the program.

By enrolling in a study abroad course, the students accept the usual risks associated with international travel. One student consulted privately with one of the faculty the day before departure with concerns about her physical size and being comfortable in the airplane seats. By enrolling in a service-learning course, they face additional unknowns. Students' course applications and oral comments reveal concerns about their feelings of inadequacy for creating relationships in the classrooms, for communicating with students, and for managing their emotions and for being up to the tasks in general.

COMMUNITY MEMBERS AS VALUE-ADDED PARTICIPANTS

In addition to the university students, we invite community members to join us in service. As such, we have sometimes traveled with as many adults as university students. The mix of service-minded individuals from many backgrounds, occupations, and ages adds expertise, diverse perspectives, and, most significantly, expanded mentoring capacity for our activities. One student commented that "adults listen better"; she valued having an audience beyond her fellow students to listen to her and serve as a sounding board for her concerns.

During our second year of the Belize program, three mothers and their three middle and high school children also joined the group. University students served as big brothers and sisters to these young people; at the same time, several university students also appreciated the nurturing relationship that developed between themselves and the mothers, even to the extent of nicknaming one community member "Mom." By providing mature perspectives and modeling their passion for service, community members serve as mentors-on-the-side to the university students. In addition, some community members bring medical backgrounds and expertise in construction, plumbing, electricity, and agriculture. During a water outage in our dormitories, they used their skills to fix the problem, thus role modeling how to react to a challenge. However, the community members also learn new techniques—the Belizean methods. Overall, the collective knowledge and wisdom within our team adds capacity to our ability to serve the Belize community in ways that they request. The complex course design creates robust learning opportunities in cross-cultural and cross-generational directions, as we illustrate later.

Fundraising

Group collaboration to fundraise in support of the various service projects at the Belize school and in their community is important. As much as possible, all participants contribute time and effort toward this goal. Through fundraising, we develop group cohesiveness and more fully recognize the components of service-learning projects. Our group also receives financial support from supporters in the university and community as we raise awareness about the need for school supplies. University students sometimes garner personal travel support by educating their families and others on their goals and projects.

Belizean Partners as Community

Our service-learning partner in Belize is also a community, and this enriches the service-learning projects and increases opportunities. Their community comprises a primary and secondary school, a church, and a women's sewing group supported by the church. The close-knit group is guided by the church's pastor, who also has official duties administering the school. Since the pastor wears multiple hats, he serves as our primary contact in communicating with the schools, determining the projects, and even securing transportation and arranging accommodations for room and board at the school's retreat center.

Over the three years of service-learning projects, we have earned the pastor's and the school administrator's respect. Trust between partners and authentic relationships is essential for reaching goals and sustaining progress toward community-driven goals (Mitchell, 2008). On the day we left after our most recent trip, the pastor said:

> This is one of the dreams I have always had. Indeed, it has become a reality. I just hope it keeps being solidified every year. We have had many [mission] teams . . . but they have been one time or two times and that's max. But you guys have really crossed over the line now three years consecutively and especially this year with this teaching strategy and teaching connection . . . [that] has cemented more the

relationship . . . cemented more this partnership. . . . I don't know if I dream too big but I want [my] school to be an example in all aspects. . . . I thank God for making this a reality. Like Moses I can sleep in peace.

The pastor's affirmation of our productive relationship assured us that our service in his community had been respectful of their needs and goals. However, his words also point out a risk in service-learning partnerships: trust takes time to develop. Authentic partnerships that are most meaningful emerge through repeated and consistent commitments to serve.

Garoutte (in chapter 8 of this volume) explains the significance of developing relationship: "It is especially important that students and faculty alike be welcomed by community members as their input and cooperation are essential for justice-focused CBL [community-based learning]." In Belize, their well-developed leadership team guides our service in specific ways to be agents of change in their school. For example, the principals requested us to lead a separate teacher development in-service in each of their buildings during our next visit with a focus specifically on literacy, English as a second language, and agricultural education strategies.

Border Crossings between Secular and Sacred Territories

Many schools in Belize are supported by faith-based institutions, as is our service-learning partner K-12 school. Teachers conduct their own daily staff devotions before school starts, and our students may choose to attend these twenty-minute sessions as a matter of following the teachers' routines and recognizing this aspect of school culture. Our students may also choose to be observers rather than participants. They often recognize through attending the devotions that religion provides a central guiding principle in many Belizean schools for students as well as teachers. Experiencing this element expands our students' understanding of culture and diversity. The university students recognize that the teachers' spiritual faith empowers the teachers. The shared faith is an asset.

Still, we are keenly aware of and sensitive to the thin line required in our democracy—legitimate restrictions exist to separate the rights of religious institutions and the state. We manage this separation by acknowledging our relationships at the beginning of conversations with potential enrollees in the study abroad course. We inform our students that our provider for logistical arrangements in travel and in some service projects is a local church. We assure students that we, as course instructors, and our community church leaders, as project organizers, will not proselytize or require personal belief statements as a requisite for program participation at any level. Clear communication about expectations helps us manage the risks here.

Our students choose the service projects and contexts that fit their needs. One student did not want to present part of a faith-based lesson that was requested by the church in Belize. We assured her that she could find another way to serve. However, she had a strong interest in drama. When she discovered that we were telling a story through a puppet show, she quickly volunteered her theatrical skills for the lesson.

How We Serve and Learn through Service

During the third iteration of the course, nine students and we as teacher educators offered to work more extensively than before in the classrooms. Before spring break, Susan Filler prepared the university students to teach an integrated miniunit of science lessons based on science standards established by the Ministry of Education in Belize. Each lesson included a rich variety of engaging hands-on activities, such as experimenting with concepts of buoyancy and replacement by having students listen to a story about pirate ships, create aluminum foil boats, weight them down with coins, and test the students' designs in tubs of water. Some of the interactive strategies were new to the Belizean students while other activities were familiar. For example, the university students used choral response to teach terminology, and the Belizean students quickly responded. Since teaching strategies and student responses have a basis in culture, we took risks by introducing different instructional methods in the lessons that were taught.

In a previous year, Filler noted that Belizean teachers and students typically used directed teaching strategies that were associated with certain content standards. Engaged learning, discovery, or inquiry methods did not appear to be familiar. When she modeled an inquiry lesson requiring observations, the class hesitated and didn't know how to react. She also noticed significant differences in assessment and teacher accountability compared to our state's system. In Belize, teacher evaluation and effectiveness is tied to student work samples, for example.

These classroom observations of cultural differences in teaching and learning alert us to a risk that we must carefully evaluate as we prepare in-service materials for the Belizean teachers and step into a leadership role in their educational system, even though we have been asked to do so. We first must consider how we as faculty can come to understand and identify the differences between culturally important classroom traditions and the Western research-based strategies on effective teaching and learning (Ibrahim, 2012). After all, what we know to work best in our world might not translate well into the Belizean culture. Yet we have recognized an assumption on our part that we know what effective teaching and learning looks like as teacher educators. Admitting to this error in thinking challenges our professional identities. Still, to avoid paternalistic arrogance, we need to be cautious, observe closely, ask questions, and dialogue with Belizean teachers and administrators (Spradley, 1980).

At the high school, the Belizean principal has an ongoing goal of transforming her school into a model focused on agricultural entrepreneurship. She is a change agent with a vision for improving her students' lives and opportunities. At her request, Lonell Moeller worked to meet this goal by sharing his expertise in agricultural curriculum by consulting with the teachers. We also supported the principal's goals through the teaching of a university student who majors in agricultural education. She came prepared to teach a small animal care class. She focused on the rabbits that the school had recently acquired and demonstrated proper techniques for working with them. In developing her lesson, we as faculty assumed that these rabbits would be raised for a food source. We recognized our faulty assumption once at the school and, fortunately, before traumatizing the Belizean students who intended the rabbits to be their pets!

In working with this unit, our student brought her college textbook on small animal care. She was thrilled to see the level of interest in this hefty book with its colored plates depicting rabbit breeds. She left this as a resource for the students, and the opportunity to donate her book to the Belizean students created a learning moment for her about social justice. She had identified a lack of resources and attempted to rectify the disparity. Cochran-Smith, Shakman, Jong, Terrell, Barnatt, and McQuillan (2009) describe similar actions as "helping to redistribute educational opportunities" (p. 349) in a very real and concrete way.

As a former agricultural education teacher and university teacher educator, Lonell Moeller was able to provide significant support by working with the science teacher, modeling teaching methods, and identifying and purchasing laboratory equipment. By recognizing these inequities across schools and the uneven opportunities for students, our faculty and students developed a sociocultural consciousness, the "awareness that a person's worldview is not universal but is profoundly influenced by life experiences, as mediated by a variety of factors, including race, ethnicity, gender, and social class" (Villegas & Lucas, 2007, p. 4).

Process of Project Completion Provides a Variety of Lessons

We are never certain of which projects we will work on or what we will be able to complete until we are at the school, the week unfolds, and the pieces come together. However, this uncertainty has also pushed us toward a more trusting collaboration, one that now recognizes the capacity or assets of the Belizean partners to accomplish the task at hand. Garoutte (chapter 8) explains the significance of this perspective in successful service-learning projects: those who intend to strengthen communities through service projects should first recognize that the community possesses its own capacities and assets. Accessing those assets promotes sustainable change because the change emerges from community engagement and expertise. More significantly, from our perspective the process of identifying local assets also helps those who serve to view the community in a different light, one in which we see possibility and promise rather than deficit and need. As Lisa Garoutte notes in chapter 8 of this volume, the recognition of these assets shapes the way we all engage with the community in Belize, to move us toward equitable partnerships rather than "charity." We have learned that our Belizean service-learning partner understands what is required to complete a project, even though we might not be fully aware of the plans for execution.

An example of this happened during our second year of program delivery when we were asked to provide financial and physical support for the construction of a school meal shelter. Preparing the concrete footings in rocky ground, mixing the concrete in small batches, and wheel-barrowing it to the foundation forms required much physical effort from our group. Then, at midmorning, we were surprised to see army trucks pulling into the schoolyard with about a dozen armed soldiers. The school principal had contacted a local Belizean national guard unit to provide additional manpower for pouring the foundation. She wanted to support our efforts in a very real way.

On other occasions, we have returned home with several unfinished jobs on our to-do lists. With our Midwestern mind-set, we value timely project completion, so not finishing a job is unsettling. We have been frustrated as leaders and participants if we leave with uncompleted work. This has happened in working with the women's sewing group. After the first year of mentoring these women in reading sewing patterns, we anticipated that upon our return in year two, the group would be organized as a co-op and have articles sewn for us to retail in the United States. When that didn't happen, we felt deflated and puzzled about how to move the sewing projects forward. At times we have characterized this as a program weakness—to be addressed because *our* expectations are not fulfilled. We have felt apologetic in returning and explaining our lack of tangible progress to program supporters back home. However, as Mitchell (2008) explains, "The types of service experiences that allow students to consider social change and transformation may not bring immediate results and, therefore, may not offer the type of gratification that students involved in more traditional service-learning classes experience when the painting is completed, homeless person is fed, or child has finished the art project. Social change oriented service takes time" (p. 54).

We have also learned that the Belizean culture has a different set of priorities. As Filler reflected, "Accomplishing a task is not the first priority of the day. Reaching a monetary or material goal is not primary. More energy is focused on sharing their life stories, their faith stories and their time. The 'task' will get done on Belizean Time. Our Belizean partners have taught us the value of relationship building."

Cultural differences also emerge as we observe the Belizean methods used to complete projects in a place where specialized tools are not readily available. While working on a large concrete project, we needed to cut steel reinforcement rods to strengthen the structure. Although we had brought hacksaw blades to the construction site, we did not have a hacksaw frame. Without this piece in hand, we were stymied in thinking about how to cut the rods. Then, a local laborer proceeded to fashion a serviceable hacksaw by bending a piece of the rod and attaching our blade. As observers of this creative problem solving, we were able to see how work gets done. On another occasion, Lonell Moeller was cutting wire mesh for screens on the rabbit cages. He diligently cut the mesh using pliers, which was a slow process considering the number of wires that needed to be cut. His Belizean partner observed the process carefully until the end. He then asked, "Would you like to see the Belizean way?" When Moeller said yes, the partner took his machete, placed it vertically on the wire mesh and proceeded to pound on the blade with a large hammer. The mesh was cut in a matter of seconds. The worker offered his machete to Moeller and said, "Would you like to try?" Coming from a part of the world where there is a separate tool for each task, we developed a new level of respect and recognition for Belizean ingenuity. The workers demonstrated originality, "putting everyday things to uses which had not occurred to others" (Dewey, 1938, p. 187).

Working hand in hand with Belizean laborers helped us as leaders develop what Freire (1998) described as a new awareness or *critical consciousness* (p. 82). This means the ability to focus on the reality of a situation by not imposing any preconceived ideas, for example, on the competencies and resources in the Belizean community. In contrast, when we first visited the community, we were more likely to make assumptions. Freire (1998) describes this as a *naïve consciousness* that relies on a subjective interpretation of the situation that is not grounded in facts. For example, when we initially heard of the meal shelter construction project, we assumed that the design would be similar to an agricultural pole barn. We brought along tools such as hammers and saws for that work. Upon arriving on site, we recognized that a different building design was required. Our growth as faculty and community leaders in understanding the difference of these two concepts developed over time, through immersion experiences, and by developing relationships.

Reflecting on Learning in Multiple Ways

Methods

In this chapter we used Scholarship of Teaching and Learning to focus on this broad and open-ended question: How did the Belize program experience shape our understandings about the requisite skills and dispositions to become culturally responsive teachers working in an international setting toward social justice goals? By using ethnographic methodology, specifically as participant observers immersed in the Belizean culture, we have been able to "step outside our narrow cultural backgrounds, to set aside our socially inherited ethnocentrism . . . and to apprehend the world from the viewpoint of other human beings" (Spradley, 1980, p. viii). This process has led us to other questions and answers to be uncovered along the way. We investigated and documented our learning by reflecting in various ways.

Following the university's Institutional Review Board guidelines, we gathered data before, during, and after each of the three study abroad experiences. The data includes individual students' collected daily written reflections during the study abroad experience; pre- and postdeparture written reflections as course assignments with specific prompts; recorded and transcribed interviews of nine selected program participants; and final program evaluations from students, faculty, and community members.

Students from multiple majors and academic backgrounds entered the course with little common training or understanding about writing reflections. As a one-credit course with limited time available to develop that skill set, we initially accepted a variety of formats for the daily reflections that built around general open-ended prompts in a journal we provided. We used specific probing prompts for the predeparture reflection and the final program evaluation, collected within two weeks after returning.

By allowing students to write their reflections during the time abroad in their own styles, we personalized the learning to meet individual needs. For example, one teacher education major with previous training in writing reflections admitted that she was "not much for journaling"; in addition, she recognized a natural tendency toward cynicism. She created a solution for meeting the course reflection requirement by listing things and people that she was thankful for each day; at the end of the week she reported that she could "relive the week" to construct a more formalized reflection. Without recognizing it, the student conducted participant observations in the sense that her wide-open initial step for gathering ideas led her to analyze the week more precisely (Spradley, 1980). Her cyclical process proved valuable and meaningful because she had personalized the reflection process in a thoughtful way (Whitney & Clayton, 2012).

Scheduled debriefings each evening, informal mealtime discussions, and extemporaneous conversations throughout the day, along with formal written reflections from specific prompts, created multiple opportunities for learning within relationship to happen during this program. As educators, we specifically identified the transformative power of the scheduled evening group times where we paused, thought, and measured the day in terms of our personal highs and lows and personal perspectives. Transformative learning happens as people begin to see the world through the eyes of others and develop new ideas about how they can work together in supportive roles (Gilpin & Liston, 2009). Having open-ended prompts and regular group reflections supported this goal.

The evening reflections also served the purpose for us as participant observers to gather data frequently and to process it daily. Maintaining a regular tradition of sharing individual stories and perspectives with the whole group also contributed to group cohesiveness and created a safe place to verbalize thoughts or to "pass" and listen to others. Establishing this reflection protocol reduced risk by giving permission for participants to either expound on the day's events or listen and absorb others' perspectives. Observing, listening, and reflecting on experience remained as an important measure of learning and growth (Dewey, 1938; Whitney & Clayton, 2012). The methodology supported our understanding that we learn as we go (Spradley, 1980).

Some of us used our time within the evening debriefings to describe what others had done that warranted recognition, and some explained the emotional impact of an experience. For example, one community member who was also a construction manager praised the perseverance and work ethic of students as they hauled concrete that day; his new awareness contradicted his previous notions about the younger generation. He also pointed out, for the benefit of all, that several Belizean students had come to the work site looking for a university student because they had missed his presence. This young man hadn't been in class with them that afternoon. Instead he had chosen to work on a school construction project because he had not felt valued by the Belizean students in the classroom. The university student had not recognized the significant interpersonal relationships he had developed with the Belizean students. By recalling this incident during the evening group time, the construction manager validated the university student's vocational choice to become a teacher. In his post-experience interview, the student recalled that affirmation as a significant moment.

The evening opportunity often produced a full range of emotional responses from our group members. We bonded with laughter, tears, and this last spring, a celebratory version of a children's song on homemade kazoos. We could be silly and serious at the same time. Group reflections demonstrated the power to impact learning and make meaning of the service (Whitney & Clayton, 2012).

Developing as a Community of Practice

After reviewing the data, including our own stories as participants and researchers, we recognized that we had developed into a community of practice focused on learning together to become agents of change in Belize (Savin-Baden & Van Niekerk, 2007). Rather than thinking of learning as a result of knowledge accumulation in an individual's head, Smith (2003) defines learning as what occurs in communities of practice as people relate to each other. For students, faculty, and community members as service learners together, our actions were tied to learning goals and ongoing reflection about the experience (Jacoby, 1996). One university student identified her reason for participating as becoming an agent of change and defined what that looked like to her. She said, "We wanted to make a difference . . . over time the small changes do add up."

Learning happened when we took advantage of brief opportunities throughout the day to converse, share a quick story, and ask questions of each other as a matter of routine. The evening ritual created a space for genuine listening and communication, whether a university student, community member, or leader chose to speak or to observe. Hearing the perspectives of fellow team members reflecting on shared experiences developed a sense of camaraderie and understanding. We identify the cross-generational learning in this space as a "shared endeavor that transforms not only teaching and learning but our relationship of one to another and of ourselves to the world" (Gilpin & Liston, 2009, p. 2). This commons fosters a collaborative process that "encourage[s] the free flow of ideas and exchange of information"; it "enable[s] dialogue between people who come together to explore new possibilities, solve challenging problems, and create new, mutually beneficial opportunities" (Cambridge, Kaplan, & Suter, 2005, p. 1). The evening discussions provided evidence that we had created a community of practice within our team.

What We've Learned

As we deconstruct the course design, the delivery mechanisms, and the various ways multiple leaders interacted, we can identify experiences that supported the teaching of social justice goals for participants (Ludlow et al., 2008). By developing personal relationships with our Belizean service-learning partners in the school, church, and community, we examined and confronted our own beliefs about other people, their cultures, and their institutions. This introspection required us to be vulnerable and to recognize our assumptions and biases. This is risky because new understandings challenge our world view and can even expose our academic weaknesses. For example, we experienced multiple times when the Belizean people proved their capacity to use community assets to solve problems, confront inequities in their society, and succeed in community building—all in spite of limited, and what we might identify as insufficient, resources. Through the stories and reflections related in this chapter, we demonstrate the learning that has occurred, specifically in our understanding of promoting social justice.

Student Understandings and Disillusionments

In addition to recognizing our differences in cultural expectations for project completion and methods, group participants have also identified a need to reconceptualize the goals. An elementary education student commented: "We saw smiles, heard laughter, [but] we did not teach a grand lesson that transformed a community, the structure was by no means finished . . . we were not determined to revolutionize the world all at once." However, she did not initially reach this conclusion without frustrations and tears during the week's work. Her expectations for being able to engage with students in the classroom had not been met, and she felt sidelined. As an energetic university student, she needed to step back from her original perspectives to consider the possibilities more realistically.

In a similar way, another student recognized her culture shock, meaning that she had entered Belize with a "naïve consciousness" (Freire, 1998, p. 82) and needed to reconcile that with the reality of what she saw as she walked through the town. The simply constructed houses often included unfinished rooms and signs of incomplete projects; previously, she had only envisioned the tourist perspective of tropical resorts and paradise. Students with travel abroad experience did not experience this culture shock, and they readily compared the Belizean landscape to what they had observed on other service trips in the Caribbean.

Different classroom experiences and perceptions of Belizean students also provided learning opportunities. One student had an opportunity to help Belizean students prepare for a dance competition. After identifying cultural differences in dance styles and competitions, she later observed, "I know Belizean values and customs are much different than mine and other Americans, but the pride we have for those values and customs are the same."

Our students were also able to experience being in an English as a second language environment since many of the Belizean students speak Spanish regularly in their homes. Students were able to observe that teachers sometimes struggle with literacy challenges. For most of the university students, being in an English as a second language environment brought a new awareness about the importance of teaching literacy and about the concept of social justice. For example, one student wrote, "I learned that students who speak English as a second language can be successful when steps are taken to provide them with the tools they need to understand and develop and showcase what they know and what they are learning." The university student recognized the need for literacy interventions. As Cochran-Smith et al. (2009) write, "When good teaching is conceptualized as challenging educational inequities so that everybody has the kinds of rich learning opportunities that have historically been reserved for the privileged, it links teachers' classroom practices with larger social responsibilities" (p. 30).

These reflections demonstrate that the students are developing the capacity to become agents of change in their praxis. Their experiences during the Belize program prompted them to be aware of differences in schools and opportunities, to question inequities, and to recognize the assets Belizeans possess to solve problems. Through this recognition, the university students participate in what Freire (1998) has called "liberating education."

Where We Go from Here

Breaking down the siloed thinking that separates us in our own communities from accessing each other's areas of expertise creates room for dialogue between collaborators in the Belize program. Freire (1998) describes dialogue as a "horizontal relationship" (p. 83), which indicates that differences in power have been reconciled. Dialogue between service-learning partners opens the door for possibilities and fresh perspectives to develop. We have been able to nurture equitable relationships by appreciating and utilizing each other's strengths and assets in accomplishing service-learning goals. Sandmann et al. (2009) developed a model of program planning that characterizes our experiences in the Belize program community of practice: "The relational model compels service-learning educators to address important questions related to the ways institutions impact the planning process. How does the institution support or impede more robust forms of democratic and inclusive service-learning programs?" (p. 31).

The university study abroad office supported a relational approach to program planning in this service-learning course by allowing us to partner with a local faith-based organization as our provider for logistical support and connections with a Belizean faith-based institution. By supporting this innovative and collaborative service-learning partnership, the university study abroad staff allowed us to explore new possibilities in relationship. We were given the freedom to plan in nontraditional ways. By reconsidering and "renegotiating relationships," we can continue to explore ways "to break out of institutional conventions without having to dismantle them" (Sandmann et al., 2012, p. 31).

After three years of experiencing the Belizean program design, we can envision more possibilities and ways to grow relationships at home and abroad. For example, the Belize program opportunity is now being offered at another university under the leadership of Filler. She plans to develop a library in the Belize primary school and add more contact time within the classrooms for preservice elementary teachers. Taking these steps increases our capacity to serve and characterizes the "grow phase" in the life cycle of a community of practice (Cambridge et al., 2005).

By developing collaborative relationships over the last three years between multiple entities both in the United States and in Belize, we have created an international community of practice centered on serving and learning from each other. Out of these experiences we suggest the following points for teacher education praxis consideration:

1. The relational planning process promotes the development of service learning as communities of practice. With time and commitment to the same service-learning partner (Sandmann et al., 2009), relationships can develop into productive collaborations characterized by power sharing, trust, and mutual respect. Further, Lave and Wenger (1991) assert that "learning is a process of participation in communities of practice, participation that is at first legitimately peripheral but that increases gradually in engagement and complexity" (p. 37).
2. By developing relationships across borders, both in their local communities and abroad, service-learning partners can recognize and collaborate with the community-based assets to increase capacity and to effectively support sustainable progress toward social justice goals.
3. Through relationships and cultural immersion experiences, service learners can begin to understand and respect how culturally based problem solving allows communities to direct and advance their own destinies.
4. Even though taking the first steps outside of our doors to serve others involves risk taking in many forms, this is part of the learning process. Further, an international service-learning program can foster the desire in participants to learn more, to stay on that road, and to identify more paths toward goals of social justice.

5. Staying on the international service-learning road *with* our students challenges us as teacher educators to take risks too. We can evaluate our own development as agents of change; we can affirm our core values of committing to equitable learning opportunities for all students. We, too, learn through relationships with others.

Six months after returning from Belize, a university student invited us to view her Belizean scrapbook. It was a visual reflection, summarizing what she had learned. A picture caption in large font expressed her clear understanding of service learning: "We helped them . . . and they helped us." She then explained what that meant in terms of her own teaching: "[Being in that place] drove my teaching, it did! I was so passionate there because I could talk about things that were exciting to me that they didn't know about!" And how had this happened? She continued, "And then, I realized how supportive the community was, with [faculty] and the other teacher, as well. It's awesome—it was just a week—it's pretty cool. It was like family. I have my very own family there." This same student had reciprocated by leaving her small-animal textbook behind—to benefit her "family."

Our reason to stay on the road focuses on this purpose: Service learning is a way of participating in a community of practice that provides opportunities for learning about culturally responsive teaching for faculty and for students both here and in Belize. Through relationships with others through service, we grow in understanding ways to promote social justice. We are transformed by engaging with community.

MARY R. MOELLER is Associate Professor at South Dakota State University. She has spent most of her career teaching high school in Brookings, South Dakota, where she implemented service learning as a way to teach authentic technical writing skills.

LONELL MOELLER is Professor Emeritus of Agricultural Education at South Dakota State University. He taught high school agriculture for six years before completing a PhD in agricultural education. At SDSU he taught courses in teaching methods, curriculum planning and evaluation, computer programming, technology in education, and agricultural business management.

SUSAN L. FILLER is an adjunct instructor at Dakota State University and has spent the majority of her educational career teaching various grades 6–12 science courses. She developed curriculum incorporating service learning with middle school students who conducted bimonthly water quality testing in area streams and lakes.

References

Anderson, J. B., Swick, K. J., & Yff, J. (Eds.). (2001). *Service-learning in teacher education: Enhancing the growth of new teachers, their students, and communities* [E-reader version]. Washington, DC: American Association of Colleges for Teacher Education. Retrieved from http://eric.ed.gov/?id=ED451167.

Bolk, T. (2010). Study abroad: An exploration of service-learning programs. *UW-L Journal of Undergraduate Research, 13*, 1–16. Retrieved from http://www.uwlax.edu/urc/JUR-online/html/2010.htm.

Boyer, E. L. (1990). *Scholarship reconsidered: Priorities of the professoriate.* Lyon's Falls, NY: Carnegie Foundation for the Advancement of Teaching.

Boyer, E. L. (1996). The scholarship of engagement. *Journal of Public Service and Outreach, 1*(1), 11–20. Retrieved from http://openjournals.libs.uga.edu/index.php/jheoe.

Bringle, R. G., & Hatcher, J. A. (2011). International service learning. In R. G. Bringle, J. A. Hatcher, & S. G. Jones (Eds.), *International service learning: Conceptual frameworks and research* (pp. 3–28). Sterling, VA: Stylus.

Cambridge, D., Kaplan, S., & Suter, V. (2005). Community of practice design guide: A step-by-step guide for designing & cultivating communities of practice in higher education. *Educause.* Retrieved from http://net.educause.edu/ir/library/pdf/NLI0531.pdf.

Cochran-Smith, M. (1991, September). Learning to teach against the grain. *Harvard Educational Review, 61*(3), 279–311. Retrieved from http://hepg.org/her-home/home.

Cochran-Smith, M., Shakman, K., Jong, C., Terrell, D. G., Barnatt, J., & McQuillan, P. (2009, May). Good and just teaching: The case for social justice in teacher education. *American Journal of Education, 115*(3), 347–377. Retrieved from http://www.press.uchicago.edu/ucp/journals/journal/aje.html.

Dewey, J. (1938). *Experience and education.* New York, NY: MacMillan.

Freire, P. (1998). Education for critical consciousness. In D. Macedo, A. Man, & A. Freire (Eds.), *The Paulo Freire reader* (pp. 80–110). New York, NY: Continuum.

Gilpin, L. S., & Liston, D. (2009). Transformative education in the scholarship of teaching and learning: An analysis of SoTL literature. *International Journal for the Scholarship of Teaching and Learning, 3*(2), 1–8. Retrieved from http://digitalcommons.georgiasouthern.edu/ij-sotl/.

Holsapple, M. A. (2012). Service-learning and student diversity outcomes: Existing evidence and directions for future research. *Michigan Journal of Service-Learning, 18*(2), 5–18.

Ibrahim, B. L. (2012). International service-learning as pathway to global citizenship. In J. A. Hatcher & R. G. Bringle (Eds.), *Understanding service-learning and community engagement: Crossing boundaries through research* (pp. 11–24). Charlotte, NC: Information Age.

Jacoby, B., & Associates. (1996). *Service-learning in higher education: Concepts and practices.* San Francisco, CA: Jossey-Bass.

Kea, C., Campbell-Whatley, G. D., & Richards, H. V. (2006). Becoming culturally responsive educators: Rethinking teacher education pedagogy. *The National Center for Culturally Responsive Educational Systems' Practitioner Brief Series.* Retrieved from http://www.niusileadscape.org/docs/FINAL_PRODUCTS/NCCRESt/practitioner_briefs/%95%20TEMPLATE/DRAFTS/AUTHOR%20revisions/annablis%20pracbrief%20templates/Teacher_Ed_Brief_highres.pdf.

Kolb, D. A. (1984). *Experiential learning: Experience as the source of learning and development.* Upper Saddle River, NJ: Prentice Hall.

Lave, J., & Wenger, E. (1991). *Situated learning: Legitimate peripheral participation.* Cambridge, England: Cambridge University Press.

Ludlow, L. H., Enterline, S. E., & Cochran-Smith, M. (2008). Learning to teach for social justice—Beliefs scale: An application of Rasch measurement principles. *Measurement & Evaluation in Counseling & Development, 40*(4), 194–214.

Lyday, W. J., Winecoff, H. L., & Hiott, B. C. (2001). *Connecting communities through service learning. Linking learning with life.* Clemson: South Carolina Department of Education.

Marbley, A. F., Bonner, F. A., Malik, S. M., Henfield, S., & Watts, L. M. (2007). Interfacing culture specific pedagogy with counseling: A proposed diversity training model for preparing pre-service teachers for diverse learners. *Multicultural Education, 14*(3), 8–16.

Meaney, K., Griffin, K., & Bohler, H. (2009). Service-learning: A venue for enhancing preservice educators' knowledge base for teaching. *International Journal for the Scholarship of Teaching and Learning, 3*(2), 1–17. Retrieved from http://digitalcommons.georgiasouthern.edu/ij-sotl/vol3/iss2/21.

Mitchell, T. D. (2008). Traditional vs. critical service-learning: Engaging the literature to differentiate two models. *Michigan Journal of Community Service Learning, 14*(2), 50–65. Retrieved from https://ginsberg.umich.edu/mjcsl/.

Plater, W. M. (2011). The context for international service learning: An invisible revolution is underway. In R. G. Bringle, J. A. Hatcher, & S. G. Jones (Eds.), *International service learning: Conceptual frameworks and research* (pp. 29–56). Sterling, VA: Stylus.

Sandmann, L. R., Kiely, R. C., & Grenier, R. S. (2009). Program planning: The neglected dimension of service-learning. *Michigan Journal of Service-Learning, 15*(2), 17–33. Retrieved from https://ginsberg.umich.edu/mjcsl/.

Sandmann, L. R., & Kliewer, B. (2012). Theoretical and applied perspectives on power: Recognizing processes that undermine effective community-university partnerships. *Journal of Community Engagement and Scholarship, 5*(2), 20–28. Retrieved from http://jces.ua.edu/.

Sandmann, L. R., Moore, T. L., & Quinn, J. (2012). Center and periphery in service-learning and community engagement: A postcolonial approach. In J. A. Hatcher & R. G. Bringle (Eds.), *Understanding service-learning and community engagement: Crossing boundaries through research* (pp. 25–48). Charlotte, NC: Information Age.

Savin-Baden, M., & Van Niekerk, L. (2007). Narrative inquiry: Theory and practice. *Journal of Geography in Higher Education, 31*(3), 459–472. Retrieved from http://www.tandfonline.com/doi/abs/10.1080/03098260601071324.

Smith, M. K. (2003). *Jean Lave, Etienne Wenger, and communities of practice. The encyclopedia of informal education.* Retrieved from www.infed.org/biblio/communities_of_practice.htm.

Spradley, J. P. (1980). *Participant observation.* New York, NY: Holt, Rinehart and Winston.

Tolkien, J. R. R. (1994). *The lord of the rings part one: The fellowship of the ring.* New York, NY: Ballantine Books. (Original work published 1954.)

Villegas, A. M., & Lucas, T. (2002). *Educating culturally responsive teachers.* Albany: State University of New York Press.

Villegas, A. M., & Lucas, T. (2007, March). The culturally responsive teacher. *Educational Leadership*, pp. 28–33.

Whitney, B. C., & Clayton, H. C. (2012). Research on and through reflection in international service learning. In R. G. Bringle, J. A. Hatcher, & S. G. Jones (Eds.), *International service learning: Conceptual frameworks and research* (pp. 145–187). Sterling, VA: Stylus.

6 Champions for Health in the Community: Critical Service Learning, Transformative Education, and Community Empowerment

Karen Meaney, Jo An M. Zimmermann, Yongmei Lu, Gloria Martinez-Ramos, and Jacquelyn McDonald

CHAMPIONS FOR HEALTH in the Community initiated from a critical service-learning (CSL) program embedded within a physical education teacher education methods course at Texas State University. What began as a challenge to preservice educators to explore health disparities among low-income families residing in San Marcos, Texas, progressed into a multifaceted project consisting of five phases (see figure 6.1). Students' participation in CSL initiated a community-based participatory research project (CBPR) that ultimately resulted in transforming students' understanding of social injustices as well as faculty's perceptions of CBPR. Moreover, uniting CSL and CBPR provided a venue for empowering community members to voice their concerns regarding environmental barriers that negatively impacted their family's health and physical activity.

Conceptual Framework

Social cognitive theory (SCT) (Bandura, 1986, 1999) served as the theoretical framework for both the CSL program and the CBPR project. SCT suggests that human learning occurs within a dynamic framework and initiates interaction between one's personal factors, environment, and behaviors. These dynamic relationships constitute an interactive model referred to as triadic reciprocality (see figure 6.2).

Within the model of triadic reciprocality, personal factors may include one's motivation, self-efficacy, knowledge, fears, and expected outcomes. The environment is perceived in three stages: imposed, selected, and constructed (Bandura, 1999). One's imposed environment includes the way things are—that is, situations an individual must interact with on a daily basis (e.g., neighborhood, school, work, and family). While individuals may have minimal influence over imposed environmental factors, they do have choices in how they interpret and react to imposed factors. These choices regarding how one reacts to the imposed environment constitute the selected environment. The resulting behaviors, the third aspect of triadic reciprocality, become one's constructed environment. Construction of one's environment demands actively engaging in one's surroundings and may often result in the acquisition of new knowledge, beliefs, and behaviors.

The service-learning environment is designed to connect scholastic knowledge and civic engagement. Through active participation in authentic learning situations, students are provided opportunities to unite theory to practice. An essential component of service, learning requires that the student's service attempt to meet a genuine need in the community. Through engagement in guided reflection activities, students link academic content to their service experiences (Cress, 2005). CSL incorporates the core elements of traditional service-learning curricula and extends the paradigm to embrace social change (Mitchell, 2008). Specifically, the classroom and community components of CSL are founded on the idea of students as agents for social change working to redistribute power through developing authentic relationships with community participants. Consequently, the CSL environment is central to students' learning.

The imposed, selected, and constructed environment is also a core component of CBPR. CBPR is a collaborative process that unites researchers and community residents to collectively design and implement studies and programs that ultimately result in social change. Within CBPR, the environment influences both community and university members' learning and behaviors. Specifically, mutual respect between university researchers and community members is critical (Wallerstein & Duran, 2003). CBPR has been used to improve public health outcomes for at-risk communities (Minkler & Wallerstein, 2008). This dynamic process enables researchers and community members to work as partners and ultimately leads to enhanced communication, trust, and rapport between both parties.

CSL and CBPR emphasize the central role of the community–university collaborative environment to promote social justice. Combining a CSL program and CBPR study is an ideal forum to raise university students' awareness of society's disparities and unite students, faculty, and community residents to enact change.

Phase I: Critical Service Learning

CSL is embedded within the ESS 4624-Principles and Practices for Teaching Physical Education undergraduate course. A primary goal of this course is to enhance undergraduate students' understanding of the need for evidence-based physical education curriculum programs and instructional strategies. Examining pedagogical research and understanding learner variables (e.g., gender, socioeconomic status, cultural beliefs, values, geographic location) that influence participation in lifelong physical activity are also instilled throughout the course. Readings, discussions, and learning activities focus on increasing students' cultural competency for teaching. Additionally, the course embeds a CSL program that challenges preservice educators to gain an understanding of as well as assist in combatting barriers youth raised in low-income families face in regard to participation in regular physical activity.

Students enrolled in ESS 4624 during the first phase of our Champions for Health in the Community (CHIC) project participated in a "neighborhood exploration" assignment that exposed the students to the Riverside (pseudonym) low-income public housing neighborhood. Students were asked to identify components of the neighborhood that may positively or negatively contribute to participation in physical activity and healthy behaviors. The majority of student narratives underscored the dilapidated neighborhood park, lack of sidewalks and lighting, and extremely limited access to recreational facilities or open green space. The students also commented on the numerous fast food outlets and one Walmart store in proximity to the neighborhood.

Discussions following the neighborhood exploration assignment enabled the students to verbally share their thoughts and feelings about how levels of income may impact individual and family physical activity, health, and wellness. Several of the students commented on how different the public housing neighborhood was compared to the community where they were raised. Other students stated that the neighborhood resembled the community where they or perhaps people they knew lived. Rich and in-depth conversation followed and explored the difficulties families living in low-income households may face in regard to participation in physical activity. Safety of the children playing outside and lack of lighting, equipment, and facilities were all discussed as significant barriers.

A major component of CSL is empowering the students to act as agents of change. Therefore, simply discussing the neighborhood exploration and barriers to physical activity was not sufficient. Based on the findings of the neighborhood exploration assignment and class discussions, the students were faced with developing solutions to assist in minimizing barriers to physical activity faced by youth in low-income families. Collectively, the Phase I students proposed one or all of the following programs be developed and implemented the following year:

- An after-school physical activity program for the children to take place in the neighborhood
- An after-school physical activity program for the children to take place at Texas State University
- A summer physical activity program for the children to take place at Texas State University

The Fun & Fit 4 Life summer camp program was implemented during the summer of Phase II of the CHIC project. In collaboration with the Riverside families, and under the guidance of the professor instructing ESS 4624, students designed and delivered a physical activity summer program for the Riverside youth at Texas State University. Ideas for the program incorporated suggestions from the Riverside parents, caregivers, and youth.

During Phase III of the CHIC project, students enrolled in ESS 4624 participated in the National Night Out picnic with the families to gain insight into what the community thought was important to incorporate in the physical activity program. The students learned via conversations with the community members that not only did the parents and caregivers want their children to participate in physical activity, but they also suggested the youth engage in lessons about the importance of a college education. In collaboration with Texas State University's Center for P-16 Initiatives, the Fun & Fit 4 Life summer camp began including college readiness activities (e.g., career exploration, goal setting, campus exploration, and leadership activities) within the camp program.

The program expanded to include two additional public housing residences in the San Marcos vicinity during Phase IV. Approximately fifty to seventy-five youth aged five to twelve living in three different public housing residences continue to participate in the Fun & Fit 4 Life summer program. The Fun & Fit 4 Life program continued through Phase V of the CHIC project and remains a critical component of ESS 4624.

Phase II: Community-Based Participatory Research Project

The CBPR project took place in San Marcos, Texas. The city of San Marcos is located in Hays County, the fastest-growing county of fifty thousand people or more in the United States (Census, 2015a). With a 2014 estimated population of 185,025, almost 38 percent identify as Hispanic. Of those, 10,339 speak Spanish at home and 2,847 self-report speaking English less than "very well" (Census, 2015b). The city is young with a median age of 23.2 with 27 percent of the population under the age of 20 and 18 percent between the ages of 10 and 20.

The median household income in San Marcos is $27,443 ($40,661 mean income) with 37.3 percent of the population living below poverty in 2013. Of 17,381 households, 3,134 earned less than $10,000 per year and 59 percent of households earned less than $35,000. Twenty-five percent of all families with children lived below the poverty line. The picture was much grimmer for female heads of households with 41.9 percent of those with children under the age of 18 living in poverty ($n = 1,009$) (Census, 2015b, c). The relationship between low income and obesity is well documented. Studies have found correlations between low income, single-parent homes, high-density fast food establishments, and lack of parks and recreation facilities (Eagle et al., 2012). National Health and Nutrition Examination Survey data for 2011–2012 showed that nationwide, 31.8 percent of all youth aged two to nineteen were classified as either overweight or obese compared to Hispanic youth at 38.9 percent. For all adults nationally, 68.5 percent were classified as overweight or obese with 77.9 percent of Hispanics identified as such. The obesity rate (BMI ≥30) among all American adults was 34.9 percent compared to 42.5 percent among Hispanic adults (Ogden, Carroll, Kit, & Flegal, 2014).

The incidence of obesity in Hays County and San Marcos is evident. In 2010, the Behavioral Risk Factor Surveillance System results for the Austin Metropolitan Statistical Area (including Hays County) found that 36.7 percent of those adults with incomes less than $25,000 and 52.4 percent of those with incomes between $25,000 and $50,000 reported a BMI of thirty or greater. This compares to 20.4 percent of those with higher incomes self-reporting as obese (Department of Social and Health Services, 2015). Texas Education Agency Fitnessgram data for the 2012–2013 academic year identified approximately 40 percent of students in the San Marcos Consolidated Independent School District as being at high risk for obesity (Texas Education Agency, 2015). All of the residents in the Riverside public housing complex live at or below the poverty level. Collectively, 232 families and 345 children reside in these complexes, and 67 percent of the residents are Hispanic.

Exploring Stakeholder's Perceptions

Grounded theory qualitative methodology is based on conducting research while including the experiences of community members who are affected by the changing social conditions in their communities. Our research for the CHIC project followed the qualitative research method described by Corbin and Strauss (1990) in which "the research process itself guides the researcher toward examining all of the possibly rewarding avenues to understanding" (p. 6). Qualitative research methods using focus group data-gathering techniques offer access to community members' ideas, language, thoughts, feelings, and memories in their own words rather than the words of the researcher; this in turn leads to the discovery of new information. In addition, this method allows community members to be included as active participants in the research process, thus minimizing researcher control over others by giving interviewees control over their interview process. This method is perceived as minimizing power differences and alienation and creating an ethic of caring and connectedness between the researcher and the interviewees. Quality social science research in the Latino community is largely dependent on a trusting and ongoing relationship between the researcher and the community (Zinn, 1979).

Our university researchers met and connected with community leaders to assure them that the research project would benefit the community and that both confidentiality and anonymity would be ensured. It was agreed that some of the focus groups would be conducted in Spanish and some in English. Our ability to gain access to the community to conduct focus groups depended on our relationship with key community gatekeepers, including social workers, key administrators, and long-term community leaders, and their willingness to assist with recruiting people to participate in our study. We made every effort to share information about our study and our roles as researchers when communicating with community leaders and at every step of the research process. Focus groups gathered information about community members' perceptions of their quality of life, physical activity, nutrition, and weight in addition to identifying the social determinants that prevent or promote physical activity and maintenance of a healthy weight.

The study involved conducting interviews over a six-month period. A total of nine focus groups of five or six persons each were conducted with residents from the Riverside neighborhood. Three of the groups consisted of children in the neighborhood who were participating in the Fun & Fit 4 Life program at Texas State University. Six groups were interviewed in a community gathering space in the same low-income neighborhood; three of the groups were comprised of youth/teenagers, and three were comprised of adults (parents and caregivers). Focus groups were conducted in both English and Spanish in homogenous language groups. Spanish-language focus groups were conducted with Hispanic families. Participants were recruited using advertisements at their neighborhood center, and community leaders were relied on to identify members of the community using a snowball sampling method. Snowball sampling is a research method used when the desired sample characteristic is rare or when studying hard-to-reach or vulnerable groups and relies on referrals from initial subjects to generate additional subjects. The snowball method was effective in achieving the desired categorical group sample from the different age groups. The researchers worked collaboratively with the neighborhood directors and community leaders to recruit participants for the study. During the focus group, we emphasized that their participation was important and that all the information would be kept confidential and anonymous and would be recorded for the purpose of recalling important information. Demographic information, such as age, socioeconomic status, language, education, acculturation, and media exposure, was collected for each group. Focus groups were audio recorded, and at the conclusion of each focus group, the researchers recorded field notes of observations, reflections, and abstractions of topics and issues that emerged. Field notes included information about the context and quality of the focus groups and evaluations of the interviewers. After the recordings from the focus groups were transcribed, a constant comparative analysis of the data was used to identify patterns and relationships or links of patterns in the data (Glaser & Strauss, 1999). Unique issues and concerns from each focus group were aggregated and compared and contrasted across all three groups.

The Focus Group Research Process

At the beginning of each focus group we stressed that there were no right or wrong answers to the question and that our goal was to learn from community members.

We aimed at being empathetic and active listeners. We probed occasionally to gain greater insights and details about their experiences. This method allowed us to be situated as researchers who wanted to build knowledge from the standpoint of learning from the community. The interviews were carried out over a period of six months and transcribed when all the interviews were completed. Following transcription of all the interviews, we listened to the tapes again while reading the transcripts to check for accuracy. All the final corrections and translations for each transcription were edited by the researchers and printed on hard copy.

The grounded theoretical framework, which allows the researcher to discover what is happening in a particular social situation and generate theory from individual experiences, is a process of examining different issues related to the problem or topic inductively through a systematic collection and analysis of data. The data must be solid, "thick," and rich so that it can be used to elicit the development of analytic issues. Field notes evaluated the context and quality of the interviews, content analysis showed patterns of concerns and issues for each group, and notes were written about the general issues based on the questionnaire.

Results of the Focus Groups

Children's Perceptions

The perceptions of children and youth living in the housing complex were explored through six structured focus groups—three for children in elementary school and three for youth in middle and high school. There was a total of twenty-nine participants in the three focus groups held with children and fifteen participants in the three groups held for teens/youth.

When asked, the children had very specific ideas of how to describe a healthy person: they talked about someone who is strong, active, a fast runner, and motivated. Teens, on the other hand, focused almost immediately on how a healthy person behaved, with comments such as "someone that eats vegetables and works out a lot" and "someone with a good lifestyle." In terms of behavior, the children said that a healthy person would "eat right" and then listed the types of foods and drinks a healthy person might consume, such as water, milk, veggies, and fruit that "doesn't come in a bottle." The children also said that a healthy person would exercise and stay fit, listing activities such as going outside, playing sports, riding a bike, walking their dog, running, and swimming. The teens had similar answers but added "getting enough sleep" and "having fun."

Both children and teens listed similar things when discussing unhealthy behaviors: eating cake and chips, sitting or lying on the couch, watching TV, and being lazy. We also asked about behaviors when eating. Most of the children indicated that although they sometimes ate as a family, many times they were also watching TV, playing on the computer, or talking on the phone. When asked about eating regular meals, most of the participants talked about what they wanted to eat. We also discovered that the children especially relied on the free breakfasts and lunches that they received at school. During the summer, lunches were still available, but the children coming to campus for the Fun & Fit 4 Life program for the most part had not had breakfast. Additionally, we discovered that the housing authority in essence provided the youth another meal after school. The teens talked a lot about the fast food they ate. Both children and teens talked about missing at least one meal a day. When asked why they didn't eat every meal, comments included "no time, I overslept," "it was too expensive," and "there wasn't enough money." Like children and teens everywhere, the participants could list many foods they wished they could eat more often: pizza, McDonalds, vegetables, Oreos, kolaches, and fruit. One child wished his mom wouldn't "buy food like strawberries that are rotten." One teen really just wanted "more variety."

When addressing the issue of being physically active, both children and youth said they didn't think many people were doing anything outside in the neighborhood: "it is just quiet; no one is around." Children said they played in the basketball court, the street, and the park. They also mentioned places other than their neighborhood where they would play: the city pool, the river, and other parks in town. Participants in the youth focus groups said they sometimes play basketball in the neighborhood park, but it is really small, and they used to play football between the houses but they aren't allowed to anymore because someone got injured. When asked about where else they do physical activities, they mentioned the river, the skate park, and tennis courts near the river. In at least one children's group and one youth group there were comments about the neighborhood not being safe for kids to play outside, especially when it starts getting dark. One child actually said she wasn't allowed to go to the neighborhood park after dark because "that is where girls get pregnant."

Adults' Perceptions

Three focus groups were conducted with adults (e.g., parents and caregivers) to examine their perspectives about healthy behavior and healthy eating and learn more about their social and physical environments and protective factors or modifiable risk factors associated with promoting healthy eating and physical activity. Two groups were conducted in English and one in Spanish. Participants were asked to describe what healthy people look like and how they behave. Parents/caregivers described a healthy person as someone who does not worry, who is thin but not skinny—"proportional"—maybe "with a bit of color." A person who is physically active, happy, optimistic, and socially engaged in civic or leisure activity is perceived as healthy. Children who are healthy are likely "dirty, from playing outside." Conversely, they perceived that people were not healthy if they lived with worries and stress or in isolation. Comments about healthy people included "They are active. They go outside, they go dancing, walking, gardening" and "Not a person that gets very depressed or isolated."

When asked, "What might a healthy person eat or drink?" many adults reported healthy eating behaviors but also reported eating unhealthy foods: "Water, vegetables, fruit, and things that aren't fried. We know those things are healthy, but we eat other things.... I eat sweets all the time." Participants highlighted that although they know that they should eat healthy foods, sometimes they don't because they feel rushed and lack access to fruits and vegetables.

Participants in the Spanish-speaking group discussed in detail how food preparation was shaped by their social circumstances and impacted their eating patterns in their everyday lives. Some respondents stated that their ability to sit down and eat a meal with their families changed after immigrating from Mexico because their lives are now more rushed or "fast paced," and they are experiencing greater stress in the United States. When asked, "How is the food different here than in Mexico? Do you prepare foods in the same way or differently?" there was a variety of responses, although most indicated a big change in eating habits: "It depends. It depends on how you prepare the food but also what you eat." "In Mexico, you know ... we would serve ourselves. Your grandmother would serve you.... I stayed with my grandmother.... She would sit the four of us down and she would serve ... a bowl of soup, a little piece of meat, and you'd eat the whole thing. But not here.... You eat by yourself."

Many parents/caregivers stated that they worry about whether their children are eating right. Some parents discussed how unhappy they are with the quality of the food that their children are eating at school: "My daughter is already a bit heavy.... She eats different things at school, because we don't have so much money as to be packing her a lunch for school. I mean, it's not good food." "I notice how fast he [my child] eats.... It depresses me because at school it's quick, quick, quick. Thirty minutes and hurry, the kids don't finish eating, and when they get home they are hungry ... very hungry."

Parents and caregivers also worry about their children being exposed to danger, drugs, and violence in their neighborhoods: "I want a place that's secure, where children can play, and I think, where can I take her [my daughter]? There's no security for them. Many older guys hang around smoking marijuana." They mentioned kids having to play football and soccer right next to a busy street and riding their bikes in the street as there were no sidewalks. Regarding other places to be active, the adults were very clear that there needed to be more opportunities "on our side of the highway." The majority of the places they listed—the city pool, big playgrounds or parks, and the activity center—all require them to drive in order to participate as they are far away and there is no safe way to walk or ride bikes to get to them. Another change noted specifically by the Spanish-speaking group was that physical activity seems to be a challenge: "Over there [Mexico], people exercise.... You walk more [in Mexico]. Or if you're going to take the bus, it's like you have to walk some ... and you can't take your time, you have to get up earlier."

In summary, adult participants stated that a healthy person is one who is socially engaged with his or her family, connected with other families, and active in a safe community. These findings highlight the importance of familism in promoting positive mental and physical health. Researchers have highlighted that family is an important cultural value. This corroborates what other researchers have found regarding the participant-described patterns and behaviors of familism that are connected to being a healthy person as well as worries and stressors that put them "at risk" of not engaging in healthy behaviors (Gonzales et al., 2011; Leidy, Guerra, & Toro, 2012). Equally important to the parents/caregivers were the barriers their families faced in regard to participating in physical activity (e.g., walking, riding bikes, recreation time at the park) due to the neighborhood environment.

Phase III: The Built Environment

"Built environment" refers to the physical makeup of the surroundings of people's daily life, including homes, schools, workplaces, entertainment and recreational options, and transportation choices. The built environment may influence population health through its impact on health behaviors that are essential for energy balance (McCormack, Giles-Corti, Lange, Smith, Martin, & Pikora, 2004; Economos, Hatfield, King, Ayala, & Pentz, 2015), including physical activity and diet. Many studies have found that a built environment that facilitates access to physical activity facilities also promotes a physically active lifestyle (e.g., Cohen, Ashwood, Scott, Overton, Evenson, & Staten, 2006; Gordon-Larsen, Nelson, Page, & Popkin, 2006; Papas, Alberg, Ewing, Helzlsouer, Gary, & Klassen, 2007; Wendel-Vos, Droomers, Kremers, Brug, & Van Lenthe, 2007; Ferdinand, Sen, Rahurkar, Engler, & Menachemi, 2012). However, as pointed out by Fang, Glass, Curriero, Stewart, and Schwartz (2010) and Ding, Sallis, Kerr, Lee, and Rosenberg (2011), a lack of standard and objective measurement for built environment is believed to be the major reason for the failure of some empirical studies to identify connections between positive built environment and increased physical activity.

To guide the measurement of the key features and qualities of built environment that are believed to contribute to promoting healthy behaviors, the Center for Disease Control and Prevention (2015) released the Built Environment Assessment Tool (BE Tool) in July 2015. Despite the need for further tests of the applicability and efficacy of the BE Tool, its development heightens the shift of health research and practitioners' focus from individual-centered to community-focused approaches. The recent decade has seen a growing body of literature on community-based studies. These studies use the neighborhood as the basic unit to examine possible associations between population health outcomes or health behavior (i.e., physical activity) with certain traits of the built environment. Various age groups have been studied, spanning from preadolescent and adolescent children (e.g., Rosenberg, Ding, Sallis, Kerr, Norman, & Durant, 2009; Carroll-Scott, Gilstad-Hayden, Rosenthal, Peters, McCaslin, Joyce, & Ickovics, 2013) to adults of twenty to sixty-five years old (e.g., Sallis et al., 2009; Adams et al.,

2011). Neighborhoods from different regions and different socioeconomic paths have been examined, including neighborhoods from Seattle and Baltimore (Sallis, Saelens, Frank, Conway, Slymen, & Cain, 2009; Adams, Sallis, Kerr, Conway, & Saelens, 2011) and those from both wealthy and disadvantaged areas (e.g., Forsyth, Oakes, Lee, & Schmitz, 2009; Carroll-Scott et al., 2013). Adams et al. (2011) explored ways to build a neighborhood profile based on built environment and found that neighbor profiles are associated with body mass index (BMI), pointing to the possibility of developing intervening measures by considering built environment for a particular neighborhood.

While age was not found to be an intervening factor on the effect of neighborhood built environment in promoting physical activity among a population, socioeconomic status of neighborhood was identified by the literature as an important confounding factor. Forsyth et al. (2009) found that unhealthy, unemployed, and retired populations tend to be more impacted by environment characteristics, meaning that these population groups are more responsive to environmental intervention. Carroll-Scott et al. (2013) endorsed this by identifying the other side of the coin—that populations of affluent neighborhoods enjoy a protective effect for healthy behaviors, including exercise and diet. This suggests that a deteriorating built environment would impact the poor more than the rich by discouraging healthy behaviors. Sallis et al. (2009) examined the interaction of built environment and income on physical activity and found that low-income populations may not benefit as much as high-income residents from increased walkability in a neighborhood until their other needs are met. This finding may indicate a need for a more holistic approach to health intervention than simply changing the built environment, especially when working with disadvantaged communities.

Participatory Photo Mapping

Following analysis of data from the focus groups, the CBPR team used participatory photo mapping (PPM) to further examine the influence of the built environment on community members living at the Riverside residences. PPM is an innovative technique that incorporates digital technology, narrative interviewing, and participatory research procedures (Dennis, Gaulocher, Carpiano, & Brown, 2009). PPM has been used by cross-disciplinary research teams to explore the impact of the built environment on community members' access to healthy lifestyles (Dennis et al., 2009). PPM is a systematic process that "adds a spatial component to traditional participatory photography methods" (Teixeira, 2015, p. 395) by incorporating geographic information systems (GIS) technology. According to Teixeira (2015), this method allows "participants to reflect on the role of space and place in their own lives" (p. 396). Additionally, the use of PPM "can shift power dynamics from government and planning agencies . . . to the hands of community members" (Teixeira, 2015, p. 396). Typically, there are four steps in PPM:

Step 1: Community participants use digital cameras to photograph their neighborhood with specific attention devoted to documenting routine use or lack of use of the neighborhood facilities. As a picture is being taken, the GIS coordinates are noted.

Step 2: The participants' photographs serve as the focal point of the interviews. Researchers ask questions in order to obtain information about why the participants have chosen to take a picture of this particular location. Narrative data collected via the interview process are then connected to particular photographs.

Step 3: Images and the narratives regarding those images are mapped within the neighborhood using the GIS data, resulting in both quantitative and qualitative assessment of the community.

Step 4: Researchers perform a member check to ensure that they have interpreted the data correctly. They then work with participants to develop an action plan designed to improve the barriers and/or expand the resources within the neighborhood.

How Was PPM Used in the Project?

The first community picnic and participatory photomapping session was held at Riverside in the fall of Phase III. Housing Authority staff and residents assisted in the planning and preparation for the event. Flyers in English and Spanish announcing the event were posted around the complex. Key residents also helped spread the word throughout the complex. On the night of the event, healthy food and drinks were provided by the research project, and families brought side dishes for a potluck dinner. Incentives for attendance included five- and ten-dollar gift cards as well as draws for "swag" donated by various departments in the university.

Approximately one hundred residents attended the event. Attendees were divided into two groups of parents (one Spanish speaking and one English speaking) and four groups of preteen and teen participants of approximately six each. Three groups completed the thirty-minute photomapping walk while three groups ate dinner. The process was then reversed. Each group was led by a research faculty facilitator and one graduate student research assistant (RA) with a digital audio recorder, a digital camera, a handheld GIS device, and a notepad to record locations of photos and general comments. Guiding questions regarding the built environment were determined in advance based on the focus groups conducted with residents in Phase II. Specifically, we were asking where participants "played" or engaged in physical activity. We wanted them to show us what was working and what wasn't working in their neighborhood. Originally, it was planned that groups would pass the recording device to each other as they responded to the questions posed by the researcher. Due to inconsistency in the recording process at the beginning of the first walk, it was quickly determined that the facilitator would hold the recorder to each participant as he or she spoke. The camera was passed to members as each identified a location or issue to photograph. The RA was responsible for recording GPS data points as photographs were taken or ideas discussed.

During the first few minutes of each tour, participants were often reluctant to contribute opinions. However, enthusiasm quickly prevailed with additional people joining the groups. Participants often led researchers to unexpected locations (e.g., the river bank). The challenge to researchers was to ensure that all comments and data points were identified and coordinated. Though it was tempting to have additional researchers assisting in the groups, it was important to balance the participants' needs for ownership in the process with the research desires of the facilitators.

GIS has been used to measure built environment and its potential to promote physical activity (e.g., Thornton, Pearce, & Kavanagh, 2011), to analyze access disparity to green space and facilities (e.g., Charreir et al., 2012), and to examine the association between a population's access to health facilities and their physical activity level (e.g., King, Thornton, Bentley, & Kavanagh, 2015).

Technology developments also provide an opportunity for transformative research through enabling a high level of public participation. Incorporating public participation into community planning and decision-making is not new in general (e.g., Blair, 2004; Sieber, 2006) nor for public health (e.g., Checkoway, 1982; Abelson, Forest, Eyeles, Smith, Martin, & Gauvin, 2003). GIS has been widely adopted for public participation due to its unique capabilities of data collection, integration, and map communication. GIS mapping, analysis, and visualization can be used together with photos to document, contextualize, and share people's observations of environment, an approach referred to as participatory photomapping. PPM has an advantage over general public participatory GIS in that it minimizes the technological challenges for public participation by allowing data to be collected and incorporated as ordinary photos, which can be taken with virtually no special training. These photos serve as great narratives of stakeholders' perspectives and knowledge of built environment; they are also a powerful means of communication to connect community with policy makers and resource holders. PPM can therefore effectively support a transformative approach at the community level and guide the understanding, management, and use of built environment to promote life quality in general (Loebach & Gilliland, 2010) and public health in particular (Dennis et al., 2009; Bukowski & Buetow, 2011).

For this project, the participants took pictures of selected locations in the neighborhood with the purpose of providing a visual representation of the local residents' perception of the built environment in the neighborhood of Riverside Homes. Issues of concern included missing sidewalks, overgrown grass and possible sighting of snakes on the playground, and presence of gang graffiti, among others. A total of thirty-nine pictures were taken, and the longitude and latitude coordinates were collected and recorded by the RA using GPS. The GPS data of these points were later brought into GIS using ArcGIS10.2 software to create a shapefile including all of the places of interest (POI) as point features and each point feature linked to a corresponding picture. For visualization and communication purposes with the local communities, the GIS shapefile was brought into Google Earth and draped on aerial photos of the study area to show the facility locations, the corresponding pictures, and brief text annotations. Linking the photos with Google Earth turned out to be very effective for communicating with both the residents and the local authorities to show the locations and the general geographical context of POIs and the associated community concerns. It is important to point out that the PPM approach taken by this project was proven to be very effective for understanding the local community's perception of and needs for their built environment; PPM was essential for visualizing both problematic places and facilities and healthy and positive features in the neighborhood. Being able to present both types of examples visually and spatially enabled the authorities to see the problems with, and the goals for, built environment management and health promotion.

Phase IV: Action Plan

The community participants (e.g., parents, caregivers, youth, San Marcos Housing Authority [SMHA] personnel) and research team collaboratively developed an action plan based on findings from the PPM and interview data. The action plan identified the community's priorities to enhance their families' participation in physical activity, health, and wellness. Collectively, the top priorities included the following: (1) crosswalks and stop signs, (2) "Children at Play" signage, (3) outdoor lighting at the park and throughout the neighborhood, and (4) park enhancement (e.g., water fountain, picnic tables, fencing, covered swings, trees for shade, garbage cans, and resurfaced basketball court).

Plans were made for the community participants, SMHA personnel, faculty, and students to present their findings and voice their concerns to the San Marcos City Council. Specifically, the collective group requested funds from the City Development Block Grant be used to improve the Riverside neighborhood. On the day of the meeting, car pools were organized to transport parents/caregivers, youth, SMHA personnel, faculty, and students from Riverside to City Hall. When the Riverside Action Plan was called to present, all stakeholders (e.g., parents/caregivers, teenagers, SMHA personnel, faculty, and students) took turns at the microphone voicing their concerns to members of the San Marcos City Council.

Approximately one month following the meeting, the city announced an allocation of $177,000 of the City Block Grant to be devoted to enhancements to the Riverside neighborhood. Lighting, crosswalks, and signage were installed in the neighborhood within one month of presenting the action plan to City Council. Plans for park renovations were developed over a period of six months. Once the plans were finalized by the contractor and presented to the city officials, a meeting was scheduled with the residents to gather the youths' and adults' perceptions and feedback for the proposed renovation. The San Marcos city representative and the contractor presented the design at the residents' meeting room within the public housing complex. Visual displays were explained and described. Included in the plans were the following: (1) covered playground and new play equipment, (2) upgraded half basketball court, (3) small skate venue, (4) trees to provide shade, and (4) wrought-iron fencing around the perimeter of the park.

Immediately following the presentation, community participants were invited to share their thoughts about the design. Interestingly, the youth in the audience provided the city officials with numerous questions and suggestions concerning the layout of the park. Of particular concern was the lack of a water fountain. The youth voiced their concerns regarding how hot the weather is in Texas in the summer and how they would really appreciate having a water fountain at the park. One male adolescent suggested that a park bench be included in the design so his mother could watch his younger siblings play on the swings. A young female adolescent asked why the city didn't include permanent garbage cans in the design—the children were always told to throw trash in a garbage can. The city officials and the contractor were receptive to the youths' suggestions and informed everyone at the meeting they would attempt to include the helpful suggestions.

Phase V: Summary

The renovation of the Riverside neighborhood park was completed over a two-year period. Following completion, one afternoon during the month of October, city officials, SMHA personnel, parents/caregivers, children, and adolescents residing at the Riverside residences, and Texas State University students and faculty, gathered at the park for the official ribbon-cutting ceremony. Everyone attending the ceremony at the Riverside neighborhood took great pride in the fact that they each contributed in some special way to the transformation of the park. What was once a run-down, dilapidated, weed-infested area surrounded by a graffiti-covered fence was reconstructed to be an inviting green space with beautiful trees, covered swing sets, picnic tables, a skateboard venue, a basketball court, and a water fountain! While the children laughed and played, the adults conversed and congratulated each other on a job well done.

Social cognitive theory underscores the interactive effects of one's environment and personal factors on behaviors. Throughout the duration of our CHIC project, it was important to understand the significant role of the environment on community members, students, and faculty. The CHIC project came to fruition due to the partnership that was nurtured between the Texas State University faculty and students and Riverside community members. This collaborative relationship founded on mutual respect enabled the development and implementation of every aspect of the project. The focus groups, participatory photomapping, and creation and presentation of the action plan would not have occurred without the strong bond between the university students, faculty, and Riverside community. Equally important to note is the critical service-learning environment that initiated this multifaceted community project. Challenging undergraduate preservice physical educators to explore the impoverished Riverside community instigated this entire project. Undergraduate students placed in a CSL environment were forced to examine disparities and injustices in the health and wellness of low-income families.

During Phase I of the CHIC project, students' perceptions of children's access to participation in physical activity were amended. University student preservice physical education teachers came to the realization that all children do not have equal opportunities for physical activity. Creation of the Fun & Fit 4 Life program in Phase II provided a venue for university faculty to listen to the needs of the community. Actually listening to the community members and developing a program for children that included components deemed important to the parents/caregivers (e.g., college readiness) laid the foundation for the collaborative relationship between the Riverside community and Texas State faculty and students. The partnership between the university students, faculty, and community cultivated during National Night Out in Phase III grew stronger while participants worked together on the action plan throughout Phase IV. The opening of the park in Phase V demonstrated the power of diverse people working together to overcome social injustices and disparities. The CHIC project built a truly collaborative partnership between the university and the community that continues today.

KAREN MEANEY is Professor in the Department of Health and Human Performance at Texas State University. Her research examines the impact of participation in service-learning programs on preservice educators and community participants.

JO AN M. ZIMMERMANN is Associate Professor in Recreation Administration at Texas State University. Her research interests focus on management issues related to improving the planning and delivery of community-based recreation services.

YONGMEI LU is Professor of Geography at Texas State University. Her major research interests include geographic information system and science (GIS) and the application of GIS to examine and model socioeconomic and environmental issues, particularly health and environment studies, crime analysis, and urban and regional analysis.

GLORIA MARTINEZ-RAMOS is Associate Professor of Sociology at Texas State University. She has focused her research and scholarship on the impact breast cancer has on the quality of life of survivors, Latino/a health and well-being, Hispanic students' transition and retention in college, and school safety.

JACQUELYN MCDONALD is Clinical Assistant Professor of Health Education at Texas State University. As both a registered nurse and registered dietitian, she has over twenty-five years of experience as a public health practitioner. Her areas of interest focus on program planning and evaluation.

References

Abelson, J., Forest, P. G., Eyles, J., Smith, P., Martin, E., & Gauvin, F. P. (2003). Deliberations about deliberative methods: Issues in the design and evaluation of public participation processes. *Social Science & Medicine, 57*(2), 239–251.

Adams, M. A., Sallis, J. F., Kerr, J., Conway, T. L., Saelens, B. E., & Frank, L. D. (2011). Neighborhood environment profiles related to physical activity and weight status: A latent profile analysis. *Preventive Medicine, 52*(5), 326–331.

Bandura, A. (1986). *Social foundations of thought and action.* Englewood Cliffs, NJ: Prentice Hall.

Bandura, A. (1999). Social cognitive theory: An agentic perspective. *Asian Journal of Social Psychology, 2,* 21–41.

Blair, R. (2004). Public participation and community development: The role of strategic planning. *Public Administration Quarterly, 28*(1/2), 102–147.

Bukowski, K., & Buetow, S. (2011). Making the invisible visible: A Photovoice exploration of homeless women's health and lives in central Auckland. *Social Science & Medicine, 72*(5), 739–746.

Carroll-Scott, A., Gilstad-Hayden, K., Rosenthal, L., Peters, S. M., McCaslin, C., Joyce, R., & Ickovics, J. R. (2013). Disentangling neighborhood contextual associations with child body mass index, diet, and physical activity: The role of built, socioeconomic, and social environments. *Social Science & Medicine, 95,* 106–114.

Census Bureau. (2015a). *Population estimate.* Retrieved from http://factfinder.census.gov/faces/tableservices/jsf/pages/productview.xhtml?src=bkk.

Census Bureau. (2015b). *Selected social characteristics in the United States: 2009–2013 American community survey 5-year estimates.* Retrieved from http://factfinder.census.gov/faces/tableservices/jsf/pages/productview.xhtml?src=bk.

Census Bureau. (2015c). *Selected economic characteristics 2009–2013 American community survey 5-year estimates.* Retrieved from http://factfinder.census.gov/faces/tableservices/jsf/pages/productview.xhtml?src=bkk.

Center for Disease Control and Prevention. (2015). National Center for Chronic Disease Prevention and Health Promotion. *The built environment—An assessment tool and manual.* Retrieved from http://www.cdc.gov/nccdphp/dch/built-environment-assessment/pdfs/builtenvironment-main.pdf.

Charreire, H., Weber, C., Chaix, B., Salze, P., Casey, R., Banos, A., . . . & Oppert, J. (2012). Identifying built environmental patterns using cluster analysis and GIS: Relationships with walking, cycling and body mass index in French adults. *International Journal of Behavior, Nutrition, and Physical Activity, 9*(1), 59.

Checkoway, B. (1982). Public participation in health planning agencies: Promise and practice. *Journal of Health Politics, Policy and Law, 7*(3), 723–733.

Cohen, D. A., Ashwood, J. S., Scott, M. M., Overton, A., Evenson, K. R., & Staten, L. K. (2006). Public parks and physical activity among adolescent girls. *Pediatrics, 118*(5), e1381-e1389.

Corbin, J., & Strauss, A. (1990). Grounded theory research: Procedures, canons, evaluative criteria. *Qualitative Sociology, 13*(1), 1–21.

Cress, C. M. (2005). What is service-learning? In C. M. Cress, P. J. Collier, & V. L. Reitenauer (Eds.), *Learning through service: A student guidebook for service-learning across disciplines* (pp. 7–16). Sterling, VA: Stylus.

Dennis, S. F., Gaulocher, S., Carpiano, R. M., & Brown, D. (2009). Participatory photo mapping (PPM): Exploring an integrated method for health and place research with young people. *Health & Place, 15*, 466–473.

Ding, D., Sallis, J. F., Kerr, J., Lee, S., & Rosenberg, D. E. (2011). Neighborhood environment and physical activity among youth: A review. *American Journal of Preventive Medicine, 41*(4), 442–455.

Department of Social and Health Services Center for Health Statistics. (2015). *Behavioral risk factor surveillance system*. Retrieved from http://www.dshs.state.tx.us/Layouts/ContentPage.aspx?pageid=35474.

Eagle, T. F., Sheetz, A., Gurm, R., Woodward, A., Kline-Rogers, E., Leibowitz, R., ... & Eagle, K. (2012). Understanding childhood obesity in America: Linkages between household income, community resources, and children's behaviors. *American Heart Journal, 163*, 836–843.

Economos, C., Hatfield, D., King, A., Ayala, G., & Pentz, M. (2015). Food and physical activity environments: An energy balance approach for research and practice. *American Journal of Preventive Medicine, 48*(5), 620–629.

Fang, J., Glass, T. A., Curriero, F. C., Stewart, W. F., & Schwartz, B. S. (2010). The built environment and obesity: A systematic review of the epidemiologic evidence. *Health & Place, 16*(2), 175–190.

Ferdinand, A., Sen, B., Rahurkar, S., Engler, S., & Menachemi, N. (2012). The relationship between built environments and physical activity: A systematic review. *American Journal of Public Health, 102*(10), e7–e13.

Forsyth, A., Oakes, J. M., Lee, B., & Schmitz, K. H. (2009). The built environment, walking, and physical activity: Is the environment more important to some people than others? *Transportation Research Part D: Transport and Environment, 14*(1), 42–49.

Glaser, B. G., & Strauss, A. L. (1999). *The discovery of grounded theory: Strategies for qualitative research*. New York, NY: de Gruyter.

Gonzales, N. A., Coxe, S., Roosa, M. W., White, R. M. B., Knight, G. P., Zeiders, K. H., & Saenz, D. (2011). Economic hardship, neighborhood context and parenting: Prospective effects on Mexican-American adolescents' mental health. *American Journal of Community Psychology, 47*(1–2), 98–113.

Gordon-Larsen, P., Nelson, M. C., Page, P., & Popkin, B. M. (2006). Inequality in the built environment underlies key health disparities in physical activity and obesity. *Pediatrics, 117*(2), 417–424.

Hirsch, J. A., James, P., Robinson, J. R., Eastman, K. M., Conley, K. D., Evenson, K. R., & Laden, F. (2014). Using MapMyFitness to place physical activity into neighborhood context. *Frontiers in Public Health, 2*, 19. doi:10.3389/fpubh.2014.00019

King, T. L., Thornton, L. E., Bentley, R. J., & Kavanagh, A. M. (2015). The use of kernel density estimation to examine associations between neighborhood destination intensity and walking and physical activity. *PLoS One, 10*(9), e0137402.

Leidy, M. S., Guerra, N. G., & Toro, R. I. (2012). Positive parenting, family cohesion and child social competence among immigrant Latino families. *Journal of Latina/o Psychology, 1*(Suppl.), 3–13.

Loebach, J., & Gilliland, J. (2010). Child-led tours to uncover children's perceptions and use of neighborhood environments. *Children Youth and Environments, 20*(1), 52–90.

Lu, Y., & Fang, T. B. (2015). Examining personal air pollution exposure, intake, and health danger zone using time geography and 3d geovisualization. *ISPRS International Journal of Geo-Information, 4*(1), 32–46.

McCormack, G., Giles-Corti, B., Lange, A., Smith, T., Martin, K., & Pikora, T. J. (2004). An update of recent evidence of the relationship between objective and self-report measures of the physical environment and physical activity behaviours. *Journal of Science and Medicine in Sport, 7*(Suppl. 1), 81–92.

Minkler, M., & Wallerstein, N. (Eds.). (2008). *Community-based participatory research for health: From process to outcomes* (2nd ed.). San Francisco, CA: Jossey-Bass.

Mitchell, T. (2008, spring). Traditional vs. critical service-learning: Engaging the literature to differentiate two models. *Michigan Journal of Community Service-Learning*, pp. 50–65.

Ogden, C. L., Carroll, M. D., Kit, B. K., & Flegal, K. M. (2014). Prevalence of childhood and adult obesity in the United States, 2011-2012. *Journal of the American Medical Association, 311*(8), 806-814. doi:10.1001/jama.2014.732

Papas, M. A., Alberg, A. J., Ewing, R., Helzlsouer, K. J., Gary, T. L., & Klassen, A. C. (2007). The built environment and obesity. *Epidemiologic Reviews, 29*(1), 129–143.

Rosenberg, D., Ding, D., Sallis, J. F., Kerr, J., Norman, G. J., & Durant, N. (2009). Neighborhood Environment Walkability Scale for Youth (NEWS-Y): Reliability and relationship with physical activity. *Preventive Medicine, 49*(2), 213–218.

Sallis, J. F., Saelens, B. E., Frank, L. D., Conway, T. L., Slymen, D. J., & Cain, K. L. (2009). Neighborhood built environment and income: Examining multiple health outcomes. *Social Science & Medicine, 68*(7), 1285–1293.

Sieber, R. (2006). Public participation geographic information systems: A literature review and framework. *Annals of the Association of American Geographers, 96*(3), 491–507.

Teixeira, S. (2015). It seems like no one cares: Participatory photo mapping to understand youth perspectives on property vacancy. *Journal of Adolescent Research, 30*(3), 390–414.

Texas Education Agency. (2015). *2012-2013 PFAI fitness assessment data by district, grade and gender.* Retrieved from http://tea.texas.gov/Texas_Schools/Safe_and_Healthy_Schools/Physical_Fitness_Asssment_Initiative/Fitness_Data/.

Thornton, L. E., Pearce, J. R., & Kavanagh, A. M. (2011). Using geographic information systems (GIS) to assess the role of the built environment in influencing obesity: A glossary. *International Journal of Behavior, Nutrition, and Physical Activity, 8*(71), 10–1186.

Wallerstein, N., & Duran, B. (2003). The conceptual, historical and practical roots of community based participatory research and related participatory traditions. In M. Minkler & N. Wallerstein (Eds.), *Community based participatory research for health: From process to outcomes* (2nd ed.). San Francisco, CA: Josey Bass.

Wendel-Vos, V., Droomers, M., Kremers, S., Brug, J., & Van Lenthe, F. (2007). Potential environmental determinants of physical activity in adults: A systematic review. *Obesity Reviews, 8*(5), 425–440.

Zinn, M. B. (1979). Field research in minority communities: Ethical, methodological and political observations by an insider. *Social Problems, 27*(2), 209–219.

7 Teacher Candidates' Dispositions for Civic Engagement and Social Responsibility: Discernment and Action

Patricia Calderwood, Stephanie Burrell Storms, Thomas Grund, Nicole Battaglia, and Emma Sheeran

Recently, our teacher preparation programs were assessed for reaccreditation by the Council for the Accreditation of Educator Preparation (CAEP). During the on-site visit, the accreditation team repeatedly asked faculty to explain how we were assessing the dispositional outcomes we had identified for our teacher candidates. In response, we explained that a small collaborative study conceived as an element of our ongoing accreditation documentation was planned. It would be an element of an upcoming capstone seminar for our second cohort of candidates completing their five-year integrated bachelor-master's teacher education programs in elementary, English, and social studies education (Pinnegar & Erickson, 2009). We intended to examine this question *with* candidates as they synthesized their learning and professional development at the transition point between the finale of their degree and certification programs and the next stage of their professional careers as educators. In particular, together we would identify their understanding, competence, and willingness to be reflective practitioners who act as change agents for equity and social justice (Lassonde & Strub, 2009). We would collaboratively examine their understanding, experience, and willingness to contextualize their work as educators within a sociocultural and philosophical framework of education, schooling, and society; reflect critically on their roles as active citizens and advocates with students, families, schools, and communities; participate in a professional community that facilitates their development toward social and educational agency; and collaborate with educators, students, parents, and community members to support student learning and development.

We are not unique among teacher preparation programs in identifying aspirational dispositional learning outcomes for our candidates (Cochran-Smith, Villegas, Abrams, Chavez-Moreno, Mills, & Stern, 2015; Henry, Campbell, Thompson, Patriarca, Luterbach, Lys, & Covington, 2013; Nelson, 2015; Whipp, 2013). Accredited teacher education programs, in addition to developing the professional and pedagogical knowledge and skills of their candidates, are also expected to support the development of dispositions for effective teaching (Nelson, 2015). Currently, teacher preparation programs are expected to turn out teachers who effectively support student learning and who are inclined, or disposed, to do so purposefully, in particular ways and for specific reasons. As we seek to determine how best to credential teachers who embody the dispositions we aspire for them, Nelson (2015) cautions us to parse our understandings of dispositions as immutable, innate characteristics of individuals (and thus, not learned), contextually flexible, learned habits, or, more complexly, some amalgam of both. The distinctions are significant for teacher educators who seek to design progammatic support to foster particular dispositions within their candidates. In the teacher education programs at our university, we have identified the dispositional goal that our teacher candidates will become reflective practitioners and act as change agents for equity and social justice through education, and we build in learning experiences to support candidates' embrace of this goal. We seek evidence that our candidates demonstrate that they have developed this disposition in four key ways: We hope that they (1) contextualize their work as educators within a sociocultural and philosophical framework of education, schooling, and society; (2) reflect critically on their roles as active citizens and advocates with students, families, schools, and communities; (3) participate in a professional community that facilitates their development toward social and educational agency; and (4) collaborate with educators, students, parents, and community members to support student learning and development.

As Nelson (2015) comments, accreditation bodies such as CAEP specify for candidates only a disposition toward fairness and a belief that all students can learn. Nelson notes that "without a sophisticated conceptual framework upon which to build program details, teacher educators risk implementing poorly designed and conceptually incoherent strategies in their efforts to develop specific sets of dispositions in their students" (Damon, 2007, in Nelson, 2015, p. 95). Teacher education programs, then, generally draw on the missions of their institutions as they articulate additional or more thoroughly articulated dispositional learning outcomes, the motivating "why" of teachers' identities. For example, our institution's mission reflects its historical and current identity as Jesuit, which includes an "obligation to the wider community of which it is a part, to share with its neighbors its resources and its special expertise for the betterment of the community as a whole ... sharing common goals and a common commitment to truth and justice, and manifesting in their lives the common concern for others which is the obligation of all educated, mature human beings" (Mission statement of Fairfield University, 2014).

As Caruana (2014) and Girtz (2014) each note, the "Ignatian Paradigm" that marks Jesuit education (a recursive interplay of context, experience, reflection, action, and evaluation) aligns well with the dispositions we hope our teacher candidates will develop and exhibit. Identifying what these dispositions look like for our candidates during their programs requires a developmental outlook, a sense that their professional dispositions in practice will become more expert and more integrated, and a hope that their dispositions will deeply resonate with those we aspire to develop in them. Attending to the scaffolding of their experiences, so that this developmental trajectory is supported, requires a constant fine-tuning of incremental benchmarks along the trail so that our candidates and we can discern progress. Further, we need to rely on a deep sense of connectedness and of trust between faculty and candidates so that we can be honest in our evaluations not only of the candidates' development but also of the quality of the learning experiences we engage in with them. We faculty need to develop and nurture our own professional dispositions, too, aligning with those we hope our candidates develop. But because dispositions are most reliably understood in the actions they spur, we *infer* our own and others' dispositions for teaching through observation of and critical reflection on actions planned and taken. We note how words and deeds reflect the implicit and explicit values, beliefs, perspectives, and stances of the actor (Alsup & Miller, 2014; Bolton & Reisboard, 2014; Bradley & Jurchan, 2013; Cummins & Asempapa, 2013; Hochstetler, 2014; Shoffner, Sedberry, Alsup, & Johnson, 2014; Schussler & Knarr, 2013; Whipp, 2013).

Schussler, Stooksberry, and Bercaw (2010) proposed a framework for understanding dispositions for teaching. They parsed dispositions into multiple domains (intellectual, cultural, and moral), noting that the inclination and ability to act in particular ways are twined, and examined teacher candidates' reflection and understanding of their inclinations, abilities, and actions. They noted that *how* candidates used reflection to understand their actions, abilities, and inclinations across domains was significant. For example, organizing the reflection to foreground oneself, rather than the students, their cultural context, or their learning needs, was common and less likely to lead to critical awareness. Perspective taking, on the other hand, interrupted thinking of students or their cultural contexts in a deficit mode.

Cummins and Asempapa's 2013 study provides support for the notion that desired dispositions for teaching are not necessarily innate but can be taught to teacher candidates. They found that building in, throughout a teacher education program, opportunity to practice thinking about and acting with desired dispositions was useful but that the developmental trajectories of the candidates' dispositions would be somewhat idiosyncratic to each person. This observation cautions us that establishing developmental benchmarks and exemplars for the desired dispositions can be challenging. Curwood (2014), espousing the value of professional learning communities in the professional development of teachers, noted that teachers' identities are socially constructed through narrative—contested, contradictory, and coherent—and embedded in the web of multiple sociocultural contexts (a shifting constellation of private/public, personal/professional) across which they move. A sense of one's own multiple identities can support perspective taking. For example, liminality of identity, a fluid state where one can hold multiple identities in shifting patterns, can facilitate candidate management of the tensions and contradictions, alignments and surprises of maturing identities that play a significant role in the development of teacher candidates' dispositions for teaching (Burrell Storms, Calderwood, & Quan, 2014; Cook-Sather, 2006; Cook-Sather & Alter, 2011; Gomez, Carlson, Foubert, & Powell, 2014; Lund, Bragg, Kaipainen, & Lee, 2014; McDonald & Kahn, 2014; Shultz & Ravich, 2013).

Warren and Hotchkins (2014) explain that "false empathy is a state of mind that ultimately places the needs, desires, and points of view of the empathizer above those needs, desires, and points of view of the intended beneficiary of an empathetic response" (p. 14), and they note that it inhibits the development of perspective taking, a critical element of authentic empathy. Marri, Michael-Luna, Cormier, and Keegan (2014) found that an orientation to a personal responsibility, rather than participatory or justice-oriented citizenship, dominated in the population of K-6 teacher candidates they studied. They cited developmental inappropriateness as a candidate-identified concern about including a justice-oriented focus in their lessons, and generally, they saw that candidates skirted around deep engagement with the political aspects of curricular topics (for example, urban food deserts) in order to address what they saw as the needs of the children (for example, to understand why they should eat more fruits and vegetables) rather than social change (activism to eliminate food deserts).

Inquiry

Our reflections are anchored in self-study, participant observation, and grounded theory (Pinnegar & Erickson, 2009). For the study, we analyzed data (eighteen curriculum maps, eighteen funds of knowledge identifications, ninety discussion posts, thirty-six conceptual papers, and eight collaborative capstone project proposals) generated by eighteen candidates during their teacher education programs' capstone course in teacher education during the summer of 2014, identifying themes and patterns that emerged. These eighteen teacher candidates were all aged between twenty-two and twenty-three years old; three white males and fifteen females (two of whom were Latina, the rest white) were finishing their five-year teacher education programs in childhood education (ten candidates: nine women and one man), social studies education (five candidates: two men, three women), and English education (three women). All of the candidates had completed their certification requirements and were awaiting their initial certifications from the state. By the end of the course, most had teaching contracts for the following year, and of those who did not, three had identified alternative pursuits and two were uncertain of their next steps. This course, their capstone, was the final requirement for their master's degree in education. During their capstone course, they were expected to identify and critically reflect on their current and aspirational dispositions for civic engagement and social responsibility at the transitional moment between completion of their teacher preparation program and first year of teaching. Further, this section of the teacher education capstone course was redesigned for the teacher candidates within this cohort, morphing into a self-study about, for, and with the students. Assigned readings (Clayton, Bringle, Senor, Huq, & Morrison, 2010; Fox, 2014; Oakes & Rogers, 2006; Ritchie, 2014), including the manuscript of an earlier study about the developing dispositions of candidates at the beginning of their programs (Burrell Storms et al., 2014) and the conceptual framework of the school, plus other assignments and learning activities, were designed to prompt critical reflection on the first-person texts of the course—their own discernment, discussion posts, conversations, and reflective papers—as they reflected on their past, current, and anticipated dispositions for civic engagement and social responsibility (Clayton & Ash, 2004; McDonald & Kahn, 2014; Mitchell, 2015; Schussler et al., 2010; Sturgill & Motley, 2014).

We turned to a participatory, critical self-study to understand, from the teacher candidates' point of view, who they are at the transitional moment between preservice and the first year of teaching (Lassonde, Galman, & Kosnik, 2009; Lassonde & Strub, 2009; Pinnegar & Erickson, 2009) and to find the fit between their sense of their attainment of our dispositional outcomes and the reasonableness of our aspirations for them. To this end, the eighteen teacher candidates were invited to coconstruct the analysis with us during their capstone course. Samples of their reflections and insights are attributed throughout the paper. Additionally, we showcase in depth the reflections and insights of three coauthoring candidates: Thomas Grund, Nicole Battaglia, and Emma Sheeran. We provide these brief biographical snapshots of faculty and coauthoring candidates as context:

> *Patricia Calderwood:* As a doctoral candidate, I spent three years as a participant observer in a small and remarkable public middle school in New York City. As a result of that experience, I began to believe that teachers really could teach for transformation and that they and their students might change our world for the better. The hopefulness that was sparked during those three years, with those teachers and adolescents, has never abandoned me but has supported me to ask, to always ask, that the teachers and teacher candidates with whom I learn and teach aspire to educate and advocate for justice and equity. I hope that they expect the same from me and that they will help me to become that educator.
>
> *Stephanie Burrell Storms:* I am a middle-class African American woman who identifies as both a teacher educator and social justice educator and who holds the belief that through education, collaboration, and action, citizens can reduce structural inequality and increase equity in schools. In the participatory action research

course I teach every year, I have witnessed teacher researchers conduct studies and collaborate with their students and colleagues to create more socially just learning environments. I hope our student coauthors will take what they have learned through this inquiry into their own classrooms.

Thomas Grund: I finished college in 2013 with a degree in German literature, already recognizing my waning interest in the subject area. Following a brief stint as a German teacher at a Saturday school, I realized that the only jobs I have enjoyed involved close work with children. With this in mind, I enrolled in a five-year accelerated master's program in elementary education. After a tedious start, my placement as a volunteer, intern, and student teacher within my residential community was revolutionary. As a self-assigned pillar of the community, I deeply appreciate and commit to teaching for social responsibility and civic engagement, working closely with community stakeholders. In the fall, I will begin my first year teaching in a fourth-grade classroom at the same school, with the intention to pursue a socially just, multicultural curriculum bolstered by aspects of yoga and mindfulness meditation.

Nicole Battaglia: I graduated in 2013 with a bachelor's degree in psychology and completed my graduate degree in elementary education in 2014. Along with taking academic courses, I spent my graduate year interning and student teaching in a neighborhood elementary school located within a low-income urban setting. During this year, I had the unique opportunity to learn in theory how to educate for social justice while simultaneously applying this knowledge to practice within the classroom. I am drawn to teaching for social justice because I believe it to be crucial that children see the responsibility they have to others and the power they hold to make a positive impact in their community and in the world. I look forward to continuing to empower my students by teaching for social justice in my own classroom throughout my career as an educator.

Emma Sheeran: I graduated in 2014 with a master's in secondary education social studies. Due to the location of the university, I, along with the other students in the education program, had the opportunity to experience on a local level the effects of the education gap. I spent four out of five years in the education program mentoring and observing students in poorly funded school districts. I witnessed the lack of commitment from the teachers and in turn saw the uninterested and negative attitude for school from the students. Because of these experiences, I am committed to disregarding outside biases and to teaching all students equally. I believe that teachers have the social responsibility to push students to reach the highest level of success. Additionally, I plan to teach students about social justice. In order to educate my students on social issues, I firmly believe in introducing students to topics that may not necessarily be found in the curriculum.

Limitations of the Study

Our observations are, as yet, early impressions. We infer dispositions primarily from students' and candidates' written self-reflections on their experiences and actions.

We have not yet examined additional sections of either the initial or capstone courses to build a longitudinal graph of outcomes for each course. We have not examined individual development from program onset to conclusion in order to track dispositional development. More varied and extensive evidence of observed behaviors during the teacher preparation process would strengthen analysis, but this first-person opportunity was not available to us during the study period. This data was collected during student teaching observation and eventually may be available from program data obtained for accreditation purposes but is not yet organized appropriately for this purpose.

Findings

During an earlier study of a larger group within which our cohort of candidates was nested (Burrell Storms et al., 2014), we noted that a romanticization strategy proved useful as a conceptual holding pen, allowing candidates to linger in consternation rather than moving to a premature reconciliation of expectations and experience. We postulated that service-learning partnerships could radicalize, transform, or offer multiple trajectories for teacher preparation, based on three observations. The first is that we observed that a reflective focus backgrounded becoming competent (in literacy or math teaching) and foregrounded critical engagement with social justice and civic engagement. We saw that shared engagement, rather than solo performance, was foregrounded and noted that the college students discerned multiple possible roles for themselves, including and excluding classroom teaching.

We also noted in that study that we anticipated longer-term outcomes by the end of their teacher preparation that would indicate a range of increased sophistication of critical reflection about their dispositions and practice, the acquisition of professional language and values, and varying depth of commitment to enacting and educating for civic engagement and social responsibility. Longer-term outcomes within this capstone course group do provide evidence that continued engagement with complex issues related to social justice and the realities of urban schools found our students coming to more mature terms with their understanding of their experience and with their reconciliations of threshold concepts about civic engagement and responsibility, social justice, and their sense of self in relation to others (Cook-Sather & Alter, 2011; Harrison & Clayton, 2012; Meyer & Land, 2005; Meyer & Shanahan, 2003). However, this does not mean that their understandings and reconciliations have traveled along a single shared path toward a common understanding, nor does it mean that, regardless of the path, all have arrived at a similar depth of understanding. Resolution of threshold concepts does not always lead to hoped-for outcomes. For this cohort, struggling with threshold concepts has led to an array of resolutions, including both the willingness to continue to struggle and the abandonment of the struggle (Clayton & Ash, 2004; Matias & Zembylas, 2014; Meyer & Land, 2005; Meyer & Shanahan, 2003).

As part of a curriculum mapping assessment of where and when in their teacher preparation programs they made progress toward meeting our aspirational goals for their professional knowledge, skills, and dispositions, candidates determined that they, in the aggregate, developed toward mastery more robustly in some courses than in others. The candidates were able to see a reasonably linear development of their knowledge and skills from introductory, foundational, and intermediate-level pedagogy courses. They identified student teaching as a significant transitional space, where most self-assessed that they had mastered almost all of the outcomes. During class discussions, candidates came to a consensus that two of the dispositional indicators (participating in a professional community that facilitated their development as social and educational change agents and collaborating with other professionals, students, and families to support student learning) had not been as effectively scaffolded as the other twelve indicators of their professional development. However, in this course, their last, approximately 80 percent of the candidates felt that they had demonstrated mastery of the four dispositional indicators, with approximately 20 percent believing that they were still developing toward that mastery. In their final reflective papers, all candidates noted that they expected to continue to mature in their dispositions within the next few years (see table 7.1).

The candidates also engaged in a "funds of knowledge" reflection designed to make visible their explicit recognition of the knowledge, skills, and dispositions they had developed and believed that they would be able to draw on during their first years of teaching. Patterns emerged as they reflected on what they knew about educational theory and practice, diversity, how people learn, current issues relevant to education and schooling, civic engagement, activist strategies, professional ideals, and organizing for social action. For example, they connected theory with practice, citing their fieldwork, internships, and student teaching as spaces where theory and practice met, noting that sometimes theory and practice aligned, and sometimes theory and practice collided. When theory and their lived professional experiences did not align, they tended to evaluate their experiences as more influential, more authentic, and more accurate.

When asked why we integrate theory and practice, students' comments reflected their predominant concerns for the adequacy of their pedagogical knowledge and skills ("We integrate theory and practice because then we are able to see exactly how the theories work and *if* they actually work in the practical sense."). A strong underlying concern for *cura personalis* (care of the whole person) was evident as well ("We are able to see what needs to be modified and what needs to be let go or heightened when we use theory for what the students really need"), relegating the dispositional bent toward activism and advocacy to a less urgent but genuine concern ("Explain the importance of social justice and the need to educate students through any theories and practices necessary while including parents and community members").

When candidates noted what they were able to do during the funds of knowledge exercise, they cited pedagogical knowledge and skills learned during their courses

Table 7.1. Candidates' self-assessment of dispositional outcomes.

Program Candidate Dispositional Outcome	Activity Indicating the Dispositional Outcome	# Candidates who self-assessed as either developing (D) or mastered (M) (n=18)
Candidates are reflective practitioners who act as change agents for equity and social justice through education. They	Contextualize work as educators within a socio-cultural & philosophical framework of education, schooling and society	D = 2 M = 16
	Reflect critically upon roles as active citizens and advocate with students, families, schools and communities.	D = 3 M = 15
	Participate in a professional community that facilitates their development towards social and educational agency.	D = 3 M = 15
	Collaborate with educators, students, parents, and community members to support student learning and development.	D = 3 M = 15

and put to the test during their fieldwork, internships, and student teaching experiences. A pattern of strong alignment between course learning and field-based application emerged. In particular, the elementary education candidates were very specific about what they could do, where they learned how (course readings and activities), and where they validated their abilities (in classrooms). One candidate noted that she knew how to "teach for social justice, utilize resources to reduce the achievement gap (e.g., technology) and engage students as well as communities (including parents)," although she confessed that she wasn't really so sure about her ability to engage with communities and parents.

Candidates wrote that they still had much to learn. Similarly to their other reflections in the funds of knowledge exercise, candidates focused on content knowledge and skills in pedagogy ("We still need to learn how to implement practices and theories of education to meet the needs of *all* students"). They emanated *cura personalis* ("We still need to learn how to work with students with special needs and how to approach an integrated classroom with professionalism. We need to learn how to differentiate without making it obvious. We need to learn how to discreetly differentiate"). They also identified dispositional aspirations for learning to teach for civic engagement and social responsibility ("We need to learn how to work on creating transformative relationships with the community"; "We can learn this through work with other schools, faculty members, community involved members, institutions, officials, etc.").

The candidates were asked to think about what they could do collectively, with each other, with other educational professionals, and with community partners. Their responses indicated willingness to collaborate with education professionals and community members ("Share what we have learned and our future teaching goals with community partners; create new goals with community partners [teachers, administration, parents]; compromise on curriculum and what can be achieved when teachers work together to achieve a common goal. We can offer ideas to our community partners on how to integrate student involvement into their practices since we have been with the students and understand their capacities. They can offer us insight on how to better prepare/teach our students in terms of social justice and civic engagement").

When we turn to the course outcomes evident in evaluated student reflective papers and capstone project proposals, we see further evidence of disjunction between the candidates' more extended reflections and the curriculum mapping and funds of knowledge activities. Most candidates earned high grades on papers one and two, but many earned mediocre grades on the final paper. In the first paper, a reflection of oneself in relation to our conceptual framework and its articulation of candidate outcomes, most but not all candidates indicated reconciliation with threshold concepts in ways that faculty had desired. In one startling disconfirming example, however, a candidate explicitly rejected the call to engage in critical pedagogy and dismissed the value of constructivist pedagogy, instead staunchly and sincerely advocating "banking education" as a sound practice, citing a miserable past year of interning and student teaching in an urban high school as the source of his conviction that adolescent students are too self-absorbed to engage critically in any curriculum. Although most of the other candidates noted that they had considerable competence in evidence-based, socioculturally and philosophically informed reflective practice, few identified as being deeply engaged with the dispositional outcomes of engagement and justice-oriented activism or advocacy, and none indicated that they had had significant collaboration with families or communities, noting that they either had little opportunity to practice these dispositions or that the dispositions were not appropriate or within their reach as teacher candidates. The second paper, identifying what they would need to support their work as educators for civic and social responsibility, similarly revealed few robust communal or justice-oriented activist stances or intentions to work with local communities. The candidates consistently focused on personally meeting the social/emotional and cognitive learning needs of their students. They labeled this as a form of social justice they knew as *cura personalis* but drew a line between what they were ready to do (impart knowledge, provide active learning opportunities) and what they were not ready to do during their first year (encourage communal or justice-oriented activism, for example). They overwhelmingly indicated a stance tightly connected to *cura personalis*. They deferred making a commitment to engaging with families and communities in any way other than providing a caring and effective learning environment for their students.

The capstone course also required a final, brief reflection from the candidates about their work and growth in this course, their next anticipated professional steps, their current and future learning needs, and their plans for educating for civic and social responsibility. Candidate investment in this final paper seemed to differ substantially from that made for the first two papers. All candidates were able to identify their learning, but not all critically reflected on it. Some candidates had "checked out" of the course once the capstone project proposal was delivered, and they had turned their attention to preparing for or continuing the search for teaching positions. For others, however, the very pointed instructions to be specific about their next steps, learning needs, and plans might have raised or illuminated some anxieties about what their realities would be like come late August. Grades for this paper were strikingly lower than for the first two papers. Very few of the reflections included in-depth consideration of how they would educate for civic and social responsibility, and only a handful of candidates indicated with specificity that they would be implementing aspects of their capstone projects during their first year of teaching. Five of the candidates (three social studies, two elementary) did not have teaching positions in place by the time they wrote their final reflections, although three of those candidates had alternate plans, while two were uncertain of their path going forward. Of the candidates who were about to begin classroom teaching positions, all expressed that their primary focus would be on building learning communities that were caring and well designed to support a diverse range of student learning needs. Several of the candidates noted that this was how they would teach for social justice (but they did not note if or how they would be teaching for civic engagement and social responsibility).

Listening to the Candidate Voices

When the teacher candidates scrutinized narratives they had written describing their dispositions as reflective practitioners, they discovered some identity inconsistencies from one narrative to the other (Curwood, 2014; Schultz & Ravitch, 2013). For example, in their curriculum maps, although many of the candidates rated their dispositional development for participating in a professional community dedicated to advocacy in improving learning for students as developing or well developed, very few called up the notion of their participation in such an activist professional community in the brief "Situating the Self" papers they wrote about their personal understandings of the school's conceptual framework.

In his second paper, Grund reflects on two collective course activities (curriculum mapping and the creation of a funds of knowledge inventory):

> Considering my cohort of current graduate students in our final course, I am slightly shocked by the number of students who express a great deal of confidence in regard to social justice and responsibility, myself included. The curriculum map in relation to learning outcomes suggests that upon completion of student teaching,

it was nearly unanimous in favor of mastery across the four suboutcomes within outcome three (reflective practitioners and act as change agents for equity and social justice through education). When I think about these words, I wonder how many of my cohort, myself included, often consider the fact that we are becoming teachers, some in urban districts, sufficient work as social advocates. I can admit that at times I think my profession is doing enough for the world just by deciding to do it. Am I working toward social justice just by choosing to teach in an urban district? I believe these discrepancies further reveal themselves in the elementary education students' funds of knowledge assignment. As the students described what they know, teaching for social responsibility does not come up under what we do know or what we still need to work on. Among my cohort I believe teaching for social responsibility falls into an extremely uncertain area.

In their second papers for the course (Finding the Courage to Teach for Civic Engagement and Social Responsibility), the candidates' voices, Grund's included, wove a collective narrative of individuals working steadily but generally uncertainly toward learning how to teach for social justice. (In this course, the meaning of the title of the capstone course, "Educating for Civic and Social Responsibility," was consistently glossed as "social justice" and "*cura personalis*" by the teacher candidates, in agreement with how they collectively and individually understood the university's mission statement). Although none of the teacher candidates rejected the call to teach for social justice, how they understood what this means for their work as educators varied. Most contextualized this as additive to their curricular work (and, to an extent, acceptable to delay while acclimating to their first year of teaching), but most of the students also identified small ways that they would incorporate awareness of social justice issues into curriculum through careful selection of texts and activities.

One way to understand the move from certainty to uncertainty is articulated by Battaglia, who explains that she feels a chasm between what she has learned during her teacher education program about teaching for social justice, how she would like to teach, and what she is able to do. A local educator, recently named teacher of the year in her district, and a recent graduate of our elementary education certification program, had visited our class to discuss how she thought about and taught for civic engagement and social responsibility: her personal narrative was cited by more than half the candidates as inspirational, as Battaglia's reflection showcases:

> On Monday, August 25th, I will have a classroom full of my own students looking to me to lead them. A real and pertinent question that I must ask myself is how am I going to teach for social responsibility? I know that emotionally, I am ready to tackle the challenging and oftentimes very uncomfortable task of introducing and seeing out lessons focused on issues of inequality that are happening in all areas around the world. I feel invigorated after listening to Mary Nelson speak about the importance of using social justice as the main thread that engages students and weaves together the teachings within all content areas as opposed to trying to insert social justice

into the classroom as a disconnected afterthought. By truly engaging students with issues and topics that reach their hearts, their minds will naturally follow. It is the responsibility of the educator to be genuinely enthusiastic and passionate about issues of social justice. It is this passion alone that will invigorate the students and lead them to become intrinsically passionate and motivated in the content areas that are interwoven within a given social justice topic.

We see in Battaglia's statement above that she has been inspired by a conversation with an outstanding teacher who is an alum of the program from which Battaglia was about to graduate. But we can also see below that Battaglia is uncertain about her ability to follow through, as her narrative continues:

Intellectually, I feel that I have much more to learn when it comes to using social justice and civic engagement as themes that incorporate learning within the content areas. I do not feel confident in my breadth of knowledge or depth of understanding when it comes to issues of inequality and injustice that are currently happening around the world. At this moment, I feel inadequately prepared as to which topics to incorporate into my classroom as well as how to present them in a way that is developmentally appropriate for each grade level. . . . I worry that introducing a social justice issue that is even only a little bit above the developmentally appropriate level will leave students feeling anxious and powerless as opposed to the desired outcome of feeling empowered. This requires a risk that should only be taken, I believe, with a very acute awareness and understanding of how to present issues in a way that is sensitive yet impactful as well as developmentally appropriate.

Despite her uncertainties, Battaglia has constructed some scaffolding to support her work as an educator. She tells us,

Spiritually, I feel very well prepared to take on the weighty task of teaching for social justice and social responsibility. My undergraduate and graduate Jesuit education has led me to truly embody many of the Jesuit tenets that were introduced to me on the first day of orientation freshman year. The tenet that speaks to me the most is *cura personalis*, care for the whole person. In my own personal development, I have come to care for my own whole person—mind, body, and spirit. Consequently, I see this as fundamentally essential to teach my students in my own classroom. I see myself using social justice issues as a vehicle to incorporate teachings in morality and goodness in a secular manner, so that I am able to fully foster growth of the mind and of the spirit within my students. Secondly, the Jesuit tenet of men and women for others, or *hominess pro aliis*, is a concept that resonates with me. I believe that we all as humans have a responsibility to each other, and I want to impart this responsibility to my students. Teaching each of my students that they have a civic responsibility to care for others and stand up for what is right, as opposed to what is easy, seems most effectively done using themes of equality and social justice issues. I want to empower my students and lead them to believe that they truly do have the power to change their community and the larger society in which they live to make their world a better place for themselves and for others. Finally *magis*, or more, is a concept that I want my students to live by in my classroom. There is always more that can be done, both in regard to self-improvement as well as the improvement of their community or society. Teaching for social justice and social responsibility as a main focus will show my students that there is always room to make things better in the world, and that school is not just about learning academics but about learning their larger role within their community and society.

Other candidates also feel uncertain about incorporating social justice into their work, planning to delay what they consider as an addition or an infusion until after they get their bearings. ("I do not think I will be straying too far away from the curriculum the first year or two. I don't believe I will feel so confident in my abilities as a young teacher to undertake extra tasks while being on target with things that are required to get done.")

Sheeran writes about her struggles to reconcile her inexperience as an educator who finds ways to care for all of her students with her lived experiences during student teaching. She is discomfited with what she must acknowledge. Finding a way to linger in the uncomfortable space of her struggle, Sheeran finds positive evidence that she can interrupt similar bias among her students. She may not yet be able to completely overcome her own biases, but she has added some supportive conceptual cocooning to soften the space of her struggles so that she can continue to linger there for a while. She says,

> While a lot of my education classes at the university have focused on social justice, I know that I still have biases that I will have to work through during my years of teaching. To be honest, I think that the only way I will get past certain biases is by witnessing change. I remember how frustrated I was during my student teaching with certain students who were practically unreachable because of their strong negative attitude toward school. Over time, I began to realize that their attitudes were strengthened by teacher and administrative opinions. Before these students even walked into high school they were stereotyped as being uninterested in their educational future because of the color of their skin and their socioeconomic status. That being said, the fact that the students were giving in to this stereotype was frustrating.
>
> After experiencing these attitudes during the first couple of classes, I decided I was going to reach them and change their views. After a couple of weeks, however, with the stresses that come from student teaching, I directed my energy elsewhere. It's a sad but true reality that I'm sure most teachers experience. It's the reality of the original goal slowly morphing into an easier, more attainable one.
>
> When I reflect on this experience, I am disappointed that I took energy away from my struggling students. But while the student teaching was taking place I recognized that I wasn't reaching some of my students and I didn't want to nag them because I didn't want to cause any kind of conflict. One girl in my class was constantly fighting with her peers, and I would hear stories of her cursing out her other

teachers. As a student teacher, I didn't want to face that type of confrontation, so I left her alone. I recognize that this was not the best approach, but at the time it was the only way I knew to act.

I believe that teachers are fortunate to have different avenues for teaching social justice and responsibility because of the profession. That being said, in the beginning I struggled to find ways to engage in social justice during my time at a local high school. Then, one day, I made the connection and figured it out. I was the head coach of the JV girls' lacrosse team and the assistant varsity girls' lacrosse coach. I never would have considered it a social justice experience, but it ended up being one.

Social justice and social responsibility come into play as a coach because you have to teach your players how to act on and off the field. There were multiple times during the season when the girls would judge opponents completely based on their zip code. To my urban students, the suburban girls were all rude and self-centered, even if that wasn't necessarily the case. This experience allowed me to teach social responsibility to my girls, but in a backward manner. I attempted to lecture them on not judging high-socioeconomic families based on their income. It poses an interesting question: Is social justice and social responsibility only for sympathizing with and helping students on the lower end of the socioeconomic spectrum? Or is it about changing peoples' views about everybody?

Although some of the candidates were comfortable that their teacher identities were secure, others, at this time of transition, were still cautiously casting about for how to enact the persona of the teacher they would like to be. Some were still grappling with the romanticization of "teacher" (Burrell Storms et al., 2014) that we observed at the beginning of their professional program, trying on personas that felt just right, that will help them feel more confident, that might inspire their students. Several of the candidates made visible a tension between a sense of responsibility and insecurity about being able to carry through with that responsibility. The struggle to conquer the insecurities is glimpsed in this self-assessment of strengths and weaknesses as a learner and teacher: "I feel overwhelmed by the prospect of teaching for social responsibility because especially as a beginning teacher I feel it is going to be hard enough to keep my head above water. However, I am passionate about this mission and see it as the only way that makes sense to educate students for the world that awaits them" (DV, personal communication, July 2014).

Synthesizing

> GRUND: As the capstone course concludes and the end of the summer draws rapidly near, I see reality, adulthood, and the responsibility of a classroom teacher sinking in. I received my class list, sent out my parent and student letters, and am "officially" a teacher—I decided I felt this way when I notified my students and their families and had a work email address to be contacted at. As I think about all of this, I have mixed feelings about the future.

In regard to setting up my classroom and planning curriculum, I feel well prepared by the university. I know how to use reverse curricular design to form an effective unit of study, and I know all the key details that I cannot neglect in planning a classroom. I know my students will feel welcome in my classroom, and I am already so excited to see each student and consider them "my kids" for the year.

My school network is extremely supportive, as I have a principal who is giving me a lot of freedom, which naturally comes with great responsibility and accountability. However, this also means I can design a classroom where I do everything my way. If I follow the standards within our district's curriculum guide, my principal has given me the go-ahead to do what I want. This is the type of teaching Fairfield has gotten me ready to do. I was always worried I'd be handed a teacher's guide or an anthology and would uncontrollably revert to doing everything my professors encouraged us to avoid. I am proud to say I have already collected over three hundred books for my students, and they will be engaged in meaningful, personal activities throughout the school year.

As a social justice educator, I have achieved a lot, and I have a long way to go. After this course, I know that I can engage students, push them to think critically, and guide them to recognize the voices of oppression and begin to identify issues in the world around them. At the same time, I don't believe I have enough experience as a social justice educator. While my first years teaching will allow me to begin working in this field, I believe my ties to Fairfield University will be critical to maintain. Should I want a classroom that actively advocates for social justice and shares civic responsibilities with the students, I will need consistent, genuine guidance and feedback. I need to see where I am going wrong—something few observers have been willing to do. I also believe I need to observe more examples of best practices in relation to social justice. While it naturally looks different in all classrooms, I want to see what other educators are doing and how I can integrate their own approach into my classroom. I am extremely fortunate and relieved to be working within a few miles of the university, because I know it means it will be that much easier for me to reach out to students and faculty.

I hope that my classroom is a place of learning and growth for my students, myself, and any individuals spending time in the room. With continued university collaboration and networking with social justice educators, I believe I can succeed in making my students critical, engaged citizens.

Aligning Candidate Reflections with Aspirational Dispositional Outcomes

As noted earlier, our teacher education programs purport to develop teacher candidates who are reflective practitioners who act as change agents for equity and social justice through education. We specifically state that, by the conclusion of their preparation programs, our candidates will

- contextualize their work as educators within a sociocultural and philosophical framework of education, schooling, and society;

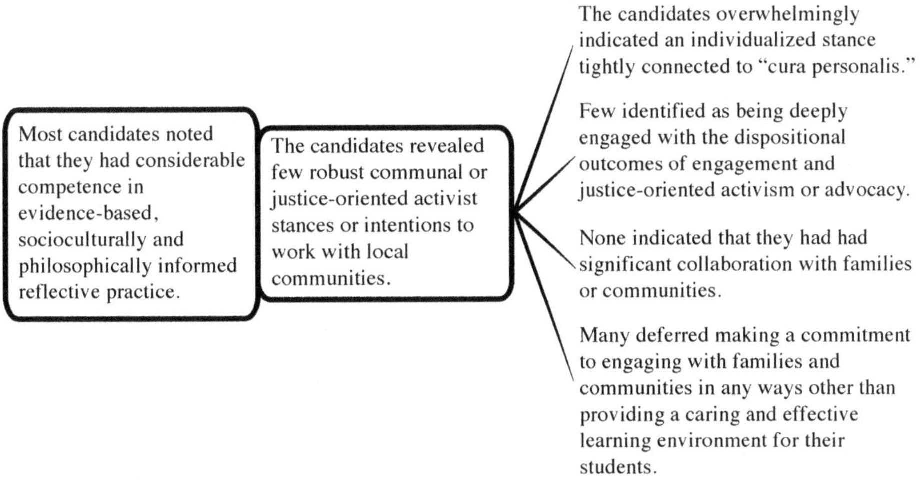

| Most candidates noted that they had considerable competence in evidence-based, socioculturally and philosophically informed reflective practice. | The candidates revealed few robust communal or justice-oriented activist stances or intentions to work with local communities. |

The candidates overwhelmingly indicated an individualized stance tightly connected to "cura personalis."

Few identified as being deeply engaged with the dispositional outcomes of engagement and justice-oriented activism or advocacy.

None indicated that they had had significant collaboration with families or communities.

Many deferred making a commitment to engaging with families and communities in any ways other than providing a caring and effective learning environment for their students.

FIGURE 7.1. Capstone candidates' extended reflections tell a complex story.

- reflect critically on their roles as active citizens and advocates with students, families, schools, and communities;
- participate in a professional community that facilitates their development toward social and educational agency; and
- collaborate with educators, students, parents, and community members to support student learning and development.

During this study, the candidates noted both alignment and misalignment between the dispositional outcomes faculty aspired to nurture in them and the opportunity to practice these during their courses, fieldwork, and practicums. In particular, candidates noted strong alignment of the first two dispositions, a moderate alignment with the third, and a weak alignment with the fourth. Drawing on Whipp's 2013 study of graduates from a teacher education program at her institution (Jesuit, as is ours), we see a mix of individual and structural orientations toward social justice, which our students regularly used as a gloss for the advocative and agentive stance we hoped that we were supporting, in their self-assessments and reflections. More than half of the candidates in our study demonstrated what Whipp (2013) notes as an individualistic orientation toward teaching. These candidates wrote about their individual responsibilities toward their generic students, with few or no references to culturally responsive teaching or social justice. For these students, a sense of agency and/or advocacy was suffocated by their notions that their first years of teaching required compliance rather than agency (Girtz, 2014; Silva & Herdeiro, 2014). Second most prominent was an individual/structural orientation, in which the notion of *cura personalis* (care for the whole person) was often cited, along with theoretical influences from education scholars, such as Nel Noddings. A few candidates in our study also anchored their self-reflections in the language of culturally responsive teaching, generally as a minor note to a more generic stance of caring. Thomas Grund, as an outlier within our group, demonstrated a more pronounced commitment toward the agentive and advocative, stating intentions to further develop his capacities.

Situating in Sociocultural Context and Critical Reflection as Active Citizens and Advocates with Students, Families, Schools, and Communities

The teacher candidates overwhelmingly judged that they had achieved mastery of our second dispositional outcome, reflective practice, by the end of their programs, on their curriculum mapping, in their conceptual papers, and during their shared analysis of the first reflective papers. However, they overwhelmingly provided evidence of reflective practice of pedagogical knowledge and skills rather than of critical reflection of their roles as active citizens or as advocates *with* students, families, schools, and communities. Most of their experiences cited were limited to teacher-student interactions and cooperating teacher–student teacher relationships. None mentioned interactions with families or communities. Advocacy was generally seen as helping students learn what the candidates were teaching, or, very commonly, expressed as *cura personalis*, the holistic care of their students. Within the papers, discussions, and reflective activities produced for this course, we notice that our candidates collectively exhibit three orientations to civic engagement noted by Westheimer and Kahne (2004). As a group, they have shown strong orientation to teaching for personally responsible engagement and for active participation in civic life in their curricular designs, although they sometimes characterize this as a social justice orientation. However, they are not, at this point, a group that is marked by the critically conscious activism that a deeply social justice orientation would prompt.

This marks a challenge for our program's sufficiency to provide a compelling and rich contextual mix of theory and practice that prompts and develops critical reflection and social justice–oriented action (Caruthers & Friend, 2014; Marri, Michael-Luna, Cormier, & Keegan, 2014; Lemley, 2014).

Participation in a Professional Community for Social and Educative Agency

During a class discussion about this dispositional outcome, the candidates offered mixed opinions about their participation in a professional community for social and educative agency. They did not identify themselves as members within a professional community, not recognizing that they were participants in a community of practice (of teaching and learning) that understood and framed its practice as one of social and educative agency. The language of this dispositional outcome was not transparent to the candidates at first, although they unanimously indicated understanding of the concept of community of practice for social and educative agency as the discussion continued. By the end of the semester, 80 percent of them self-assessed as at mastery on this disposition. However, given that very few candidates provided evidence of their actual (in the first reflective papers) or potential (during the final reflection) agentive engagement, it is possible that the candidates are overstating their competence in this arena. The capstone project proposals were mixed as to their expression of membership in a professional community, although most of the candidates demonstrated a moderate to strong attempt to work as transformative agents for their future students. The 20 percent who rated themselves as "developing" within professional community for social and educative agency may be more willing to admit just how ambitious a stretch participation in such a professional community might be and to thus make a more modest self-appraisal.

Collaboration to Support Student Learning and Development

Similar to Whipp's findings (2013) we learned that many of our candidates subscribe to an ethic of care more robustly than one of critique. They take an individualistic stance more easily than a structural one, although they acknowledge the structural as contextual, informing their individualistic approaches. Most of our candidates acknowledged that their collaborative endeavors were not broadly based or inclusive of parents and community members. They cited collaborations with their mentor teachers and peers but noted little to no experience working in partnerships with families or community agencies. Few had had opportunity to collaborate with curricular or health specialists located in the schools in which they interned, student taught, or did fieldwork.

If we are to effectively support our candidates to push the boundaries of their collaborative efforts, our preparation programs need to build in meaningful opportunities to engage with families and community organizations while they are learning their profession. Further, we need to find more opportunities to integrate our allied professions' faculty and candidates into our teacher preparation. Until that happens, we cannot thread out the dispositional elements—the willingness to collaborate broadly—from actual experience in collaboration.

Backing Away

We are concerned that the teacher preparation process might interrupt candidate development toward our more challenging dispositional outcomes (Burrell Storms & Calderwood, 2015). The credentialing aspects of teacher preparation can shift candidates' reflective focus from critical engagement with social justice and civic engagement toward becoming pedagogically competent. We are aware that solo performance, rather than shared engagement, is foregrounded. Throughout their field experiences and student teaching, our teacher candidates discern that classroom teaching is subject to numerous (and onerous) regulations and requirements. As a consequence, they and we note that their commitment to education as a civic and social responsibility can come to be seen as an additional or optional, rather than foundational, focus.

For some of our candidates, a yearlong internship and student teaching experience in a desperately struggling school system is overwhelming, and they retreat from deep engagement within such a community as a self-protective measure (Matias & Zembylas, 2014; Smith & Crowley, 2014). As an example, in his first paper, one of the candidates rejected the Freirean critique of banking education and the notion that adolescents are able to attend to any concerns larger than their immediate contexts. During class sessions, he described his year of interning and student teaching in an underresourced, failing urban high school as one of "suckitude." Although he sees himself as an effective educator despite his misery of the past year, he will not willingly return to urban teaching in a high-needs area, and, in the familiar suburban environment he prefers, will strive to inspire his students as an admirable role model with regard to developing personal talents, a resolution that effectively allows him to disengage from further developing the third and fourth dispositions of collaborative activism and agency. His choice, as a striking example, raises urgent questions for our faculty. How can we scaffold the field-based learning experiences we provide to meet the developmental needs of *all* our candidates, so that they can experience a satisfying and empowering sense of what it might be like to be a change agent with their students and their local communities?

Implications

The findings from this self-study have specific implications for our specific teacher education programs. We here note implications for identifying, developmentally scaffolding for, and assessing candidate dispositions in meaningful ways. With regard to identifying our aspirational dispositions, we need to continue to be guided by our Jesuit heritage of engagement and service, understanding how to address systemic issues of educational equity through all the tools at our disposal, including the *cura personalis* that resonates so powerfully with our teacher candidates. We also need to continue to be guided by our school's conceptual framework, which is deeply grounded in four tenets of our university's Jesuit identity (see figure 7.2). But it is time to invite our candidates' insights and inspirations into an ongoing conversation about how to (even, perhaps, whether to) most effectively support their development of dispositions for teaching that reflect our collective values and beliefs.

Harkening back to our earlier studies (2014, 2015), we believe that some of the interruptions that a teacher preparation process brought to the dispositional foundation that had been built during the candidates' earlier service learning course might be addressed by turning to a community-engaged partnership model for at least the field experiences and student teaching portions of the professional preparation. We are convinced that commitment to a partnership can balance growth in pedagogical

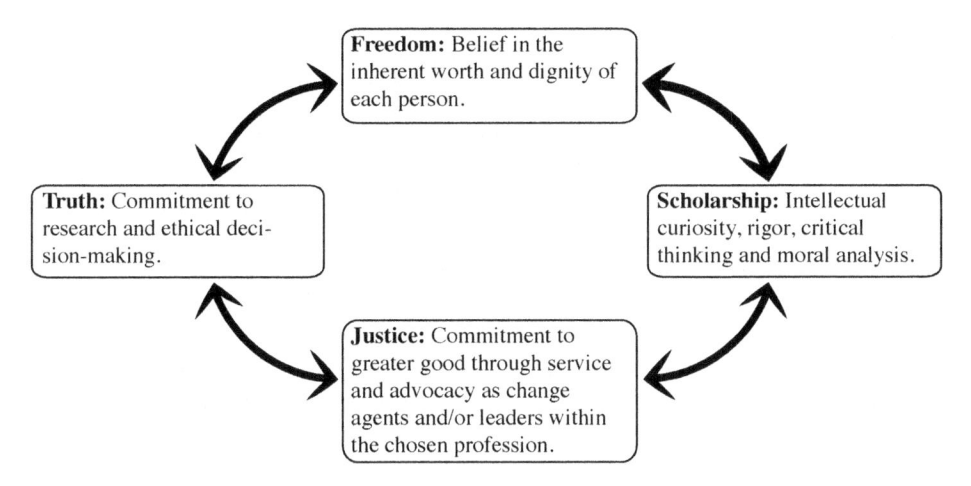

```
        ┌─────────────────────────┐
        │ Freedom: Belief in the  │
        │ inherent worth and dignity of │
        │ each person.            │
        └─────────────────────────┘
```

Truth: Commitment to research and ethical decision-making.

Scholarship: Intellectual curiosity, rigor, critical thinking and moral analysis.

Justice: Commitment to greater good through service and advocacy as change agents and/or leaders within the chosen profession.

FIGURE 7.2. Four tenets underlying candidate dispositions.

competence with critical engagement with social justice and civic needs of the school partners. We believe that programmatic, faculty, and candidate commitment to the partnership builds a professional community that facilitates teacher candidate development toward social and educational agency and encourages collaboration among educators, students, parents, and community members to support student learning and development.

With regard to scaffolding more effectively to support candidate development of the desired dispositions, we need to model and better support perspective taking (George Dover, 2009) rather than simply asking candidates to reflect on their experiences. Building in sustained, meaningful interactions of mutual and reciprocal benefit with local communities and their neighborhood school and other organizations would provide more, and more authentic, opportunities to decenter candidates' points of view; support deep, sustained engagement with challenging threshold concepts; and offer authentic opportunities for our candidates to act as and to see themselves as effective and collaborative change agents. We need to provide an extensive range of exemplars that seem attainable in practice. Across programs, we need to explicitly include attention to the dispositions as they might most commonly be evident in practices closely aligned with course content, and we should build in problem-solving discussions of dispositionally challenging aspects of engaged, collaborative civic and social agency to support student learning.

We faculty need to come to terms with the most common developmental trajectories, which, at least for this cohort of candidates, arc toward more modest, less radical dispositional inclinations and actions than we anticipated when drawing up our list of candidate outcomes. Not all of our candidates will, by the end of their programs, be ready or willing to move beyond the gentle, caring curricula they tell us they will create *for* their students and the individualized attention they will try to provide. But we do not need to abandon our aspirations, for some of our candidates have great courage and determination and are ready to push hard against the forces that might rein in their willingness to take other steps. We need to decide how we account for the full range of our candidates' dispositional outcomes—will we rank order the dispositions, considering the most activist, critically conscious inclinations and actions as more sophisticated or more evolved? Can we support such an evaluative system if we don't adequately scaffold for this profile in our program courses and activities or if we ourselves fall short as role models for our candidates?

Regardless of whether we are casting a wider net to find evidence of identified dispositions, we need to challenge our conceptualizations of our courses and of our required field experiences to provide more robust support for the development of dispositions for engagement and advocacy with local communities. For example, we have not yet tightly organized the teacher preparation programs so as to systematically and consistently require the candidates to engage meaningfully and with increasing sophistication with the local communities we serve, but we could do so with multiple small but significant changes to the programs and one bold curricular adjustment—to switch to a course in participatory action research rather than the more traditional introduction to educational research course we now require. We can also require a course in multicultural foundations of education in the five-year teacher education programs in lieu of broader-based diversity courses from which they choose now. The multiple small changes to course curricula could be aligned and developmentally configured. For example, we can require that candidates and faculty together construct, over a series of courses, long-term, meaningful engagement with local communities that extend beyond classrooms. Although a moderate number of our candidates work intentionally and consistently within one or two schools within a local community as they choose field placements, teaching internships, and student teaching placements in local schools, a much smaller number of our candidates extend their engagement into community life outside the schoolyard. For this population, all of whom live on or near campus, including a more organic immersion into local community activity could be accomplished to a much greater extent than we see now. To this end, our professional school has committed to a multifocal, long-term community partnership with our service-learning school. Within the partnership, teacher candidates will collaborate with faculty, local educators, students, parents, and community members to support student learning and development. This professional community may facilitate candidates' development toward social and educational agency.

A next step in tracking dispositional outcomes is to analyze and compare dispositional outcomes in our five-year and post-BA teacher education programs. We need to organize candidate data over time (reflections, lesson plans, student teaching observations) so as to track individual development of dispositions for agency and activism. Another next step is to follow up with our alumnae to learn when, if, and how they exhibit our aspirational dispositions over the longer term (interviews, surveys, and observation). We need to know where, why, and how they teach in their early and more experienced lives as teachers. What are they doing in their classrooms and with their students, families, and communities to promote civic engagement and social responsibilities in line with our dispositional aspirations for them?

Finally, we faculty can rise more robustly and more visibly to model the dispositional attributes we have identified for our teacher candidates. Like our candidates, we faculty embody considerable variance in how, and even whether, we act in collaboration with families and communities to support student learning and development—the most challenging dispositional attribute we have set for our students.

PATRICIA CALDERWOOD is Professor of Educational Studies and Teacher Education at Fairfield University.

STEPHANIE BURRELL STORMS is Associate Professor of Multicultural Education and Director of Secondary Education in the Department of Educational Studies and Teacher Preparation Department.

THOMAS GRUND is an elementary school teacher.

NICOLE BATTAGLIA holds a graduate degree in elementary education.

EMMA SHEERAN holds a graduate degree in secondary education social studies.

References

Alsup, J., & Miller, S. (2014). Reclaiming English education: Rooting social justice in dispositions. *English Education, 46*(3), 195–215.

Bolton, M., & Reisboard, D. (2014). Improving pre-service teacher dispositions. *Journal of Teaching Effectiveness and Student Achievement, 1*(1), 24–32.

Bradley, A. P., & Jurchan, J. (2013). Dispositions in teacher education: Complex but comprehensible. *Education, 3*(1), 98–104.

Burrell Storms, S., & Calderwood, P. (2015). Service learning influences teacher candidate development of dispositions for civic engagement and social responsibility. Roundtable presentation accepted for AERA annual conference, April 2015.

Burrell Storms, S., Calderwood, P., & Quan, M. (2014). Student learning and discernment in a service-learning course. Unpublished manuscript.

Caruana, V. (2014). Using the Ignatian pedagogical paradigm to frame the reflective practice of special education teacher candidates. *Jesuit Higher Education, 3*(1), 19–28.

Caruthers, L., & Friend, J. (2014). Critical pedagogy in online environments as thirdspace: A narrative analysis of voices of candidates in educational preparatory programs. *Educational Studies, 50*(1), 8–35.

Clayton, P. H., & Ash, S. L. (2004). Shifts in perspective: Capitalizing on the counter-normative nature of service-learning. *Michigan Journal of Community Service Learning, 11*(1), 59–70.

Clayton, P. H., Bringle, R. G., Senor, B., Huq, J., & Morrison, M. (2010). Differentiating and assessing relationships in service-learning and civic engagement: Exploitative, transactional, or transformational. *Michigan Journal of Community Service Learning, 16*(2).

Cochran-Smith, M., Villegas, A., Abrams, L., Chavez-Moreno, L., Mills, T., & Stern, R. (2015). Critiquing teacher preparation research: An overview of the field, part II. *Journal of Teacher Education, 66*(2), 109–121.

Cook-Sather, A. (2006). Newly betwixt and between: Revising liminality in the context of a teacher preparation program. *Anthropology & Education Quarterly, 37*, 110–127.

Cook-Sather, A., & Alter, Z. (2011). What is and what can be: How a liminal position can change learning and teaching in higher education. *Anthropology & Education Quarterly, 42*(1), 37–53.

Cummins, L. L., & Asempapa, B. (2013). Fostering teacher candidate dispositions in teacher education programs. *Journal of the Scholarship of Teaching and Learning, 13*(3), 99–119.

Curwood, J. S. (2014). Between continuity and change: Identities and narratives within teacher professional development. *Teaching Education, 25*(2), 156–183.

Damon, W. (2007). Dispositions and teacher assessment: The need for a more rigorous definition. *Journal of Teacher Education, 58*(5), 365–369.

Fairfield University. (2014). Mission statement of Fairfield University. Retrieved from http://www.fairfield.edu/aboutfairfield/missionvalueshistory/missionstatement/.

Fox, K. R. (2014). Exploring literacy in our own backyard: Increasing teachers' understanding of literacy access through community mapping. *Journal of Praxis in Multicultural Education, 8*(2), 1.

George Dover, A. (2009). Teaching for social justice and K-12 student outcomes: A conceptual framework and research review. *Equity & Excellence in Education, 42*(4), 506–524.

Girtz, S. (2014). Ignatian pedagogy and its alignment with the new teacher bar exam (edTPA) and action research frameworks. *Jesuit Higher Education, 3*(1), 75–80.

Gomez, M. L., Carlson, J. R., Foubert, J., & Powell, S. N. (2014). "It's not them, it's me": Competing discourses in one aspiring teacher's talk. *Teaching Education, 25*(3), 334–347.

Harrison, B., & Clayton, P. H. (2012). Reciprocity as a threshold concept for faculty who are learning to teach with service-learning. *The Journal of Faculty Development, 26*(3), 29–33.

Henry, G. T., Campbell, S. L., Thompson, C. L., Patriarca, L. A., Luterbach, K. J., Lys, D. B., & Covington, V. M. (2013). The predictive validity of measures of teacher candidate programs and performance toward an evidence-based approach to teacher preparation. *Journal of Teacher Education, 64*(5), 1–15. doi:0022487113496431

Hochstetler, S. (2014). The critical role of dispositions: What's missing in measurements of English teacher candidate effectiveness. *The Clearing House: A Journal of Educational Strategies, Issues and Ideas, 87*(1), 9–14.

Lassonde, C., Galman, S., & Kosnik, C. (Eds.). (2009). *Self-study research methodologies for teacher educators*. Rotterdam, The Netherlands: Sense.

Lassonde, C., & Strub, D. (2009). Promoting self-study as a habit of mind for preservice teachers. In C. Lassonde, S. Galman, & C. Kosnik (Eds.), *Self-study research methodologies for teacher educators* (pp. 207–225). Rotterdam, The Netherlands: Sense.

Lemley, C. K. (2014). Social justice in teacher education: Naming discrimination to promote transformative action. *Critical Questions in Education, 5*(1), 26–51.

Lund, D., Bragg, B., Kaipainen, E., & Lee, L. (2014). Preparing preservice teachers through service-learning: Collaborating with community for children and youth of immigrant backgrounds. *International Journal of Research on Service-Learning in Teacher Education, 2.* Retrieved from journals.sfu.ca/cje/index.php/cje-rce/article/download/1744/1756.

Marri, A., Michael-Luna, S., Cormier, M. S., & Keegan, P. (2014). Urban pre-service K-6 teachers' conceptions of citizenship and civic education: Weighing the risks and rewards. *Urban Review, 46*(1), 63–85.

Matias, C. E., & Zembylas, M. (2014). "When saying you care is not really caring": Emotions of disgust, whiteness ideology, and teacher education. *Critical Studies in Education.* Advance online publication. doi:10.1080/17508487.2014.922489

McDonald, D., & Kahn, M. (2014). "So, you think you can teach?": Reflection processes that support pre-service teachers' readiness for field experiences. *International Journal for the Scholarship of Teaching and Learning, 8*(2), article 18. Retrieved from http://digitalcommons.georgiasouthern.edu/cgi/viewcontent.cgi?article=1436&context=ij-sotl.

Meyer, J. H. F., & Land, R. (2005). Threshold concepts and troublesome knowledge (2): Epistemological considerations and a conceptual framework for teaching and learning. *Higher Education, 49,* 373–388.

Meyer, J. H. F., & Shanahan, M. (2003, August). The troublesome nature of a threshold concept in economics. Paper presented to the tenth Conference of the European Association for Research on Learning and Instruction, Padova, Italy.

Mitchell, T. D. (2015). Using a critical service-learning approach to facilitate civic identity development. *Theory into Practice, 54*(1), 20–28.

Nelson, P. (2015). Intelligent dispositions: Dewey, habits and inquiry in teacher education. *Journal of Teacher Education, 66*(1), 86–97.

Oakes J., & Rogers, J. (2006). *Learning power: Organizing for education and justice.* New York, NY: Teachers College Press.

Pinnegar, S., & Erickson, L. (2009). Uncovering self-studies in teacher education accreditation review processes. In C. Lassonde, S. Galman, & C. Kosnik (Eds.), *Self-study research methodologies for teacher educators* (pp. 151–168). Rotterdam, The Netherlands: Sense.

Ritchie, S. (2014). Teaching for social justice in three voices. *Journal of Critical Thought and Praxis, 2*(2), 5.

Schultz, K., & Ravitch, S. (2013). Narratives of learning to teach: Taking on professional identities. *Journal of Teacher Education, 64*(1), 35–46.

Schussler, D. L., & Knarr, L. (2013). Building awareness of dispositions: Enhancing moral sensibilities in teaching. *Journal of Moral Education, 42*(1), 71–87.

Schussler, D., Stooksberry, L., & Bercaw, L. (2010). Understanding teacher candidate dispositions: Reflecting to build self-awareness. *Journal of Teacher Education, 61*(4), 350–363.

Shoffner, M., Sedberry, T., Alsup, J., & Johnson, T. S. (2014). The difficulty of teacher dispositions: Considering professional dispositions for preservice English teachers. *The Teacher Educator, 49*(3), 175–192.

Silva, A., & Herdeiro, R. (2014). The work, perceptions and professional development of teachers. *Teaching Education, 25*(2), 184–201.

Smith, W. L., & Crowley, R. M. (2014). Pushback and possibility: Using a threshold concept of race in social studies teacher education. *The Journal of Social Studies Research, 39*(1), 17–28.

Sturgill, A., & Motley, P. (2014). Methods of reflection about service learning: Guided vs. free, dialogic vs. expressive, and public vs. private. *Teaching & Learning Inquiry, 2*(1), 81–93.

Warren, C. A., & Hotchkins, B. K. (2014). Teacher education and the enduring significance of "false empathy." *The Urban Review*, pp. 1–27.

Westheimer, J., & Kahne, J. (2004). What kind of citizen? The politics of educating for democracy. *American Educational Research Journal, 41*(2), 237–269.

Whipp, J. (2013). Developing socially just teachers: The interaction of experiences before, during and after teacher preparation in beginning urban teachers. *Journal of Teacher Education, 64*(5), 454–467.

8 Transforming Student Ideas about Community Using Asset-Based Community Development Techniques

Lisa Garoutte

SERVICE LEARNING AND community-based learning (CBL) are increasingly important pedagogical tools in higher education. The potential benefits of service learning and CBL are as varied as the type of experiences, which range from traditional service (sometimes called a "charity" model) to efforts aimed at creating lasting, sustainable change in the community (Lewis, 2004; Peterson, 2009). The primary goal in traditional service learning is to create enriching educational opportunities for students while also providing a service to the community (Mooney & Edwards, 2001). Those who follow a social change model, on the other hand, are typically focused on creating more equitable communities rather than offering assistance for a short period of time. Working with the community, rather than doing for/to the community, is key with this kind of work (Eby, 1998; Steiner, Warkentin, & Smith, 2011). While the distinction between the two may not seem great, there has been significant debate between the two camps.

One of the primary criticisms leveled at traditional service learning is that it can leave students with the perception that disempowered groups are hopelessly dependent on outside actors and thus have neither the skills nor ability to help themselves. As a result, this type of work has the potential to reinforce student stereotypes about oppressed groups rather than challenge students to think beyond those confines (Camacho, 2004; Eby, 1998; Mitchell, 2008; Peterson, 2009). As such, power relationships are reinforced in ways that sustain an unjust status quo.

Despite these concerns, many point to the pitfalls of not involving students with the community. Not only are there significant educational benefits to doing so (see, for example, Battistoni, Longo, & Jayandadhan, 2009; Chesler, Ford, Galura, & Charbeneau, 2006; Eyler & Giles, 1999; Mobley, 2007; Murphy & Rash, 2008; Peterson, 2009; Schamber & Mahoney, 2008), but maintaining a strict separation between the academy and surrounding areas reinforces an "us versus them" mentality, which is, in and of itself, problematic for building community. It is for this reason that many faculty have turned to the social justice model of community-based learning. Indeed, the Scholarship of Teaching and Learning (SoTL) provides a great deal of insight into how to best engage in CBL for social justice. While the literature is instructive, it also makes clear the difficulty of doing this work well.

At best, properly engaging in community-based learning with a social justice goal is complex and requires a great deal of work before, during, and after the semester. Before meeting with students, and before even developing a project or identifying community partners, faculty must be engaged in the community, building trust and growing genuine relationships (Lewis, 2004). Once the semester is underway, this work expands as faculty must continue to nurture their community relationships while also facilitating the project and guiding students to create their own meaningful relationships within the community. It is especially important that students and faculty alike be welcomed by community members as their input and cooperation are essential for justice-focused CBL. Intensive conversations with students about issues of race, class, and gender, for example, are also necessary for success (Green, 2003). Finally, maintaining positive relationships after the semester's end and ensuring needs have been adequately met are essential to change-focused community-based learning.

Of course, these difficulties do not mean that this type of work is not worth doing. But the time and effort it requires can deter busy faculty, even those with the best intentions. The realities of academic life only add to these challenges: the academic calendar, course rotations, and competing demands for student time are a few examples of structural constraints that make true social justice CBL so difficult. It can be especially challenging for pretenure faculty who may face greater pressure to publish than those who are already tenured (Lewis, 2004). This concern weighs heavily on those at institutions where the tenure and promotion structure privilege traditional scholarship and service to the institution over social justice work in the community. A preference in many disciplines for "pure," "objective," and "unbiased" research is another roadblock faced by faculty (Stoecker, 1996).

The question, then, becomes one of practicality as well as ideals. How can one engage students in community-based learning, address concerns of social justice, and avoid the potential pitfalls of a charity approach to community work? In this chapter, I argue that using elements of asset-based community development, known as ABCD or asset mapping, helps to better ground students in their community while also providing them with a more structural perspective. Preliminary experiences with asset mapping begin to help students develop an understanding of community that is neither strictly individualistic nor deterministic while also fostering a sense of belonging to the community with which they engage. These experiences prepare students to interact with their community in a way that promotes collaboration rather than charity, help them realize how they and others are connected to social systems that exist beyond them, and help them understand how they are both products of and creators of those structures. So while this may not be change in and of itself, it is certainly an important step on the way to social justice. Further, the activities and exercises suggested can be completed either in a single course or, ideally, implemented over several courses and semesters. This flexibility helps circumvent the academic constraints discussed above.

Below, I outline the basic tenets of asset-based community development and locate these ideals within the SoTL work related to social justice. I then move to a discussion about how this model can be adapted for classroom use to provide a building block for social awareness. Quantitative analyses of student perceptions before and after the asset-mapping experiences are included, as are comparisons between students who did and did not participate in asset mapping. Results demonstrate the development of a more structural understanding of community and a significant change in student investment in their communities as a result of ABCD practices.

Asset Mapping, Community Empowerment, and Community-Based Learning

In 1993, Kretzman and McKnight released their seminal work on asset-based community development: *Building Communities from the Inside Out: A Path toward Finding and Mobilizing a Community's Assets*. The text is a response to traditional efforts to rebuild troubled communities. In it, Kretzman and McKnight criticize community development efforts that ignore the skills, abilities, and resources of those within the community. By focusing on the problems of a community, public and private actors attempting change create dependency rather than empowerment. In doing so, they argue, outside actors attempt to "fix" both the people and community identified as incapable of self-sufficiency rather than recognizing the capacities that already exist within the community. Such an approach, they argue, is demeaning to members of the community, most of whom are already marginalized by society. At the same time, it feeds the perception that those doing the helping are superior; their resources, skills, and contacts are privileged in relation to those who are perceived as deficient. In other words, Kretzman and McKnight share the same concerns about community building that Eby (1998), Peterson (2009), Stoecker (1996), and others express about traditional models of community-based learning.

In response to these concerns, Kretzman and McKnight propose an alternative approach called asset-based community development. The asset-based approach, they argue, overcomes many of the pitfalls associated with traditional forms of community development by focusing on the strengths, or assets, of a given community. Indeed, the belief that all communities are asset-rich is at the core of the ABCD model. These assets can take many forms: individuals, citizens' associations, and local institutions are, according to Kretzman and McKnight (1993), sources of assets (p. 7).

The asset-based community development process includes several key steps. First, assets need to be identified. This occurs when community members canvas the community to see the area and meet and talk with as many people as possible within the geographic and social boundaries of the community. Assets are defined as any resources that exist within the community. In the context of ABCD, assets are defined fairly broadly: anything that has the potential to benefit the neighborhood, even if it is currently considered useless, is an asset. Individuals' knowledge and skills, for example, are assets. Places of business are also assets, as are governing bodies. Empty buildings and lots, places of worship, racial and ethnic diversity, and schools are likewise identified as key assets by those engaging in ABCD. This wide definition is useful because it challenges us to consider the parts of our community that we know, or think we know, in an effort to see their full potential. That said, it can be overwhelming to reexamine everything within a community in this light. To that end, the Bonner Foundation (2012) has identified assets as falling into five basic categories: individual, institutional, organizational, cultural, and physical assets.

Second, a profile of the community is created. The community profile serves as an asset guide. It provides lists of assets and includes as much information as possible about each one. The profile must also point to the relationships that exist between the various assets. For example, if organizations have the same board members or strive to reach similar goals, this should be noted in the community profile. Connections should also be made between people with similar skills and interests, historical and cultural connections between parties, and approaches to problem solving, among others.

Third, a visual asset map that physically demonstrates the profile is created. Engaging in each of these steps requires that those aspects of the community typically considered mundane or useless (e.g., the homeless population, teenagers, the elderly, empty buildings and plots of land) are understood as useful entities that are significant resources for the community. They are, in other words, acknowledged as valuable resources and treated as important, vital, and capable, rather than as lacking and dependent.

Asset-based community development is, as said above, a method for creating positive, sustainable change in a community. Yet until this point, the emphasis has been only on the significant assets, or resources, of a community; no attention has been given to areas of concern or problems that need to be addressed. This is an intentional effort to move community development efforts away from a deficiency model (i.e., focusing on what is "wrong" with an area and its people) and toward a strength-based approach. When creating a community profile, however, those engaging in ABCD notice those assets that are not being taken advantage of, connections between assets that could be strengthened or utilized in a more efficient manner. These realizations, along with conversations that take place during the canvasing project, lead community developers to identify areas of concern for the community.

At this point, community members create and eventually implement a plan of action. The action plan is entirely based on those assets that already exist in the community. While existing assets are used in new ways or mobilized for the first time, and/or new relationships between assets are formed, nothing from outside of the community is brought in. The community is, in other words, treated as self-sufficient rather than deficient. In asset-based community development, plans of action, once implemented, create long-term sustainable change. It is also important to note that action plans are created and implemented by community members themselves. As such, community members are cocreators of their developing neighborhoods rather than passive recipients of outsiders' gifts.

This process fits well into the best practices of community-based learning that come out of the SoTL literature, especially if the goal is to move toward greater social justice. As described above, CBL with a social justice focus should not be about helping the "less fortunate." Instead, it is about empowering communities and creating more equitable structures (Lewis, 2004). As Petrov (2013) writes, the goal is to "increase solidarity between students and the communities they serve" (p. 310) and to understand "that all members of society are entitled to dignity and respect, no matter their socioeconomic status, and that all members of society are not positioned equally within it" (p. 311). These same concerns—building relationships, valuing individuals, and emphasizing human dignity—come through in both the theory and practice of ABCD. For these reasons, I use elements of ABCD in several of my courses. Below, I describe how I alter pieces of the ABCD process for classroom use, and I consider the benefits of adapting ABCD in this way.

Adapting Asset-Based Community Development Ideas for Classroom Use

I collected data about the use of classroom exercises inspired by ABCD in three sociology courses at a Loras College, a small Midwestern Catholic liberal-arts institution. Two of these were sections of Introduction to Sociology populated primarily by first-year students. I also worked with students on an asset-based project in a general education course for seniors in a variety of majors. The general education course and one of the introductory courses took place in the traditional sixteen-week semester. The other introductory section worked on their ABCD-inspired project during a three-week January term course. January term is an intensive, experiential term in which students take only one course.

The January term class was the first time I used ABCD-inspired projects in the classroom. This group of students studied a local neighborhood that had been working with city officials to engage in asset-based community development. During this course, students met with community leaders and citizens of the neighborhood to better understand both the history and current situation of the area. Because the students were new to college and had little previous experience with this neighborhood, their project focused on identifying assets and discussing possible asset-based solutions to previously identified community concerns. Action plans were not shared with community members as they were engaged in their own, separate ABCD project.

The following semester, I wanted to provide a more authentic asset-mapping experience for students. Doing so required that they work in a community of which they were members. To that end, my semester-long Introduction to Sociology class engaged in an asset-based project on our campus. Because they were focused on a community they were already members of, I felt comfortable asking students to develop and propose plans based on their asset-mapping experiences. In this case, some student groups did take their proposals to the campus community, though only one group was successful in implementing the change (increasing institutional and emotional support for students dealing with mental illness).

A year later, I was approached by a colleague serving on a community-relationship board. This group was focused on fostering stronger connections between our college and nearby residents. After meeting with members of this group, most of whom represented neighborhood organizations, we agreed my senior-level general education students would be able to assist them in bridging relationships between the campus and surrounding neighborhood. They, too, proposed long-term action plans that were developed in concert with community leaders.

When using ABCD-inspired exercises in the classroom, faculty should begin by introducing students to the underlying principles and methods of asset mapping. Students are typically both unaware of ABCD and tied to the ideals of traditional service; at least that is the case at my Catholic institution where service projects are a regular part of campus life. Asking students to consider critiques of a model for which they are typically praised for participating in can be difficult. I had the most success when I started talking with students about the concepts of empowerment and justice generally and how that should look within a community. From there, I brought in the ABCD approach by focusing heavily on the concepts of assets, sustainability, and cocreators of change. I found that by focusing on the benefits of asset mapping from the outset, and linking them to student ideals about justice, I created more excitement around the practice of ABCD and reduced student resistance.

Strong outside resources are also essential in this regard. Both Cone, Kiesa, and Longo (2006) and the Bonner Foundation (2012) have asset-mapping materials designed for students. The Asset-Based Community Development Institute run out of Northwestern University (founded by John McKnight and Jody Kretzman) is another useful resource. Their website (www.abcdinstitute.org) lists a variety of videos, podcasts, tools, and a discussion group that are helpful for those participating in ABCD projects. I also found guest speakers who have done this type of work to be valuable. In my experience, both city leaders and Girl Scout council staff are eager to talk about

Transforming Student Ideas about Community | 149

Canvas
- Identify Community
- Get to Know Community Members
- Familiar with Community Resources

Identify Assets
- Consider Strengths
- Community Profile
- Connections Between Assets

Action Plan
- Identify Concerns
- Plan Based on Assets within Community
- Share & Implement Action Plan

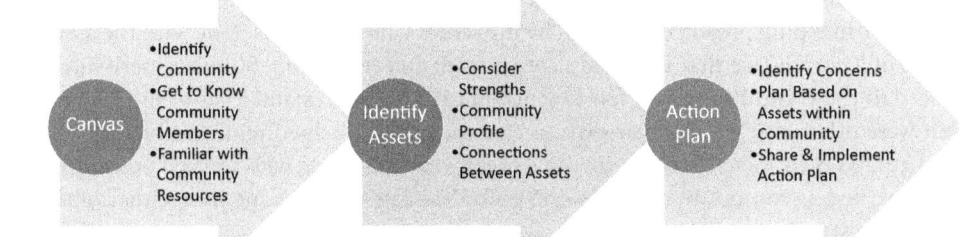

FIGURE 8.1. Flow chart of ABCD practices for classroom use.

their experiences with asset mapping. Speakers have the additional benefit of complementing theoretical readings about ABCD with discussions of how this style of community development is played out in the real world.

Once familiar with the ABCD philosophy, students begin to use the practices in their course work. Figure 8.1 indicates how ABCD-inspired activities might play out in the classroom, though faculty should adjust the experiences to best fit the needs of their students and community partners. Ideally, this process should be conducted in conjunction with community leaders or groups that have been identified by the professor before classes begin. When working closely with community members isn't possible, students can engage in ABCD-style practices on their own campus.

Depending on the project, the first step may be to identify the community being studied. This was the case for my general education students working with a local community group to help improve relationships between Loras College and the surrounding neighborhood. Neither the community group nor my students had a clear idea about who or where "the neighborhood" was. As such, my class was first charged with identifying what defined the college's neighborhood within Dubuque, Iowa. To do so, students considered geographic boundaries (large bluffs and busy streets, for example), perceptions of those surrounding the campus, as well as contemporary and historical patterns of interaction between the college and surrounding areas. During that process, students had intense conversations about what makes a community, the role of culture and inclusion and exclusion, and who gets to make those decisions. After coming to an agreement about their definition of the neighborhood, students consulted with community members to determine if the definitions lined up. This type of reciprocity in the project was not only useful for verification and validity but also created a better power balance between students and the community.

Once the community was identified, students canvased the neighborhood to identify assets. The ways in which students canvas can and should be altered based on specific course needs. For example, heavier faculty involvement was needed for my first-year students working off campus than others. For my January term course, I set up tours of the neighborhood; organized meetings and panels of citizens, community leaders, and city employees; and walked students through past research on the area. The asset-mapping project engaged in by my seniors, however, was done with the assistance of a committee that included faculty, staff, and neighbors. Students were introduced to the committee and a few key neighborhood leaders and long-term residents but were otherwise left on their own to canvas. While I helped with troubleshooting and guided their focus, they led the way. Meanwhile, students who worked on campus were treated as community experts and given less assistance by me than either of the other two student groups.

When canvassing, students spent significant time in the community. This includes tours, meetings, informal conversations, interviews, and other types of interactions with community members as appropriate for the project. While canvassing, students, faculty, and community partners were exposed to a wide variety of perspectives. For example, my January term students took walking tours of the neighborhood with both long-term and relatively new residents. Given the history and culture of the community, this distinction led to very different accounts of the neighborhood. This is key, as the goal of canvassing is to better understand the richness of the community and what it means to the people who live there.

Students typically needed help realizing how asset-rich communities are and recognizing assets that may not be widely appreciated or valued. For example, my January term students were readily able to identify the educational assets of the homeless women they spoke with but had a more difficult time recognizing the same women's personal assets of perseverance, determination, and generosity; their familial and friendship networks were likewise overlooked as potential assets. The students working on campus, meanwhile, noted the expertise of faculty and staff but had a more difficult time identifying the significant strengths of students. As a result, we had many conversations about how our experiences shape what we see, what we miss, what we appreciate, and what and who we devalue. These conversations are related back to readings on ABCD and, when possible, course content.

After assets were identified, students completed a community profile. The profile listed all resources identified during canvassing and made connections between those resources. Students considered interpersonal, professional, geographic, and cultural connections between the various assets. Creating a visual asset map is one way to facilitate this. Visual maps can be drawn in any number of ways, but I have typically relied on two formats in my classes. First, the visual map can be placed on an actual road map, as seen in figure 8.2. In this type of map, students indicate where services, individuals, or other assets are located. In this example, each type of asset (e.g., neighborhood businesses, campus groups, parks, and religious organizations) was represented with a different color pin. The heads of the pins are numbered, and a key (not shown) states which asset can be found at the location. Relationships between the various assets are represented by thread; each type of relationship (between on-campus organizations and religious groups, for instance) was also represented by a different

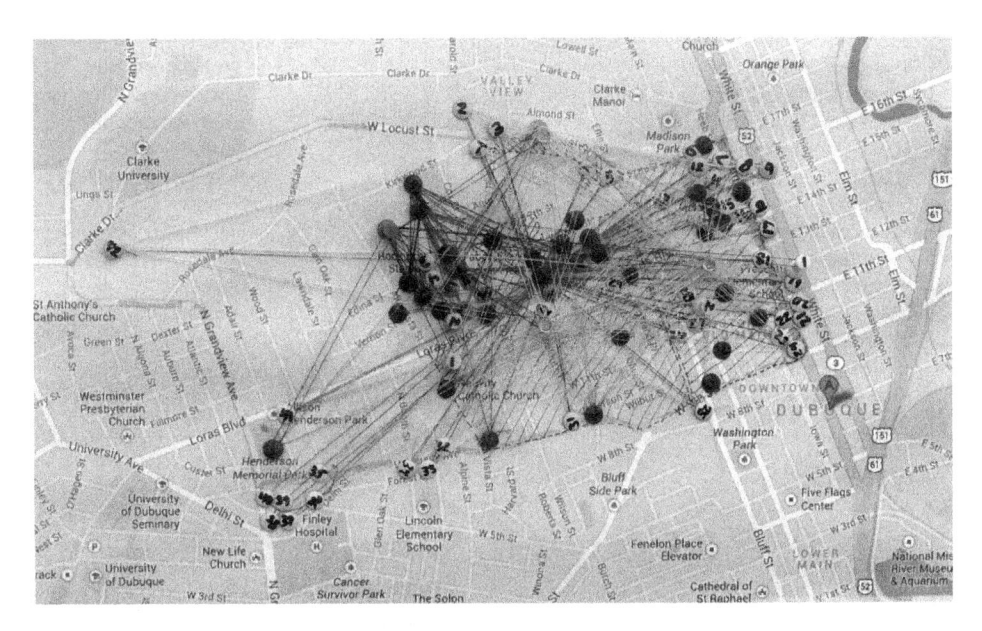

FIGURE 8.2. Example of a visual asset map based on a street map.
Source: Map Data ©2013 Google, DigitalGlobe

color. This method highlighted not only the relationships between various assets but the physical proximity between them.

Another option is based on a concept-map model (figure 8.3). In this type of map, students grouped various resources on paper, making sure to highlight connections within and between the various categories. Here, connections between resources are shown using various types and colors of lines (dotted lines and dashes, for example). This method was usually easier for students and is best used when the location of assets is less important. Regardless of the method, all asset maps helped make the assets more concrete in the minds of students and created a useful starting point for future work in the area.

The last step in the ABCD model is developing and implementing an action plan that grows out of the canvasing process and creation of the community profile. This plan should be clear and specific and have attainable outcomes. Further, action plans should be sustainable in the long term. They should not, therefore, be reliant on a single individual or organization. Rather, successful action plans draw on a wide base of assets and are as inclusive as possible so as to achieve greater success and empowerment for community members (Kretzman & McKnight, 1993).

When students developed an action plan, I required them to develop two or three options that they believed would build on the identified assets and assist with problem solving. Each plan has a step-by-step blueprint for implementing and maintaining the

152 | Garoutte

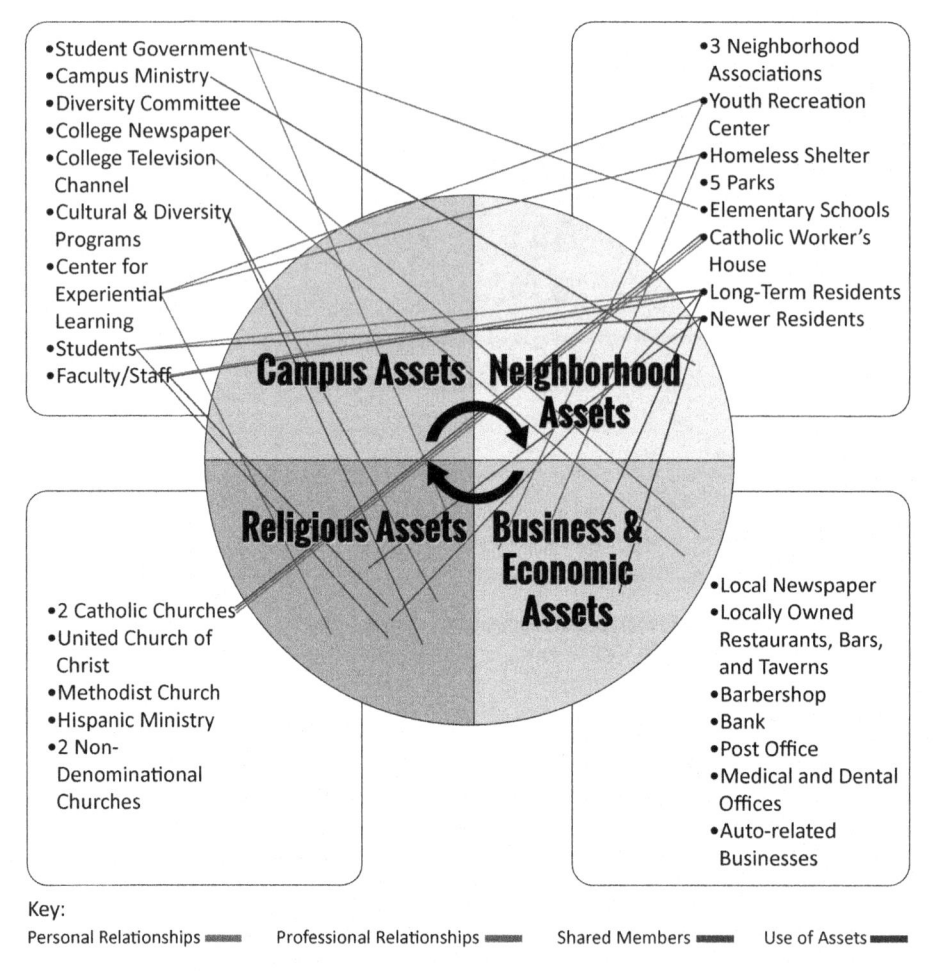

Campus Assets
- Student Government
- Campus Ministry
- Diversity Committee
- College Newspaper
- College Television Channel
- Cultural & Diversity Programs
- Center for Experiential Learning
- Students
- Faculty/Staff

Neighborhood Assets
- 3 Neighborhood Associations
- Youth Recreation Center
- Homeless Shelter
- 5 Parks
- Elementary Schools
- Catholic Worker's House
- Long-Term Residents
- Newer Residents

Religious Assets
- 2 Catholic Churches
- United Church of Christ
- Methodist Church
- Hispanic Ministry
- 2 Non-Denominational Churches

Business & Economic Assets
- Local Newspaper
- Locally Owned Restaurants, Bars, and Taverns
- Barbershop
- Bank
- Post Office
- Medical and Dental Offices
- Auto-related Businesses

Key:
Personal Relationships ▬▬ Professional Relationships ▬▬ Shared Members ▬▬ Use of Assets ▬▬

FIGURE 8.3. Example of a visual asset map based on concept map style.

plan. This process generally requires instructor push-back, especially when working with first- and second-year students, as they are more likely to underestimate the complexity of creating social change. When students work with community organizers to develop the plan, as is preferred, the complexity of developing a sustainable solution will be more apparent.

After designing several potential plans, students pick one and defend it as the most realistic, most steeped in assets, and most likely to be effective. For example, one of the most frequent complaints my general education students heard from people living near campus is that they did not feel welcomed on campus. Students worked in groups of four to develop several solutions to this problem, including setting up a website, sending neighbors tickets to upcoming events on campus, and putting together festivals for neighborhood kids. The student groups presented these plans to the community groups involved in the project. The committee that commissioned our work was excited by the action plans but, unfortunately, dissolved before it was able to implement them. Nonetheless, even when action plans aren't implemented, students gain useful experiences that "transform what they have learned and done through an asset-based process into a concrete and tangible goal for the future" (Garoutte & McCarthy-Gilmore, 2014). Yet the question remains, to what extent did participating in asset mapping promote a move toward greater social awareness?

Data and Methods

In order to better understand whether and how students become more fully prepared for social justice work as a result of asset mapping, survey data were collected from four classes that relied heavily on ABCD-inspired projects. Three of these courses were described above: two Introduction to Sociology courses and a general education course for seniors. The fourth class, an upper-level general education course, was taught by a colleague in another discipline with whom I have collaborated on previous asset-mapping projects (Garoutte & McCarthy-Gilmore, 2014). Like one of the introductory sociology classes, this class was also taught during the three-week January term. Students in this class mapped resources for Latinos and Latinas in the Dubuque community. Ninety students from across these four classes participated in the Institutional Review Board–approved study.

Overall, these students had significant experience with service learning before enrolling in the ABCD-based classes. Among the test group, 84.4 percent of these students had previously been in a college course with a significant community component. This level of engagement is common for students on our campus. It also suggests that any gains made by students as a result of their asset-mapping experiences are above and beyond the benefits they may have received from more traditional forms of service learning.

A control group of ninety-five students was also included in the analyses. The control group was drawn from three Introduction to Sociology classes and an upper-level general education course that did not include ABCD-based activities. These classes were chosen for two primary reasons. First, they drew from a student population similar to those in the asset-mapping courses. The introductory classes were filled primarily with first-year students and a few sophomores; the general education classes were populated primarily by seniors. Further, students in the control group had similar rates of previous community-based learning: 82.1 percent of the control group and 83.2 percent of the test group had previous CBL experience. A chi-square test indicates that the difference between the two groups is insignificant ($p = 0.578$).

The second reason for including these courses in the control group relates to course content. Each of the classes from which the control group was drawn had a significant focus on community. Students in the control group therefore spent significant time learning about communities and how they operate and the relationship between individuals and the larger social world. The ABCD-based courses had similar content. As a result, it is likely that if greater gains were made among the asset-mapping students than those in the control group, then the asset-mapping component was largely responsible.

Student respondents in both the test and control groups completed a survey about their ABCD experiences. The survey included both open-ended and quantitative, Likert-scale questions intended to gauge both involvement in and understanding of community. Students were first asked to rate their level of participation in their own communities. They could respond that they are "very involved" (coded 1), "involved" (2), "somewhat involved" (3), "not very involved" (4), or "not at all involved" (5) in the community. Those who participated in the ABCD courses answered the question both at the beginning of the semester (before asset mapping) and at the end of the term (after their ABCD experiences). Because greater community involvement is key for social justice work, movement toward higher levels of involvement suggest better preparation on the part of students for this type of work.

At the end of the semester, those in the asset-mapping classes were also asked whether their asset-mapping experiences promoted their involvement in the community. Students were asked if they strongly agreed (coded 1), agreed (2), somewhat agreed (3), somewhat disagreed (4), disagreed (5), or strongly disagreed (6) with the statement "My asset-mapping experiences promoted my involvement in the community." This question was asked in part to better understand how students understood their experiences with asset-based community development. It was also used because it seems likely that students who engaged in asset mapping could feel less involved in their community as a result of better understanding its complexities and size. This question is thus another measure of ABCD-style activities' ability to encourage greater connections between students and surrounding neighborhoods.

Involvement in a community is a good start, but it is not enough. If students hold views of the world that do not account for the role of social structure in daily life, then it will be unlikely they will be able to engage in future social justice work in a way that builds communities upward, rather than fostering dependency. To that end, students were surveyed about their understanding of community in two ways. First, students responded to the prompt "Explain the relationship between individuals and the community" by writing their answers in the space provided. Again, students who participated in the ABCD-based courses answered this question in both a pre- and post-test. Those who did not engage in asset mapping explained this relationship at the end of the semester, after they had spent time dealing with issues of community through traditional learning formats. Responses were coded as demonstrating understanding of a reciprocal relationship between community and individuals (coded 2), showing only a one-sided understanding of this relationship (1), or as having little to no understanding of it (0). The asset-mapping students were also asked if their ABCD activities facilitated a stronger understanding of community generally, the specific community they mapped, and the link between individuals and communities. When responding to these questions, students used the same "strongly agree" to "strongly disagree" scale described above. Greater awareness of how communities operate and increased familiarity with a specific community are essential for empowerment efforts for change. To be considered successful as a tool for promoting social awareness and justice work, asset mapping should push students in this direction.

Two types of analysis were completed to assess the potential benefits of asset-based community development. First, changes in community involvement and understanding before and after participation in asset mapping were tested using a paired-sample t-test. Differences in mean responses from the asset-mapping group and the control group were compared using an independent sample t-test. Because the control group had learned about community using traditional pedagogies, differences between the test and control groups allow us to begin to understand how ABCD-inspired work in the classroom compares directly to a more traditional means of achieving the same goal. As is the case with the pre- and posttests, greater community involvement and a better understanding of the relationship between people and their surroundings is suggestive of greater ability to participate in genuine efforts for social justice. If students who participated in asset mapping improve in these areas, then it will be considered successful in that regard.

Results

The analyses begin with an evaluation of how asset mapping affects student investment in community. Table 8.1 compares means for community involvement among asset-mapping students both before and after they engaged in ABCD-inspired practices. Numbers closer to one suggest greater community engagement. As seen below, the mean response moves from "somewhat involved" (3.22) to "involved" (2.89). Although the numerical change is small, the difference is significant. Students report higher levels of involvement after asset mapping than before. It should be noted that this change comes after a short duration (three weeks for two of the classes, sixteen weeks for the other two), and, in most cases, after previous service-learning experiences.

When asked if this shift is the result of their ABCD experiences, students overwhelming agree that it was. Seventy-four students, or just over 87 percent, agree that asset mapping promotes their involvement in the community, as shown in table 8.2. Only eleven of the eighty-five students who answered this question disagree. These are typically students who described themselves as "very involved" before asset mapping began. Notably, not a single student strongly disagreed with this statement.

Table 8.1. Paired-Sample T-Test of Community Involvement Among Asset-Mapping Students.

	Pre-Test	Post Test	Significance
"Overall, how involved are you in your community"	3.22	2.89	.000*

N= 83 Responses are scaled as follows: 1=Very Involved, 2=Involved, 3=Somewhat Involved, 4=Not Very Involved, 5=Not At All Involved

Table 8.2. Frequencies of Responses to "Asset Mapping Promoted My Involvement in the Community."

	Promoted My Involvement in the Community
Strongly Agree	5 (5.9%)
Agree	35 (41.2%)
Somewhat Agree	34 (40.0%)
Somewhat Disagree	0 (0%)
Disagree	11 (12.9%)
Strongly Disagree	0 (0%)

Table 8.3. Independent Sample T-Test of Community Involvement.

	Mean
Control Group	3.32
Asset Mapping Group	2.90

N=180; p = .005; Responses are scaled as follows: 1=Very Involved, 2=Involved, 3=Somewhat Involved, 4=Not Very Involved, 5=Not At All Involved

Table 8.3 presents the results of an independent sample *t*-test that compares the mean scores for community involvement of those who participated in asset mapping and those who did not. The findings corroborate the students' claims that ABCD experiences support increased interest in the community. The difference between the two groups is significant. Students involved with ABCD projects report feeling more connected to the larger community than those who were exposed only to more traditional pedagogical techniques.

Community involvement is important but so too is a firm understanding of how those communities work. Students generally come to our classes with an individualistic view of the world (Brezina, 1996; Brislen & Peoples, 2005; Davis, 1992), yet the relationships between the two are more complex. Moreover, a stronger understanding of the reciprocal nature between individuals and the social structure is more in line with a social justice framework of community-based learning. Indeed, the results of this study show that students who participate in asset-mapping experiences do develop a more nuanced understanding of this relationship.

Students in the test group were asked to explain this relationship between individual actors and their society both at the beginning of the semester (pretest) and at the end of the term (posttest). Answers were analyzed using a paired-sample t-test, the results of which are shown in table 8.4. At the beginning of the semester, the mean score was 0.79, which indicates no real understanding of this relationship. Typical answers at this time were "People should try to do the right thing" and "Don't know." By the end of the semester, however, students' scores increased to a mean of 1.26, which is a statistically significant shift toward greater structural understanding of the relationship between individuals and the community. More typical answers in the posttest include "Individuals both challenge and are constrained by the community; they influence each other," "One effects [sic] the other," and "Individuals make up the community, but the community shapes the individual."

Comparisons between the test group and control group also demonstrate improved community understanding as a result of participating in ABCD-based projects. As seen in table 8.5, those who engage in asset-based activities better understand the relationship between social structure and individuals than those who do not. Indeed, the mean score for the control group is closer to the pretest scores of the asset-mapping group than the posttest scores, even though the control group answered the question at the end of the semester in which course content emphasized this very topic. In other words, students begin to understand that individuals do not exist in isolation and are, in fact, affected by their community as a result of asset-inspired activities. The students themselves attribute this change to their asset-mapping experiences. Table 8.6 presents frequency distributions about what aspects of community they believe asset mapping helped them better understand. Nearly 99 percent of students either strongly agree or agree that ABCD taught them about the concept of community generally. The same number report that they now better understand the mapped community as a result of their asset-based community development experiences. In fact, only one student disagrees with these statements. Likewise, all but one of the students agree that their improved understanding of the individual–community link is the result of asset-based community learning.

Taken as a whole, these finding suggest that students make considerable strides in their ideas about community as a result of their ABCD experiences. In particular,

Table 8.4. Paired Sample T-Test of Student Understanding of Community/Individual Relationship Among Asset-Mapping Students.

	Pre-Test Mean	Post-Test Mean	Significance
Explain Individual-Community Relationship	0.79	1.26	.000*

N=84 Responses are scaled as follows: 0= No Understanding of Relationship 1=Address One Direction of Relationship 2=Address Reciprocal Relationship Between Individual and Society

Table 8.5. Independent-Sample T-Test of Student Understanding of Individual/Community Relationship.

	Control Group (No Asset Mapping)	Test Group (Asset Mapping)	Significance
Explain Individual-Society Relationship	0.55	1.26	.001*

N=185 Responses are scaled as follows: 0= No Understanding of Relationship 1=Address One Direction of Relationship 2=Address Reciprocal Relationship Between Individual and Society

Table 8.6. Frequency Distribution of What Students Learned from Asset-Mapping.

	Taught Concept of Community	Better Understand The Mapped Community	Taught Relationships Between Individuals and Community
Strongly Agree	42 (49.4%)	45 (52.9%)	41 (48.8%)
Agree	42 (49.4%)	39 (45.9%)	41 (48.8%)
Somewhat Agree	0 (0%)	0 (0%)	0 (0%)
Somewhat Disagree	0 (0%)	0 (0%)	0 (0%)
Disagree	1 (1.2%)	1 (1.2%)	1 (2.4%)
Strongly Disagree	0 (0%)	0 (0%)	0 (0%)

students are more likely to understand how community structures affect individuals, gain a better understanding of the communities they map, and feel a greater sense of connection to, and involvement with, community. These changes are, obviously, not social change in and of themselves and, as a result, fall short of the social justice ideals that many argue in favor of. That said, these changes do represent a move toward greater social awareness, which is a significant step toward social justice, and provide support for bringing ABCD-inspired practices into the classroom.

Discussion

Scholars have been debating methods of community-based learning for some time. Many critics of traditional service learning suggest that direct service-learning efforts have the potential to reinforce stereotypes and power relationships between students and community members. They argue that this model entrenches privilege and, essentially, is a means of using local community members—especially those who are most vulnerable (e.g., poor citizens) to benefit relatively privileged college students' confines (Camacho, 2004; Eby, 1998; Mitchell, 2008; Peterson, 2009).

In response, many have called for an approach to community-based learning that is focused on creating real, lasting change in the community. Such efforts require cooperation between faculty, students, and community members. For this to be done well, students and faculty have to invest significant time building bridges between members of the community and campus and engage in long-term relationships in order to grow trust between the two groups. The goal is worthy but challenging to properly enact.

Here, I have suggested that faculty consider adapting elements of ABCD for classroom use as a means for creating a strong basis for social awareness among students. This model of social change focuses on the assets of communities and individuals who are often thought of as lacking resources. Members of the community work together to identify their strengths and solve problems using those resources. The result is sustainable community development that empowers local residents. This involves canvassing the community, talking extensively with—and listening to—residents, and identifying assets with the help of those community members. Creating a community profile and identifying relationships between assets helps students better understand the great richness and diversity in all communities and provides for students a sense of how communities both create and limit opportunities. Students then work from these identified strengths of the community to propose a plan of action to address an issue of concern to community members.

While using these techniques in a single course is unlikely to create lasting change in a community, it does appear to transform the way students think about the social world. Results indicate that after engaging in asset-based experiences, students are (1) more likely to be invested in their communities and (2) less likely to use an individualistic perspective to understand the world around them. In other words, they develop more nuanced understandings of, and stronger connections to, their neighborhoods and the social environments they inhabit. As a result, students' ideas about the community and individuals, the relationship between the two, and their place in the community are significantly changed.

Furthermore, this work can be done in a way that does not overburden already busy faculty while promoting reciprocal relationships between students and community members. Asset-based community development projects can, as described here, be confined easily to a single semester. They may also, however, be expanded to last much longer, depending on the interest of the community and ability of faculty. As such, the practice and outcomes of these projects are more in keeping with the goals of community-based learning with a social justice focus.

LISA GAROUTTE is Associate Professor of Sociology and Codirector of Gender Studies at Loras College. Her pedagogical interests include using experiential learning, quantitative data, and classroom activities to promote a stronger understanding of equality and justice.

References

Battistoni, R M., Longo, N. V., & Jayandadhan, S. R. (2009). Acting locally in a flat world: Global citizenship and the democratic practice of service-learning. *Journal of Higher Education Outreach and Engagement, 13*(2), 89–107.

Bonner Foundation. (2012, April 12). Community asset mapping: A critical strategy for service. Retrieved from http://bonnernetwork.pbworks.com/f/BonCurCommAssetMap.pdf.

Brezina, T. (1996). Teaching inequality: A simple counterfactual exercise. *Teaching Sociology, 24*(2), 218–224.

Brislen, W., & Peoples, C. (2005). Using a hypothetical distribution of grades to introduce social stratification. *Teaching Sociology, 33*(1), 74–80.

Camacho, M. (2004, Summer). Power and privilege: Community service learning in Tijuana. *Michigan Journal of Community Service Learning*, pp. 31–42.

Chesler, M., Ford, K., Galura, J., & Charbeneau, J. (2006). Peer facilitators as border crossers in community service learning. *Teaching Sociology, 34*(4), 341–356.

Cone, R., Kiesa, A., & Longo, N. V. (2006). *Raise your voice (A student guide to making positive social change)*. Boston, MA: Campus Compact.

Davis, N. (1992). Teaching inequality: Student resistance, paralysis, and rage. *Teaching Sociology, 20*(3), 232–238.

Eby, J. (1998). Why service-learning is bad. Retrieved from http://www.messiah.edu/agape/pdf%20files/wrongsvc.

Eyler, J., & Giles, D. E., Jr. (1999). *Where's the learning in service-learning?* San Francisco, CA: Jossey-Bass.

Garoutte, L., & McCarthy-Gilmore, K. (2014). Preparing students for community-based learning using an asset-based approach. *Journal of the Scholarship of Teaching and Learning, 14*(5), 48–61.

Green, A. (2003). Difficult stories: Service-learning, race, class, and whiteness. *College Composition and Communication, 55*(2), 276–301.

Kretzmannn, J. P., & McKnight, J. L. (1993). *Building communities from the inside out: A path toward finding and mobilizing a community's assets*. Skokie, IL: ACTA.

Lewis, T. (2004). Service learning for social change? Lessons from a liberal arts college. *Teaching Sociology, 32*(1), 94–108.

Mitchell, T. D. (2008, Spring). Traditional vs. critical service-learning: Engaging the literature to differentiate two models. *Michigan Journal of Community Service Learning*, pp. 50–65.

Mobley, C. (2007). Breaking ground: Engaging undergraduates in social change through service learning. *Teaching Sociology, 35*(2), 125–137.

Mooney, L., & Edwards, B. (2001). Experiential learning in sociology: Service learning and other community-based learning initiatives. *Teaching Sociology, 29*(2), 181–194.

Murphy, J., & Rash, D. (2008). Service-learning, contact theory, and building black communities. *The Negro Educational Review, 59*(1–2), 63–78.

Peterson, T. H. (2009). Engaged scholarship: Reflections and research on the pedagogy of social change. *Teaching in Higher Education, 14*(5): 541–552.

Petrov, L. (2013). A pilot study of service-learning in a Spanish heritage speaker course: Community engagement, identity, and language in the Chicago area. *Hispania, 96*(2), 310–327.

Schamber, J. F., & Mahoney, S. L. (2008). The development of political awareness and social justice citizenship through community-based learning in a first-year general education seminar. *The Journal of General Education, 57*(2), 75–99.

Steiner, S., Warkentin, B., & Smith, M. (2011). Community forums: A unique approach to community service-learning. *Canadian Journal of Education, 34*(1), 282–307.

Stoecker, R. (1996). Sociology and social action: Guest editor's introduction. *Sociological Imagination.* Retrieved from http://www.soc.iastate.edu/sapp/soc506socialaction.pdf.

9 Transforming Awareness into Activism: Teaching Systems and Social Justice in an Interdisciplinary Water Course

Cathy Willermet, Anja Mueller, and David Alm

> If situations cannot be created that enable the young to deal with feelings of being manipulated by outside forces, there will be far too little sense of agency among them. Without a sense of agency, young people are unlikely to pose significant questions, the existentially rooted questions in which learning begins.
> —Maxine Greene *The Dialectics of Freedom,* 1988

> I believe that an education bereft of a systematic study of key social issues (local, regional, national, and international) and how they can be addressed by individuals, alone or in cooperation with others, is sorely incomplete.
> —Samuel Totten *The Importance of Teaching Social Issues: Our Pedagogical Creeds,* 2014

MOST REAL-WORLD PROBLEMS have fuzzy boundaries and require complex solutions. The more disciplines integrate their efforts at solving these problems, the more successful they will be at finding solutions (Begg & Vaughan, 2011; Holley, 2015; Lawrence, 2010). "Wicked" problems are a special class of problem arising from extreme degrees of uncertainty, risk, and social complexity (Brown, Deane, Harris, & Russell, 2010). Examples of wicked problems include inequities in health, global poverty, campus violence, racial genocide, and so on (Rittel & Webber, 1973). We define global access to affordable, clean water as a wicked problem.

Wicked problems are particularly difficult to solve because there is no "right" solution that solves it completely (unlike, say, a math problem); rather, there are better and worse solutions, depending on the context of both the problem and its solution (Brown et al., 2010; Lawrence, 2010; Rittel & Webber, 1973). For our students to be empowered to effect change, they must learn to collaborate with others, particularly across disciplines, since, as Freeman (2000) suggests, "our educated capacity in one discipline (or more realistically in one sub-discipline) tends to be associated with trained incapacity in other fields of relevant knowledge" (p. 484).

Water insecurity and water pollution are major issues in the world (Freeman, 2000; Pawar, 2013). Water is necessary for healthy ecosystems and human health and society but is controlled and regulated by economic and political forces (Pawar, 2013). Fair water sharing in terms of distribution and allocation to all stakeholders is complex; everyone, including the poor, need access to enough safe drinking water, but there are often high, often unevenly shared costs of accessing this water. Freeman (2000) argues that

> water resources policy problems are wicked then because they challenge us to confront water policy problems on four fronts simultaneously: (1) we must transcend our disciplinary camps and face the uncertainties that ride with combining our sciences; (2) we must integrate two types of knowledge (i.e., our scientifically processed traditions of knowledge must be adapted to site-specific circumstance with the assistance of people who know important, but different things than scientists know); (3) water resource issues simultaneously affect conflicting stakeholders and biotic complexity across multiple levels; and (4) individual rationality of particular actors must be constrained by local organizations in ways that empower people to provide themselves and wider society with sustainable common property regimes that can manage the interdependence of people, water, and biota in resource acquisition, allocation, and maintenance. All of this requires effective local organizations that can provide the social and organizational capacity for work that cannot be accomplished by individual citizens as resource appropriators or environmentalists, by central bureaucratic managers, or by scientists. (p. 487)

Interdisciplinary courses focused on wicked problems are one way to help students develop these skills. Interdisciplinary thinking integrates ideas from several fields or perspectives, including across scientific disciplines (Lawrence, 2010; Spelt, Biemans, Tobi, Luning, & Mulder, 2009). An interdisciplinary approach is essential to solving wicked problems, where both the problem and solution are unknown (Barisonzi & Thorn, 2003; Eisen, Hall, Lee, & Zupko, 2009; Freeman, 2000; Willermet, Mueller, Juris, Drake, Upadhaya, & Chhetri, 2013). A solid foundation in a discipline increases students' ability to bridge disciplines. Interdisciplinary understanding, then, integrates knowledge from two or more disciplines to produce cognitive enhancement (Boix-Mansilla & Duraisingh, 2007). Interdisciplinary education encourages students to analyze problems from multiple perspectives. Students are taught to contextualize both problems and solutions within a larger world context, to empathize and compromise with multiple stakeholders, and to tolerate ambiguity and complexity in solutions

(DeZure, 2010; Willermet et al., 2013). It is often the integration of disciplines and the resulting synthesis of knowledge that provide the context for appropriate solutions (Brewer, 1999).

Critical pedagogy takes the position that there exists a power imbalance that causes inequity and injustice (Freire, 1970). The resulting oppression favors some stakeholders over others. A critical pedagogy approach to an issue raises awareness of this imbalance and allows solutions that rebalance social justice to be developed (Darder, Baltodano, & Torres, 2009; Freire, 1970; hooks, 1994; Ladson-Billings, 1995; Shulman, 2002). We want students to be skilled in moving from awareness to action, to reflect and act on a situation in order to alter it. As faculty, we must intentionally develop these skills in ourselves as well as in our students, making education a transformative experience for all.

The Awareness/Action Gap

Promoting responsible citizenship related to water, a limited resource, requires the development of awareness, sensitivity, attitude, skills, and active participation in water issues (adapted from Hungerford & Volk, 1990). Awareness of the issues—such as water scarcity, ownership, pollution, and cost, to name a few (e.g., Pawar, 2013)—can cause students to be overwhelmed with the sheer scope of the social policy dimensions involved to solve water access problems. When overwhelmed, a student's sense of personal agency, or belief that she or he can influence a problem effectively, is diminished (Zimmerman & Cleary, 2006).

Awareness of an issue is a necessary but not sufficient condition to create a change in behavior. A change in behavior can come from increased education about an issue (e.g., Mosca, Mochari, Christian, Berra, Taubert, Mills, & Simpson, 2006) but not necessarily so. Additional behavior change motivators are situation factors, such as a personal experience with the issue (Eriksen & Gill, 2010); personality factors, such as attitudes and an internal locus of motivation; and development of skills needed to obtain the change (Hungerford & Volk, 1990). In order for students to feel they can be agents of change, they need a desire for action, an understanding of how best to act, and training in the skills needed to act.

Students with personal experience with water issues (water availability or quality) would feel a stronger need for action. A change in personal agency, then, often involves experiencing a concern locally. Personal agency involves a person's right to speak and act for him- or herself (Henze, 2000). In the water course, we repeatedly make the point that when outside influences coopt agency of stakeholders through, say, externally driven water development projects, this generally leads to unsuccessful outcomes. Rather, the needs and experiences of others for whom one wishes to act must be central to the action of those wishing to help. Connecting local social knowledge, technological knowledge, and an action plan, then, can most effectively employ the students' agency.

However, "as many environmental problems have social, economic and cultural causes, the solutions are often social, not just environmental" (Eriksen & Gill, 2010, p. 815). A societal change requires people's motivations to move from local, individual concerns toward collective action (Hau, 2000). Barr (2008) describes the gap between intentions and action as complex, the rationalistic model of behavioral change (Awareness→ Information→ Decision→ Action) being too simplistic to be useful. Students may be intellectually interested in activism but experience behavioral barriers, including a resistance to self-reflection and transgressing boundaries, which students often find stressful (hooks, 1994). Students have access to so much information about social problems and yet find it difficult to act; they despair into inactivity (Greene, 2009). Can we influence students, then, through a single course?

The Course: Water as Life, Death, and Power

The initial impetus for this course came from students in the Central Michigan University chapter of Universities Allied for Essential Medicines (UAEM). The students involved in UAEM were actively engaging their peers with global health inequities issues and asked faculty advisors to develop undergraduate courses that combined interdisciplinary teaching with solving real-world problems, combining theory with activism. To this end, we developed and taught (twice now) an interdisciplinary course around the wicked problem of inequities in access to and affordability of clean water. We do this through the disciplinary lenses of anthropology, biology, and chemistry. The name reflects the social justice slant to the course: Water as Life, Death, and Power (hereafter called the "water course").

Students were assigned to interdisciplinary groups based on their major and year. For a final project, the groups had to develop a proposal to an existing NGO, governmental agency, or other organization to solve a water problem. Project topics were up to the group but had to contain the following elements: (1) a relationship to water, (2) demonstrated interdisciplinary thinking, (3) implementation strategies, (4) a way to measure success, and (5) an advocacy or activism aspect. Student groups were required to present the following items over the course of the semester as stages of their project: a concept map, an elevator pitch, an abstract, and two progress reports. The final project was a poster presentation at the campus-wide Student Research and Creative Endeavors Exhibition. Students were required to present some final deliverable, be it a model, proposal, or white paper. All proposals needed to have an identified agency to which they were targeting their advocacy. Students were encouraged to actually present their ideas to this agency in person, via email, or through the postal system.

Shulman (2002) notes that engagement in scholarly teaching supports "moral action aimed at cultural change" (p. vii). We developed this water course using an integrated team approach through cooperative interdisciplinarity (Boden, 1999; Klein, 2010) with open inquiry activities designed to encourage reflection on moral actions people could take to elicit a cultural change. A key component of the water course, then, focused on empowering students to develop and act on projects centered on water issues. Students worked in teams to research issues and develop grassroots campaigns with the goal of improving a water-issue outcome. Students, however, generally have little to no knowledge of or experience with translating their interests and awareness into action.

Measuring Awareness in the Water Course

We have previously documented increased activism and awareness if water issues in our students through the utilization of student surveys (Mueller, Juris, Willermet, Drake, Upadhaya, & Chhetri, 2014). Here we employed textual analysis to elicit themes identifying increased awareness in our students.

The water course was designed to increase awareness and improve activism skills. The first time we taught this course, our assessment plan centered on measuring interdisciplinary understanding, which we argue is essential to solving wicked problems (Brown et al., 2010; Willermet et al., 2013). Using an interdisciplinary rubric, we documented increased interdisciplinary understanding (Mueller et al., 2014). Here we looked in more detail at the awareness of specific water issues and themes.

To capture awareness, we asked students to respond to an open-ended prompt about water issues at both the beginning and end of the semester. The prompt was "When you think about 'water issues,' what comes to mind?" The prompt was designed to elicit ideas from which we could identify common themes. We were interested to learn whether dominant themes changed in substance or frequency from the beginning to the end of the semester.

We identified themes using both repetitions of common words and of elements conspicuously missing (Ryan & Bernard, 2003). We initially generated sorted words (cutting and sorting method) to generate common word lists. Then the text was analyzed via Jason Davies's (2015) online word cloud generator to confirm word repetition concordance. Subthemes were identified using the key words in context (KWIC) method (Ryan & Weisner, 1996). These are qualitative methods commonly used with short text analysis (Ryan & Bernard, 2003; Ryan & Weisner, 1996; Tesch, 1990).

In the beginning of the semester (table 9.1, sample 1), fourteen students responded to the open-ended prompt, generating 203 coded responses with 99 unique terms in the word list. The words were then sorted into subthemes using the KWIC method. At the end of the semester (table 9.1, sample 2), fifteen students responded to the prompt, generating 282 coded responses with 143 unique terms in the word list. The words were sorted into subthemes using the same method as above. We recognize the potential for student responses to reflect what they may have interpreted as what we instructors "wanted to hear." We controlled for this potential bias by scoring the activity as completed/not completed. We informed the students that points for this activity were

Table 9.1. Themes emerging from the open-ended prompts.

Theme	Sample 1 N_1	Sample 2 N_2
Clean water is essential to life	40	31
Water is economically useful	22	23
Water is endangered	92	151
The water problems are global, but mainly far away	10	1
We have ways to address our water problems	19	19

issued solely on the basis of completing the activity without regard for the length or specificity of their answers. We aggregated responses for subsequent analysis.

Several themes emerged from both lists: (1) clean water is essential to life; (2) water is economically useful; (3) water is endangered; (4) the water problems are global but mainly far away; and (5) we have ways to address our water problems (see table 9.1). A sixth theme referred to those who bear responsibility (see below). Some striking differences could be seen between the two samples. For example, mentions of the idea that the water supply is threatened increased by 160 percent ($N_1 = 92$, $N_2 = 151$). Other themes seem unchanged, as in the theme *We have ways to address our water problems* ($N_1 = 19$, $N_2 = 19$). However, an examination of the subthemes can shed some light on what may have changed in students' minds.

The tone of the subthemes shifted from the beginning to the end of the semester. For example, although students in both samples expressed the theme *Clean water is essential to life* ($N_1 = 40$, $N_2 = 31$), students expressed twice as often the explicit statement that access to clean water is a basic human right ($N_1 = 5$, $N_2 = 10$). Students also indicated an increased awareness that water issues can be local: in the first sample, more students stated that water availability is an issue for people living in developing countries ($N_1 = 10$, $N_2 = 4$), while in the second sample they mentioned water issues in the U.S. almost exclusively ($N_1 = 1$, $N_2 = 11$), a drop of 90 percent. Examination of the differences in the subthemes embedded in *Water is endangered* show nearly twice as many mentions that water is depleted by economic activity ($N_1 = 5$, $N_2 = 35$), an increase of 700 percent. Terms repeatedly mentioned included who pays for water, privatization, ownership, power, and the rights of corporations/industry. Finally, while students did not change their opinions about having ways to address water problems ($N_1 = 19$, $N_2 = 19$), they shifted from focusing more on increasing water treatment, a technological fix ($N_1 = 13$, $N_2 = 8$), to increased legislation and citizen responsibility, a social fix ($N_1 = 6$, $N_2 = 11$).

Finally, a pattern emerged regarding those who bear responsibility for solving the scarcity/access to clean water issue (see table 9.2). In sample 1, mention was made of

Table 9.2. Subtheme differences within the theme *Water is endangered.*

Subtheme	Sample 1 N_1	Sample 2 N_2
Ecosystem issues are to blame	26	20
Water access issues are to blame	18	33
Economic issues are to blame	5	35
Pathogens are to blame	6	18
Pollution/solids are to blame	21	21
Chemicals in the water are to blame	9	16
Emotional worries are to blame	7	8
TOTALS	92	151

governmental agencies, regulations, and legislation (Clean Water Act, Environmental Protection Agency, environmental justice; $N_1 = 6$). Citizen responsibility for conserving water, or protecting the Great Lakes, was equally important ($N_1 = 6$); responsibility was mentioned twelve times. However, sample 2 looked quite different. Responsibility was mentioned sixty-one times. Political and governmental issues were mentioned twenty-six times, and students mentioned shared political responsibility at the local, state, national, and international levels. Citizen cooperation and local community involvement in actions and solutions were mentioned fourteen times. Corporate power, corporate liability, and unsustainable industry practices were mentioned a total of twenty-one times.

What does all this mean? At the beginning of the semester, students were focused on vague water issues in "Third World" countries. At the end of the semester, their focus was more local and specifically mentioned political control and human rights. Interestingly, students in sample 1 mentioned the Great Lakes as being perhaps vulnerable but largely protected due to their sheer volume. As these students are in a Michigan university, this is perhaps not surprising. However, the list of specific endangered locales in sample 2 included Michigan cities that lie on the Great Lakes. The focus on local actions, local politics, and industry reflect a reframing of the water issues from unspecified global water issues to local issues with government, community, and industry actors. This is positive, as it can result in increased student agency. It is more difficult to move from awareness to action if the problem is seen as vague and far away.

Reflections on Teaching the Course

Each of us came to this class from different disciplines and teaching experiences. However, we all shared the values of effective teaching and interests in social justice and, of course, in the wicked problem of availability of and access to clean water. Here are some of our personal reflections on the challenges and benefits of collaboratively and explicitly teaching toward the goal of raising awareness and encouraging activism on water issues.

> ALM: I think that we academics are no different from other humans in that we tend to see the world primarily through the tools that interest us the most. With a background in plant physiology and ecology, and an ongoing interest in simulation modeling, I have often approached complex problems by considering the situation as a set of abstracted, interacting systems and trying to represent these interactions with some sort of diagram or modeling tool, such as a causal network diagram. I find this sort of thing useful, and I am eager to teach the skills when I have the opportunity. And as a biologist, I have used many lectures to raise awareness of the types of biological knowledge needed to understand various environmental problems. However, simultaneous coteaching was a new experience that required some adjustment. It takes significant extra time, for example, to discuss and clarify criteria in order to make decisions. How much detail should be covered for a given topic and which topics to cover—these questions are difficult enough when you're doing it by yourself; when you have three opinions it takes more time. Fortunately, our regular weekly meetings were enough to get the job done, and it was worth the effort. The most enlightening aspect for me, personally, was the value of explicit teaching of activism and action. In the beginning, I thought of the activism component of the student projects as being minor, "some day we'll do this," as if the real world was someplace else, sometime in the future. These were "student" projects, after all, and some people are drawn to activism while others are not. I now see the value of guiding students to make a solution action plan and take real steps, now, however small. The understanding that they gain regarding their own agency is something that I had to see to appreciate the value of teaching it.

> MUELLER: I think two things are necessary to effectively collaborate and teach together across fields: trust and the willingness to learn from each other. What inhibits the process are inherent biases and that most people have developed a specific approach to solve problems that they are comfortable with and that is related to their field. To overcome that so that you can effectively, collaboratively teach, you need to have the time to listen and eventually incorporate different problem-solving approaches into your own thinking.
>
> The students have to go through the same process in their groups. We formed the groups based on diverse backgrounds, so everybody worked with people from different fields and backgrounds (i.e., different approaches to solving problems). But since we as faculty had just gone through the same process, we had become aware of some of our inherent biases. With that we could specifically point out these biases to the students, making it easier for the students to overcome those barriers. Making all students listen to the others was more difficult; most students eventually figured it out, but in some cases

personality stood in the way. I think what made the process easier for the students was that the groups chose projects that were important to them. Since they were personally affected by the project they chose, their willingness to do everything to solve the problem increased, and that included listening to others that they were originally not comfortable with.

WILLERMET: I think the best way to highlight to students the advantages of interdisciplinary work is to model it for them. Collaborative teaching, then, is essential. This course would have been much less effective if we had come in separately to teach our three content areas. The students needed to see us collaborate and support each other's knowledge. Also, they needed to see us sometimes see issues differently and watch how we respectfully worked that out. And we sometimes explicitly discussed the interdisciplinary nature of the topic at hand (What are the political ramifications of this? With whom might we talk for a perspective on this?). Students were encouraged to use these skills when working in their own groups. As students are interested in the tough questions (their chosen topics were wicked problems, all) they were motivated to try to solve them with a team of people bringing different skills to the project. Our explicit and continued insistence on interdisciplinary team-based solutions, supported by specific agency-based skill development, helped students to shape their projects into ones that could, if implemented, have a real impact. For example, everyone now knows not only what a "white paper" is but also how to write one.

Teaching this way is more time-consuming, as we had to essentially teach the whole course (not just a third of the course) and attend weekly one-hour meetings. We had to be organized a week in advance (no last-minute lecture prep)! But it was so rewarding. On a professional level, I was able to learn new things, both content and teaching related. On a personal level, I felt supported and enjoyed the teamwork and camaraderie we developed over the semester.

Comments by students underscore that they are linking awareness and activism in their own minds:

- "I think it's important for different fields to come together and develop a solution to the increasingly urgent water crisis."
- "I am much more curious about water issues! I want to know more. I don't like what I know and I want to help!"
- "I didn't realize how serious the water issue is in the US and globally. Hopefully more people take action to help slow down water depletion."
- "It is troubling that the cost of even dirty water is so high in some areas, and until everyone has access to clean, affordable water global equality will not be possible." (Willermet et al., 2013).

As Eriksen and Gill (2010) mention, solutions are often social. Bridging the gap between awareness and action often requires a goal that seems reachable, and local problems that students have experienced or can operationalize can be a step into action, removing those behavioral barriers and reducing the stress mentioned in hooks (1994). Here we have documented both an increased awareness of water issues and increased awareness of the actors and possible actions needed to begin to address them. Can we influence students, then, through a single course? We believe so; through the discussion of issues, and practice with the means to address them, we aspired to inspire, to encourage students to develop into active participants in the larger world.

CATHY WILLERMET is Associate Professor in the Department of Sociology, Anthropology, and Social Work at Central Michigan University.

ANJA MUELLER is Professor in the Department of Chemistry and Biochemistry at Central Michigan University.

DAVID ALM is a fixed-term faculty member in the Department of Biology as well as the Department of Business Information Systems at Central Michigan University.

References

Barisonzi, J., & Thorn, M. (2003). Teaching revolution: Issues in interdisciplinary education. *College Teaching*, 51(1), 5–8.
Barr, S. (2008). *Environment and society: Sustainability, policy, and the citizen*. Hampshire, England: Ashgate.
Begg, M. D., & Vaughan, R. D. (2011). Are biostatistics students prepared to succeed in the era of interdisciplinary science? (And how will we know?) *The American Statistician*, 65(2), 71–79.
Boden, M. A. (1999). What is interdisciplinarity? In R. Cunningham (Ed.), *Interdisciplinarity and the organization of knowledge in Europe* (pp. 13–24). Luxembourg City, Luxembourg: Office for Official Publications of the European Communities.
Boix-Mansilla, V., & Duraisingh, E. D. (2007). Targeted assessment of students' interdisciplinary work: An empirically grounded framework proposed. *The Journal of Higher Education*, 7(2), 215–237.
Brewer, G. D. (1999). The challenges of interdisciplinarity. *Policy Sciences*, 32(4), 327–337.
Brown, V. A., Deane, P. M., Harris, J. A., & Russell, J. Y. (2010). Towards a just and sustainable future. In V. A. Brown, J. A. Harris, & J. Y. Russell (Eds.), *Tackling wicked problems: Through the transdisciplinary imagination* (pp. 3–15). London, England: Earthscan.
Darder, A., Baltodano, M. P., & Torres, R. D. (Eds.). (2009). *The critical pedagogy reader*. New York, NY: Routledge.
Davies, J. (2015). Online word cloud generator [Computer software]. Retrieved from www.jasondavies.com/wordcloud/about/.
DeZure, D. (2010). Interdisciplinary pedagogies in higher education. In J. Frodeman, J. T. Klein, & C. Mitcham (Eds.), *The Oxford handbook of interdisciplinarity* (pp. 372–386). Oxford, England: Oxford University Press.
Eisen, A., Hall, A., Lee, T. S., & Zupko, J. (2009). Teaching water: Connecting across disciplines and into daily life to address complex societal issues. *College Teaching*, 57(2), 99–104.

Eriksen, C., & Gill, N. (2010). Bushfire and everyday life: Examining the awareness-action "gap" in changing rural landscapes. *Geoforum, 41*, 814–825.

Freeman, D. M. (2000). Wicked water problems: Sociology and local water organizations in addressing water resources policy. *Journal of the American Water Resources Association, 36*(3), 485–491.

Freire, P. (1970). *Pedagogy of the oppressed*. New York, NY: The Seabury Press.

Greene, M. (1988). *The dialectics of freedom*. New York, NY: Teachers College Press.

Greene, M. (2009). In search of a critical pedagogy. In A. Darder, M. P. Baltodano, & R. D. Torres (Eds.), *The critical pedagogy reader* (pp. 84–96). New York, NY: Routledge.

Hau, C. S. (2000). On representing others: Intellectuals, pedagogy, and the uses of error. In M. R. Hames-Garcia & P. M. L. Moya (Eds.), *Reclaiming identity: Realist theory and the predicament of postmodernism* (pp. 133–170). Berkeley: University of California Press.

Henze, B. R. (2000). Who says who says? The epistemological grounds for agency in liberatory political projects. In M. R. Hames-Garcia & P. M. L. Moya (Eds.), *Reclaiming identity: Realist theory and the predicament of postmodernism* (pp. 229–250). Berkeley: University of California Press.

Holley, K. A. (2015). Doctoral education and the development of an interdisciplinary identity. *Innovations in Education and Teaching International, 52*(6), 642–652.

hooks, b. (1994). *Teaching to transgress: Education as the practice of freedom*. New York, NY: Routledge.

Hungerford, H. R., & Volk, T. L. (1990). Changing learner behavior through environmental education. *The Journal of Environmental Education, 21*(3), 8–21.

Klein, J. T. (2010). A taxonomy of interdisciplinarity. In R. Frodeman, J. Thompson Klein, & C. Mitcham (Eds.), *The Oxford handbook of interdisciplinarity* (pp. 15–30). Oxford, England: Oxford University Press.

Ladson-Billings, G. (1995). Toward a theory of culturally relevant pedagogy. *American Educational Research Journal, 32*(3), 465–491.

Lawrence, R. K. (2010). Beyond disciplinary confinement to imaginative transdisciplinarity. In V. A. Brown, J. A. Harris, & J. Y. Russell (Eds.), *Tackling wicked problems: Through the transdisciplinary imagination* (pp. 16–30). London, England: Earthscan.

Mosca, L., Mochari, H., Christian, A., Berra, K., Taubert, K., Mills, T., & Simpson, S. L. (2006). National study of women's awareness, preventive action, and barriers to cardiovascular health. *Circulation, 113*, 525–534.

Mueller, A., Juris, S. J., Willermet, C., Drake, E., Upadhaya, S., & Chhetri, P. (2014). Assessing interdisciplinary learning and student activism in a water issues course. *Journal of the Scholarship of Teaching and Learning, 14*(2), 111–132.

Pawar, M. (2013). Water insecurity: A case for social policy action by social workers. *Australian Social Work, 66*(2), 248–260.

Rittel, H. W. J., & Webber, M. M. (1973). Dilemmas in a general theory of planning. *Policy Science, 4*, 155–169.

Ryan, G. W., & Bernard, H. R. (2003). Techniques to identify themes. *Field Methods, 15*(1), 85–109.

Ryan, G. W., & Weisner, T. (1996). Analyzing words in brief descriptions: Fathers and mothers describe their children. *Cultural Anthropology Methods Journal, 8*(3), 13–16.

Shulman, L. S. (2002). *Ethics of inquiry: Issues in the scholarship of teaching and learning*. Stanford, CA: Carnegie Foundation for the Advancement of Teaching and Learning.

Spelt, E. J. H., Biemans, H. J. A., Tobi, H., Luning, P. A., & Mulder, M. (2009). Teaching and learning in interdisciplinary higher education: A systematic review. *Educational Psychology Review, 21*, 365–378.

Tesch, R. (1990). *Qualitative research: Analysis types and software tools*. New York, NY: Falmer.

Totten, S. (2014). *The importance of teaching social issues: Our pedagogical creed*. New York, NY: Routledge.
Willermet, C., Mueller, A., Juris, S. J., Drake, E., Upadhaya, S., & Chhetri, P. (2013). Water as life, death, and power: Building an integrated interdisciplinary course combining perspectives from anthropology, biology, and chemistry. *Journal of the Scholarship of Teaching and Learning, 13*(5), 105–123.
Zimmerman, B. J., & Cleary, T. J. (2006). Adolescents' development of personal agency: The role of self-efficacy beliefs and self-regulatory skill. In F. Pajares & T. Urdan (Eds.), *Self-efficacy beliefs of adolescents* (pp. 45–69). Charlotte, NC: Information Age.

IV.
Classroom Practices of Reflection and Counternarratives

10 Swinging with a Double-Edged Sword: Using Counterstories to Fight for Social Justice in the Classroom

Scott D. Farver and Alyssa Hadley Dunn

> Many stories matter. Stories have been used to dispossess and to malign. But stories can also be used to empower, and to humanize. Stories can break the dignity of a people. But stories can also repair that broken dignity.
> —Chimamanda Ngozi Adichie (2009)

ON THE FIRST day of class, we watched "The Danger of a Single Story," a highly regarded TED Talk by Nigerian author Chimamanda Adichie (2009). Its overarching themes of combatting stereotypes and recognizing multiple voices set the stage for our overall course, which focused on examining issues of power, privilege, and oppression in K-12 schools and society. After watching, we did a "chalk talk," a silent activity where students compiled their reflections on the board in words, phrases, or images. They drew arrows or check marks to indicate agreement or connection with other people's ideas. This "conversation" lasted for about five minutes, with moments of silence when students stood back reading quietly and more "talkative" moments when multiple students were writing on the board at once. Finally, I asked students to read the entire board and share any portions that stood out to them. Five students picked the same comment: "I feel like people only know me by a single story. I want to be more than what the media says I am." The author of the comment did not take ownership of the comment, nor did I ask the person to identify her- or himself. However, in a written reflection later, a student wrote: "It was me. I wrote the note about being a single story. I was so happy with the way people said they didn't want me to feel that way and they wanted to hear what made me ME beyond the stereotypes. I hope I have the courage to speak up throughout the semester to tell them. The fact that we started with this video makes me think I will be supported in developing that courage." By providing a space for students to see beyond a single story—and by following this up throughout the semester with opportunities for students to share their own experiences in the form of counterstories—I hoped to model for them the importance of fighting for social justice both personally and professionally. This chapter underscores the importance of counterstorytelling as pedagogy and also the delicate nature of employing such a practice.

The guiding question for this text is "How can the Scholarship of Teaching and Learning (SoTL) be used to make education a transformative experience for *all* learners and teachers?" As teacher educators, we take this call seriously in our work, which centers on issues of social justice and equity in education. The classes that we teach focus broadly on issues of diversity, power, privilege, oppression, and equity, including difficult and often controversial topics like race, ethnicity, gender, sexuality, linguistic hegemony, immigration, religion, and (dis)ability. We believe strongly that our pedagogy has the potential to be transformative for our students and ourselves (hooks, 1994) as we evolve in our quest toward humanization through a constant state of becoming (Blackburn, 2014). That is, we do not believe we have reached some mirage of mastery in social justice education, but we realize that we, like our students, are constantly learning and growing from our lived experiences.

We enter the conversation within the Scholarship of Teaching and Learning from a unique perspective. As mentioned in an earlier chapter, some scholars may see their roles as university teachers as secondary (or even a hindrance) to what they may consider to be their "real" work of research, particularly if they work at a research-intensive university. This balance is not to be taken lightly, especially when considering tenure and promotion requirements that may place significantly higher value on research and grant-getting than teaching. SoTL, though, challenges us not to view scholarship and teaching as mutually exclusive but rather as mutually supportive in order to best serve the students we teach. It is also a place for us as practitioners to reflect on previous theory and build on and add to that knowledge (Hutchings & Huber, 2008).

Our work as former K–12 public school teachers and our current positions as teacher educators, or those who prepare the next generation of K–12 teachers, allows us to see teaching at the university level as an extension of our former careers. As former teachers who believe teaching can be transformative, we come naturally to viewing our work through an SoTL lens—that teaching in and of itself is scholarly (Boyer, 1990; Menges & Weimar, 1996). By sharing and critically reflecting on pieces of our practice, we hope to link our pedagogy and our research. SoTL allows us to do just that.

To explain the work of disrupting harmful dominant narratives, we take up the metaphor of our pedagogy being a sword. In this metaphor, our teaching allows us to cut through damaging rhetoric or beliefs in order to help future teachers recognize systems of oppression and privilege. It is our hope that in doing this, we help our students resist such narratives in order to become caring educators to their future students. However, we have found that in using this strategy, there can be unforeseen effects. While we use our sword to do what we consider to be "good" work, we sometimes have neglected the other side of the sword, which is just as sharp and can undermine the work we are trying to do. We encourage those who engage in SoTL and who examine our experiences to remember not only the power of the weapon we choose but also its unintended consequences.

Connecting SoTL to Critical Race Theory

In analyzing our experiences as teacher educators in light of SoTL, we also draw on Critical Race Theory (CRT), a framework that grew out of Critical Legal Studies in the 1980s. CRT was initially used by activists and scholars in examining and transforming relationships between race, racism, and power (Delgado & Stefancic, 2012). At the core of CRT is the belief that racism is a normalized part of life in the United States (Bell, 1992). CRT hopes to unmask this entrenched racism (Ladson-Billings, 1998) and gives scholars a framework to investigate multiple forms of oppression in the daily lives of people of color (Pérez-Huber, 2010). Following a central tenet of CRT, we believe lived experiences of People of Color* to be not only acceptable "funds of knowledge" (Moll, Amanti, Neff, & Gonzalez, 1992) but critical to understanding issues of power, oppression, and subordination (Bernal, 2002; Delgado & Stefancic, 2012; Yosso, Parker, Solórzano, & Lynn, 2004). Important narratives, or counterstories, come from "those whose experiences are not often told" (Solórzano & Yosso, 2002, p. 32) and speak against dominant ways of knowing that currently shape how we are socialized to understand various concepts. The intent of these counterstories is to disrupt such racist epistemologies. As Ladson-Billings (1998) writes, "Stories by people of color can catalyze the necessary cognitive conflict to jar dysconscious racism" (p. 14). As such, we encourage these counterstories from our university students of color in order to interrupt dominant ways of knowing in our classrooms and to coconstruct knowledge (Freire, 1994). Counterstories are ways for Students of Color to counter mainstream discourses that are laden with White privilege and that exist both inside and outside of our classrooms.

However, by seeking out examples of counterstories in our practice and enacting this pedagogy in "real time" through class discussions and activities, we realize some challenges exist. Our attempts to humanize can sometimes backfire and lead to our creation of dehumanizing spaces that are antithetical to our goals. Thus, though we try to counter the hegemony commonly found in classroom spaces through the use

---

*We choose to capitalize racial terms (such as "White," "Black," or "People of Color") as a reminder that these are not just descriptors of skin tone, but complex labels with deep implications for the people and groups being described (Vaught, 2011). However, not all authors take this position. When using direct quotes, we use the author's preferred style.

of such counterstories, we have also experienced the difficulties of engaging in those practices. In the following piece, we each highlight examples where a counternarrative from a student in our class has proven transformative in students' understanding of issues of diversity and oppression. We also each give an example of a time when opening up space for counterstory has perhaps backfired and reinforced dominant ways of thinking. Our hope is that SoTL would allow our experiences to serve as both inspiration and cautionary lesson for those who wish to engage in similar ways of transformative teaching in their own university classrooms.

The Transformational Power of Counterstories

Counterstories offer instructors and their students many opportunities to transform "typical" classroom learning. The long-standing history of ethnocentric and majoritarian curriculum in higher education, when coupled with pedagogies that reinforce dominant ways of knowing and demonstrating knowledge (such as lecture-style instruction and standardized examinations), make counterstories especially important in smaller courses or those more apt to be discussion based and flexible in their pedagogical approaches. In the two examples highlighted below, we briefly explain the context of our classrooms and then describe an instance where the use of counterstories in our teacher education courses proved to be effective and powerful. That is, we offer these instances as evidence that counterstories hold promise and possibility for transformative learning. SoTL would hold that these experiences would add to our collective knowledge base in order that all educators and their students would benefit.

Scott in New Mexico

I taught a master's-level capstone course for practicing teachers where they conducted an Action Research (AR) project at their school in order to improve their practice. Since AR draws heavily on positionality and issues of identity (Brydon-Miller & Maguire, 2009), I wanted my students to further investigate their own identities and any privileges they might have that could impact their research. Most students were receptive to learning about ideas of intersectionality in identities and the privileges some of those identities grant. However, one White male student I will call Ron was having trouble wrapping his head around the idea of unearned privilege. His comments reflected post-racial ideology (Alemán, Salazar, Rorrer, & Parker, 2011) and hung heavily on the myth of meritocracy (Laughter, 2013). In short, he argued that he worked very hard in his life, and those who did not have what he did had, conversely, just not worked hard enough.

I had anticipated this type of resistance and had adapted an activity that I hoped would reveal to students like Ron that there is such a thing as privilege. This seemed to be a common narrative that I wanted to confront. To this end, I engaged my students in an activity called a "privilege walk."

Our class walked outside into the predusk parking lot and began the privilege walk. Students lined up at a starting point, and I read a series of scenarios. Some scenarios that granted certain privileges ("You grew up in a family with two parents") allowed students to take one step forward. Other scenarios ("My family used food stamps when I was growing up") called for students to take a step backward. The goal was for students like Ron to have a stark visual example of the privileges they enjoyed by physically being further ahead of other students on the walk. True to what I thought, Ron ended up at the very front of the group, far ahead of a Native American female student in the back. I remember thinking that night, "I think he really gets it now." As I looked around, though, I realized that in forcing Ron to confront his privilege, I had needed a student for him to compare himself against.

Tanya (pseudonym) stood alone at the back of our group, far behind all the others. A Native American female, Tanya was perhaps the most engaged in our course as she was determined to learn how to improve her practice in order to better serve the special education students in her community deep in the reservation. I had taught Ron a lesson, but at what cost to Tanya? As I took in the scene before me, my joy at providing this lesson for Ron turned my stomach. How was Tanya going to react to this? What had I done?

As we trudged inside, I worried about how Tanya and the other students would react. Her identities were not privileged, and we had all seen it in stark detail in the fading light under the desert sky. As soon as we got back to the classroom, Ron was the first to speak. He talked about how he had not realized that the things he had were privileged. To him, they were "natural." Previously, he believed he had earned everything, yet now he was unsure and could see some of his privileges. His deep voice was soft as he described what it was like to look back and see the other students far behind him, with Tanya at the rear. I glanced at Tanya to see how she was reacting. I could not tell what she was thinking. I reminded the class that while it might be helpful to share our stories, no one was being forced to do so. A few other students shared what the experience had meant for them and then, finally, Tanya spoke. Her voice was soft, but everyone in the room was silent as she began telling her story. About divorced parents. Living on the reservation. Brothers and sisters and aunts and uncles living under one roof. But to her, that was her reality. Growing up, she had never seen herself as "underprivileged." She had the things she had and that was it. For her, it was "normal" as well.

Tanya's bravery in sharing her story continues to impress me long after this incident. I had been so laser-focused on presenting Ron with a compelling counterstory to his narrative of White privilege that I had never considered the cost at which this might come to students like Tanya. I apologized to her during break, telling her that I had not meant to make her feel bad. Instead of being angry, though, or at least disappointed by my misguided tactics, Tanya was understanding and compassionate. Though the activity had brought up some painful memories, it had helped her see how pervasive the issue of privilege was. I had been able to solicit her voice, but at what cost? Although in the end this turned out to be a powerful turning point in our class, I had been focusing on the wrong person. My thoughts before and during the activity had been on how I could get Ron to see his privilege. I had not thought about what this activity might mean for students like Tanya. Though her counterstory was powerful to Ron and the others in the class, I had forced her into an uncomfortable position.

Alyssa in France

It was Paris in the late spring, and for most of the students on the study abroad trip, this was the adventure of their dreams. There were strolls to be had along the Seine River, photographs to take in front of the Eiffel Tower, and crepes to be consumed on every corner. But beyond the tourist version of Paris, our goal for the study abroad class was much deeper. A colleague and I had developed a comparative multicultural program in which we examined language, religion, and immigration for people of color in France as compared to the United States. We wanted students to understand the "real" Paris in all of its complexities, to see beyond the single story of the City of Light, and to venture into neighborhoods that were not often found on group tours. Our class time was spent doing walking tours on immigration in Paris in ethnic-centered neighborhoods and learning about the history of Black Paris and the history of French education. We visited local schools and universities, spoke with students and their teachers, and learned more from these hands-on and interactive experiences than a textbook could ever provide. While the trip discussed here was before the shootings in Paris in 2015, the topic of our class was a prescient one, as immigration in France was at an all-time high and the attacks on *Charlie Hebdo* had happened just months earlier.

On this third trip abroad, however, one student had a drastically different experience than her peers. Aya (pseudonym) was Muslim and wore a hijab, which meant that, according to French laws, she could not enter public buildings or schools unless she removed her head covering. This law, commonly referred to as *laicite* and in contrast to US doctrine that grants freedom of religion, was meant to provide the French with freedom "from religion" (Scott, 2010, p. 92). In practice, this policy resulted in exclusionary treatment for Muslims in France. Rather than viewing the hijab as something that could be easily removed upon entering a public building, many Muslim women see it as part of their identity, no less complicated to remove than one's skin or eye color. Because Aya did not wish to remove her hijab, we designed an alternative assignment for her when she was not allowed inside the public schools where other students were visiting. After being separated for these days, when we got back together as a large group to debrief people's experiences, my coinstructor and I wrestled with how much to ask of Aya. Did we ask her to share her story? If so, how did we make room for her feelings without spotlighting her?

In the end, Aya took it upon herself to talk with her classmates both in small groups and the whole class. She told them how she felt as she watched Muslim girls stop at the entrance of the high school and remove their hijabs before entering and what it felt like for her to watch her classmates enter the school to visit while she and I had to wait outside and explore the neighborhood streets instead. As instructors, we merely offered up the time and space for her to share, encouraged her to do so when and if she felt comfortable, and stepped in only if other students seemed to be pushing back to the point of disrespect. An added complexity for Aya was that many of her classmates were Black, and many of them had firsthand experiences of racial discrimination of their own to share. Yet they were moved and persuaded by the idea of "one" France where everyone was "French first" and their ethnicities came second. They harkened back to James Baldwin and other writers and thinkers from the diaspora who had made Paris their home and who wrote compellingly about the ways France offered freedoms that the United States did not. For them, *laicite* seemed to make sense because, on the surface, it promoted equality. As instructors, Aya's story allowed us to emphasize the difference between equality and equity and to call into question what was, perhaps, lost in a culture that valued national unity over individual diversity.

Challenges of Counterstories in the Classrooms

Just as counterstories can give students multiple perspectives and combat stereotypes, so, too, can they reinforce dominant ideologies. In our experiences of giving students space to share their stories, sometimes this sharing does not go as we anticipate. We draw here on SoTL in an effort to be transparent about our teaching practices, offering an educative perspective for ourselves and others. For us, these challenges are just as important, if not more so, than the successes, as they remind us to be conscious of how we frame our class discussions and how we interrogate students' beliefs. The two anecdotes below, where we highlight some difficulties with using counternarratives, are included not as an indictment of the students themselves nor of this particular pedagogy. Rather, we see understanding the challenges of counterstories as vital to using them in transformational ways.

Scott in Michigan

The semester had been going fairly well. I was teaching a cohort of undergraduates who had self-identified as, and thus enrolled in a program for, future "global educators." Our course was centered on immigration, language, and culture. The goal of the course was to help students problematize popularized ideas of immigrant experiences, to combat the idea of a single immigrant story. Of my nineteen sophomores, all were female. Seventeen were White. Most students engaged in our class discussions, videos, and activities, offering their opinions and interpretations of the readings and what this new knowledge might mean for them as future educators. However, two of the students were from China and seemed to be having trouble finding their voice in the classroom and connecting with the other students. At one point, there was a physical distance between them and the White students as they all filed into class, with the two students from China sitting in a corner with a physical gap between them and the next student. While the Chinese students engaged in all of the written assignments and had strong opinions, they seemed hesitant to share these opinions and personal experiences with the class. When I approached them about it after class one day, they indicated they were hesitant to speak English in front of other native speakers, but they were enjoying the content and felt like they were learning a lot. Without wanting to pressure them too much, I encouraged them to speak out more and reminded them that our course was a place to share experiences as they related to our themes and readings. I was hopeful that our week on examining the myth of the "model minority" would help them find their voices and join in whole-group discussions, since our readings and videos included stories of Cambodian students who challenged the prevailing idea that all Asian students acted a certain way (Pass or Fail in Cambodia Town, 2014). I wanted them to be able to speak back and offer their counterstory to this prevailing myth as well. They promised that they would try.

Coming to class that day, my hope was for students to be able to confront ideas of "positive" stereotypes, which, in actuality, are very problematic for people within those groups. For example, the positioning of all Asian American students as successful because of a reigning belief that they possess a particularly strong work ethic and an inherent, almost genetic, focus on schooling, while seeming to be a "good" stereotype, can be harmful to many of those same students (Wing, 2007). This can produce an "othering" that reproduces racial inequalities (Park, 2008) that can be especially damaging for Asian students who do not live up to these particular "positive" identity constructions thrust on them (Ngo, 2010). I wanted my White students to see this through our readings and videos but also to hear how this myth might be impacting their classmates from China. I was hoping their particular counterstories would support the other readings and activities to really drive home the point that such stereotypes were anything but "positive."

The students from China did find this subject compelling, yet when I went to their small groups to listen to their observations, I was a bit startled. While each was talking much more than she had in the past, one student was proudly extolling the work ethic of Chinese students and explaining how much harder they worked than their US counterparts. I seemed to have painted myself into a corner. To be sure, one of my students from China was speaking in class, but the story she shared was not the counternarrative I had anticipated or wanted. In fact, it was reinforcing the misconception I hoped she would speak against.

After hearing the student share her opinion in the small group, I gently pushed back, asking if this was just her experience or if she believed this idea would apply to all Chinese students. Much to my chagrin, she insisted that this was true for all students from China—that all students were very hard workers and cared a lot about school—much more than students in the United States. I kept prodding because I wanted to steer her thinking past her own experience so she could "zoom out" and see the bigger picture about how such a belief might be destructive. Wasn't the video compelling? Hadn't the article painted a much different picture? Didn't she see the danger of this single story of the "model minority"? My questions seemed not to have an impact, as she was holding fast to her experience as truth and was excited to share with the whole class in our large group discussion.

In this moment, I needed to be able to both acknowledge this personal truth from this individual student yet push her and the others to see the bigger picture. As she shared her schooling experience in China and her opinion on the "model minority" in the whole-group setting, the White students listened in rapt attention, perhaps not used to hearing her talk so much. In the end, I was able to acknowledge her personal experience of working hard, but I also wanted to push on ideas of meritocracy and how this myth might negatively impact other Asian youth in a variety of ways. Other students were able to build off this and relate it to other "positive" stereotypes they had encountered in the past and how they might be damaging, such as supposedly positive stereotypes that that all African Americans are athletic or that all women are caring. In the end, some were able to counter this "counterstory." However, I had not anticipated that this student's counterstory would reinforce the problematic view I wanted to confront.

Alyssa in Atlanta

By the fourth week of class, the group of students was clearly divided, both physically and ideologically. The class consisted predominantly of Black students; on one side sat ten Black students, and on the other side, five Black students and five White students. The White students had come to align themselves with these particular Black students for very specific reasons that became almost immediately apparent in our class discussions. The class, like most of the courses I taught, focused on cultural diversity in urban schools. The undergraduates in this course were preparing to become middle-school teachers in a major metropolitan area. Though the majority of students were racially similar, they came from a wide variety of ethnic and socioeconomic backgrounds, the intersections of which led to some uncomfortable conversations in class.

The discomfort first appeared when we read an article about the myth of meritocracy, in which McIntosh (1989) argues that it is privilege (based on race, socioeconomic status, gender, language, or other dominant identity marker) rather than hard work or merit that leads subgroups to gain and maintain dominance over others. Several White students pushed back against this idea, claiming that their parents and grandparents had worked hard for what they had today and that their hard work is what mattered most, not their legacy of racial supremacy. One Black student countered with her own example of a hardworking family who had yet to achieve "the American dream." It was when I asked for other students' perspectives that the dynamic began to shift. I mistakenly believed that most of the Black students in my class would agree with the author's points, but several Black students in a row raised their hands and agreed with the White students. For example, one said that her parents had gone to college and therefore believed in meritocracy. Another shared that his parents had "just moved" when the neighborhood school he previously attended did not prove to be challenging enough for him academically. "If other people's parents cared as much as mine did," he went on to say, "they would just move, too."

In their reflections later, it became clear that there was a division in the class. On one side were the self-described "critical" Black students who sought to challenge the status quo of schools today and engage in an ongoing antiracist struggle. One of these Black students wrote in a journal that "our class discussions with my fellow Black peers remind me of what my mom says that 'your skinfolk aren't always your kinfolk.'" On the other side were the other Black students, who the first group called "bougie" but who thought themselves to be "above race." The White students were quick and able to align themselves with this group of Black students because their ideas gave the White students validation in saying, for example, that racism didn't exist and that class was more important than race. As one White student wrote in her reflective journal, "I felt weird saying that I think we are post-racial because the readings said something very different, and I was thinking my classmates would agree with the readings. But then when [Jared] said he also thought we were post-racial, I realized it was okay for me to think that because he was Black and saying it." Another student wrote, "During our class discussion, I thought Dr. Dunn was biased in the way she talked about police brutality and racism. Yes, there are a lot of statistics and stories, but I still think that the issue is that the Black people who got hurt were hurt because they were not respecting the policemen. If they behaved, everything would be fine. [Jasmine] and [Kelton] agreed with me, and that made me feel better because they said they had never experienced racism from police as Black people."

This smaller group of Black students appeared to be practicing and advancing respectability politics, or adopting mainstream (White) values and social ideas as they policed other members of their racial group. For classroom learning, this meant that their stories reinforced the dominant discourse rather than countered it. Instead, their narratives illustrated that Whiteness and White supremacy is insidious, sometimes to the point of being accepted by People of Color who may inadvertently perpetuate that majoritarian and marginalizing discourse.

As the instructor, I had to maintain a delicate balance of allowing students to share their stories while, at the same time, pushing them to see that their experiences may have been the exception rather than the rule. But, in doing so, I was also asking them to realize they had been oppressed, which is a strange place for a White instructor to be in, to be asking students to reexamine their own experiences and see them in new ways that may be hurtful and unsettling.

Toward Making Counterstories Part of the Scholarship of Teaching and Learning

The Scholarship of Teaching and Learning encourages us to link our teaching and our research in order to improve both. Thus, the cases we highlight in this chapter have allowed us to view our university classrooms and our pedagogical practices not as separate from our research but, rather, connected to it. It is our hope that by critically examining the ways in which we engage our students to promote equity and diversity through the use of counterstories, we will be able to not only improve our own instruction and the learning of our students but to humbly offer our examples in order to "advance the larger profession of teaching" (Huber & Hutchings, 2005, p. 1). Engaging in SoTL has helped us consider how we can effectively use counterstories to allow our students the space to speak back to dominant narratives. Though the examples given here did not all necessarily result in immediately positive outcomes, our hope is that by examining and critiquing our experiences using these counterstories, we may learn and grow. SoTL would encourage others to take this knowledge and learn from it as well so that these experiences might be added to the theories and experiences that came before us.

As we continue to push for social justice in our teaching about racist systems of oppression and privilege, we will continue to use counterstories. As we swing our sword to disrupt destructive discourse in our practice, however, we must remember to so with care. Though we may be able to use counternarratives in our teaching, we do so knowing that there is a risk of these stories being taken up in ways that might not reflect our intentions. We urge other educators to continue this cautious and self-reflective swinging, as we will.

SCOTT D. FARVER is a doctoral student in curriculum, instruction, and teacher education at Michigan State University. He served in the Philippines as a US Peace Corps volunteer and was an elementary school teacher near the Navajo Nation.

ALYSSA HADLEY DUNN is Assistant Professor of Teacher Education at Michigan State University. She is author of *Teachers without Borders?: The Hidden Consequences of International Teachers in U.S. Schools* and (with Andrea J. Stairs and Kelly A. Donnell) *Urban Teaching in America: Theory, Research, and Practice in K–12 Classrooms*.

References

Adichie, C. N. (2009, July). *The danger of a single story* [Video file]. Retrieved from https://www.ted.com/talks/chimamanda_adichie_the_danger_of_a_single_story.

Alemán, E., Salazar, T., Rorrer, A., & Parker, L. (2011). Introduction to postracialism in US public school and higher education settings: The politics of education in the age of Obama. *Peabody Journal of Education, 86*(5), 479–487.

Bell, D. A. (1992). *Faces at the bottom of the well: The permanence of racism.* New York, NY: Basic Books.

Bernal, D. D. (2002). Critical race theory, Latino critical theory, and critical raced-gendered epistemologies: Recognizing students of color as holders and creators of knowledge. *Qualitative Inquiry, 8*(1), 105–126.

Blackburn, M. V. (2014). Humanizing research with LGBTQ youth through dialogic communication, consciousness raising, and action. In D. Paris & M. T. Winn (Eds.), *Humanizing research: Decolonizing qualitative inquiry with youth and communities.* Thousand Oaks, CA: SAGE.

Boyer, E. L. (1990). *Scholarship reconsidered: Priorities of the professoriate.* Princeton, NJ: Carnegie Foundation for the Advancement of Teaching.

Brydon-Miller, M., & Maguire, P. (2009). Participatory action research: Contributions to the development of practitioner inquiry in education. *Educational Action Research, 17*(1), 79–93.

Delgado, R. (Ed.). (1995). *Critical race theory: The cutting edge.* Philadelphia, PA: Temple University Press.

Delgado, R., & Stefancic, J. (2012). *Critical race theory: An introduction* (2nd ed.). New York: New York University Press.

Freire, P. (1994). *Pedagogy of the oppressed* (M. B. Ramos, Trans. 20th anniversary ed.). New York, NY: Continuum.

hooks, b. (1994). *Teaching to transgress: Education as the practice of freedom.* New York, NY: Routledge.

Huber, M. T., & Hutchings, P. (2005). *The advancement of learning: Building the teaching commons.* San Francisco, CA: Jossey-Bass.

Hutchings, P., & Huber, M. T (2008). Placing theory in the scholarship of teaching and learning. *Arts and Humanities in Higher Education, 7*(3), 229–244.

Ladson-Billings, G. (1998). Just what is critical race theory and what's it doing in a nice field like education? *International Journal of Qualitative Studies in Education, 11*(1), 7–24.

Laughter, J. C. (2013). "I am my brother's keeper; I am my sister's keeper": Rejecting meritocracy and embracing relational pluralism. In D. J. Carter Andrews & F. Tuitt (Eds.), *Contesting the myth of a "post racial" era: The continued significance of race in U.S. education* (pp. 13-24). New York, NY: Peter Lang.

McIntosh, P. (1989, July). White privilege: Unpacking the invisible knapsack. *Peace and Freedom Magazine*, pp. 10–12.

Menges, R. J., & Weimer, M. (1996). *Teaching on solid ground: Using scholarship to improve practice.* San Francisco, CA: Jossey-Bass.

Moll, L. C., Amanti, C., Neff, D., & Gonzalez, N. (1992). Funds of knowledge for teaching: Using a qualitative approach to connect homes and classrooms. *Theory into Practice, 31*(2), 132–141.

Ngo, B. (2010). *Unresolved identities: Discourse, ambivalence, and urban immigrant students.* Albany: State University of New York Press.

Park, L. S. H. (2008). Continuing significance of the model minority myth: The second generation. *Social Justice, 35*(2), 134–144.

PBS. (2014, November). Pass or fail in Cambodia Town [Video file]. Retrieved from http://www.pbs.org/video/2365363645/.

Pérez-Huber, L. (2010). Using Latina/o critical race theory (LatCrit) and racist nativism to explore intersectionality in the educational experiences of undocumented Chicana college students. *Educational Foundations, 24*(1–2), 77–96.

Scott, J. W. (2010). *The politics of the veil.* Princeton, NJ: Princeton University Press.

Solórzano, D., & Yosso, T. (2002). Critical race methodology: Counter-story telling as an analytical framework for education research. *Qualitative Inquiry, 8* (1), 23–44.

Vaught, S. E. (2011). *Racism, public schooling, and the entrenchment of White supremacy.* Albany, NY: State University of New York Press.

Wing, J. Y. (2007). Beyond black and white: The model minority myth and the invisibility of Asian American students. *The Urban Review, 39*, 455–487.

Yosso, T., Parker, L., Solórzano, D., & Lynn, M. (2004). From Jim Crow to affirmative action and back again: A critical race discussion of racialized rationales and access to higher education. *Review of Research in Education, 28*, 1–25.

11 When Walking the Walk Changes the Talk: Using Critical Reflection to Inform Practices of Social Justice Research and Social Justice Education

Sabrina Ross and Alma Stevenson

SOCIAL JUSTICE EDUCATION is concerned with processes of teaching and learning that are directed at helping students critically reflect on dehumanizing sociopolitical conditions and the actions they can take to alter those circumstances (Adams, Bell, & Griffin, 2007). With its focus on improving social conditions, social justice education is closely aligned with Scholarship of Teaching and Learning (SoTL) practices that emphasize connections between reflective, inquiry-oriented teaching and social transformation (Gilpin & Liston, 2009). Social justice education and transformative SoTL practices share an emphasis on critical reflection—identification and interrogation of beliefs that influence thoughts and actions, and transformation of beliefs that are not supportive of one's educational goals (Brookfield, 1995). Critical reflection facilitates processes of social justice education and transformative practices of SoTL because it enables educators to identify connections between their individual teaching practices and broader educational and political goals (Brookfield, 1995); perceiving these connections is a necessary step toward social justice (Gilpin & Liston, 2009).

In this chapter, our goal is to illuminate the significance of critical reflection for social justice education by focusing on the role of critical reflection in ensuring alignment between social justice claims and social justice practice. Consistent with qualitative principles of reflexivity and credibility (Weis & Fine, 2000), we employ a first-person writing style in this chapter to highlight our own situatedness in the social justice inquiry we engage. We use a multivocal format of qualitative writing (Creamer, 2006) to highlight the diversity of our interpretive experiences and perspectives. The pronouns "we" and "our" are used when the writing reflects our shared interpretations; the pronouns "I" and "my" are in individual narrative accounts to reflect differing perspectives, experiences, and/or interpretations.

We use the phrase "walking the walk and talking the talk" to emphasize necessary connections between teaching about social justice and engaging in actions that support social justice. Through processes of critical reflection engaged during implementation of a summer literacy program for African American youth, one of us (Ross) recognized teaching practices that were inconsistent with the goals of social justice education. Using Brookfield's (1995) four lenses of critical reflection (autobiographical, students' perspectives, colleagues' perspectives, and theoretical literature) to operationalize connections between critical reflection and social justice education, we discuss the ways in which critical reflection on our practices of social justice education resulted in changes to our summer literacy program as well as changes in the undergraduate teaching of one author (Ross).

Organization of the Chapter

The organization of this chapter corresponds to the four lenses of critical reflection proposed by Brookfield (1995): autobiographical, students' perspectives, colleagues' perspectives, and theoretical. Section one, "The Lenses of Critical Reflection," details these four lenses and also presents our justification for their usage in this chapter. Section two, "Talking the Talk," uses individual narratives to present the personal experiences and teaching philosophies that inform the social justice education we attempt to provide as teacher educators. This section corresponds to the autobiographical lens of critical reflection. Section three, "Walking the Walk," discusses our conceptualization and implementation of a culturally relevant literacy program to support African American students. This section corresponds to Brookfield's (1995) second and third lenses of critical reflection (students' perspectives and colleagues' perspectives); it explores unanticipated student responses to our social justice curriculum and changes we made to the literacy program following our critical reflection on those responses. Section four, "Changing the Talk," revisits Ross's autobiographical lens and its connections to teacher education. The lack of compatibility between one of those practices (i.e., an oversimplified discussion of culturally responsive teaching) and Ross's social justice aims is discussed. Corresponding to Brookfield's final lens of critical reflection (theoretical literature), this section emphasizes the importance of critical reflection for social justice by highlighting connections between pedagogy, inquiry, and social justice efforts. We conclude the chapter with a discussion of the significance of the present work for the Scholarship of Teaching and Learning.

The Lenses of Critical Reflection

In his classic text *Becoming a Critically Reflective Educator*, Stephen Brookfield (1995) makes the argument that developing effective teaching practices requires faculty members to understand and identify the power relationships that influence processes of teaching and learning and the taken-for-granted ideas about one's teaching that limit transformation. Arguing that power dynamics manifest themselves in every aspect of the educational process, he states that the critically reflective educator uses awareness of these power dynamics to challenge oppressive norms and values so that more democratic teaching environments can be cultivated (Brookfield, 1995). Additionally, by questioning previously taken-for-granted assumptions about their own teaching, Brookfield (1995) contends that critically reflective educators are able to "stand outside their practice and see what they do in a wider perspective" (p. 16). The attainment of such a broad view of teaching and learning is vital because it provides critically reflective educators with moral, intellectual, and political grounding that can guide their practice.

Critically reflective teaching is an ongoing process that is accomplished through synthesis of what Brookfield (1995) refers to as "four critically reflective lenses" (p. 29). These lenses are: (1) autobiographies of learning and teaching; (2) students' perspectives; (3) colleagues' experiences and perspectives; and (4) theoretical literature. He argues that autobiography significantly influences how and what one teaches and that careful analysis of one's experiences of teaching and learning can shed light on why certain teaching practices are embraced and retained over others. Referring to the powerful connections between autobiography and teaching, he writes:

> Our experiences as learners are felt at a visceral, emotional level that is much deeper than that of reason. The insights and meanings for teaching that we draw from these deep experiences are likely to have a profound and long-lasting influence.... We may think we're teaching according to a widely accepted curricular or pedagogic model, only to find, on reflection, that the foundations of our practice have been laid in our autobiographies as learners. (Brookfield, 1995, p. 31)

While autobiographical reflection is an important part of the process of understanding and improving teaching and learning, Brookfield argues that it is insufficient. Also important are the perspectives that students hold about the teacher and about the teaching and learning process. Students' perspectives provide valuable evidence of teaching quality. These perspectives aid in responsive teaching by confirming or disconfirming that the teacher's intended message is being received (Brookfield, 1995). However, because of the inherent power dynamics involved in education, Brookfield argues that students, when questioned directly about teacher performance, may fear retribution for honest feedback. Brookfield recommends the use of anonymous student feedback for this reason.

After autobiographical reflection and taking students' perspectives into account, the perspectives of colleagues provides additional valuable information that teachers can use to better understand and transform teaching. The benefit of seeing one's teaching practices from colleagues' perspectives is that alternative interpretations and solutions are made available. Discussing the many pedagogical benefits that can be derived from the wisdom of colleagues' perspectives, Brookfield (1995) writes:

> Talking to colleagues about what we do unravels the shroud of silence in which our practice is wrapped. Participating in critical conversation with peers opens us up to their versions of events we have experienced. Our colleagues serve as critical mirrors reflecting back to us images of our actions that often take us by surprise. As they describe their own experiences dealing with the same crises and dilemmas we face, we are able to check, reframe, and broaden our own theories of practice. (p. 35)

The final lens of critical reflection is theory. Like colleagues' perspectives, reviewing theoretical/scholarly literature related to pedagogy can broaden the teacher's perspective and illuminate the broader sociopolitical context of what might otherwise be perceived as individual failings. Thus, rather than falsely assuming that the teacher is responsible for everything that occurs within her or his classroom, the critically reflective teacher uses theoretical literature to identify psychological, economic, cultural, and/or other factors that necessarily influence how and what students learn (Brookfield, 1995). Through the synthesis of the autobiographical lens, the lens of student perspectives, the lens of colleagues' perspectives, and the lens of scholarly literature, the critically reflective educator is better able to understand processes of teaching and learning and to question ideological assumptions that could hinder teaching success (Brookfield, 1998).

Brookfield's Critically Reflective Teaching and Our Practices of Social Justice Education

Brookfield's (1995) critically reflective teaching has much in common with other critical approaches to teaching and learning that emphasize teachers' and learners' sociopolitical context, such as Freire's (2001) critical pedagogy, Ladson-Billings's (1995a, 1995b) culturally relevant pedagogy, Gay's (2000) culturally responsive teaching, and Paris's (2012) culturally sustaining pedagogy. In this chapter, Brookfield's approach is used to frame our organization and discussion of practices of social justice research and education because, unlike the other approaches cited above, the four lenses of critically reflective teaching are easily operationalized and applied to the processes of teaching and learning that we hope to illuminate in this chapter. Using Brookfield's framework, we present our autobiographical lenses to position ourselves as teachers and learners and to better contextualize our motivations for the social justice work that we seek to engage in our teaching and our inquiry. We share our interpretations of the lens of students' perspectives to frame our discussion of unexpected processes of teaching and learning that occurred during our summer literacy program. We discuss the lens of colleagues' perspectives as it relates to critical conversations that we engaged in with each other about the program to enhance student learning. Our usage of Brookfield's framework for critically reflective teaching concludes with the lens of theoretical literature and a discussion of how knowledge gained from our experience with the literacy program inspired specific changes in Ross's teacher education practices.

Talking the Talk

Ross's Autobiographical Lens

As a black woman and social justice worker employed within a system of US higher education that largely presumes women of color to be incompetent (Gutierrez y Muhs, Niemann, Gonzales, & Harris, 2012), my ways of understanding the world and my place in it are closely linked to my knowledge of other black women's experiences of racial, gender, and class discrimination; their survival strategies; and their collective knowledge to resist oppression (Collins, 2000). These understandings help to guide my sense of purpose and my pedagogy. My sense of purpose is derived from my family. Although my immediate and extended family did not possess high levels of formal education, they nevertheless saw education as a route to a better life for me. They nurtured my inquisitiveness and encouraged me to excel in school so that I could use my education to make a better life for myself and to also serve others.

I progressed through secondary education and a bachelor's and master's degree with increasing awareness of social inequalities. Due to my cultural upbringing, I also possessed a strong desire to work against those inequities. However, it was not until I began my doctoral studies that I received the conceptual tools, in the form of critical theory, critical pedagogy, and black feminist thought, to understand the educational practices that I could engage to work for social transformation. It is important to emphasize that my appropriation of the theory and language of critical pedagogy was nuanced. Although I agreed with many of the ideas expressed in literature related to critical pedagogy, my lived experiences as a black woman prevented me from accepting these theoretical approaches wholeheartedly. Like other social justice workers of color, I found it necessary to combine methods of critical pedagogy with a theoretical perspective that more closely approximated my own sociocultural experiences (see, for example, Berry, 2010; Jennings & Lynn, 2005; Lynn, 1999).

I understand critical pedagogy to be an approach to teaching for freedom that bridges teaching and politics through dialogue; critical pedagogy identifies relations of domination and empowers learners to engage in critical reflection and work for social justice (Freire, 2001; Kincheloe & Steinberg, 1997; Shapiro, 2003). While critical pedagogy recognizes ways in which social markers of race, class, gender, and sexuality position individuals differently within systems of inequality (Giroux, 1985), it overemphasizes the abilities of teachers, especially female teachers of color, to facilitate democratic learning spaces when the classroom learning environment often mirrors wider social arrangements of inequality (Hoodfar, 1992; Ng, 1993).

As a corrective to this overemphasis, black feminist perspective acknowledges the historical and contemporary marginalization of black women and other women of color and actively grapples with issues of central importance to groups characterized by social, political, economic, and historical contexts of injustice (Collins, 2000).

By identifying ways in which individuals realize penalties and privilege based on their social locations within interlocking and socially constructed systems of oppression, black feminist thought seeks to empower marginalized groups to develop critical consciousness capable of overcoming structures of oppression (Collins, 2000). My critical black feminist perspective guides me to encourage the development of critical consciousness in my students while also remaining cognizant of ways in which the social markings of race and gender that inscribe all of our bodies necessarily impacts the learning environment (Ng, 2005). Thus, in teaching for social justice, I try to engage students in analysis of structures of oppression that occur within and beyond the formal educational environment. I also try to encourage critical self-reflection on ways in which their social positions afford aspects of both privilege and marginalization, and I encourage them to explore actions they can take to lessen the oppression of others.

Related to my engagement in social justice research, my cultural upbringing and educational training guide me toward work with groups who have historically not been well served by the US educational system. My focus in social justice research is twofold: First, it is to highlight the unique cultural strengths and funds of knowledge (Gonzales, Moll, & Amanti, 2005) that are possessed by historically marginalized students and to use those strengths as empowering scaffolds to their learning in the formal educational environment (Ladson-Billings, 1994). Second, it is to challenge deficit perspectives of historically marginalized groups, with the understanding that the pervasiveness of such deficit-oriented perspectives influences the perceived value that society places on these groups (Haddix, 2009). Thus, my critical black feminist lens guides my focus toward teaching and research that challenges the status quo. It allows me to use the educational privilege that has improved my life in the service of others, as my cultural upbringing and educational training dictate.

Stevenson's Autobiographical Lens

I was born and raised in Mexico in a family that values all individuals on the basis of the ethics of their behaviors rather than the value of their material possessions. Although my early education was in private institutions, social justice and fairness were essential parts of my upbringing. My father always modeled equity and generosity in his business and private interactions. As I matured, though, I learned that not all people, nor society in general, were as caring and fair. Through my daily interactions with people from different social strata, I saw the dramatically contrasting lives and opportunities of my countrymen and women and thereby understood the inequality of the Mexican sociopolitical system.

These inequities were reinforced and reproduced by the system of schooling that educated me from kindergarten to my bachelor's degree. Some of my most vivid memories are of how some teachers favored students whose families' wealth allowed them to donate substantial sums to the institutions while they displayed frustration and neglect toward other students from less privileged backgrounds, or who were intellectually challenged. I also witnessed fair and just teachers who provided all students with the same opportunities to learn and treated all with equal respect. These caring teachers planned instruction and created activities that allowed space for learning through exploration and encouraged participation without coercion.

When I moved to the United States and decided to further my education, I found my public and academic identity redefined by the fact that I was and am a person who speaks English as a second language. I experienced the challenges of studying, working, and interacting in mostly English monolingual environments in a culturally hegemonic Anglo society. These experiences, integrated with my own preexisting values, provided me with the knowledge and sensitivity necessary to understand students from diverse social, cultural, and linguistic backgrounds.

In time, I was fortunate to enroll in public institutions of higher education where my cultural background and linguistic skills were appreciated. I was able to express my thoughts in my Spanish-accented second language of English without criticism from my peers. In fact, the diverse experience I brought to our studies was celebrated and encouraged. These experiences reinforced my belief in placing students' cultural and linguistic backgrounds at the center of the curriculum, a practice I worked to actualize in my own teaching.

At the time, I was a doctoral student, a college instructor, and an elementary school classroom teacher and therefore deeply engaged in questions of pedagogy from multiple perspectives almost every hour of every day. My experiences were rich and wide-ranging and allowed me to form strong beliefs about education. Therefore, as I studied various educational theories, I focused on those that aligned with my own knowledge and values. I welcomed strategies to develop critical thinking skills and socioeconomic awareness (Freire, 2001) among students. I affirmed approaches to preserving and building on students' home cultures while teaching them how to negotiate the power codes of mainstream society (Delpit, 2006; Ladson-Billings, 1995a) so as to improve their socioeconomic status. In these ways, I instilled among my elementary students an essential awareness about their life challenges, opportunities, and choices. Meanwhile, I sensitized my college students—mostly preservice teachers—in the hope that they would practice these principles of social justice, equity, and respect with their own students.

As I have progressed in my own journey of learning and teaching, I have become more knowledgeable and conversant regarding culturally responsive literacy (Gay,

2010), wherein students' cultural ways of learning (Gutierrez & Rogoff, 2003), funds of knowledge (Moll et al., 2005), and multiliteracies (New London Group, 1996) are acknowledged, affirmed, and integrated into instruction. Thus, guided by a desire for democratic praxis, I have developed my own curricular and pedagogical principles grounded on the premise that education should provide students with the opportunity to analyze, evaluate, and participate in emancipatory sociocultural and economic transformation (Freire, 2001).

Educators favor practices that are reflective of their own experiences as learners (Brookfield, 1998) and the values and beliefs that constitute their perspective on the world. My upbringing, schooling, and experiences in my bilingual and bicultural personal and professional worlds have guided my praxis and my commitment to pedagogical practices that favor educational equity (Banks, 2006; Freire, 2001; Ladson-Billings, 1995a; Nieto & Bode, 2007). This is what has made me an educator for social justice and an advocate for historically marginalized minorities and their fair access to social and personal advancement.

Walking the Walk

This section describes processes of teaching and learning that occurred during a four-week literacy program developed for African American youth during the summer of 2012 in a rural region of the southeastern United States. Although the program was open to male and female students, the curriculum was developed to specifically enhance reading engagement and proficiency among African American male youth, whose disproportionately low rates of literacy achievement (Rashid, 2009; Tatum, 2008) are associated with a host of negative life outcomes that severely limit African American males' social, economic, and political well-being (Rashid, 2009; Hernandez, 2011). The literacy program was based on three principles of culturally responsive pedagogy (CRP): commitment to students' academic success, development and/or maintenance of students' cultural competence, and development of students' critical consciousness of the wider social and political contexts that affect their everyday lives (Ladson-Billings, 1995a, 1995b). Consistent with practices of CRP, we selected a variety of culturally and linguistically diverse literary and audiovisual texts for use in the program that we hoped students would find personally relevant and meaningful. We used those texts to bridge discussions of academic content, social context, equality, and justice with students. Also consistent with practices of CRP, we used a critical literacy approach to better understand the literacy practices of our student participants. Critical literacy is an approach that seeks to empower marginalized groups by making connections between the texts they read and the social contexts that influence their lives. A goal of critical literacy is to encourage those who are critically literate to identify and work to alter those social contexts that negatively impact their lives and the lives of other marginalized groups (Freire, 2001; Freire & Macedo, 1987).

Preparation for the literacy program involved securing a seed grant to fund program materials, developing a curriculum for the program that was compatible with our social justice goals, and identifying program dates and duration. Youth participants in the literacy program attended a local chapter of a national organization that provides programs and services to youth in the southeast after school and during summer and winter when school is not in session. Dates for the program were identified in coordination with the local chapter's director. Based on our summer college teaching schedules, we conducted the program for three days each week (i.e., Tuesdays, Wednesdays, and Thursdays) from nine o'clock until noon during the months of June and July of 2012. A total of eleven African American students (nine boys and two girls) participated in the program.

Our work with the summer literacy program represented both a teaching and a research opportunity. We wanted to provide culturally relevant literacy instruction to further engage the students we were working with in reading, but we also wanted to systematically explore the processes of teaching and learning that occurred during the program to extend research and practice related to African American youth and literacy. As part of our systematic exploration, we used a variety of methods of qualitative data collection, such as field notes, personal journaling, student work products, and small and large group interviews. We describe the research setting, goals, curriculum, and findings related to the summer literacy program in detail elsewhere (see Stevenson & Ross, 2015).

The curriculum that we developed seemed to be a fine example of the culturally relevant teaching that has enabled African American students to achieve academic engagement and success (Ladson-Billings, 1994, 1995b). However, there was a clear disconnect between what we hoped students would receive from our curriculum and the initial responses of the male students to it. Despite our efforts to design a curriculum with learning activities that the students would find fun and educational, the male participants were frequently unengaged with the curriculum as we originally presented it to them. We found ourselves spending as much time on their classroom management as we were spending on literacy instruction. To better understand the reasons for their lack of engagement with the curriculum, we used several methods of information gathering during the program to shed light on the perspectives our African American male students held.

Students' Perspectives

While we did not have available to us the anonymous student feedback that Brookfield (1998) recommends for obtaining students' perspectives, we did have numerous classroom observations, student artifacts, and conversations with students that illuminated their perspectives about the summer literacy program. Because our interactions with and interpretations of students in the literacy program differed, we present these interpretations and the conclusions we each drew about the literacy program separately.

Ross's Interpretation of African American Male Students' Perspectives

Of all the information available to me to discern students' perspectives of the literacy program, the most salient was the informal classroom observations that I conducted. Whenever I was not directly involved in student instruction or when students were working in small groups or engaged in unstructured activities, I was usually observing them and taking notes about their activities. For the boys, these activities regularly involved rapping, singing, and other similar engagement with hip-hop culture. When they were provided with time to engage in free play, they formed circles and took turns trying to best each other with rap through a hip-hop practice referred to as a cypher (Kirkland, 2013). They would be so engrossed in this practice that they did not want to return to instructional activities when free time had ended. Even when they were provided with specific reading tasks to work on in small groups, I frequently discovered them to be off task, engaging in freestyle raps or drawing images of themselves as participants in hip-hop culture when I visited their tables to check on their work. It was obvious that hip-hop culture was very important to these students. Even though we had included aesthetic activities such as poetry and song in the literacy program, it became clear to me that this inclusion was not sufficiently tapping into the passions of the African American male students in our program.

I also had a salient conversation with two African American male participants (who frequently misbehaved during the program) that helped me to understand factors external to our literacy program that nevertheless impacted students' perceptions of the program. We were taking students for a restroom break after they finished snacks. Our practice was to walk all of the male students to the entrance of the boys' restroom together and have them wait in line to enter. An instructor was needed to monitor the line to make sure that only one male student entered the restroom at a time. Prior to our establishing this practice, the boys would engage in what we felt was dangerous horseplay and roughhousing in the restroom. No such practice was necessary for our two girls, and they were able to go to the restroom independently and return to the classroom in a timely fashion and without incident. During one restroom break, two boys began roughhousing as we assembled them in line. As a result, they were not permitted to take their restroom break with the other male students that day. They remained in the classroom with me as the other male students left.

This had been one of many acts of misbehavior the two had engaged in that day. Frustrated, I asked them why they were misbehaving when I knew that they were capable of good behavior. I told them that we were trying to provide them with fun activities that they could also learn from, but learning was not taking place because they were interrupting it. I told them that I expected them to stop getting into so much trouble, and I asked them to explain their behavior to me. My frank discussion mirrored a culturally responsive method of engagement that Lisa Delpit (2006) refers to as acting with the authority that African American children deem worthy of respect. It caught their attention and, at least for a time, seemed to make them reflect on the consequences of their misbehavior that extended beyond simply "getting in trouble." As I waited for some explanation, they began talking over each other, explaining that they didn't want to be pulled out of a sports competition to come to "tutoring." They said that they weren't "slow" and didn't want to miss a fun activity to get tutored by us.

I was aware that personnel from the local chapter were describing our literacy program as "tutoring" to parents interested in letting their children attend. This shorthand description of our program was somewhat unavoidable. We lacked direct access to the parents, so we had to rely on staff members to distribute our informational flyers and consent forms. Parents often wanted a brief summary of the program before reading the paperwork we provided; when they asked the staff members what the program was about, the staff members told them it would provide tutoring in reading. This description was desirable to the parents, but it stigmatized the program to some of the participants who, as I learned, thought the program was for "slow" students.

Prior to my conversation with these students, I had not realized that students were being pulled out of a fun activity to attend our literacy program. Our scheduling of the program avoided conflict with our university teaching responsibilities. After the director of the local chapter approved the schedule, we did not inquire about potential conflicts with fun activities the students might be involved with. In talking with the students, I confirmed with the director that they were indeed pulled away from an informal indoor basketball tournament that youth leaders had organized for the students. Based on my informal student observations and my conversations with students, I understood that we needed to make curriculum alterations that tapped into the passion that many of the students had for rap and hip-hop culture and that could take away some of the tutoring stigma that surrounded our program.

Stevenson's Interpretation of Students' Perspectives

Summer programs can be challenging because students do not feel like they are in a formal school setting and they know that disengagement will not bring the same consequences as "real school," such as failing a grade. For this reason, it can be more difficult to keep students motivated in a program like ours. Although we had diligently designed instructional activities including materials that we thought would be culturally relevant for rising fourth- and fifth-graders, things did not go as smoothly as we had planned, starting with the fact that our students were two years younger than anticipated! The early challenges we faced forced me to closely attend to the students' reactions across multiple contexts: during lesson presentations, when they were receiving instructions, during individual activities, and while working in small groups. It is on the basis of these observations and field notes that I base my interpretation of our students' perspectives during the summer literacy program.

INSTRUCTIONAL STRATEGIES

We had planned our instructional activities to use with what we interpreted as potentially enabling literature for our students, including prize-winning and popular children's picture storybooks. During the first week, we presented the students with read-alouds such as *Thank You, Mr. Falker* by Patricia Polacco, a story about dyslexia and bullying with white characters. Most students were clearly disengaged. We had hoped this book would serve as an enabling text to help set a positive tone and acceptance of learning differences during the program. However, most of the students did not sit still, much less listen attentively. I realized that both the content and mode of our lesson materials and presentations would need to be adapted. I also noticed that, like many young children, the students were especially drawn toward literature with fictional characters. We added a couple of picture storybooks that not only had animal characters but that were potentially useful to develop the students' critical thinking skills. Also, their desire to imitate basketball players and fascination with rappers inspired us to expand to a multimodal approach incorporating music, videos, and illustrations as part of our instruction and student responses.

I was especially interested in learning how much the students knew about African American literature and historical events and figures. I was surprised to realize that the students did not know of significant leaders, such as Frederick Douglass and Harriet Tubman, let alone literature portraying African American characters as inspiring role models (Tatum, 2006). Our state's early elementary social studies curriculum is narrowly focused on nationalistic symbols and patriotic "heroes," including Christopher Columbus, George Washington, and Abraham Lincoln. African Americans such as Harriet Tubman and George Washington Carver are also in the standards but did not seem to be in the minds of our students, raising questions about the adequacy and balance of the instruction they had received.

Role models of all colors can be beneficial for children of any background. Students can gain understandings of and respect for other ethnic groups by learning about role models from different cultural frames of reference. However, if the role models children see are mostly Eurocentric and only representative of mainstream culture, children may come to assume that most heroes and successful people are from that background, an assumption that is clearly not in the best interest of children of color (Brookfield, 1998). Our students' lack of knowledge about African American heroes was truly worrisome. All students deserve to be presented with role models that reflect their own culture, linguistic skills, beliefs, and values (Tatum, 2006).

When we presented the students with culturally relevant stories, books, and videos regarding African American heroes, most of the students became particularly attentive. For example, they were on task when we showed them an animated video about Harriet Tubman. Moreover, the often-indifferent students stood up and started singing along and clapping to a video of Jeanette Winter's (1992) *Follow the Drinking Gourd* accompanied by gospel music. The familiar music and multimedia presentation of the story also sparked the students' curiosity and interest regarding constellations, engaged them in a discussion, and motivated them to participate in the follow-up assignment wherein they wrote their own version of the story.

The students also became more engaged when we exposed them to multiple ways to represent their understandings of content and ideas through rap, music, collages, illustrations, and open discussions. For example, after reading Joe Hayes's (2006) *The Gum-Chewing Rattler*, the students were given a choice to write a poem and perform it in rap style. Not surprisingly, some of the students enthusiastically volunteered to beat box while their peer presenters recited their poems. The same level of interest was generated when students were asked to take sides and defend their perspectives regarding Jon Scieszka's (1997) *The True Story of the Three Little Pigs*. This activity also provided the students with an opportunity to use their evaluative and argumentative skills. The students were particularly attentive and engaged when we read Ellen Levine's (2007) *Henry's Freedom Box: A True Story from the Underground Railroad* and asked them to write their own story of a time when they had worked to overcome adversity.

Even without access to computers for all students, we were able to engage them in multimodal approaches to representing their ideas using resources drawn from their own cultural background (New London Group, 1996; Kress, 2009). The curricular power of black characters and heroes, the seemingly innocent storybooks with animal characters, and multimodal activities overcame their reluctance to participate in the different instructional activities to some extent.

REDIRECTING BEHAVIORS

During the second week of the program, we noticed that the students' behaviors were interfering with their learning and with the progress of the program. At this point, I thought back to some of my experiences teaching and observing in early elementary classrooms. After talking to my colleague, we decided to introduce a traffic light system for giving the students feedback regarding their classroom behavior. Each student's name was written on a clothespin and pinned on the green light. We explained that if they misbehaved, their name would move to yellow, and if the issues persisted, eventually to red, which would have the consequence of a note sent home to their family. However, this actually seemed to make the students' behaviors more disruptive; moving their names from green to yellow was evidently upsetting for most of them. It appeared that this common early elementary behavior management strategy was not going to work.

Then I remembered a positive strategy I had used when teaching fourth-grade students: sending home notes praising well-behaved students. We found a premade certificate online that said "Job Well Done." We explained to the students that every time they went through the day successfully, without fighting and having completed their work, we would send a note to their family about their good behavior. At the same time, we divided the class into small groups, separating those who were prone to fight or did not work well together. These strategies were much more successful. The majority of the students exhibited better behavior, and the program progressed more smoothly. It was amazing how reversing the feedback—focusing on what they were doing well instead of what they did wrong—impacted their attitude. The students wanted to take the certificate home and worked to earn it.

The students' reactions to our feedback made me reflect on how easy it is for a teacher to negatively impact students by openly pointing out students' disengagement or misbehavior. At first we chose an approach, the traffic light, which seemed harmless from within our cultural frame but made the students feel uncomfortable. They were openly exposed as the "misbehaved." That exposure prompted a defiant attitude instead of encouraging a solution to the behavioral problems. When we turned the emphasis to reinforcing good behavior, the dynamic shifted in a dramatically positive direction.

Colleagues' Perspectives

A final method of information gathering that we used during the summer literacy program was ongoing purposeful and critical conversations with each other about the program. After each literacy session, we discussed program successes and challenges. We talked about pedagogical strategies that we found effective and those that we wanted to modify or eliminate altogether. We were also able to share relevant literature with each other to help in further understanding the classroom challenges we faced and to provide theoretical justification for our instructional modifications. These sessions were helpful because they enabled us to see classroom issues within a broader perspective (Brookfield, 1995). By conversing with one another about our varied interpretations of classroom events and about changes we wanted to implement, we were able to strengthen our instructional delivery and student engagement in ways that we would not have been able to realize without these critical conversations. Through these critical conversations, we were able to better process our individual thoughts and concerns and reconcile our interpretations of what students were receiving from the program. These conversations pointed us to literature that gave us broader perspectives on the significant role that hip-hop culture plays in helping African American male learners construct and communicate knowledge about themselves and their understandings of the world (Emdin, 2013; Kirkland, 2013; Kirkland & Jackson, 2009) and on the necessary and evolving nature of CRP (Paris, 2012; Ladson-Billings, 2014).

Based on our critical conversations, we made a number of curricular changes. We more thoroughly integrated aspects of hip-hop culture into our learning activities to help students see connections between the hip-hop culture they were enamored with and practices of literacy. We also incorporated more kinesthetic activities into our curriculum to help students release extra energy that might be diverted to misbehavior and to partly make up for the sports tournament they were missing to participate in our program. Finally, we engaged in very intentional conversations with the students about historical and present-day inequalities, cultural figures who worked to end social inequality, and the role that education played in the lives of those individuals. We tried to communicate to students that our program was not a tutoring program but an educational program and that education could be an important tool for anyone who wanted to make life better for themselves or for others. It would be inaccurate to state that our curricular changes solved all of the problems that we had with student misbehavior. The changes did, however, result in improved behavior for some students and enabled us to focus less on classroom management issues. The changes also confirmed for us the ways that the participants' practices of literacy were also practices of identity construction and development (Kirkland & Jackson, 2009). We felt that although the program had started out on shaky ground, by program's end we believed that we had experienced moderate success in accomplishing our goals for the participants. They had been introduced to a wide range of literary and audiovisual texts and had used those texts as the basis for varied literacy practices, such as journals, artwork, and raps. On the final day of our literacy program, we had a graduation ceremony and provided participants with certificates of completion, books, and stickers encouraging them to keep reading. As we called out their names and asked them to come forward to receive their certificates, most of the students were very quiet and attentive. The seriousness with which they shook our hands and took their certificates both caught us off guard and reminded us that the program held real significance for the students.

Changing the Talk: Ross's Critical Reflection on Her Undergraduate Teaching

The critical conversations that directed us toward new theoretical literature on African American male literacy and CRP also forced me to rethink the teaching practices that I was engaging in in my undergraduate diversity course. In teaching for social justice in that course, my primary goal is to address the cultural mismatch between a predominantly white, middle-class, and monolingual teaching force and the increasing numbers of diverse students enrolled in public schools as a barrier to these students' educational achievement (Brown, Brown, & Rothrock, 2015; Gay, 2000; Ladson-Billings, 1995a, 1995b; 2006). CRP is a cornerstone of my diversity course because it provides a framework and a methodology through which I can attempt to address this cultural mismatch.

Critical reflection on the summer literacy program and on my own undergraduate teaching with preservice educators forced me to acknowledge that I was presenting CRP to them as a static (as opposed to a fluid and evolving) practice. CRP is a fairly straightforward concept to understand, but its nuances are difficult to communicate to preservice teachers, most of whom have not had sustained contact with culturally and linguistically diverse learners. Because the knowledge in my diversity course frequently challenges long-held commonsense cultural notions endorsed by preservice teachers, they often respond with varying forms of resistance (Fierros, 2009; Ng, 1993; Wang, 2008; Williams & Evans-Winters, 2005) to my curriculum and to the racialized and gendered social markings that I bring into the classroom (Hoodfar, 1992; Muhtaseb, 2007; Ng, 1993; Williams & Evans-Winters, 2005). While self-identified white educators have certainly noted the difficulties of managing white student resistance in social justice–oriented courses (see, for example, Gillespie, Ashbaugh, & DeFiore, 2002; Gordon, 2005; Mazzei, 2008; Pennington, 2007), educators of color have pointed out ways in which the resistance of white students in their social justice–oriented classes is not only used as a form of punishment aimed at interrupting classroom learning but is also used to call into question their legitimacy of authority, qualifications, levels of expertise, and suitability for employment (Chaisson, 2004; Ladson-Billings, 1996; Perry, Moore, Edwards, Acosta, & Frey, 2009).

Based on my desires to reduce the challenges to my knowledge and authority that disrupted classroom learning in my diversity course, I realized that I was providing a very prescriptive introduction of CRP to my undergraduate students. In order to demonstrate my in-depth knowledge of the topic, I cited theory related to CRP and statistics on why CRP was necessary and provided numerous lesson plans across various content areas to demonstrate how CRP could be implemented across the K–12 curriculum. What I failed to provide, however, were explicit discussions of how practices of CRP are context specific and how those practices will necessarily change over time and based on the specific needs of the groups of students that one is working with.

Critical reflection enabled me to realize that, in inadvertently downplaying the complexity of CRP, I was guilty of the same superficial treatment of CRP that Paris (2012) and Ladson-Billings (2014) admonished. I realized that truly honoring the social justice claims of my diversity course meant that I would have to complicate my presentation of CRP even though such complications would make me more vulnerable to student resistance and complaints that I "did not know what I was talking about" (Perry et al., 2009). As a result of the processes of autobiographical reflection, critical conversations, and critical reflection on my teaching discussed in this chapter, I have complicated my presentation of CRP to my undergraduate students by honestly discussing its inherent messiness and uncertainty. This change has made teaching the diversity course more difficult but also more consistent with principles of CRP and of social justice education.

Significance for the Scholarship of Teaching and Learning

We have discussed in this chapter our autobiographical motivations for social justice research and social justice teaching. We have described conceptualization and implementation of a culturally relevant summer literacy program that we developed, detailing program challenges and the critical conversations that enabled curricular changes for improvement. Finally, we discussed ways in which critical reflection on the processes and outcomes of the literacy program resulted in curricular changes to Ross's undergraduate teaching. In highlighting connections between our processes of critical reflection and our social justice research and pedagogy, this chapter contributes to transformative SoTL practices in two significant and interrelated ways: First, through its theoretical grounding in processes of critical reflection and its emphasis on the need for compatibility between social justice talk and social justice walk, this chapter reflects the broad applicability of "third wave" SoTL scholarship (Gurung & Schwartz, 2010). Relatedly, by connecting local knowledge generated from the unique perspective of teacher researchers (Lytle & Cochran-Smith, 1992) to broader social justice aims, this chapter contributes to the diversity of literature that comprises the teaching commons other SoTL practitioners can draw on in their own social justice work.

SABRINA ROSS is Associate Professor of Curriculum Studies at Georgia Southern University. Her scholarship involves intersections of race, gender, and power within formal and informal educational contexts.

ALMA D. STEVENSON is Assistant Professor of Literacy at Georgia Southern University. Her research explores sociocultural perspectives on literacy, literacy in science, and the role of language and literacy in culture, identity, and academic achievement. She began her career as an educator of immigrant, special needs, bilingual, and mainstream students in the Mexico–US borderlands.

References

Adams, M., Bell, L. A., & Griffin, P. (2007). *Teaching for diversity and social justice* (2nd ed.). New York, NY: Routledge.
Banks, J. A. (2006). Improving race relations in schools: From theory and research to practice. *Journal of Social Issues, 62*(3), 607–614.
Berry, T. R. (2010). Engaged pedagogy and critical race feminism. *Educational Foundations, 24*(3–4), 19–37.
Brookfield, S. (1995). *Becoming a critically reflective teacher.* San Francisco, CA: Jossey-Bass.
Brookfield, S. (1998). Critically reflective practice. *The Journal of Continuing Education in the Health Professions, 18*(4), 197–205.
Brown, K., Brown, A., & Rothrock, R. (2015). Culturally relevant pedagogy. In M. F. He, B. Schultz, & W. Schubert (Eds.), *The SAGE guide to curriculum in education* (pp. 207–215). Thousand Oaks, CA: SAGE.
Chaisson, R. L. (2004). A crack in the door: Critical race theory in practice at a predominantly White institution. *Teaching Sociology, 32*(4), 345–357.

Collins, P. H. (2000). *Black feminist thought: Knowledge, consciousness, and the politics of empowerment* (2nd ed.). New York, NY: Routledge.

Creamer, E. (2006). Experimenting with voice and reflexivity in social science texts. In C. F. Conrad & R. C. Serlin (Eds.), *The SAGE handbook for research and education: Engaging ideas and enriching inquiry* (pp. 529–543). Thousand Oaks, CA: SAGE.

Delpit, L. D. (2006). *Other people's children: Cultural conflict in the classroom*. New York, NY: The New Press.

Emdin, C. (2013). Pursuing the pedagogical potential of the pillars of hip-hop through sciencemindedness. *International Journal of Critical Pedagogy, 4*(3), 83–99.

Fierros, E. G. (2009). Using performance ethnography to confront issues of privilege, race, and institutional racism: An account of an arts-based teacher education project. *Multicultural Perspectives, 11*(1), 3–11.

Freire, P. (2001). *Pedagogy of the oppressed*. New York, NY: Continuum.

Freire, P., & Macedo, D. (1987). *Literacy: Reading the word and the world*. London, England: Routledge.

Gay, G. (2000). *Culturally responsive teaching: Theory, research and practice*. New York, NY: Teachers College Press.

Gay, G. (2010). *Culturally responsive teaching: Theory, research, and practice* (2nd ed.). New York, NY: Teachers College Press.

Gillespie, D., Ashbaugh, L., & DeFiore, J. (2002). White women teaching White women about White privilege, race cognizance and social action: Toward a pedagogical pragmatics. *Race Ethnicity and Education, 5*(3), 237–253.

Gilpin, L., & Liston, D. (2009). Transformative education in the scholarship of teaching and learning: An analysis of SOTL literature. *International Journal of the Scholarship of Teaching and Learning, 3*(2), 1–8.

Giroux, H. A. (1985). Critical pedagogy, cultural politics and the discourse of experience. *Journal of Education, 167*, 22–41.

Gonzales, N., Moll, L., & Amanti, C. (2005). *Funds of knowledge: Theorizing practices in households, communities, and classrooms*. New York, NY: Routledge.

Gordon, J. (2005). Inadvertent complicity: Colorblindness in teacher education. *Educational Studies, 38*(2), 135–153.

Gurung, R. A. R., & Schwartz, B. M. (2010). Riding the third wave of SOTL. *International Journal for the Scholarship of Teaching and Learning, 4*(2), 1–6.

Gutierrez, K. D., & Rogoff, B. (2003). Cultural ways of learning: Individual traits or repertoires of practice. *Educational Researcher, 32*(5), 19–25.

Gutierrez y Muhs, G., Niemann, Y., Gonzales, C., & Harris, A. (2012). *Presumed incompetent: The intersections of race and class for women in academia*. Boulder: University Press of Colorado.

Haddix, M. (2009). Black boys can write: Challenging dominant framings of African American adolescent males in literacy research. *Journal of Adolescent & Adult Literacy, 53*(4), 341–343. doi:10.1598/JAAL.53.4.8

Hayes, J. (2006). *The gum-chewing rattler*. El Paso, TX: Cinco Puntos Press.

Hernandez, D. J. (2011). *Double jeopardy: How third-grade reading skills and poverty influence high school graduation*. Baltimore, MD: Annie E. Casey Foundation.

Hoodfar, H. (1992). Feminist anthropology and critical pedagogy: The anthropology of classrooms' excluded voices. *Canadian Journal of Education, 17*(3), 303–320.

Jennings, M. E., & Lynn, M. (2005). The house that race built: Critical pedagogy, African-American education, and the re-conceptualization of a critical race pedagogy. *Educational Foundations, 19*(3/4), 15–32.

Kincheloe, J. L., & Steinberg, S. R. (1997). *Changing multiculturalism*. Philadelphia, PA: Open University Press.

Kirkland, D. E. (2013). *A search past silence: The literacy of young Black men*. New York, NY: Teachers College Press.

Kirkland, D. E., & Jackson, A. (2009). "We Real Cool": Toward a theory of Black masculine literacies. *Reading Research Quarterly, 44*(3), 278-297. doi:10.1598/RRQ.44.3.3

Kress, G. (2009). *Multimodality: A social semiotic approach to contemporary communication*. New York, NY: Routledge.

Ladson-Billings, G. (1994). *The dreamkeepers: Successful teachers of African American children*. San Francisco, CA: Jossey Bass.

Ladson-Billings, G. (1995a). Towards a theory of culturally relevant pedagogy. *American Educational Research Journal, 32*(3), 159-165.

Ladson-Billings, G. (1995b). But that's just good teaching! The case for culturally relevant pedagogy. *Theory into Practice, 34*(3), 159-165.

Ladson-Billings, G. (1996). Silences as weapons: Challenges of a Black professor teaching White students. *Theory into Practice, 35*(2), 79-86.

Ladson-Billings, G. (2006). It's not the culture of poverty, it's the poverty of culture: The problem with teacher education. *Anthropology & Education Quarterly, 37*(2), 104-109.

Ladson-Billings, G. (2014). Culturally relevant pedagogy 2.0: a.k.a. the remix. *Harvard Educational Review, 84*(1), 74-84.

Levine, E. (2007). *Henry's freedom box: A true story from the underground railroad*. New York, NY: Scholastic Press.

Lynn, M. (1999). Toward a critical race pedagogy: A research note. *Urban Education, 33*(5), 606-626.

Lytle, S., & Cochran-Smith, M. (1992). Teacher research as a way of knowing. *Harvard Educational Review, 62*, 447-474.

Mazzei, L. A. (2008). Silence speaks: Whiteness revealed in the absence of voice. *Teaching and Teacher Education, 24*, 1125-1136.

Moll, L., Gonzalez, N., Neff, D., & Amant, C. (2005). Funds of knowledge for teaching: Using a qualitative approach to connect homes and classrooms. In N. Gonzales, L. Moll, & C. Amanti (Eds.), *Funds of knowledge: Theorizing practice of households, communities and classrooms* (pp. 120-139). New York, NY: Routledge.

Muhtaseb, A. (2007). From behind the veil: Students' resistance from different directions. *New Directions for Teaching and Learning, 110*, 25-33.

Nest Entertainment. (2007). *Animated hero classics: Harriet Tubman* [Video file]. Retrieved from https://www.youtube.com/watch?v=gojj7DUYe58.

New London Group. (1996). A pedagogy of multiliteracies: Designing social futures. *Harvard Educational Review, 66*(1), 60-93.

Ng, R. (1993). "A woman out of control": Deconstructing sexism and racism in the university. *Canadian Journal of Education, 18*(3), 189-205.

Ng, R. (2005). Embodied pedagogy as transformative learning: A critical reflection. Canadian Association for the Study of Adult Education. Retrieved from http://www.oise.utoronto.ca/CASAE/cnf2005/2005onlineProceedings/CAS2005Pro-Ng.pdf.

Nieto, S., & Bode, P. (2007). *Affirming diversity: The sociopolitical context of multicultural education* (5th ed.). Boston, MA: Allyn & Bacon.

Paris, D. (2012). Culturally sustaining pedagogy: A needed change in stance, terminology, and practice. *Educational Researcher, 41*(3), 93-97.

Pennington, J. L. (2007). Silence in the classroom/whispers in the halls: Autoethnography as pedagogy in White pre-service teacher education. *Race Ethnicity and Education, 10*(1), 93–113.

Perry, G., Moore, H., Edwards, C., Acosta, K., & Frey, C. (2009). Maintaining credibility and authority as an instructor of color in diversity-education classrooms: A qualitative inquiry. *Journal of Higher Education, 80*(1), 80–106.

Rashid, H. M. (2009). From brilliant baby to child placed at risk: The perilous path of African American boys in early childhood education. *The Journal of Negro Education, 78*(3), 347–358.

Scieszka, J. (1997). *The true story of the three little pigs*. New York, NY: Puffin Books.

Shapiro, S. (2003). Re-membering the body in critical pedagogy. In H. S. Shapiro, S. B. Harden, & A. Pennell (Eds.), *The institution of education* (pp. 333–351). Boston, MA: Pearson.

SingAnAmericanStory. (2012, February 24). *Follow the drinking gourd* [Video file]. Retrieved from https://www.youtube.com/watch?v=pw6N_eTZP2U.

Stevenson, A., & Ross, S. (2015). Starting young: Emergent Black masculinity and early literacy. *Journal of African American Males in Education, 6*(1), 75–90.

Tatum, A. W. (2006). Engaging African American males in reading. *Educational Leadership, 63*(5), 44–49.

Tatum, A. W. (2008). Toward a more anatomically complete model of literacy instruction: A focus on African American male adolescents and texts. *Harvard Educational Review, 78*(1), 155–180.

Wang, H. (2008). "Red eyes": Engaging emotions in multicultural education. *Multicultural Perspectives, 10*(1), 10–16.

Weis, L., & Fine, M. (2000). *Speed bumps: A student-friendly guide to qualitative research*. New York, NY: Teachers College Press.

Williams, D. G., & Evans-Winters, V. (2005). The burden of teaching teachers: Memoirs of race discourse in teacher education. *The Urban Review, 37*(3), 201–219.

Winter, J. (1992). *Follow the drinking gourd*. New York, NY: Dragonfly Books.

12 Consciousness Raising for Twenty-First-Century Faculty: Using Lessons from Diversity Flashpoints

Alejandro Leguizamo and Jennifer Campbell

GIVEN THE INCREASED diversification of student communities across college campuses, it is imperative to raise faculty consciousness about potential diversity flashpoints in their classrooms. This chapter presents a case study of Roger Williams University (RWU), a midsize New England private comprehensive university that is striving to increase diversity in its student body and to convey the importance of diversity issues to the entire faculty community. With support from the Office of the Provost, the Faculty Senate Diversity Committee used the mandatory fall faculty conference to increase faculty awareness of diversity issues by framing the conversation financially, pedagogically, and ethically in order to facilitate learning and build community.

Founded in the nation's smallest state as a junior college in 1956, RWU began granting undergraduate degrees in the 1960s and graduate degrees in 1992. The university moved from Providence to Bristol, Rhode Island, in 1969. The beautiful campus is built on land acquired by the Wampanoag people in a historical town once home to the largest slave port on the Eastern Seaboard. Despite being located at the intersections of white privilege, immigrant history, and native and slave cultures, the university did not fully begin to explore and embrace its own position in those connected histories until very recently.

The University's Efforts with Respect to Diversity

Like most change, the transformations that have led to the latest and most progressive institutional mission and core values have been too slow for some and too rapid for others. And when the subject at hand is the topic of diversity (difference, inclusion, integration) that touches all facets of the institution (admissions, curriculum, students, staff, faculty, finance, scholarship, residential life) dissonance is readily amplified. It is rare if not impossible to find all members of a complicated institution on the same page at the same moment. But in order to thrive in an increasingly competitive educational environment where fewer students have more choices, Roger Williams University is a prime example of the way "New England colleges and universities need to focus their recruitment strategies on increasing college participation among New England Hispanics and African-Americans. . . . And they need to increase their market share of students from outside the Northeast" (Brodigan, 2005, p. 13). Statistics show that Rhode Island, like four of the six Northeast states, suffers from both a decline of K–12 students in the pipeline and an additional loss due to out-migration (Handy, 2008).

Alejandro Leguizamo was instrumental in establishing the diversity committee within the institution's faculty senate in 2009 in response to discrete incidents of bias and a long history of inaction. Initially founded to serve the local population, Roger Williams University had often struggled to shed its reputation as a school for "rich white underachievers." Herculean efforts to improve campus climate were lost to public view, letters against affirmative hiring were distributed on the day new faculty arrived, a whites-only scholarship was sponsored by a student club, and a former president of the board of trustees became embroiled in his use of the "n-word" at a board meeting. Graduation rates for students of color were woeful. The creation of the standing committee was intended to ensure longevity of faculty input and perspective.

The charge of the faculty senate diversity committee has been to monitor issues of diversity on campus by ensuring that efforts are neither isolated nor forgotten. The committee, along with the university's administration, has been working on increasing the institution's awareness, understanding, and sensitivity to diversity issues. The committee created and maintained an archive of past efforts, sought to index courses offered with an emphasis on diversity, supported Sexual Advocacy for Everyone (SAFE) trainings, and sponsored National Coalition Building Institute (NCBI) workshops. Jennifer Campbell became the chair of that committee in 2014. Members of the diversity committee continue to implement a number of events with the intent of highlighting diversity issues in the university. The committee sponsors a multicultural film series/festival, in which foreign, diversity-related, and LGBTQ-specific films are showcased during each semester. A number of faculty have supported this endeavor and either require or encourage their students to attend and write essays about the films. Furthermore, the diversity committee established a subcommittee specific to LGBTQ issues. A faculty member from that subcommittee eventually became the advisor to the SAFE student group, a role that had previously been limited to staff from Student Affairs. Members of the committee have sought support and cosponsorship for other activities that make RWU aware of its historical ties to slavery and to the Native American cultural groups on whose land the campus has been built. And the committee has tried to lend energy and support to the creation of new interdisciplinary minors, "Gender and Sexuality" and "Latin American and Latino Studies," that fill long-standing curricular gaps.

In recognition of both negative institutional history and positive national trends, the most recent university administration has been supportive of diversity-related endeavors under the concept of "inclusive excellence." These endeavors include the adoption, in 2012, of an official statement:

> At Roger Williams University, we recognize and emphasize our responsibility to prepare students to live and work in an increasingly diverse and global society. Inclusive Excellence is our institutional approach to support the advancement of cultural sensitivity and global awareness across campus and to build a culture that inspires diversity in every aspect of the university. Inclusive Excellence is central to our role as a teaching institution, providing opportunities for greater learning, understanding and growth for all of our students within local and global contexts. Inclusive Excellence values a workforce that is reflective of and capitalizes on the intellectual potential of colleagues that will enrich the University. Our goal is to instill respect for each member of our community and to create, promote, and support an environment in which all members of the University community are provided opportunities to understand and respect diverse opinions and experiences.

In addition, the university established yearly minigrants for diversity-related projects for which everybody in the university community is eligible to apply, as well as support for various student-focused organizations (see http://rwu.edu/about/diversity-inclusion).

More recently, in part as a result of a student petition that garnished more than one thousand signatures, modifications have been made to RWU's general education program. The petition demanded a new course be created to address diversity issues. Given constraints with respect to the number of required courses in the program, an existing course based on the social sciences was deemed to be a good conduit for this effort, and its focus has been turned to various diversity-related foci. In addition, a new position was implemented for a dean of general education. The new dean has increased efforts to include diversity issues in all courses within the program (which deal with science, philosophy, literature, history, political science, and aesthetics).

Nonetheless, the university has struggled in attracting and retaining students from diverse backgrounds, as can be seen from table 12.1. In fact, results from the National Survey of Student Engagement (NSSE) from 2010 indicated that Roger Williams University lagged significantly behind other New England private and Carnegie Class schools in relation to students' exposure and comfort with diversity issues. More troubling, the NSSE data showed that our students' curricular, cocurricular, and extracurricular engagement with diversity issues actually declines during their four-year baccalaureate experience at the university. Furthermore, through participation in various university committees, regular contact with staff from the university's

Table 12.1. *Roger Williams University at a glance (2014 - 2015).*

Faculty	Full Time 207 (219 by 2015)				Part Time 282	
Full Time Faculty Composition by Race (2015)	White 86.3%	Black 3.7%	Asian 5.5%	Am. Indian 1%	Unkn. 3.7%	
Full Time Faculty Composition by Ethnicity (2015)	Non-Latino 93.2%		Latino 4.2%		Unkn. 2.7%	
Full Time Faculty Gender (2015)	Male 56.6%				Female 43.4%	
Students Enrollment: 4,884 (4,610 Undergrads)	Full Time Undergrads 87%				Part Time Undergrads 13%	
Undergraduate Student Gender	Male 49.5%				Female 50.5%	
Six-Year Graduation Rates (2008 Cohort)	Male 56%				Female 67%	
Undergraduate Student Age	24 and under 88%				25 and over 12%	
Undergraduate Student Residence	Out of State 87%		In state 8%	Foreign Countries 4%	Unknown 1%	
Undergraduate Student Race/ Ethnicity	White 73%	Latino 4.9%	Black 2.5%	Asian 2.2%	Am. Indian 0.9%	Foreign 5%	Unkn. 11.5%
Six-Year Graduation Rates (2008 cohort)	White 63%	Latino 74%	Black 13%	Asian 67%	Am. Indian 0%	Two+ Races 65%	Foreign 48%	Unkn. 62%

Notes: Data obtained from the National Center for Education Statistics.
Downloaded from: http://nces.ed.gov/collegenavigator/?id=217518#programs.

Intercultural Center, and conversations with students from diverse backgrounds as well as LGBTQ students, members of the diversity committee became well aware of students' experiences of microaggressions, or diversity flashpoints, in our classrooms.

Having defined diversity much more broadly than the visible categories of race and ethnicity to include religious difference, sexual identity, gender identification, socioeconomic class, and regional difference, RWU understands that recruitment of visible diversity is only one small step on the path toward inclusion. Recruitment of any one group without sustained support for retention will not move the university forward. In fact, "enrollment of underrepresented groups is but a pragmatic first step toward the broader social goal of integration. Presence on campus neither guarantees integration into campus life nor does it lead to realization of the pedagogic benefits of diversity" (Tienda, 2013, p. 473). In a study of over 14,000 students at ninety-five institutions, Densen and Chang (2015) consider the ways "students' satisfaction with their college's respect for diverse beliefs" (p. l) is a moderating factor in students' benefits with cross-racial interaction. The authors conclude,

> When it comes to educational practice, the context in which students engage with diversity, even when only individually perceived, is equally important in adding value to students' learning and experiences and addressing those dynamics extends beyond initiatives that only address access. *Our findings show that when this context is not seriously addressed in ways that improve both the quality of students' interaction and their perception of diversity efforts on campus, having more contact can actually dampen rather than improve educational benefits for some students.* (Densen & Chang, 2015, p. 27, emphasis added)

In other words, diversity mismanaged may be, if not worse than no diversity at all, directly harmful to students' education.

These findings amplify the importance of faculty-student interaction, both as a pedagogical exchange and insofar as faculty represent, symbolically and pragmatically, the values of their institution. Even when, or perhaps precisely because, the institution as a collective body moves toward its new mission, faculty-student interaction remains a significant factor in the ability of an institution to recruit, retain, and educate all students. We know that mentoring has positive effects despite, when unrecognized and unrewarded, amounting to "cultural taxation" when the work of mentoring is laid at the feet of faculty of color (Williams, 2015). Instead, the work of integrating campus culture, transforming curriculum, and increasing the numbers of students able to thrive on campus must be shared by all faculty members, including those who do not recognize the role they play in changing the dynamic.

Fall Faculty Conference

Before the start of every fall semester, the Provost's Office at RWU hosts the fall faculty conference, which faculty are required to attend. The conference is comprised of addresses by the university's president and provost and the leaders of the faculty senate as well as the presentation of information about the entering first-year cohort. In addition, a portion of the conference is reserved for a presentation/training. In late 2013, the diversity committee developed a proposal to use the presentation/training time at the 2014 fall faculty conference for a diversity-related topic, which was eagerly accepted by the university's provost, Andrew Workman. Having long discussed "the diversity paradox," wherein sensitivity trainings and consciousness raisings are offered to all but attended only by those who are already sensitive and conscious, the diversity committee understood this to be a unique opportunity for faculty development.

The program for the 2014 fall faculty conference comprised an introduction by the diversity committee, a presentation by an invited speaker, and a faculty activity. It was framed in terms of student retention and success rather than "just diversity" to make everyone aware of the financial and pedagogical costs—in addition, of course, to the ethical costs—of leaving flashpoints unaddressed. Its purpose was to raise faculty's consciousness around their behavior in the classroom, their interactions with students, and how they may impact student retention and success.

Conference Speaker

The diversity committee invited Dr. Thomas Kling, professor of physics at Bridgewater State University in Bridgewater, Massachusetts, to speak to our faculty about student retention and success. Dr. Kling oversees student retention and enhancement across mathematics and sciences at his university. Two members of RWU's diversity committee had attended a diversity-related conference at Bridgewater State University in June of 2013 and were impressed by Dr. Kling's presentation about the efforts his university had been making, with great success, to increase student retention and success in the STEM fields.

In his presentation to the RWU faculty, Kling (2014) identified a three-level approach to increase student success and retention. His approach centered on assessment, faculty development, and updating pedagogical practices. Kling (2014) recommended that a thorough assessment be conducted with respect to student performance, retention, range of diversity, microaggressions on campus, universal design, and campus climate. He encouraged faculty to participate in continuing education around pedagogical practices. Specifically, he noted that techniques that involve students to a greater extent than lecturing are more helpful in keeping students engaged. At Bridgewater State University, Kling added, a system was implemented, beginning with the STEM fields, where learning became inquiry based; students worked in small groups that were led by fourth-year students, and every student participated; the focus was on learning and not on skills deficits; and entering classes were connected with upper-level students, faculty, and staff, both socially and academically. Kling (2014) reported gains in both student performance and retention at his institution and underscored the notion that methods designed to increase students' success in general (such as project-based learning, group work, mentoring, etc.) proved to be successful not only with students from underrepresented or marginalized groups (students of color, students from lower socioeconomic status, or first-generation students) but with students in general.

Conference Activity

The diversity committee determined that it would be helpful for faculty attending the fall faculty conference to participate in an activity that highlighted the impact of faculty behavior on students at our own campus—in particular, for faculty to learn of microaggressions, or diversity flashpoints, to which students have been subjected, or exposed, as part of their classroom experience. Faculty members were randomly assigned to tables of eight to ten people with whom they analyzed diversity flashpoint vignettes obtained through a student survey (described below).

Defined by Garcia and Hoelscher (2008) as a "potentially explosive interpersonal situation between faculty and students that arises out of identity differences . . . a diversity flashpoint incident results in some people present recognizing a broken connection among those working together on the common task of teaching and learning. Left unaddressed, this broken connection is likely to lead to defensiveness, reduced communication, and disengagement" (p. 56). This definition of a flashpoint makes clear not only the relationship between diversity issues and retention but the importance of being able to manage these types of incidents for any teacher interested in fostering significant student learning, leadership, teamwork, and collaboration. While taken individually these stories may seem of little lasting consequence, looked at collectively they give shape and voice to a larger pattern of "broken connections" that impede the mission of teaching and learning. And the vignettes collected here at RWU made one vital idea very clear: "flashpoints" are not only about the interaction between one student and one teacher; a flashpoint that is not transformed into an "educable moment" affects *every* student in the class, as borne out by the fact that 50 percent of the respondents to the student survey were bystanders and witnesses. Given the scholarship of Densen and Chang (2015) quoted earlier ("*Our findings show that when this context is not seriously addressed in ways that improve both the quality of students' interaction and their perception of diversity efforts on campus, having more contact can actually dampen rather than improve educational benefits for some students*" [p. 27, emphasis added]), the idea that flashpoints affect not only the students directly subjected to them but also students who witness them takes on startling consequences relevant to student learning, campus climate, and overall student retention.

Student Survey

In order to obtain flashpoints experienced by our students, we decided to conduct a survey. After obtaining approval by our institution's human subjects review board, a short survey (see appendix A) was emailed to all students in the university, including undergraduate, graduate, and law students. We received thirty-four responses, of which five were not usable given what appeared to be a problem with the survey program used (Qualtrics). The respondents were mostly female (69 percent) and mainly freshmen (47 percent) or seniors (24 percent). Interestingly, respondents were evenly divided in terms of whether they had been involved in the flashpoint or had witnessed it (49 percent versus 51 percent, respectively). Thirty-eight percent of the events described involved interactions between faculty and students, and 14 percent involved student interactions in the presence of faculty, whereas 32 percent involved only students (without faculty presence) and 17 percent involved mainly other situations. No flashpoints involving only faculty were reported. Most flashpoints involved race/ethnicity (49 percent), gender (38 percent), or sexual orientation (30 percent). The members of the diversity committee then selected five vignettes obtained through the survey to share with faculty and elicit discussion. Each vignette included the event in question (redacted to strip it of any potential identifier and for ease of reading), how the student felt about it, and its resolution, if any. The selected vignettes are included in appendix B.

Faculty Discussion Guidelines and Evaluation of the Activity

Faculty were given a packet of information about how to approach a discussion of the diversity flashpoint vignettes as well as an evaluation form. Faculty were given the following instructions:

> Please note the vignette your table is being assigned to discuss.
> Please choose a table facilitator. The role of this person will be to keep the conversation focused and to encourage discussion among table members. This person will also record and submit the answers to the three questions at the end of this handout at the conclusion of the exercise.
> Following the theoretical framework suggested by Garcia and Hoelscher, we have designed discussion questions for each vignette in order to share knowledge, generate discussion, and improve practice. (They call their method The Four Rs: Recognize, Reflect, Respond, and Reassess.)
> Your goal is to spend 30 minutes in a table discussion that can result in a five-minute reporting out that highlights, explains, and heals the broken connection so that significant teaching and learning can happen for every member of the community. Following the conceptual framework from *Managing Diversity Flashpoints*, we offer the following brief suggestions for sparking and managing the conversation:
> Recognize:
> *What identities and life experiences seem to be colliding?
> Reflect:
> *What might be the short- and long-term implications of the incident for those involved?
> Respond:
> *How could the flashpoint have been productively managed? (Again, remember all the stakeholders, including "silent" witnesses.)
> You will be invited to share your answers with the entire conference at the end of the exercise.

Postactivity Discussion

Like all consciousness-raising activities, the discussion was simultaneously full of insights and fraught with tensions. Many faculty members were duly unsettled by the insensitive and hurtful comments students reported hearing in pedagogical contexts. Many faculty were uncomfortable realizing that colleagues who had allegedly spoken those words were in the room at the time. Some faculty were able to reflect on how their own teaching practices might be improved simply by taking the time to learn to pronounce names correctly or by being sure not to ask any student to represent the thoughts of a group, and, importantly, by telling students explicitly at the beginning of a course how and to whom to communicate if they feel uncomfortable or disrespected. This last point became a larger structural question as well: "Who does tell students how to report the kind of incident our survey collected?"

After completion of the activity, faculty were invited to provide the diversity committee with anonymous evaluations of both the speaker and the activity. The majority of the responses ($n = 71$, 34.3 percent response rate) were positive with respect to the speaker (72 percent) and the activity (75 percent). A faculty member who did not find the experience helpful wrote, "No. Awful. Boring. Different demographic [Dr. Kling's presentation]. Not a lot of take away points. We aimed low and got what we brought." On the other hand, another faculty member wrote, "Appreciated the message that by treating/engaging EVERY student—we can reduce the likelihood that someone feels target[ed] or marginalized (or the likelihood that someone is targeted).... Activity was meaningful—helpful to have a range of real RWU scenarios that require ACTION and reflection that we can ALL use" (emphasis in the original).

Assessment of Long-Term Effects

In May 2015, the diversity committee surveyed faculty to assess the impact of the 2014 fall faculty conference. The brief questionnaire can be found in appendix C. Forty-four faculty participated in the survey, which represents a 20 percent response rate. Although more than half of the faculty that participated in the survey stated that the conference had no impact on them (55 percent), 27 percent stated that their awareness of diversity issues in the classroom was raised, but they were not sure how to proceed, and 18 percent reported that their awareness was raised and they had taken steps to modify their pedagogy.

Faculty who reported that their pedagogy had changed, and others, offered various comments. For example, some faculty described steps they have taken based on their increased awareness of diversity issues. One wrote, "Began to address issues of gender more pointedly, for instance." Another one stated, "More inclusive material, more discussion." Other faculty felt that they had already taken steps in the past and hence the conference did not have much impact: "When I say that the [conference] presentation had no impact it is because I already try to incorporate those ideas into my classrooms. I feel I am very successful at this." On the other hand, one faculty member brought up an issue he or she had with the approach taken at the conference:

> Respectfully, I do not think the discussion was very effective. There was and continues to be a presumption that "flashpoints" are as presented and interpreted by students. There is never a discussion that this is a two-way street. Because someone perceives something to be the case does not make it so. Sure, faculty need to be sensitive to and aware of how issues impact students. But students (and our colleagues) need to be aware that their interpretations are not always accurate. This is about a dialogue which is, by definition, bidirectional. The bidirectional dimension to this is largely lost. It feels very much like a lecture instead of a conversation.

Faculty were also asked what approaches might be helpful in the future in order to increase their awareness of diversity issues. Of the options provided (see appendix C), where faculty could choose more than one, 52 percent chose "Hearing from students directly about their experience in the classroom (during divisional faculty meetings)"; 43 percent chose "Regular communication with examples of diversity flashpoints, why they're flashpoints and how to address them"; 34 percent chose "Incorporate diversity flashpoints training in the New Faculty Learning Community"; 32 percent chose "Regular communication with literature on the subject" and "Availability to consult with other faculty on these matters in a somewhat formal manner (as opposed to "break room" consultations)"; and 27 percent chose "Future faculty conferences on the subject." The least-chosen options were "Nothing" (11 percent) and "Online diversity trainings" (7 percent).

Subsequent Efforts

Clearly, one consciousness-raising event will not reach all those exposed to it, nor will it provide guidance for those who are, or who become aware of being, in need of it. Therefore, the activities described in this chapter represent only a beginning.

Since the 2014 faculty conference took place, the university's administration, faculty, and students have been involved in diversity-related endeavors that seek to raise awareness and understanding and further our process of becoming a diverse and accepting community.

The administration, for example, created a position of chief diversity officer, which would report directly to the university's president and be part of his or her cabinet. The university is in the process of finding the right person for that position. The university also created the position of associate provost for the advancement of teaching and learning. That office oversees a number of academic student services as well as the general education program and is charged with the development of a center for teaching and learning for the faculty. Through that office, the diversity committee has distributed information for faculty on how to foster increased communication and success in a diverse classroom, including diversity based on ethnicity, socioeconomic status, gender, ability, and developmental conditions (e.g., autism spectrum disorders). Moreover, efforts have begun to recruit faculty who are interested and experienced in teaching topics from a diversity standpoint to teach in our general education program.

Faculty at the university continue to be active in nurturing student understanding and appreciation of diversity through many means, more recently in our core liberal arts classes. For instance, social sciences–based courses that are part of our general education curriculum have been transformed to focus directly on issues of diversity through the inclusion of themes chosen by individual faculty. One course focuses on cross-cultural aspects of addiction; a second course covers a wide range of diversity issues through the lenses of social justice reading assignments and socially conscious stand-up comedy. An upcoming section of the course will focus on refugees, given the contemporary issues related to that phenomenon. Moreover, the science-based course in the same program has incorporated lessons through which students explore and dispel myths of biologically based racial differences. These are but small samples of the work many faculty have undertaken in order to engage our students in diversity-related academic and personal journeys.

Students have also remained involved in the process of increasing diversity and acceptance on our campus. Two recent efforts are worth mentioning. First, students who are engaged with the university's intercultural center have organized an event in which a number of them will share for members of the administration and the faculty experiences of diversity flashpoints they have endured in our classrooms. We expect to record the event to make it available to faculty who are not able to attend. Second, inspired by the "Black Out" movement started by students of color at the University of Missouri, students at RWU organized a protest and presented our current president, Dr. Farish, who was in attendance, with a number of demands related to diversity on campus. Dr. Farish then called for a task force comprised of himself, members of the administration, students, and Jennifer Campbell to address the demands made by the student group. The demands mainly involve increasing diversity in hiring at the university, training of faculty and staff on diversity issues, increased diversification of our curriculum, and the expansion of our intercultural center.

Conclusions

In this chapter we sought to describe an example of how faculty's consciousness on diversity issues in a predominantly white institution can be raised. It is, of course, evident that one effort, event, or training is not sufficient. Raising the consciousness of university educators is a process, and any one faculty member may fall at any place on a continuum that ranges from having complete disdain for these efforts and disregard for diversity issues to being well versed on them and actively revising pedagogy in order to provide all students, but especially those from marginalized populations, with a supportive environment that is conducive to learning.

We learned from the endeavor described in this chapter that a number of students are greatly impacted by their experiences in the classroom. It is not surprising that faculty could have such an impact on students, since students look at their professors for knowledge, guidance, and examples for how to *be* in a particular discipline. The presence of diversity flashpoints on college campuses can have a detrimental effect on the students' self-esteem (e.g., Nadal, Wong, Griffin, Davidoff, & Sriken, 2014), negatively impact campus climate for students of color (e.g., Solorzano, Ceja, & Yosso, 2000; Yosso, Smith, Ceja, & Solorzano, 2009), and impact success in college (e.g, Harper, 2009). Therefore, it is imperative to raise faculty consciousness and to train faculty on how to foster engagement, learning, and success in a diverse classroom as part of an overall labor to create a campus community that is welcoming to diverse students, especially those from marginalized populations. The first step in minimizing the occurrence of diversity flashpoints in the classroom is for faculty to be aware of them so that they can avoid creating them. Further training can then help faculty learn how best to manage them when they arise in the classroom, among students during class discussions, or in assignments turned in by students.

We also learned that students are impacted by diversity flashpoints when they witness them. It is striking that about half of the vignettes we received from students as part of the first survey involved students witnessing flashpoints directed at other students and their expression of distress and anger as a result. We cannot assume that only those who are the targets of diversity flashpoints are impacted by them. Bystanders can have strong reactions to the interactions they witness in the classroom and, while the extent of that impact remains unclear, it is evident that these students, at the very least, experience discomfort.

Based on the students' responses, we learned that they are very hesitant to intervene when exposed to diversity flashpoints. Both those who were targeted by faculty and bystanders reported that they did not confront faculty when the flashpoint took place. Their reasons ranged from not wanting to interrupt the lecture/discussion to fear of retaliation from the faculty member. The effect of diversity flashpoints in the classroom cannot be dismissed. They contribute to an environment that is unconducive to learning and growth if not outright toxic for students.

In sum, faculty in the twenty-first century need to become ever more conscious of their pedagogical and interactional approach in classrooms that are becoming increasingly diverse. This is the case not because those teaching in institutions of higher education are behaving in overtly oppressing or discriminatory ways. Rather, the great majority of faculty mean well in their classrooms and may engage in subtle but impactful behaviors that often go unanalyzed, unchallenged, and therefore unchanged, creating a negative impact on their students' experience in the classroom. Having one's consciousness raised does not prevent professors from becoming involved in diversity flashpoints at all. It helps us become more aware of our interactions with students and others, helps us think about the impact our words have on others, prevents diversity flashpoints, and, by providing students with a more civil and comfortable learning environment, it can contribute to their success as students. The example we share with this case study could easily be replicated with fairly minimal resources, and the process can help faculty elsewhere assess their students' experiences in their classrooms.

ALEJANDRO LEGUIZAMO is Associate Professor of Psychology at Roger Williams University. His research focuses on multicultural issues among sex offenders and on predictors of psychological well-being among diverse populations. He is also a trained forensic psychologist and has worked in a variety of psycho-legal contexts.

JENNIFER CAMPBELL is Professor of Writing Studies, Rhetoric, and Composition at Roger Williams University and is currently serving as Coordinator for First-Year Writing. At all levels, her writing courses afford students the opportunity to explore diversity and social justice issues.

References

Brodigan, R. (2005). Demographic perfect storm: New England confronts a shortage of college-bound students. *Connection: The Journal of New England Board of Higher Education, 19*, 13–14.

Densen, N., & Chang, M. J. (2015). Dynamic relationships: Identifying moderators that maximize benefits associated with diversity. *Journal of Higher Education, 86*, 1–37.

Garcia, J. E., & Hoelscher, K. J. (2008). *Managing diversity flashpoints in higher education.* Lanham, MD: Rowman & Littlefield.

Handy, T. J. (2008). Differentiate or die. *New England Journal of Higher Education, 22*, 13–14.

Harper, S. R. (2009). Niggers no more: A critical race counternarrative on Black male student achievement at predominantly white colleges and universities, *International Journal of Qualitative Studies in Education, 22*(6), 697–712. doi:10.1080/09518390903333889

Kling, T. P. (2014, September). *Increasing student retention and success.* Paper presented at the 2014 Fall Faculty Conference, Roger Williams University, Bristol, Rhode Island.

Nadal, K. L., Wong, Y., Griffin, K. E., Davidoff, K., & Sriken, J. (2014). The adverse impact of racial microaggressions on college students' self-esteem. *Journal of College Student Development, 55*, 461–474. doi:10.1353/csd.2014.0051

Roger Williams University. (2015). *History & traditions.* Retrieved from http://www.rwu.edu/about/who-we-are/history-traditions.

Solorzano, D., Ceja, M., & Yosso, T. (2000). Critical race theory, racial microaggressions, and campus racial climate: The experiences of African American college students. *Journal of Negro Education, 69*, 60–73.

Tienda, M. (2013). Diversity does not equal inclusion: Promoting integration in higher education. *Educational Researcher, 42*, 467–475.

Williams June, A. (2015, November 8). The invisible labor of minority professors. *Chronicle of Higher Education.* Retrieved from http://chronicle.com/article/The-Invisible-Labor-of/234098.

Yosso, T., Smith, W., Ceja, M., & Solorzano, D. (2009). Critical race theory, racial microaggressions, and campus racial climate for Latina/o undergraduates. *Harvard Educational Review, 79*, 659–691.

Appendix A

RWU Diversity Survey (for students)

1. Your gender?
2. What is your current class year?
   a. Freshman
   b. Sophomore
   c. Junior
   d. Senior
   e. Grad
   f. Law
3. In the circumstance you are describing, please indicate whether you were involved or a witness by checking in the appropriate box:
   a. Involved
   b. Witness
4. In the circumstance you are describing, please indicate whom it involved:
   a. Faculty-Student
   b. Student-Student (in the presence of Faculty)
   c. Student-Student (not in the presence of Faculty)
   d. Faculty-Faculty
   e. Faculty-Staff
   f. Other
5. Which of the following areas did the event involve? Select all that apply:
   a. Race/Ethnicity
   b. Socioeconomic Class
   c. Gender
   d. Sexual Orientation
   e. Ability
   f. Spiritual Tradition/Religion
   g. Place of Origin
   h. Other
6. Please describe what happened.
7. Please describe how you felt.

8. Did anyone (including you) intervene/respond to this event?
    a. No
    b. Yes
9. Please describe your reasons for *intervening or not intervening* in this event.
10. Were you aware of how the event was resolved (or what happened in the end)?
    a. No
    b. Yes
11. If Yes, describe how the event was resolved.
12. Would you have preferred that the event be handled differently?
    a. No
    b. Yes
13. If Yes, describe how you would have preferred the event be resolved.
14. If you could make three recommendations as to what would make studying (e.g., classroom-related activities) at RWU a more inclusive/welcoming experience, what would they be?
15. If you could make three recommendations as to what would make living (e.g., extracurricular and housing-related activities) at RWU a more inclusive/welcoming experience, what would they be?

Appendix B

Vignettes Selected for the Faculty Conference Activity

Vignette 1. "A professor treated a female, African American student, different than the rest. She never pronounced the student's name correctly and failed to attempt to learn it. She disregarded anything the student said to participate in class. One day when the student was not in class, the professor made a negative comment about her."

This vignette was provided by a second-year student who witnessed the events. The student reported feeling "angry and ashamed." The student added, "It did not feel my place to intervene. The professor chose favorites and if I called her out she would have liked me less and my participation grade would suffer." When answering the question of how he or she would have preferred the event to be handled, the student wrote, "I would prefer [the professor] treat everyone equally."

Vignette 2. "The professor was explaining the male rape scene from the movie *Deliverance* and said how he would never allow himself to be raped."

The first-year student who witnessed the professor making this statement reacted in the following way: "I felt as if the professor was saying that people 'allow' themselves to get raped. He made it seem like being raped was an option and that if you didn't want to be raped then you simply have to not allow it. He never thought for a second that even if someone fights as hard as they can, that they could still be overpowered and still get raped." The student added, "I didn't intervene because I really like the professor and respect him, and I didn't want to interrupt the class."

Vignette 3. "I had a teacher my first semester who was very racist to races besides White. She would tell the class that the people who did not speak English did not do too hot in the class and she would talk down to these classmates as well. At one point in the class she told us that we only had to take an in-class essay to prove to the school that we actually knew what we were doing [as opposed to] those Saudi Arabia kids who cheat on their essays. I know the school has in-class essays to see how students are doing within the writing classes. I know they are not to see if international students are cheating or not."

The student who provided the above vignette was a first-year student. The student stated, "I believe what this teacher was saying was very inappropriate and hurtful for students. I did not agree with what she was saying as I am a teacher in training, no teacher should be treating her students like this or with this attitude." The student stated that he or she did not intervene because "she is a teacher, and if I intervened I believed she would just judge me for it, and tell me that I was not minding my own business even though she told the whole class."

> Vignette 4. "A student in class who identifies as a lesbian female was consistently identified as male by the professor. Even though the professor was corrected multiple times (mostly indirectly) by the student herself. The professor constantly referred to the student as 'him' and 'he.'"

The student who witnessed this event was a fourth-year student. He or she stated, "The situation made me feel frustrated because I wanted to say something to [the] professor outside of the class but the student asked me not to because 'the professor is old and I'm used to this.' This was so troubling to hear from a student." The student tried to intervene: "I intervened as much as the student felt comfortable. I wish I could have done more but I did not want to go against the student's wishes." The student added, "I wish someone was able to correct the professor on a one to one basis so that the student would not feel embarrassed. Also, this professor needs some kind of education so that she does not make this 'mistake' again."

> Vignette 5. "This instance is one of the MANY occurrences of stereotypical comments and statements that have been made in many of my classes. In discussing socioeconomic status, a fellow student made a comment that people who live in urban/inner cities use their spare time to commit crimes, whereas individuals in suburban areas are more likely to spend their time being involved with the community and getting jobs. This comment (as well as the many others I have heard) is extremely [disturbing] due to the general consensus the class had in agreement to this statement. It is truly frightening to see that students are giving into/believing the stereotypes they hear. Another comment was made about single-parent households. A student stated that those who are raised in single-parent households are not raised as well as others who are raised in two-parent households."

The above vignette came from a first-year student who was involved in the class. The student reacted, "I was angry. Most of the class agreed to what that student had said after our class had a dialog on what social stratification was." The student did not intervene: "The class ran over time. This comment was made in response to a presentation that was given. At the end of class, I spoke with my professor who counted seven comments of biased statements as well as microaggressions. She did express her genuine concerns over what was said. She assured me that she will be speaking with these students." Although the student felt that the event was resolved by the professor speaking to the other students, the student added, "I wish I had more time at the end of class to discuss the statements made. I was infuriated that we left the class off with a stereotype that MANY students nodded in agreement." The student recommended: "(1) Have professors trained in how to respond to biased comments. (2) Have professors set up a system where comments can lead to a grade deduction in participation. (3) When professors are discussing race in class, they should make students aware of stereotypes and then debunk them." The student also recommended, in terms of university-wide factors, "(1) Have [residence assistants] trained on matters of diversity. None of this [National Coalition Building Institute training] crap. I am honestly VERY disappointed in the NUMEROUS discriminatory comments I have heard in the PRESENCE of an RA. (2) Have more programs for students to have open dialogs on race, sexuality, etc. (3) Emphasize that biased incidents will not be tolerated and will [be] handled the same way alcohol-related issues are handled (through conduct, fines, mandatory meetings)."

Appendix C

IMPACT OF 2014 Fall Faculty Conference Faculty Survey

1. As part of the 2014 Faculty Conference, Dr. Tom Kling presented on the work Bridgewater State University has been doing with respect to student retention and success. We also presented a number of diversity flashpoints shared with us by students and you analyzed them using the framework provided. In your evaluation forms, the great majority found either or both experiences helpful.

    We'd like to gauge what impact, if any, the conference had on your pedagogy, now that a number of months have passed.
    a. The conference had no impact.
    b. My awareness of diversity issues in the classroom was raised, but I am not sure how to proceed from here.
    c. My awareness of diversity issues in the classroom was raised, and I have taken steps to modify my pedagogy.
    d. My pedagogical approach has changed dramatically.
2. If your pedagogical approach has changed, how has it changed?
3. What do you think would be helpful for us as a faculty in order to increase our awareness of diversity issues/flashpoints as we work to create a supportive learning community for ourselves and the students? (check as many as you'd like)
    a. Nothing
    b. Regular communication with examples of diversity flashpoints, why they're flashpoints, and how to address them
    c. Hearing from students directly about their experiences in the classroom (during divisional faculty meetings)
    d. Availability to consult with other faculty on these matters in a somewhat formal manner (as opposed to "break room" consultation)
    e. Incorporate diversity flashpoint training to the New Faculty Learning Community
    f. Online diversity trainings
    g. Regular communication with literature on the subject
    h. Future faculty conferences on the subject

13 "The Way I View the World Has Changed": Student and Teacher Reflections on Transformative Social Justice Education

Annemarie Vaccaro, Athina Chartelain, Sarah D. Croft, Brooke D'Aloisio, Tiffany Hoyt, and Brian Stevens

LEARNING ABOUT AND doing social justice is a lifelong journey. For some of us, that journey begins with, or is intensified through, a particular life event or educational experience, such as an academic course about diversity. Annemarie Vaccaro, the instructor of two graduate-level courses about social justice in higher education, writes the first section of this chapter. She describes the courses as well as specific assignments designed to yield critical reflection and social justice action. The second portion of the chapter is coauthored by Athina Chartelain, Sarah D. Croft, Brooke D'Aloisio, Tiffany Hoyt, and Brian Stevens, former students who offer evidence from course assignments and postcourse retrospection about the transformative nature of these social justice educational experiences. In the introduction to this text, editors Liston and Rahimi reminded readers of Shulman's (2002) argument that educators have an "obligation to inquire into the consequences of one's work with students" (p. vii). This chapter serves as one example of how teachers and students can engage in transformative learning communities during an academic course and well after it ends.

Since creating a more socially just world requires change, this chapter explicates how transformative social justice education can prompt action on behalf of learners. Through critical reflection on our experiences, we (as teachers and learners) offer specific insight into the ways the courses in general, and reflective writing assignments in particular, prompted transformative learning and social justice action. Encapsulating all of our rich educational experiences in one short chapter would be impossible. Instead, we have chosen to focus on four specific topics related to our transformative learning: the shift in our world views, the process of critical reflection, the emotional nature of social justice education, and the social justice action we were inspired to engage in.

Course and Paper Overview

Athina Chartelain, Sarah D. Croft, Brooke D'Aloisio, Tiffany Hoyt, and Brian Stevens are former students in one of two graduate courses that addressed social justice topics of oppression, privilege, identity, and cultural competency in higher education. Both courses are designed to help emerging educational professionals become more inclusive and socially just in their practice. To design these courses, I, Annemarie Vaccaro, use critical perspectives such as inclusive pedagogy (Tuitt, 2006), feminist pedagogy (Maher & Tetreault, 1994, 2006; Tisdell, 1995), transgressive education (Freire, 1970/2006; hooks, 1994), transformative learning (Brookfield, 1995, 2000; Dirkx, 1998; Mezirow, 1991), matrix of domination (Collins, 2000), and the multiple dimensions of oppression (Hardiman & Jackson, 2007). Unfortunately, there is not enough space in this short chapter to discuss each of these pedagogical perspectives. However, overlapping themes from these perspectives that undergird the courses included valuing students as active agents of the learning process; sharing power with students by inviting them to make decisions about curriculum, pedagogy, and classroom expectations; acknowledging the influence of sociopolitical structures on everyday life; encouraging students to engage in deep self-reflection about their social identities and assumptions about the world; infusing active learning into the classroom; inspiring inclusive and socially just action; role modeling risk taking and compassionate questioning by the instructor; and seeking paradigm-shifting learning outcomes as opposed to mere comprehension of course materials. Taken together, these pedagogical elements served as a foundation for our course learning communities.

To structure these courses, I used a basic framework that contains three components: learning about the matrix of oppression, engaging students in deep self-reflection, and calling students to action (Vaccaro, 2013). I believe students must first gain a foundational knowledge about the matrix of domination, where individuals experience and resist marginalization on three levels: individual, group, and system (Collins, 2000; Hardiman & Jackson, 2007). In this course rooted in critical and transformative paradigms, students are asked to go beyond mere comprehension of key concepts (e.g., identity, oppression, privilege) to engage in critical reflection (Brookfield, 1995, 2000; Mezirow, 1991) on self and society. They are also invited to begin planning socially just action within their personal and professional spheres of influence.

Woven into the courses is an emphasis on the nature of privilege and oppression in the United States as well as an emphasis on multiple and intersecting social identities (e.g., race, class, gender, sexual orientation, religion, ability) (Abes, Jones, & McEwen, 2007; Choo & Ferree, 2010; Museus & Griffin, 2011; Shields, 2008). The course allows students to identify their social identities and make meaning of them in the context of the matrix of domination. Learning about complex social justice topics requires careful scaffolding from simple to more complex ideas and thoughtful attention to student readiness. Sanford (1966) noted that educators must consider student readiness and then apply the right balance of challenge and support so students can achieve the maximum amount of development. He also argued that students must be ready for these challenges or they can regress or resist growth. Indeed, much has been written about student resistance to learning about oppression and privilege (Goodman, 2011; Watt, 2007). Since students come from a range of privileged and oppressed intersecting identities, lived realities, and prior social justice educational experiences, some were ready to delve more quickly and deeply into social justice topics than others. In an attempt to honor differences in student readiness, I scaffold curriculum and assignments and offer feedback based on individual student growth. Not all students begin the class in the same place, grow at the same rate, or leave with the same social justice skill sets. This is a reality of doing social justice education (Vaccaro, 2013).

As a partner in the educational commons, as opposed to a faculty member who does banking education (Freire, 1970/2006), I try to role model risk taking and a willingness to engage in the lifelong work of social justice (Vaccaro, 2013). One way I do this is by candidly sharing struggles and triumphs from my own social justice learning journey. I am honest about being in various stages of readiness throughout my own life.

Naming and situating our social identities in the context of the matrix of domination (Collins, 2000) is a crucial first step in "understand[ing] how one is affected by and participates in maintaining systems of oppression, privilege, and power" (College Student Educators International/Student Affairs Administrators in Higher Education [ACPA/NASPA], 2015, p. 30). Classroom discussions emphasize the process of critical reflection on self in the context of systems of oppression. Students are encouraged to critically reflect on their diverse identities and their lived realities with oppression and privilege in course papers (see below). Chartelain identifies as a working-class woman of color who is heterosexual, able-bodied, and Christian. Stevens self-identifies as a straight, middle-class, white male without any religious affiliation. D'Aloisio identifies as a white, middle-class, heterosexual woman who currently has no physical disabilities and is not religious. Croft identifies as a straight, middle-class, white woman who does not currently have a disability and is not religious. Hoyt identifies as a straight, lower-middle-class, white woman who does not currently have a disability and is more spiritual than religious. I (Vaccaro) self-identify as a queer, middle-class, white woman who does not currently have a disability and who is not religious.

Because students engage in a learning community where interactions are paramount, I (Vaccaro) encourage students to respect, and learn from, the various cognitive and affective locations of their peers. A cornerstone of the classes is active engagement with course materials and classmates. Classroom discussions and activities invite students to engage in what Liston and Rahimi (in the introduction to this volume) refer to as the "heart of transformative practice"—engagement with classmates who are different from themselves.

Aligning with critical pedagogical tenets (e.g., active learning, self-reflection, action) listed earlier, I assign semistructured self-reflection papers for both courses. In the doctoral course, students keep a reflective journal throughout the semester and craft a social justice autobiography for a final project. Master's students write a cultural competency reflection paper in the middle of the term and an action plan at the end. The semistructured reflection papers prompt students to delve deeply into their personal and professional connections to social justice concepts. Deep self-reflection is an essential part of socially just, inclusive pedagogy and also a foundation for competency development in emerging professionals (ACPA/NASPA, 2015; Pope, Reynolds, & Mueller, 2004). Brookfield (2000) explained how critical reflection illuminates power and inequity and forces us to question our hegemonic assumptions. Moreover, critically reflective practice offers educators the opportunity to "help ourselves and others lead more authentic and compassionate lives in a world organized according to ideals of fairness and social justice" (Brookfield, 2000, p. 47). To signify the importance of connecting critical reflection and action, the papers ask students to develop concrete plans for social justice action. Brief descriptions of the paper assignments are included next.

Social Justice Autobiography Paper Description—Doctoral Course

> As a leader within the field of education, you must continuously assess your personal development, confront your weaknesses, and acknowledge your strengths. The purpose of this assignment is to give you the opportunity to reflect on the content of this course and your experiences (or lack of) as a diverse and socially just individual. As such, you will be expected to maintain a journal reflecting upon your personal journey during this class. In your entries, apply course readings, class discussions, and presentations to your reflections. Within your reflections, please consider addressing areas of personal resistance, new knowledge/perspectives, change, and/or insights. You may consider questions such as: How have my educational experiences related to course materials?; How have my experiences contributed to my understanding of myself/others as people who live within oppressive systems?; and What significant experiences have I had that contributed to my perceptions of racial, gender, sexual orientation, class, religion, ability, etc. identities in education?

Cultural Competency Reflection Paper—Master's Course

Self-reflection is incredibly important to being a culturally competent practitioner. We must be able to recognize our strengths as well as our assumptions and biases. This paper invites you to candidly reflect upon your transformation in this class. In the paper, please address the following: Reflect on the theory of oppression. What were the most moving and most difficult parts to understand? Why? What is privilege? What types of privilege do you hold? Discuss your reflections on intersectionality. What does it mean for your life? How have your social justice awareness, knowledge, and skills evolved since the first day of class? How have you changed? In what areas are you still struggling? Finally, talk about 2-3 ways you will apply your learning to become a more socially just practitioner (Pope et al., 2004). Integrate relevant course readings into this paper for a thoughtful, reflective, and academic analysis.

Action Plan Paper Description—Master's Course

One of the more advanced student affairs competencies is to engage in "opportunities for self-reflection and self-evaluation on issues of equity, diversity, and inclusion" (ACPA/NASPA, 2010, p. 13). Reflect upon this competency and your learning in the course and develop an action plan. Describe 2-3 ways you will engage in self-reflection and self-evaluation after this course ends. Also, consider 2-3 ways you can engage with programs, services, and policies aimed at making your assistantship, work setting, or home life more inclusive. Be sure to explain how key social justice concepts shaped your thinking about this plan.

Student Perspectives on Transformative Social Justice Education

To write this chapter, each of us reread our course papers and crafted additional retrospective writings about the ways the learning community shaped our personal and professional world views and behaviors. In the following pages, we share selections from our course papers as well as postcourse reflections to offer insight into our shifting paradigms and desires to become socially just educators. This chapter reflects a deep desire on the part of us as educators and learners to "continue to investigate ways to improve our conditions as learners, teachers, and researchers" (introduction, this volume). To exemplify continued investigations as well as the reality that "transformative learning is not an independent act but is an interdependent relationship built upon trust" (Baumgartner, 2001, p. 19), we share our insights in the form of a conversation situated within the Scholarship of Teaching and Learning.

These two social justice courses were often the first (sometimes only) academic setting where we were asked to engage in critical reflection on our social identities within the matrix of domination (Collins, 2000). The courses transformed our world views. As many scholars have argued, transformed world views often result from triggering events, disorienting dilemmas, and cognitive dissonance (Baumgartner, 2001; Mezirow, 1991). Others, however, have noted the impetus for paradigm shifts can result from "long cumulative process[es]" such as learning in a social justice course (Taylor, 2000, p. 300). As a result of these transformative social justice courses, we came to see ourselves, and the world around us, in a different light. Our paradigms about diversity and the inclusiveness of our society (and educational institutions) were forever altered once we began to recognize the matrix of domination and question oppressive dominant ideologies that perpetuate oppression (Brookfield, 2000; Goodman, 2011; Collins, 2000; Vaccaro, 2013). A dominant ideology refers to the "means by which relations of power, control and dominance are maintained and preserved within any society" (Augoustinos, 1998, p. 159). Some common dominant ideologies perpetuated in the United States include the ideas that inequality is largely a vestige of the past, that the playing field is equal and every person has an equal opportunity to succeed, and that oppression only manifests in overt acts of exclusion. In this course, we began to see these ideologies for what they really are—myths that perpetuate oppression. In turn, our world views began to shift.

> VACCARO: Years ago, as a graduate student, I did not have the opportunity to enroll in a social justice course. My paradigm-shifting moments happened in a variety of work settings. One of my goals as a teacher was to create a learning community where you could be introduced to, and explore, different world views. Many of you talked about altered world views in your course assignments. Will you share some of those reflections?
>
> HOYT: The lessons I have learned have been invaluable in changing my outlook on life. The theory of oppression opened my eyes to how widespread and covert oppression really is. When I contemplated oppression before taking this class, I only considered intentional thoughts and beliefs people put into action to stifle another group. Most often, I would have cited other countries with genocides and tyranny, or I would have discussed the most racist people and remarks I could think of. I never realized how often the things done to oppress others are done automatically and unconsciously throughout entire systems. I am also guilty of using lines like "everyone is equal," "I don't see color in people," and "everyone can succeed if they try hard enough." The readings and discussions in class have shown me that I was wrong in saying each of those things because it invalidates the identities of people and denies privilege as a factor in success.
>
> CROFT: The class opened my eyes to the daily hints of oppression disguised as naïvety or obliviousness. The class demanded an acknowledgment of my own privileges, for better or for worse. Before this class I was scraping the surface. I could recognize oppression but I didn't stop to evaluate the role I play in it.
>
> D'ALOISIO: It was not easy for me to realize that the playing field is not level and that meritocracy is a myth and that racism and oppression not only still exist but are even more prevalent in many cases today. But once I did realize these facts, I

felt as though everything else in the world made sense; I felt enlightened. It was an uglier picture than the one I was used to, but it made me feel empowered to make change. My experiences in this course have completely changed the way I view the world and who I am in it.

Prior to taking these courses, our paradigms were informed by "naïvety," "obliviousness," and dominant ideologies in the form of "myths." Through critical reflection, we came to understand societal and educational inequity is widespread, systemic, and often covert. Our eyes were opened to a new reality. Once seen, we could not unsee the realities of oppression and privilege that surround us.

Shifting our world views was not an easy process. Transformative social justice education is not merely a cognitive exercise; it is also deeply emotional work. Learning about privilege and reflecting on manifestations of marginalization can be especially emotional (Goodman, 2011; Vaccaro, 2013; Watt, 2007). As D'Aloisio noted, it required us to see an "uglier picture" of our world and, sometimes, ourselves.

> VACCARO: Social justice education is both a personal and professional journey that has engendered a roller coaster of emotions for me. As such, I attempted to design learning communities where everyone was inspired, challenged, and supported while wrestling with the emotions associated with social justice education.
>
> CHARTELAIN: This class has been an emotional roller coaster for me. There were high moments when I allowed myself to take on a particular lens and learned about an unknown issue related to my privilege. For example, I am heterosexual; I never have to second-guess what others will perceive of me when they see me with the opposite sex. I can comfortably walk the streets with my male beau and not be ostracized. Another privileged population I associate myself with is the able-bodied. My full body functions, and I never have to base my restaurant choice on whether or not they can accommodate my physical ability. In times like those, I felt empowered to effect change on college campuses. On the contrary, there were times when I felt discouraged and hopeless because despite extensive research, issues such as racism, classism, and sexism are still prevalent in higher education institutions today, and they continue to shape my daily life as a working-class woman of color.
>
> HOYT: In my journey, I felt a huge range of emotions. I was incredibly excited to finally be learning about issues and ideas that have always been seen as taboo in other courses. We were finally having *real* conversations about race, gender, religion, sexual identities, and social class. I felt like I was really going to learn from other people and be able to share things about myself that I don't normally talk about. When discussing my own marginalized gender and social class identities, I was confident and felt as though I finally had words to describe some of the experiences I've had in my life. On the other hand, I felt guilty and angry when talking about other people's marginalized identities; I felt guilty about being so ignorant to other people's challenges and angry when I realized

no one had ever taught me about it before. I still feel shocked that children and adults are so ignorant, because people are afraid to talk about issues that are at the core of all human interactions, and schools are unable or unwilling to teach children such valuable information. In addition to these feelings, I continue to feel overwhelmed at the amount of information I am still unaware of.

D'ALOISIO: My knowledge in this area has increased as a result of this class, and I am grateful to have had the opportunity to be in a safe place to learn about privilege in an educational space that many others never have. Many of the articles that spoke of white, able-bodied, and/or heterosexual privileges opened my eyes. This was an extremely challenging experience for me—it was comfortably uncomfortable.

STEVENS: I had written countless reflections of my experiences in divesting my privilege. Each effort followed the same formula. I traced an evolution from ignorance to enlightenment that began with a mea culpa for myself prior to college and usually concluded with a paragraph outlining the miracle of my transformation. This autobiography was different. Setting played a critical role in differentiating this assignment from anything I had written before. I was challenged to train a critical eye on my beliefs and actions. My standard self-flagellation approach to writing about my privilege would not suffice in this situation, and this was what made this particular assignment so impactful. I was challenged to move out of a safety zone that I had created by acknowledging my privilege. I was also challenged to interrogate the extent to which I have not fully divested this privilege. It was not enough to simply admit guilt and outline the number of ways that I have improved in the decades since high school. The autobiography forced me to acknowledge that my commitment to social justice was not as strong as I believed and wanted others to believe. It allowed me to raise the bar and be more critical of myself as a person and as a professional.

As Liston and Rahimi noted in the introduction to this volume, critical and transformative education is inherently about social change. Therefore, transformative social justice education is only effective when it inspires us to take action (Vaccaro, 2013). Adams, Bell, and Griffin (2007) explained: "The goal of social justice education is to enable people to develop the critical analytic tools necessary to understand oppression and their own socialization within oppressive systems, and to develop a sense of agency and capacity to interrupt and change oppressive patterns and behaviors in themselves and the institutions and communities of which they are a part" (p. 2). As such, reflection papers and classroom conversations revolved around doing social justice work in our personal and professional lives. This call to action (Vaccaro, 2013) was always situated within our spheres of influence—namely our families, workplaces, and local communities.

VACCARO: Social justice is not merely an exercise of intellect. In fact, I would argue that teaching about social injustice without inviting, encouraging, and supporting social change is an unjust form of education. However, we each enter (and depart) the learning community with varying levels of readiness to challenge oppression perpetuated by friends, families, peers, and strangers. I was impressed by the ways you have, or plan to, translate course concepts into social justice action. Can you share some of those strategies?

HOYT: My reflections have already changed the personal and professional relationships I have with others. In my professional life, I make a point to bring diversity and intersectionality into conversations. When supervising undergraduate students, I now ask them to speak more about their personal experiences and describe what their identities mean to them. I also see myself looking at students differently and trying to understand where they are coming from in order to better meet their needs. In my personal life, I challenge boundaries more often and risk having more difficult conversations. Prior to my work in class, I would ignore racist comments or be passive with people who made ignorant remarks. Now, I challenge friends and family to see where their ideas are coming from and how society has shaped their views. Even though it usually causes some friction, I feel happier when I speak up and find ways to educate other people about marginalized identities. In future jobs, I know I will be looking for supportive environments rich with diverse people who are willing to engage in sensitive conversations and open up other students to do the same.

CHARTELAIN: One way I see myself doing social justice action is by using inclusive language to make students feel comfortable. For example, I no longer say "my boyfriend" or "my man." Placing a gender on significant others perpetuates this idea that heterosexuality is the norm and that everyone should align with it. Instead, I use "significant other" or "partner."

D'ALOISIO: I have stopped apologizing for being a woman. In my autobiography, I wrote: Nearly every time I raised my hand to speak, my sentence began with "I'm sorry, but . . ." or "This is probably wrong, but . . ." or "I'm not really sure, but . . ." as if I always had to justify why I was about to waste everyone's time and try to contribute to the conversation. What was I sorry for? This incessant apologizing was not particularly unique to my educational experiences; I found myself doing the same thing in social settings and with my family. It was not until I started to witness my own women students apologizing for their classroom contributions that I began to notice this was a problem rooted in women's oppression. If I cannot model a confident woman role for my students, how can I help them gain confidence in themselves? My goal is to serve as a strong woman role model and supportive ally for my students. I can't do this by apologizing for my gender or trying to "act like a man."

CROFT: Maybe I can't change the world right now, but I can change myself, and this class was an eye-opening experience. The course has caused a reevaluation of my character and the lens through which I view my surroundings. This paper alone empowered me to reach out to a past ethnic studies professor and admit a mistake. I have come full circle from that previous undergraduate learning experience. My professor grew up in the peak of the civil rights movement. For the first few weeks of class, I remember being frustrated at the way she talked about my race. I was the only white student in class and often felt singled out.

The world was still black and white to her—we hadn't made any of the progress I thought had happened in my time. I was ignorant in blaming her views on age and upbringing. I felt she focused too much on her difficult past and since I've only seen the present, I wouldn't understand where she was coming from. By the end of that undergraduate class, I was able to admit racism still existed and stopped feeling defiant. However, this graduate social justice class has now made me realize I *still* was not as open-minded as I could have been. As a result of this class, I emailed that professor to reconnect.

Croft's comment leads nicely into our final point. Social justice action does not necessarily mean constructing elaborate plans to change the world. An important aspect of action is continuing to educate ourselves and engage in the unending process of critical reflection (Brookfield, 1995, 2000; Mezirow, 1991; Vaccaro, 2013). Social justice education is both a process and a goal (Bell, 2013). The goal is to transform societies (and our educational institutions) into more equitable spaces. The process is an ongoing learning journey. As such, situating ourselves and our activism within the societal contexts of oppression and privilege will be a lifelong process. Some societal contexts regarding the matrix of domination remain constant, while other manifestations evolve or become subtler over time (Sue, 2010). Therefore, there will *always* be more to learn about being a socially just person and educator.

VACCARO: While I may be the instructor, I am also a learner. My journey toward self-reflection is ongoing.

CROFT: I know this journey is far from over, but I feel more aware of the process and the direction I'd like to head in.

CHARTELAIN: While I notice areas in which I improved, I also still have a long journey to go in order to enhance my cultural awareness.

HOYT: I still have some work to do to change some of my own attitudes and beliefs.

STEVENS: It is critical to note that I am still very much a work in progress. This experience has been enlightening for me because it helped me to train a more critical eye on how I operate in my day-to-day life—personally and professionally.

D'ALOISIO: I am a work in progress for sure.

As a result of this course, and our critical reflections, we understand that there is still much social justice work to be done. We are indeed works in progress.

Conclusion

As we have shown, thorough narratives, critical reflection on self and society, emotional investment in learning, and a commitment to social justice action are difficult educational endeavors. Yet they are important foundations for transformative social justice education. Our shifting world views resulted from recognizing and questioning the matrix of domination and dominant ideologies that perpetuate oppression (Brookfield, 2000; Freire, 1970/2006; Goodman, 2011; Collins, 2000; hooks, 1994; Vaccaro, 2013). Such paradigm shifts can result from triggering events, disorienting dilemmas, and cognitive dissonance (Baumgartner, 2001; Mezirow, 1991) or long-term interactions in a transformative social justice learning community. We hope that through our sharing snapshots from our educational experiences, readers will be motivated to engage in their own transformative social justice learning process. Because the goal of social justice—a safe, validating, and equitable society—has not yet been achieved, all of us have a responsibility to engage in critical reflection and social justice action. A good place to start is in a social justice learning community like the one described in this chapter.

ANNEMARIE VACCARO is Associate Professor in the Department of Human Development and Family Studies, College Student Personnel Program at the University of Rhode Island. Her research focuses on social justice in higher education.

ATHINA CHARTELAIN is a Student Success Coach at the Massachusetts College of Pharmacy and Health Sciences. She holds a graduate degree in human development and family studies.

SARAH D. CROFT is a Study Abroad Advisor at Johnson and Wales University. She holds a graduate degree in human development and family studies.

BROOKE D'ALOISIO is Lecturer of Financial Mathematics in the College of Business Administration at the University of Rhode Island. She has studied factors that predict success with business students in higher education.

TIFFANY HOYT is Area Coordinator at Bridgewater State University and holds a graduate degree in human development and family studies.

BRIAN STEVENS is Assistant Director in the Office of Undergraduate Admissions at Rhode Island College and a doctoral student. His professional and research interests center on equity in access to higher education for traditionally underrepresented students.

References

Abes, E. S., Jones, S. R., & McEwen, M. K. (2007). Reconceptualizing the model of multiple dimensions of identity: The role of meaning-making capacity in the construction of multiple identities. *Journal of College Student Development, 48*(1), 1–22.

ACPA/NASPA. (2010). *ACPA/NASPA professional competency areas for student affairs practitioners: A joint publication of ACPA & NASPA.* Washington, DC: Author.

ACPA/NASPA. (2015). *Professional competency areas for student affairs educators*. Washington, DC: Author.
Adams, M., Bell, L. A., & Griffin, P. (Eds.). (2007). *Teaching for diversity and social justice: A sourcebook*. New York, NY: Routledge.
Augoustinos, M. (1998). Social representations and ideology: Towards the study of ideological representations. In U. Flick (Ed.), *The psychology of the social* (pp. 156–196). Cambridge, England: Cambridge University Press.
Baumgartner, L. M. (2001). An update on transformational learning. In S. B. Merriam (Ed.), *The new update on adult learning theory. New directions for adult and continuing education* (pp. 15–24). San Francisco, CA: Jossey-Bass.
Bell, L. A. (2013). Theoretical foundations. In M. Adams, W. Blumenfeld, C. Castaneda, H. W. Hackman, M. L. Peters, & X. Zuniga (Eds.), *Readings for diversity and social justice* (3rd ed., pp. 21–25). New York, NY: Routledge.
Brookfield, S. D. (1995). *Becoming a critically reflective teacher*. San Francisco, CA: Jossey-Bass.
Brookfield, S. D. (2000). The concept of critically reflective practice. In A. L. Wilson & E. R. Hayes (Eds.), *Handbook of adult and continuing education* (pp. 33–49). Hoboken, NJ: Wiley.
Choo, H. Y., & Ferree, M. M. (2010). Practicing intersectionality in sociological research: A critical analysis of inclusions, interactions, and institutions in the study of inequalities. *Sociological Theory, 28*(2), 129–149. doi:10.1111/j.1467-9558.2010.01370.x
Collins, P. H. (2000). *Black feminist thought: Knowledge, consciousness, and the politics of empowerment* (2nd ed.). New York, NY: Routledge.
Dirkx, J. M. (1998). Transformative learning theory in the practice of adult education: An overview. *PAACE Journal of Lifelong Learning, 7*, 1–14.
Freire, P. (2006). *Pedagogy of the oppressed*. New York, NY: Continuum. (Original work published 1970.)
Goodman, D. J. (2011). *Promoting diversity and social justice: Educating people from privileged groups* (2nd ed.). Thousand Oaks, CA: SAGE.
Hardiman, R., & Jackson, B. W. (2007). Conceptual foundations for social justice education. In M. Adams, L. A. Bell, & P. Griffin (Eds.), *Teaching for diversity and social justice: A sourcebook* (2nd ed., pp. 35–48). New York, NY: Routledge.
Hooks, B. (1994). *Teaching to transgress: Education as the practice of freedom*. New York, NY: Routledge.
Maher, F. E., & Tetreault, M. K. (1994). *The feminist classroom: An inside look at how professors and students are transforming higher education for a diverse society*. New York, NY: Basic Books.
Maher, F. E., & Tetreault, M. K. T. (2006). Learning in the dark: How assumptions of whiteness shape classroom knowledge. In A. Howell & F. Tuitt (Eds.), *Race and higher education: Rethinking pedagogy in diverse college classrooms* (pp. 69–96). Cambridge, MA: Harvard Educational Review.
Mezirow, J. (1991). *Transformative dimensions of adult learning*. San Francisco, CA: Jossey-Bass.
Museus, S. D., & Griffin, K. A. (2011). Mapping the margins in higher education: On the promise of intersectionality frameworks in research and discourse. *New Directions for Institutional Research, 151*, 5–13. doi:10.1002/ir.395
Pope, R. L., Reynolds, A. L., & Mueller, J. A. (2004). *Multicultural competence in student affairs*. San Francisco, CA: Jossey-Bass.
Sanford, N. (1966). *Self and society*. New York, NY: Atherton.
Shields, S. A. (2008). Gender: An intersectionality perspective. *Sex Roles, 59*(5), 301–311.
Shulman, L. S. (2002). Forward. In P. Hutchings (Ed.), *Ethics of inquiry: Issues in the scholarship of teaching and learning* (pp. v–vii). Menlo Park, CA: Carnegie Foundation for the Advancement of Teaching and Learning.

Sue, D. W. (2010). *Microaggressions in everyday life: Race, gender, and sexual orientation*. Hoboken, NJ: Wiley.
Taylor, E. W. (2000). Analyzing research on transformative learning theory. In J. Mezirow & Associates (Eds.), *Learning as transformation: Critical perspectives on a theory in progress* (pp. 285–328). San Francisco, CA: Jossey-Bass.
Tisdell, E. J. (1995). *Creating inclusive adult learning environments: Insights from multicultural education and feminist pedagogy*. Retrieved from ERIC database. (ERIC Information Series No. 361).
Tuitt, F. (2006). Afterword: Realizing a more inclusive pedagogy. In A. Howell & F. Tuitt (Eds.), *Race and higher education: Rethinking pedagogy in diverse college classrooms* (pp. 243–369). Cambridge, MA: Harvard Educational Review.
Vaccaro, A. (2013). Building a framework for social justice education: One educator's journey. In L. Landreman (Ed.), *The art of effective facilitation: Reflections from social justice educators* (pp. 23–44). Sterling, VA: Stylus.
Watt, S. K. (2007). Difficult dialogues, privilege and social justice: Uses of privileged identity exploration framework in student affairs practice. *The College Student Affairs Journal, 26*(2), 114–126.

14 Using Attitude Measures and Student Narratives about Diversity to Enhance Multicultural Teaching Effectiveness

Robert Lake and Kent Rittschof

Attitudes on Diversity among University Students

Educators around the world are faced with numerous challenges associated with effectively promoting the learning engagement of a diverse population of students. As part of many university programs in the United States attempting to help future educators understand cultural diversity, one or more undergraduate courses specifically dealing with diversity issues are typically required. Goals associated with such diversity courses usually include the enhancement of greater understanding of the many types of student diversity and the implications for social justice within educational settings. Toward addressing these goals, awareness of commonly held misunderstandings about diversity is often central to the curriculum.

While teacher education programs usually examine whether teacher candidates have sufficiently learned the required material from diversity courses, these programs often overlook whether the candidate's attitudes have changed in ways that coincide with the research-based information provided in the course and the general awareness expected of many schoolteachers. This chapter describes a study that begins to address this neglected aspect of teacher candidate assessment within the context of a university course dealing with multiculturalism.

Furthermore, considering that teacher candidates study across college or university settings in the physical sciences, social sciences, or humanities, this examination of teacher candidates has relevance to many fields of study. That is, attitudes of future educators are influenced by the context of pluralistic and diverse ways of seeing, knowing, and being in the world as they study across different domains.

Theoretical Perspective

This inquiry is framed in the literature of multicultural education in America. A broad survey of the major works in this field reveal several evolutionary periods of this discipline that emerged through the historical struggle for social justice (Banks, 1993). The first period emerged during the Jim Crow period through the work of Dubois (1903) and Woodson (1933), who were instrumental in initiating the study of black history. The next major period of research arose out of the civil rights movement with the Coleman Report (1966), with whom the terms "social capital" and "white flight" had their origin. The civil rights movement was a catalyst for the emergence of ethnic studies (Banks, 1973) as well as the women's rights, gay and lesbian rights, Chicano rights, and disability rights movements, to name a few. The term "multicultural education" began to be used in the latter half of the 1970s (Grant, 1977; Hilliard, 1974; Klassen & Gollnick, 1977). During the culture wars of the 1980s, multicultural education was aligned with minority language advocacy (Nieto, 1986) and brought direct challenges to issues of race, class, and gender in schools (Sleeter & Grant, 2009). By the close of the twentieth century, multicultural education was fully immersed in the literature of social justice, critical educational practices, and equality issues for all minorities.

The conceptual framework of the institution's education college where the present study took place informs the choice of the literature and theoretical perspective of the curriculum under investigation. The following excerpt from the conceptual framework appears on the syllabus of the course of central interest:

> We believe that Reflective Educators for Diverse Learners, as the theme for our conceptual framework, considers all learners and represents a vision of professional practice for undergraduate students, graduate students, and faculty, joining together to form a community of learners. Therefore, we believe that all educators, at all levels, must acknowledge the multifaceted nature of their work and engage in an informed pedagogy that both recognizes and celebrates the diversities of contemporary life. *Reflective Educators for Diverse Learners* is the framework that permeates various orientations to the foundation of education, students' reflections upon their educational experience, observations of teachers in practicum, and the portraiture of schools. (Georgia Southern University, College of Education, 2006)

In addition to gaining further perspective from some of the key literature in the field of multicultural education by leading theorists such as Banks (2006), Sleeter and Grant (2009), and Nieto and Bode (2008), the instructor also adapted an "additive approach" (Valenzuela, 1999). This method draws on each student's "funds of knowledge" (González, Moll, & Amanti, 2005) as a starting point and lens for recognizing, affirming, and valuing the cultural wealth (Martin, 2002) and diversity of any and all of those who are "other." This includes ethnicity, religious or nonreligious world views, socioeconomic status, and sexual orientation. For example, one of the first assignments given is a personal culture presentation that includes personal samples of home language use, including maxims, metaphors, and accents; celebrations; music; and food. This assignment serves as a "home base" for exploring and affirming diversity.

The theoretical framework and course content was further informed by Maxine Greene's (1995) notion of social imagination through the lenses of personal and humanizing narratives of those who are considered "other." For example, stories of the lives of Muslim teachers and children raised by gay couples, stories of racial violence and hate crimes, historical narratives, and movies based on true stories were all continually woven into the course content. Greene (1995) says, "I have learned the value of connective details. Without them, it is extraordinarily difficult to overcome abstraction in dealing with other people. A fearful oversimplification takes over in the blankness" (p. 95). Thus, teacher candidates were encouraged to share and reflect on personal narratives as a means of developing a capacity to move beyond static views of diversity and *become* agents of social justice as a result. As Greene (in Ayers, Hunt, & Quinn, 2009) writes elsewhere, "teaching for social justice is teaching for the sake of arousing the kinds of vivid, reflective, experiential responses that might move students to come together in serious efforts to understand what social justice means and what it might demand" (pp. xxix–xxx). This notion of teaching for social justice as a means to awaken "vivid reflective responses" (Greene in Ayers, Hunt, & Quinn, 2009) is perhaps best illustrated with narratives from the students themselves.

In one example, a student asked if he could share his personal situation with the class. He opened with "I have three dads." Needless to say, he had everyone's attention right away. He explained that he lives with his father and his father's gay partner and that he really respects the gay partner because of the interest the partner takes in his life and how well the partner communicates with him compared to his biological father. He also stays with his mother and stepfather quite often. One reason this story had an impact within the class context was that the student was very well liked by all in the class and had outstanding leadership qualities.

Another student in the class related the following account of her experience at the end of the fall 2015 semester:

> When I saw that this class was going to be a part of my Pre-Professional Block (PPB) experience, I did not have any assumptions or preconceptions regarding the class. I came in with an open, or more of an "empty" mind. I was going to go with the flow and learn about diverse cultures and take the final. Then I would move on to the next phase of the education program. That definitely was not the case. First of all, we learned about more than diverse cultures and races. We covered topics from disabilities and the Lesbian Gay Bisexual and Transgender (LGBT) community. I

did not expect to be covering the latter whatsoever. We approached the elephants in the room without beating around the bush which I formerly found intriguing yet terrifying. Approaching those hot topics without slowing down has made me more likely to come forward with my beliefs. Being more transparent about what I believe has made me want to become more well-read on today's issues. This also makes me want to listen to people that are diverse from myself. A thirst for learning and celebrating diversity makes a better student which will lead to becoming an outstanding teacher. I want to be that outstanding teacher, and this class has given me the tools to do just that and much more. (L. Chute, personal communication, December 3, 2015)

Our framework for understanding was also influenced by several decades of inquiry on preservice teachers' beliefs on diversity and the major themes within the body of research. Castro (2010), for example, tracked themes in research from the middle 1980s through the late 2000s and converged on the following four themes in research as most current: (1) a lack in understanding multicultural issues, (2) contradictory attitudes/perceptions concerning diverse populations and social justice, (3) importance of personal background on attitudes, beliefs, and multicultural concepts, and (4) instructional practices that foster changes in preservice teachers' beliefs about diversity, social justice, or multicultural education. We find that each of these research themes is relevant to our current investigation. We are particularly interested in major factors that influence change in college students' attitudes. Garmon's (2004, 2005) well-considered research into change factors led to identification of disposition-related influences and experience-related influences on attitude change. Disposition factors include (a) openness, (b) self-awareness/self-reflectiveness, and (c) commitment to social justice. Experience factors include (a) intercultural experiences, (b) educational experiences, and (c) support group experiences. Each of these factors is also relevant to our current investigation, though the educational experiences factor is most directly examined in the present inquiry.

Action Research Questions

The overarching question of interest was whether students who successfully completed an undergraduate diversity course changed their attitudes about diversity issues addressed in the course. The issues investigated included two gender categories of homosexuality and women's equality, as well as the two broad categories of race and social class. We were interested in whether students would demonstrate change in their reported diversity attitudes across four issue categories that coincided with the information provided in the course. Specifically, we sought to determine whether changes in attitude would tend toward agreement with statements consistent with course curriculum and toward disagreement with statements that were inconsistent with course curriculum.

A secondary but crucial question of interest was whether a preexperimental single-group approach to examining change with a widely used instrument would generate valid, meaningful analysis on attitudes through repeated measures change data (Dimitrov & Rumrill, 2003; Morris & DeShon, 2002), despite the limitation of no control group for comparison. That is, by incorporating a contemporary item response theory (IRT) analytic approach to investigate change, we examined whether a single-group pre/post study design would yield measures that could inform teaching and continuous improvement of instruction. The importance of using a single-group design was to investigate using an action research approach that can be frequently and easily repeated by an instructor and that avoids the logistical constraints of control-group experimental research designs, such as the exclusion of participants from treatment or, alternately, the locating of nontreatment participants each semester. By using this single-group preexperimental design, it should be emphasized that generalizing beyond the particular group examined would not be supported. Although a lack of control group also prevents specific comparisons of whether any change would occur in the absence of treatment, the steps taken to support honest responding and our use of an IRT Rasch (1960/1980) scale approach with effect size adjustments were implemented to maximize meaningful data reflecting change. The design was also based on the assumption stemming from Garmon's work (2004, 2005) and our practical experiences that significant changes in diversity attitudes are not likely to occur easily by themselves. As Gay, Mills, and Airasian (2006) have noted relative to pretest-posttest design decisions, "certain prejudices, for example, are not likely to change unless a concerted effort is made" (p. 253). With these ideas in mind, we designed this research process in support of a valid, sustainable approach that assists with continuous improvement of instructional effort.

In particular, by taking advantage of a set of Rasch methods for constructing scaled linear measures and determining change in attitudes, we were able to examine our research question beyond the broad issue of whether expected change takes place. We sought to examine and compare the relative degree to which change in diversity attitudes may occur both overall and for a variety of subtopics from within the four general categories of homosexuality, women's equality, race, and class. By specifying and examining these measures of change, we sought to identify instructional areas that may need to be addressed differently. This measurement approach, in comparison to traditional investigations using raw scores, averages of raw scores, and percentages, allows us to simultaneously take into account both the level of attitudes and the relative difficulty participants have with endorsing particular attitudes. Thus we are able to improve on levels of certainty about the meaning behind the attitude assessment results and better examine potential sources of change, bias, and inconsistent responding that can affect the measurement of attitudes (Curtis, 2004). Specifically, Rasch measurement includes several diagnostic indices that permit item-specific and person-specific scrutiny on data reliability and measurement fit, for example. In addition, any measured changes in attitudes were assumed to reflect influences that include instruction but that may not be limited to instruction, such as maturation or other courses.

Furthermore, we recognize the potential complexity of human attitudes, particularly with respect to controversial topics. For instance, an attitude toward an issue may include both an automatic, "implicit" attitude as well as a different "explicit" attitude (Wilson, Lindsey, & Schooler, 2000). Although most attitude measures do not differentiate between such implicit and explicit attitudes, we maintain that studying student attitudes while remaining aware of complexities and possible limitations can nonetheless provide valuable insights that support the development of effective teaching.

Method

Context and Design

The study took place during the fall 2009/spring 2010 semesters within a preservice education course called Exploring Socio-Cultural Perspectives on Diversity in Educational Context. The institution where the course was delivered was a university located in the heart of the rural American South, a region that is generally characterized by traditionally conservative values when compared to metropolitan areas. The course was a live, face-to-face semester requirement that met twice weekly for ninety minutes. Participants were simultaneously enrolled in two other required preservice education courses: Exploring Teaching and Learning, and Investigating Critical and Contemporary Issues in Education.

A preexperimental single group pretest-posttest design was used. The first author conducted a pre- and postsemester survey of students' attitudes toward diversity. The survey data was used to construct attitude measures then calculate measured attitude change. Attitude measures reflected the relative agreement with statements that were consistent with research on diversity as well as statements that were inconsistent with research on diversity.

Participants

Undergraduate sophomore-level college students ($n = 88$) who were enrolled in and successfully passed a three-credit course on diversity issues at a medium-sized university in the southeastern United States participated as part of a class activity. All students were enrolled in the course as a prerequisite to entering one of several teacher certification programs at the institution. This course is part of a block of three courses that are taken in conjunction with a fifty-hour field placement component. There were two sections of students in the fall of 2009 and one section in the spring of 2010. An aggregate of the gender and ethnicity of the student participants was as follows: sixty-nine white women, fourteen African American women, two African American men, and thirteen white men.

Instruments

The Human Relations Attitude Inventory (HRAT; Koppelman & Goodhart, 2005) assesses cultural attitudes. It consists of a sixty-four-item survey on the topics of homosexuality, race, social class, and women's equality (see table 14.3 for specific subtopics). Each item consisted of a statement followed by a five-point Likert scale of "strongly agree," "agree," "uncertain," "disagree," and "strongly disagree." The instrument is intended for assessment of students who studied the Koppelman and Goodhart (2005) textbook *Understanding Human Differences: Multicultural Education for a Diverse America* used in the course. An example item statement from the instrument that was inconsistent with course curricula is as follows: "Minorities do not achieve as much in our society because they do not aspire to achieve as much as white people do." An example item statement that was consistent with course curricula is as follows: "Racial segregation in our schools and neighborhoods remains a problem." We found no prior validity studies on the HRAT within searches of international databases of the literature. Therefore, both the qualitative and quantitative analyses of validity and reliability within this investigation were crucial to our interpretations. (The complete HRAT instrument is available online at http://wps.ablongman.com/wps/media/objects/4105/4204210/Human_Relations_Attitude_Inventory.pdf.)

A content validity evaluation of the instrument was first conducted by the two authors of this chapter in order to identify items from the instrument that were most relevant to the course content pertinent to the investigation. In addition, the two authors screened for items that tended to express overgeneralizations of course information and yield data from items that would not address the research question well. Mutual agreement was used to identify forty-six of the sixty-four items that possessed appropriate levels of content validity for this investigation. These forty-six items consisted of thirty-one items that were statements reflecting course-inconsistent views of diversity. The remaining fifteen items were statements reflecting course-consistent views of diversity.

In addition, three items from the standard end-of-course student evaluation instrument were aggregated to provide additional context to the findings. These three items addressed the amount of perceived learning and the change in interest level following the course.

Procedure

The researchers administered the entire HRAT within classrooms during the first week of class and again during the last week of class. Students were given one hour to complete the paper-and-pencil inventory. Procedures were designed to encourage and support the same level of honest response on both the pretest and posttest and minimize responding based primarily on social desirability biases. Students read the following instructions: "For each statement, select the response most representative of your own thinking and select the space corresponding to that response. Make each response a separate and independent one. Please respond to all statements. Respond as honestly as possible and work through the inventory as quickly as possible. Do not include your name when submitting the form. Note: Reference to "minority" or "minorities" in this inventory is to racial minorities in the U.S. (i.e., African Americans, Hispanic Americans, Asian/Pacific Island Americans, and American Indians) and does not include white ethnic groups and/or religious minorities." Students were also told that their responses would have no bearing on their grade in the course.

Results

Measurement Properties

The thirty-one items reflecting course-inconsistent perspectives were analyzed separately from the fifteen items reflecting course-consistent perspectives in order to examine whether students responded reliably on the issues regardless of the framing of the questions. In addition, we did not assume that ratings of "strongly disagree" on any course-inconsistent statements necessarily equated to ratings of "strongly agree" on any course-consistent statements, for example. Measurement validity characteristics were examined using an IRT Rasch (1960/1980) model approach. Rasch analysis is a contemporary latent trait approach that allows an examination of both the items and the students on a common interval measurement scale to gauge the comparative differences among both students and the items (Smith & Smith, 2004). Rasch measures of attitudes take into account the levels of difficulty in endorsing each survey item statement, unlike traditionally used counts and averages of ratings. Using the Rasch model, ordinal raw score ratings from the Likert instrument were converted to an interval scale of logistic units, or logits, that are scaled with the mean at zero. Fit analyses were then conducted using the infit and outfit procedures to help examine unidimensionality, an important measurement validity requirement (Bond & Fox, 2007) addressing the question of whether a single identifiable construct (i.e., diversity attitudes) was measured by all the selected diversity items and categories of issues those items represent. These analyses were conducted first separately on each pretest and posttest data set for both the course-inconsistent and the course-consistent subsets of items in order to maximize the diagnostic potential. Measurement change between pretest and posttest were examined in logits and effect sizes in conjunction with variability, error, and reliability indices to help emphasize magnitude and direction. The Winsteps (Linacre, 2011) computer program was used for analysis.

Both the pretest and the posttest scores of course-inconsistent items were approximately normal in distribution, with skewness of 0.17 (SE = 0.26) and kurtosis of -0.34 (SE = 0.51) for the pretest and skewness of 0.37 (SE = 0.26) and kurtosis of

-0.02 (SE = 0.51) for the posttest. Likewise for course-inconsistent item score normality with skewness of -0.21 (SE = 0.26) and kurtosis of -0.41 (SE = 0.51) for the pretest and skewness of 0.18 (SE = 0.26) and kurtosis of -0.52 (SE = 0.51) for the posttest. Initial examination of standardized fit statistics revealed one item that misfitted the Rasch model on both the pretest (z infit = 2.5, z outfit = 2.7, and posttest, z infit = 3.8, z outfit = 3.8). Standardized weighted infit and unweighted outfit levels that are above 2 indicate underfit to the Rash model, resulting from an improbable pattern of responding on that item. Item number seven, the misfitting item, read: "One's gender has little to do with one's educational opportunity." Though misfit alone was not used to determine inappropriateness of any items, this consistent underfit on both pretest and posttest and its potentially ambiguous wording were used to decide on removal of this single item (Bohlig, Fisher, Masters, & Bond, 1998), leaving forty-five items with more favorable measurement characteristics in this modification of the sixty-four-item HRAT.

Pretest and posttest distributions of difficulty measures for both the course-consistent and the course-inconsistent item subsets all showed productive matches (i.e., correspondence) of item difficulties and person attitude distributions for the majority of students and items. Distributions for both items and students were primarily within 1 and -1 logits, indicating that overall differences among most students were not extreme, for the most part. Table 14.1 depicts item and person statistics summaries. Instrument reliability levels were relatively consistent and sufficiently high, either at or above the 0.92 level. Error rates for items (average of 0.12 to 0.14) and persons (0.21 to 0.34) were at consistent levels for the respective number of items under examination. Fit statistics indicated good overall model fit though the combined analysis identified a potential misfit of the measurement model for three more items (infit, outfit >2) that will be examined further with future samples of students to determine whether misfit items exist across student samples. Overall, the modified HRAT consisting of forty-five items showed appropriate measurement properties with this type of student sample and the diversity course being examined. Measurement properties of scaled measures, reliability, error, infit, and outfit yielded suitable levels for meaningful analysis using the modified instrument.

Likert Scale Statistics

Prior to examining measures derived from the raw data, an overview of the Likert scale counts provides important preliminary perspective on the data. While these raw counts are highly informative, comparisons of counts do not reflect the precise magnitude differences among items and among students that influence the measurement scale for attitudes. Table 14.1 (bottom section) shows overall counts of ratings from "strongly agree" to "strongly disagree," which indicate that most students were in disagreement with course-inconsistent statements and most students were likewise in agreement with course-consistent statements, both before and after the course. Many

Table 14.1. Item and person statistics on pretest and posttest.

Statistic	Course Inconsistent		Course Consistent	
	Pretest	Posttest	Pretest	Posttest
Items				
Number of Items	30	30	15	15
N (Participants)	88	88	88	88
Mean Raw Score	247.7	227.9	307.9	323.5
SD Raw Score	48.0	45.1	41.7	37.4
Max Raw Score	347.0	328.0	386.0	380.0
Min Raw Score	149.0	146.0	249.0	250.0
Item Reliability	.94	.94	.92	.94
Persons				
Number of Items	30	30	15	15
N (Participants)	88	88	88	88
Mean Raw Score	84.5	77.6	52.5	55.1
SD Raw Score	13.0	13.5	4.8	5.2
Max Raw Score	112.0	110.0	64.0	69.0
Min Raw Score	50.0	52.0	41.0	46.0
Person Reliability	.86	.87	.62	.72
Likert Rating Counts				
Strongly Agree	174	125	173	230
Agree	641	540	581	652
Uncertain	661	515	326	248
Disagree	851	1036	212	161
Strongly Disagree	313	424	28	29

students were uncertain about statements. In addition, when compared with pretest counts, posttest counts showed 5.9 percent average decreases in "uncertain" ratings, 12 percent overall increases in "disagree" or "strongly disagree" categories for course-inconsistent statements, and 9.7 percent overall increases in "agree" or "strongly agree" categories for course-consistent statements. Counts also indicate the numbers of posttest ratings that do not coincide with course information.

Counts on issue-specific items also yielded posttest shifts to the "disagree" and "strongly disagree" categories on course-inconsistent statements for 9.7 percent of ratings with homosexuality items, 8.6 percent of ratings with race items, 13.1 percent of ratings with social class items, and 12.4 percent of ratings with women's equality items. Similarly, with course-consistent statements, counts yielded posttest shifts to the "agree" and "strongly agree" categories for 19.3 percent of ratings with homosexuality items, 4.3 percent of ratings with race items, 12.8 percent of ratings for social class items, and 8.4 percent of ratings with women's equality items. Averaging these pretest to posttest shifts toward course consistency in attitude ratings across statement types yields changes of 14.5 percent for homosexuality, 6.5 percent for race, 13 percent for social class, and 10.4 percent for women's equality. Although these general percentage shift trends provide a broad view of the change in attitudes, they do not account for the relative endorsement difficulty of the individual subissues within the four categories, nor do they represent precise measures of change. Discussion of endorsement difficulty and measures of change among subissues and their implications follow.

Measures of Difficulty Endorsing Diversity Issues

Linear measures constructed from a second combined Rasch analysis were used to conduct valid comparisons of the two survey administrations. Analyses included combining pretest and posttest data in two distinct ways, known as "racking and stacking" the data, to place pretest and posttest data on common frames of reference and measurement scales prior to making item and person comparisons (Wright, 2003). Racked data allowed a focus on items and associated diversity issue measures of endorsement difficulty while stacked data allowed a focus on student attitudes and changes. Although items such as these that assess attitudes are different than items assessing ability, we use the term "difficulty" considering that higher levels reflect ideas that are not as agreeable to the students as a whole or are more difficult to endorse. This should not be confused with being more difficult to answer correctly, considering that there are no incorrect answers in attitude survey items.

Measures of endorsement difficulty are on the logit scale with zero as the mean score. Endorsement difficulty statistics are provided in table 14.2 in aggregate and table 14.3 by item both as context for the findings on student attitude and for future comparisons. These statistics on specific subtopics addressed by each item can be usefully considered as instructional revision is planned. For example, items with small levels of measured change, as shown in the far right column, represent subtopics or questions that were interpreted in a similar way both before and after the course regardless of the changes in viewpoints among students. Very little change in endorsement difficulty between the two assessments is normal, indicating consistent measurement. However, when change occurs we expect positive change (increased difficulty) with course-inconsistent items and negative change (decreased difficulty) with course-consistent items due to the most probable influence of the course on the way issues are interpreted. That is, we expect the items that are consistent with course material to become more easily endorsed by students who might, as a result of the course, develop a stronger rationale for endorsing those items, stemming from what they learned. Similarly, items that are inconsistent with the course might become more difficult to endorse as a result of a weakened rationale for the perspective, stemming from what

Table 14.2. Item measures on pretest and posttest rack analysis.

Statistic	Course Inconsistent	Course Consistent
Items Racked		
Mean Item Measure	.00	.00
SD Measure	.48	.52
Max Measure	.84	.92
Min Measure	-.93	-1.33
Mean Error	.12	.14
SD Error	.01	.02
Max Error	.15	.22
Min Error	.09	.10
Mean Z Infit	.0	.1
SD Z Infit	1.0	.5
Max Z Infit	2.0	1.4
Min Z Infit	-2.2	-1.0
Mean Z Outfit	.1	.2
SD Z Outfit	1.1	.6
Max Z Outfit	3.2	1.7
Min Z Outfit	-2.2	-.9
Item Reliability	.94	.93
Item Separation	3.82	3.56

was learned. Relatively large change can reflect a measurement problem known as differential item functioning (DIF), indicating an item that is not functioning repeatedly in relative unison with the other items (Smith & Smith, 2004). This can result from differences in the ways perspectives in particular issues are being considered at different times.

Although the majority of items across the four main categories had relatively little change, as shown in table 14.3, a few items had large and unexpected change. For instance, nine of the ten course-inconsistent items dealing with homosexuality did not show large amounts of change from pretest to posttest. However, the course-inconsistent item on the specific subtopic of homosexual fantasizing (number thirty) showed a relatively large and unexpected decrease in endorsement difficulty (-0.58 logits), suggesting a possible change in the way many students viewed this item and possibly the corresponding issue. Connecting this type of specific data to the instructional context of that particular subtopic within the course material and discussion of homosexuality can be a useful part of considering possible enhancements.

Items that were at, near, or above one standard deviation (0.5 logits) of unexpected change in difficulty measures are shown in bold in the far right column of table 14.3 to highlight use of the item data for informing instructional revision. While the category of homosexuality had one item with large unexpected change, within the race category none of the items showed unexpected change at or above one standard deviation. Still, item number sixty-one on racial segregation showed 0.38 logits of unexpected change, making some reexamination of this subtopic worth considering. Within the social class category, only item number forty on stereotypes of the working class led to a large and unexpected change of 0.92 logits. Notable also in this category was item number forty-eight on affecting children, which had 0.4 logits of change in the unexpected direction, also making that subtopic worth reexamining. Within the category of women's equality, three of twelve items showed large and unexpected change, including item number thirty-nine on working hard at -0.51 logits, number forty-seven on hating men at -0.48 logits, and number fifty-nine on sexist attitudes at 0.75 logits. Each of these noted issues was scrutinized closely with respect to future instruction following this analysis.

Similarly, large change in the expected direction indicates that the perception of that item or its represented issue changed more than most from pretest to posttest but in the direction suggested by course content. As an example, within the category of women's equality, item number nineteen on victims of sexism led to a large change (-1.07 logits) that was supported by the course. Using this type of data can likewise be a constructive part of course reflection as recent revisions and new approaches are evaluated for their possible influence. Furthermore, in addition to examination of change, the relative difficulty among items and their subtopics shown before instruction and after instruction, without regard to change, may also serve to inform instructors' ideas about how new students perceive the various issues. As an example, item number fifty-six dealing with adults on welfare was relatively difficult for students to endorse, at 0.92 logits prior to the course. Instructors may benefit from being aware of that type of finding.

Using the data from table 14.3, average change from all forty-five items relative to the course-consistent direction showed that the greatest amount of overall postcourse change among these items occurred for the category of homosexuality at 0.45 logits, followed by women's equality at 0.22 logits, then race at 0.09 logits, and lastly social class at -0.01 logits. Pretest and posttest data columns in table 14.3 regarding the difficulty to endorse confirm that race and social class subtopics were also the more challenging issues with respect to the course content. Generally, however, these data on endorsement difficulty indicate the importance of focusing on subissues within the broader categories of issues in order to gain specific awareness of the most likely influences of the course experience on students.

Table 14.3. Posttest fit statistics for the HRAT instrument, followed by pretest, posttest and change measures for difficulty to endorse.

Course Inconsistent Items on *Homosexuality*	Z Infit	Z Outfit	Pre	Post	Change
10. unnatural	.5	.4	-0.19	-0.07	0.12
14. gay rights	-1.5	-1.2	0.11	0.64	0.53
26. many partners	-1.4	-1.5	0.23	0.52	0.29
30. fantasize	5	.7	0.30	-0.28	**-0.58**
38. promiscuous	.5	1.1	0.33	0.05	-0.28
46. child molesters	-.3	-.6	0.72	0.68	-0.04
54. same sex relationships	1.5	1.6	0.17	0.13	-0.04
62. proves	.3	.5	0.40	0.52	0.12
66. violent crimes	-1.2	-1.2	0.15	0.51	0.36
70. a choice	1.6	1.4	-0.72	-0.74	-0.02
Course Consistent Items on *Homosexuality*					
22. mental illness	-.3	.0	0.58	-0.25	-0.83
34. many contributions	.2	.6	0.44	-0.44	-0.88
Course Inconsistent Items on *Race*					
09. do not achieve	-.1	-.3	0.73	0.84	0.11
17. skin color	1.8	2.6	-0.91	-0.81	0.10
33. affirmative action	-.3	-.4	-0.16	-0.06	0.10
41. all-white communities	-.4	-.3	0.23	0.31	0.08
45. stopped complaining	-1.6	-1.8	-0.14	-0.07	0.07
57. same opportunity	.2	.1	-0.48	-0.30	0.18
65. victims of racism	2.0	2.8	-0.93	-0.91	0.02
Course Consistent Items On *Race*					
21. institutional racism	1.4	1.4	0.49	0.65	0.16
37. get hired	-.1	-.1	0.47	0.22	-0.25
53. cultural racism	-.9	-.9	-0.03	-0.64	-0.61
61. racial segregation	-.5	-.4	-0.13	0.25	0.38
Course Inconsistent Items on *Social Class*	Z Infit	Z Outfit	Pre	Post	Change
12. will power	.1	.7	0.07	0.24	0.17
20. want to work	-.9	-.5	0.03	0.00	-0.03
24. welfare assistance	.1	.1	0.23	0.06	-0.17

36. homeless	-.3	-.1	0.28	0.75	0.47
44. dependent	.0	.0	-0.90	-0.49	0.41
52. tax dollars	-.8	-.9	-0.46	-0.63	-0.17
Course Consistent Items on *Social Class*					
32. poverty	-.3	-.3	-0.58	-0.50	0.08
40. stereotype working class	.9	1.7	-0.44	0.48	**0.92**
48. affecting children	.3	.4	-0.28	0.12	0.40
56. adults on welfare	.3	.7	0.92	0.07	-0.85
Course Inconsistent Items on *Women's Equality*					
15. feminists	-.2	.0	-0.29	0.44	0.73
23. discrimination	.1	.2	-0.58	-0.20	0.38
31. sexism	-.8	-.9	-0.76	0.15	0.91
39. work hard	1.2	1.3	-0.07	-0.58	**-0.51**
47. hate men	-1.1	-.9	0.46	-0.02	**-0.48**
55. paid about the same	.0	.5	0.28	0.50	0.22
63. rapes are perpetrated	.6	1.4	0.40	0.30	-0.10
Course Consistent Items on *Women's Equality*					
11. sex role stereotypes	-.2	-.1	0.75	0.37	-0.38
19. victims of sexism	-.2	-.2	-0.26	-1.33	-1.07
43. occupations	-.4	-.2	-0.51	-0.70	-0.19
59. sexist attitudes	-.1	.2	-0.14	0.61	**0.75**
67. violence against women	-.5	-.4	0.14	-0.33	-0.47

Note: Items are labeled by instrument number and an identifying topic term. Higher measured change corresponds with increased difficulty to endorse, and lower measured change corresponds with decreased difficulty to endorse. The complete instrument is available at http://wps.ablongman.com/ab_koppelman_humandiff_2/77/19966/5111404.cw/content/index.html.

Measures of Attitude Change on Diversity Issues

Linear measures of student attitudes from stacked data were compared. These analyses allowed us to determine (a) whether student attitude measures primarily did or did not correspond with course information, (b) whether there was a change between pretest and posttest attitude measures, and (c) what the relative size of the overall effects was. Comparisons of attitudes were again made relative to course-consistent and course-inconsistent items separately, as shown in aggregate in table 14.4.

Table 14.4. Person measures on pretest and posttest stack analysis.

Statistic	Course Inconsistent	Course Consistent
Persons Stacked		
Mean Person Measure	-.36	.52
SD Measure	.58	.61
Max Measure	.95	3.04
Min Measure	-1.88	-.65
Mean Error	.21	.33
SD Error	.01	.05
Max Error	.27	.54
Min Error	.20	.28
Mean Z Infit	-.1	-.1
SD Z Infit	1.8	1.4
Max Z Infit	6.7	3.8
Min Z Infit	-4.3	-4.2
Mean Z Outfit	-.1	-.1
SD Z Outfit	1.8	1.4
Max Z Outfit	6.4	3.4
Min Z Outfit	-4.0	-4.0
Person Reliability (Cronbach Alpha)	.87	.62
Person Separation	2.62	1.54

For course-inconsistent items, pretest to posttest measures indicated sixty students (68 percent) changed their attitudes about diversity toward correspondence with the course information, four students (5 percent) showed no change in attitude, and twenty-four students (27 percent) changed their attitudes toward the opposite direction of course information. However, fifteen of those twenty-four students (17 percent overall) whose attitudes changed away from course information had posttest attitudes that primarily corresponded with the course information but to a lesser degree than their attitudes on the pretest. Thus, only twelve students (14 percent) showed attitudes that both changed in the opposite direction of course information and were primarily not in correspondence with the course information. Also, seventy-five students (85 percent) either changed their attitudes as hypothesized or remained primarily correspondent with the diversity course content. Figure 14.1 shows the locations of student attitude measures plotted for pretest by posttest on course-inconsistent items. In figure 14.1, negative measures reflect more course-consistent attitudes, as they represent

Student Change in Attitudes On Diversity Issues

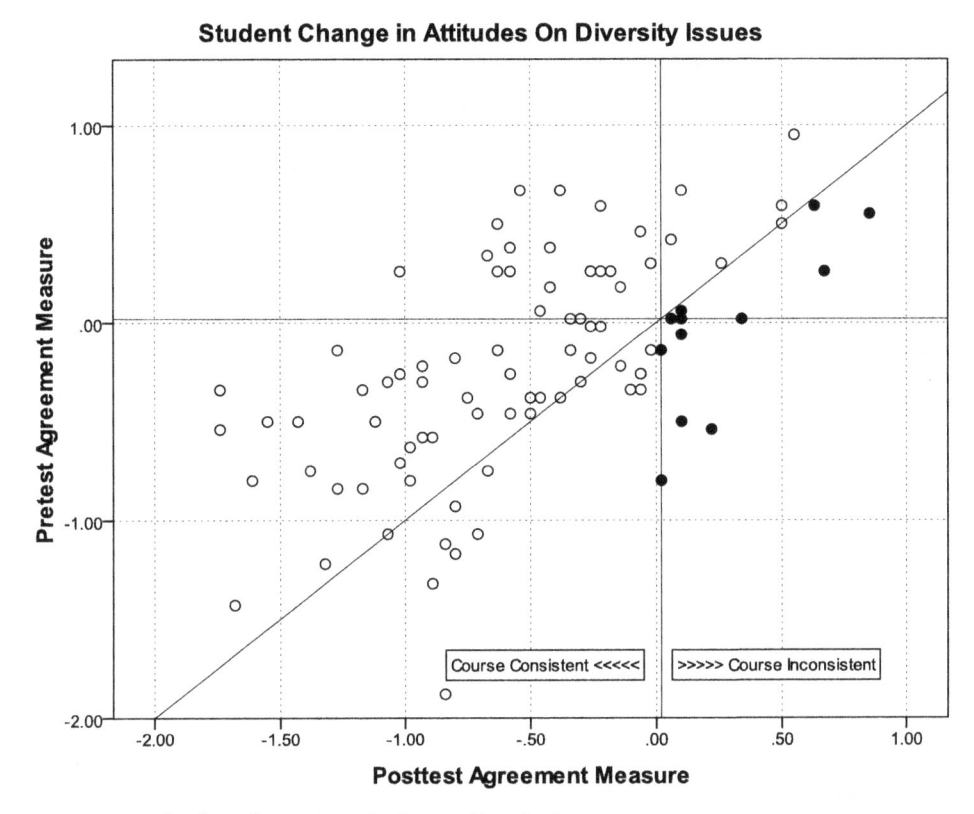

FIGURE 14.1. Student change in attitudes on diversity issues.

lower agreement with statements that were not consistent with the course. Hence, student attitude locations to the left of the diagonal represent movement in the course-consistent direction. This type of plot can be a very effective means of visualizing the differences and similarities in change across a group of students.

Measures for students illustrated in figure 14.1 are also on the logit scale with zero as the mean score. To further assist with interpretation relative to the level of agreement and disagreement, 0.02 logits was the measured point corresponding with an average uncertainty level (Likert rating of 3) for course-inconsistent items. Thus, measures above 0.02 shown in figure 14.1 tended toward the agreement range while those below tended toward the disagreement range. The mean pretest measure of attitudes toward course-inconsistent items was -0.21 logits, 95 percent CI [-0.33, -0.1] (SD = 0.55), and the mean posttest score was -0.50 logits, 95 percent CI [-0.63, -0.38] (SD = 0.58), a statistically significant difference of -0.29 logits, 95 percent CI [-0.40, -0.19] (SD = 0.50), t (174) = 3.42, p = 0.001, favoring average change that continued toward greater

Agreement with Diversity Statements

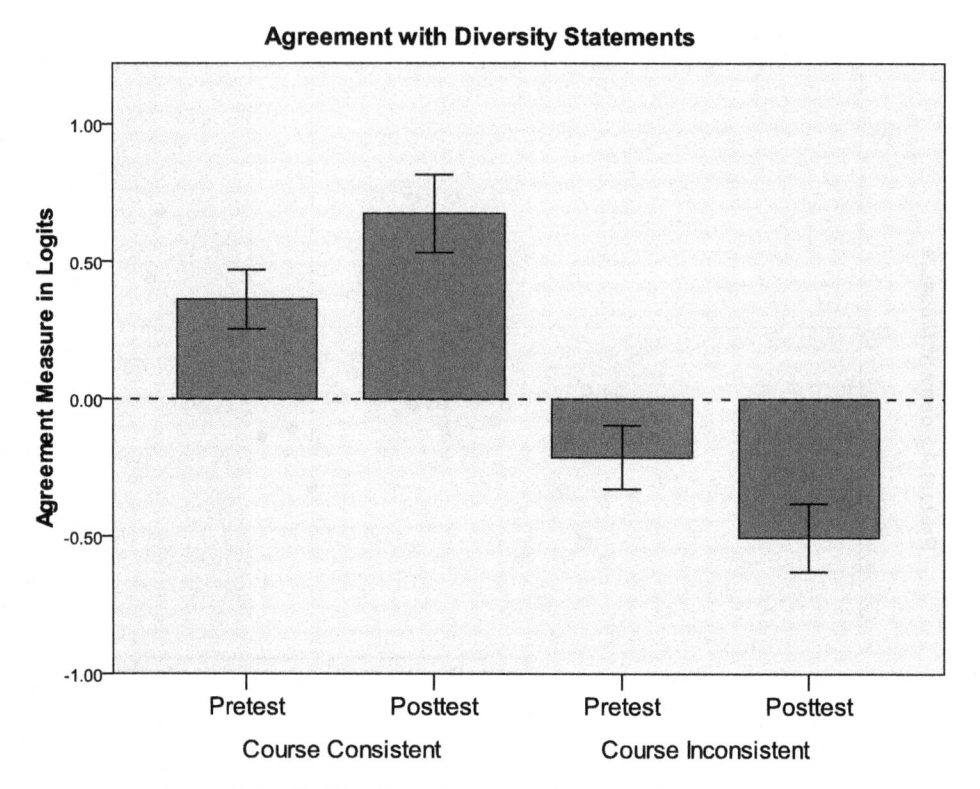

FIGURE 14.2. Agreement with diversity statements.

course-correspondent attitudes. After correcting for the correlation between means (r = 0.61) using Morris and DeShon's (2002) equation, Cohen's d = 0.45, a medium effect size for course-correspondent attitude change (Cohen, 1988).

For course-consistent items, figure 14.2 shows that pretest to posttest change in attitude paralleled that of course-inconsistent items but in the opposite direction as expected. Measures indicated fifty-eight students (66 percent) changed their attitudes about diversity toward correspondence with the course information, three students (3 percent) showed no change in attitude, and twenty-seven students (31 percent) changed their attitudes in the opposite direction of course information. However, eighteen of the twenty-seven (20 percent overall) whose attitudes changed away from course information had posttest attitudes that remained primarily correspondent with the course information but to a lesser degree. Thus, only ten students (11 percent) showed attitudes changing in the opposite direction of course information and also primarily not corresponding with the course information. In all, seventy-six students (86 percent) either changed their attitudes as hypothesized or remained primarily consistent with the diversity course content.

The measured point corresponding with an average uncertainty level (Likert rating of 3) for course-consistent items was -0.33 logits. The mean pretest score for attitudes on course-consistent items was 0.36 logits, 95 percent CI [0.26, 0.47] (SD = 0.51), and the mean posttest score was 0.68 logits, 95 percent CI [0.53, 0.82] (SD = 0.67), a statistically significant difference of 0.31 logits, 95 percent CI [0.19, 0.44], $t(87) = -5.02$, $p = 0.001$. Again, correcting for the correlation between means ($r = 0.54$) according to Morris and DeShon (2002), Cohen's $d = 0.52$, also a medium effect size though slightly higher than that for course-inconsistent items.

Student Learning and Interest Level Perspectives

Three items from the end-of-course student evaluations were examined to provide student perspective on their learning and interest levels. These perspectives were considered an important part of the context for interpreting the diversity attitudes findings. The first item examined was "Compared to other courses of similar credit value: How much did you learn from this course?" An aggregate of the four course sections was examined. Data were similar across all sections, showing that overall 8 percent responded with either "much less" or "less," 26 percent responded with "about the same," and 66 percent responded with "more" or "much more." The other two items examined related to course interest. The first of this pair of items was "What was your interest in this subject matter *before* taking this course?" and the second was "What was your interest in this subject matter *after* taking this course?" The percentages of before-course versus after-course interest reported respectively were 21 percent (before) versus 6 percent (after) who reported "no interest at all" or "mildly interested," 42 percent (before) versus 20 percent (after) who reported "average," and 36 percent (before) versus 74 percent (after) who reported "interested" or "very interested." Overall, self-reports of postcourse learning and change in interest levels showed some variation among students but were predominantly supportive of perceived learning relative to other courses and increased interest in the subject following the course.

Summary of Findings

Instrument measurement characteristics were favorable though imperfect and possibly improvable with the forty-five selected items from Koppelman and Goodhart's (2005) HRAT survey. Survey items were a good match for this student sample, but there was some redundancy among items toward the center of the distributions. Also, for this type of student group there appeared to be a need for a few items that are at both difficulty-level extremes than any of the current items. Fit statistics suggest the need for continued evaluation of a few existing items (see table 14.3 infit and outfit columns) as other student samples are assessed. While there was good evidence for the overall unidimensionality of this portion of the HRAT instrument, endorsement difficulty changed slightly from pretest to posttest and varied among items and their corresponding issues. Clearly, change was not limited simply to student attitudes but also appeared to occur with regard to student interpretations of some issues and questions about themselves relative to others. These findings support the benefit of further research on the dynamics of interpreting individual diversity attitude items and issues across time and experiences. On the whole, the Rasch statistics as shown in tables 14.2, 14.3, and 14.4 provided strong reasons to consider the linear measures that were constructed from the Likert data, while imperfect, to support valid, useful comparisons of interest.

Change in course-consistent attitudes was shown by a large majority of students who reported different levels of item endorsement following the course, the pretest to posttest changes in student measures, and the effect sizes that were just below and just above one-half of one standard deviation on course-consistent and course-inconsistent item types, respectively. That is, most students demonstrated measurable change in their reported diversity attitudes between the beginning and the end of the diversity course in line with the information provided in the course. Findings also identified a number of students whose attitudes changed in opposition to the course information. This outcome corresponded with the instructor's recognition that a few students within each class continually exhibited resistance to many of the issues of diversity, which, at the very least, offered us a vantage point into the vigorous challenge by some students to the intent of the diversity curriculum. By isolating the data from these nine students (figure 14.1), the nature and magnitude of their resistance relative to the attitudes of the rest of the class was more easily examined.

Whether questions were framed to be consistent or inconsistent with course information did not appear to greatly affect their reported attitudes, a finding of importance to future investigations and the use of reverse coding of survey data. One of the benefits of having questions framed differently is the ability to verify whether each student completed the survey in a consistent rather than careless or random manner, regardless of whether other possible threats to internal validity, such as a pretesting, maturation, or history, influence student responses. The fact that the course-consistent versus the course-inconsistent question framing effect sizes differed by only $d = 0.07$ provides support for the relative consistency of the measures.

Item endorsement difficulty measures indicated that a few subissues warranted particular attention toward future instructional revision, as indicated by apparent differential item functioning. Thus, measures of endorsement difficulty were shown to be a useful tool for examining changes on subissues that can occur among students following instruction. With difficulty measures using the same scale as attitude measures, change magnitude for difficulty could be considered from a similar frame of reference as that of attitudes.

Discussion

As Nieto and Bode (2008) have emphasized, our students' understanding of diversity supports effective education in a changing world. Among other reasons for this is the increasing interdependence of our communities that requires that students better understand one another, including varieties among people in a global society. In this investigation, we sought to track the component of growth in student understanding that was reflected in attitudes toward acceptance of human differences. The evidence of student growth shown in this investigation is a type often overlooked by standard assessment practices in higher education. The Rasch measures provided a means to specify whether and how the diversity course influences went beyond learning the required material on diversity research. Most students in the course changed the way they think about diversity issues and to a substantial degree. While these students' attitudes typically became more accepting of diversity among people, findings also provided evidence for the need to adjust the way several subtopics across the categories of race, homosexuality, social class, and women's equality are taught within the course. For instance, the results of this survey have been used to bring a greater focus to the race category in subsequent semesters using the guiding framework described at the beginning of this chapter. The instructor recognized that a greater variety and better balance of personal narratives than previously achieved in the classroom would logically be instrumental in helping students develop the connections that lead to change. To illustrate, the following vignette is from a student who was enrolled in a semester after the results of the survey were interpreted. In this excerpt from an assignment, the student comments on the story of a classmate who up until recently was an "unregistered alien." The classmate was, in fact, one of the highest-achieving students from the prior year, and her story appeared to profoundly touch many in the class.

> What I view as the turning point was when a female student in class opened up about the Mexican coyotes. I had never heard this term before, and in all honesty I just assumed that people who crossed the border merely had to walk across a fence when a guard's back was turned and they were in. It was seeing the raw human struggle that changed me. All of a sudden, the term illegal alien was no longer some abstract concept attached to a subhuman, taco eating fiend, it was someone's mother. It was a she, and that started a change in me (N. Adams, personal communication, December 12, 2010)

Changes in Student Perspectives on the Difficulty to Endorse

Beyond the general trends that express consistency with the targeted goals of the curriculum, some of the specific topics of instruction that were made salient in table 14.3 bring to light some areas of focus that may call for an adjustment in future curricular design as well as areas that appear to be addressed well. One of the most unexpected areas of focus had to do with issues of women's equality. For example, item thirty-nine reads, "Women shouldn't be given the rights feminists are demanding; women must first work hard and earn them." With this item there was a -0.51 logit change (relatively easier to endorse) toward greater inconsistency with the targeted goal of instruction, which was surprising given the fact that the majority of students who took this survey were women. Another example in this topic area is expressed in the misinterpretation of feminists as "women who hate men" (item forty-seven). There was a -0.48 logit change also in an opposite direction (easier to endorse) of the instructional orientation with this item. Related to this finding, the instructor has already chosen as an example the kind of personal narrative mentioned earlier for use in dispelling feminist stereotypes (Kress, 2012). Furthermore, with item fifty-nine, which reads, "Most men in our society are not aware of their sexist attitudes," there was a change of 0.75 logits (more difficult to endorse) also in the direction inconsistent with the instructional orientation on this topic. On the other hand, item nineteen on sexism, which reads, "Both females and males are victims of sexism" showed a relatively large decrease in difficulty to endorse of -1.07 logits, consistent with the more expected influence of the course orientation. This change likely occurred because of the salient course material highlighting that men as well as women are victims of sexual harassment and bullying.

Resistance and Entrenchment among Some Students

Of additional interest to the instructor was the evidence provided by data that exposure to diversity issues led to a small portion of students possibly becoming more deeply entrenched, or polarized (Kuhn & Lao, 1996), in views that are contrary to the information and discussion provided by the course. This finding suggests the need for closer analysis of attitudes on specific issues for this type of attitude-entrenched subgroup. The fact that these data could help identify the number of students (see figure 14.1) who most clearly resisted the curriculum and compare that measured resistance level to those who did not resist using the same measurement scale allowed a useful means of more thoroughly understanding student viewpoints. Additionally, if further investigations indicate this possible entrenchment effect to be common across different populations, deeper examination of the reasons is a next step toward improving instruction on diversity. The various dispositional and experiential factors identified by Garmon (2004, 2005) appear to be useful for consideration within focused inquiries on attitude polarization and entrenchment that may result from student engagement with diversity topics.

Benefits, Challenges, and Reflections for Future Planning

Overall, despite the lack of an experimental control group, the analyses of change were of real value to the instructional improvement process of this course, in part because these repeated measures were calibrated on the same scale for improved comparison. Additionally, honesty in responding, encouraged through the survey instructions and procedures, was supported by data. The students who provided responses in resistance to the curriculum served as one indicator that there was not apparent pressure to respond dishonestly yet in a socially desirable manner according to what students might assume the instructor or institution would prefer. However, it is crucial to be aware with this type of change analysis that effects observed can be due to influences beyond the instruction, such as other experiences at either pretest or posttest.

The survey administration and interpretation were found to be sustainable in terms of the effort and time needed during a semester. Data entry and analysis were considered the most time-consuming aspects for attempting to sustain the use of this type of study each semester. Access to a systematic analysis process, preferably with a campus testing and assessment office, would perhaps allow the best means to sustaining this type of pretest-posttest process involving the construction of Rasch measures from the survey data. Such a resource was not available at the institution where this study occurred. Still, the fact that this type of analysis is becoming increasingly accessible to educators through personal computing tools and software now available is encouraging (Bond & Fox, 2007; Linacre, 2011).

Having reflected on success and challenges faced with pedagogical strategies used and the data from this investigation, the course instructor has initial evidence to support that the course-consistent attitude changes observed among most students can result from (a) deliberate effort to create a nonthreatening class environment that attempts to welcome and value all perspectives, (b) direct teaching that addresses misinformation, and (c) using personal narratives toward the goal of creating empathy across differences in gender and sexual identity. More specifically, the instructor sets the tone at the very beginning of the semester by assuring students that the purpose of the course is not to make students feel guilty about their backgrounds in terms of race, class, gender, or ethnicity. In addition, the more controversial topics, such as homosexuality, are covered toward the end of the semester, after there has been a sense of group trust established. One way this is achieved is through two configurations of class meetings. One configuration involves the instructor presenting material in a whole-class setting with much interaction from the students. Many narratives like those mentioned in the beginning of this article come out of this type of meeting. The second configuration of class meetings involves the students working in groups of three or four while responding to group study-guide questions as they collaboratively prepare a single group document. This smaller setting can encourage more openness and trust in a way that the students tend to appreciate. Also during the semester, each student is required to interview in depth someone who is "other" than them. Though these strategies were considered crucial to instructional effectiveness, it is important to consider whether these strategies or other course characteristics encouraged the attitude entrenchment found among a small number of students. This question will be the topic of subsequent investigation.

Finally, the course instructor has used the measures of change from this study alongside results from course examinations of required topics. By examining both performance and attitude data together, he can carefully consider where he might place greater focus on specific areas of instruction with the intent of more effectively using multiple forms of evidence to inform future practices.

Three Years After: Revisions and New Insights toward Ongoing Improvement of the Teaching/Learning Process

In the three years after this initial research was conducted, information about attitudes toward gender issues and poverty have been addressed within the course in a more concentrated manner. For example, the instructor now schedules diverse women guest teachers to address gender equality. These guest speakers not only contributed to instructional variation but helped validate some of the perspectives students were considering while providing some additional perspective. The instructor has also recently strengthened the personal narrative aspect of the course by adding another interview assignment at the suggestion of some of the students after discovering how much there was to be learned from the first interview assignment they completed. Indeed, the students agreed that the best "textbook" that they could read was the lives of diverse "others." A large majority of the students affirmed that their views of people from other cultures, including LGBTQ individuals, were positively changed through the stories they heard in personal interviews. For example, one of the students from the spring of 2015 chose to interview a student who was a victim of homophobic bullying in school and had suffered rejection from his father. Here are a few of my grading comments to the interviewer: "It is clear that _____ trusts you or he wouldn't have given you the answers to the questions that you so wonderfully framed for him as an individual. It is sad that his father cannot accept him for who he is, but I love the fact that he channels his feelings of rejection into creativity. Most of all I am glad you got to know _____ better through this work. Personal story surrounds prejudice with love and takes it apart, one detail at a time" (R. Lake, personal communication, 2015).

Moreover, as a result of the interpretations of findings from this research, stories from students' field experiences about working with students from low-income families have been given greater centrality in class discussions. This was accomplished by encouraging the students to bring stories from firsthand accounts of the lives of individual children in their field experience observations to be shared in class when we discussed the effects of poverty on the learning process. New readings that address ways of reaching children in poverty were also added to the syllabus in 2015 as well as including *Reaching and Teaching Students in Poverty: Strategies for Erasing the Opportunity Gap* by Paul C. Gorski (2013). The instructor looks forward to seeing what kind of impact this work might have on attitudes about poverty.

In addition to these specific instructional modifications that resulted from our interpretations of findings, our ongoing scrutiny and reflection on our data and that of subsequent investigations on these issues has provided us with further insights. The Rasch measures, being on a common linear scale, have allowed us to consider and compare differences among the course topics using table 14.3 measurements of item-by-item difficulty. Recall that these Rasch item measures reflect the same measurement scale rather than the item-distinct Likert averages using only item averages of raw score ratings. Thus, our measures constructed from the raw Likert data provide more meaningful sets of comparisons than average raw score averages do because the common measurement scale allows valid comparisons of magnitude. An imperfect analogy of this measurement advantage would be if we were comparing baskets containing peaches rather than student attitudes. When comparing baskets of somewhat different-sized peaches using weight as a measurement rather than only the count of peaches, we have a more meaningful basis for distinguishing the peach content perhaps for the purposes of estimating ingredients for peach cobbler, or for consistent pricing when selling the various-sized peaches by the basket, for instance. To extend this analogy relative to our diagnostic processes, we benefit from also inspecting the baskets of peaches first to ensure none of them are rotten or underripe and to ensure that no unintended fruits or other objects ended up in the peach baskets we sell so that we can remain confident we are selling mostly peaches. Similarly, we examine the attitude measures constructed from student data for fit to determine whether our data actually represent diversity attitudes rather than something else.

Revisiting this data and the change represented by the measures allowed us to think carefully about whether differences we observed among topic areas of homosexuality, race, women's equality, and social status as well as differences of item subtopics within these broader topics were relatively minor or relatively important. Taking the time to revisit and reflect on these differences, and the possible reasons the differences were found, has helped us to consider revisions with respect to magnitude of findings. As we reflect on our findings, it is crucial for us to keep in mind the lack of a control group as an important limit on what we can interpret. That is, without a comparison group who did not experience the course, we cannot be certain that any change we observe resulted from the course experiences. However, examining whether any notable change occurs at all is a first step in determining whether carrying out a subsequent true experiment using a control group will be of value.

Table 14.3 shows change in logits from pretest to posttest within the far right column. For course-inconsistent items, we expected positive change, meaning the items became more difficult to endorse. In contrast, for course-consistent items, we expected negative change, meaning the items became easier to endorse. As mentioned previously, we bolded the change observed for items that exceeded the standard deviations in the unexpected direction. These items were examined closely to determine whether there was any possible reason for the highly unexpected findings. Five of the forty-five items (11 percent) showed highly unexpected responses, including items on fantasizing, stereotyping working-class people, working hard, hating men, and sexist attitudes. What we discovered is that these issues were either not addressed explicitly or the wording of the items led the issue to contrast somewhat with the instruction. This was not surprising when we considered that the course instruction was not explicitly aligned with the survey items. However, it did allow reflection on whether these issues required any different treatment. For example, these data supported the idea that women's equality and sexism issues could be taught in conjunction with expert guest speakers who were also women. We also intend to use these measures and unexpected findings to compare with future student data using the instrument.

One of the other clear benefits of having constructed measures that allow us to improve our awareness of magnitudes among both student attitude levels and item/topic difficulty levels is that we can visualize the magnitudes through graphic depictions of the data. Figure 14.1, for example, has allowed us to better understand the degree of differences among our students' attitudes through the spatial depiction of the student measures that allow distances to proportionally represent the measured differences. This use of a two-dimensional graphical display to support our thinking about student differences increases our appreciation for both where (on the scales), how much, and how many of our students both differ from and agree with one another relative to their diversity attitudes before and after our instruction. This depiction of expected change, unexpected change, and consistent responding is both satisfying and humbling as we plan for the ongoing challenges of developing impactful teaching and supportive learning environments. Figure 14.1 reminds us that most of our student measures reflected some type of attitude change and that even among those with expected attitude change (above/left of the diagonal) many of the differences among attitudes were still considerable. In addition, we must also appreciate the finding that ten students (left of the horizontal and right of the diagonal) began and completed the course with relatively course-consistent attitudes but shifted to slightly lower levels in their course consistency in their attitudes. This suggests that the course experience did not appear to greatly change attitudes for these ten students across the issues but may have still slightly altered their views in unexpected ways.

Figure 14.2 illustrates two slightly different overall change magnitudes (effects sizes $d = 0.52$ and $d = -0.45$) that were both near one-half of one standard deviation in change, depending on the respective course-consistency framing of the attitude items. When we investigated students' responses to all sixty-four items of the HRAT in a separate investigation (Rittschof & Lake, 2011), the magnitude of change observed was even greater, at $d = 0.66$, indicating that the addition of diversity items that were not course specific did not deflate the amount of attitude change reported. On the contrary, a modest increase was observed. That is, this subsequent investigation result suggests that our students' attitudes in diversity changed in a way that was broader than the course-specific issues.

Finally, it is worth mentioning that since this initial research was conducted in 2010, the course content has become increasingly relevant to current events and has the potential to increase in its impact on the attitudes and identities of future educators and their students as agents of social justice. Building on a premise that preservice teacher educators have a responsibility to resist static views of course content and become role models of social justice advocacy, we are convinced by our research on students along with our other experiences that careful engagement in a self-reflective praxis of teaching and learning can enable us to challenge and inspire future teachers to also engage in their own beneficial self-reflection on students' quantitative data and personal narratives as evolving participants of change in this increasingly diverse and complex global landscape of the twenty-first century.

ROBERT LAKE is Associate Professor of Social Foundations of Education at Georgia Southern University. He is author of *Vygotsky on Education* and *A Curriculum of Imagination in an Era of Standardization: An Imaginative Dialogue with Maxine Greene and Paulo Freire*.

KENT RITTSCHOF is Professor of Educational Psychology at Georgia Southern University and Chair of the Department of Curriculum, Foundations, and Reading. His expertise is in learning, cognition, and psychological foundations of education.

References

Ayers, W., Hunt, J. A., & Quinn, T. (2009). *Teaching for social justice: A democracy and education reader*. New York, NY: Teachers College Press.
Banks, J. (1973). *Teaching ethnic studies*. Washington, DC: National Council for the Social Studies.
Banks, J. (1993). Multicultural education: Historical development dimensions and practice. *Review of Research in Education*, 19(1), 3–49.
Banks, J. (2006). *Cultural diversity and education: Foundations, curriculum and teaching*. Boston, MA: Allyn & Bacon.
Bell, L. (2002). Sincere fictions: The pedagogical challenges of preparing white teachers for multicultural classrooms. *Equity and Excellence in Education*, 35(3), 236–244.
Bohlig, M., Fisher, W. P., Jr., Masters, G. N., & Bond, T. (1998). Content validity and misfitting items. *Rasch Measurement Transactions*, 12(1), 607.
Bond, T. G., & Fox, C. M. (2007). *Applying the Rasch model: Fundamental measurement in the human sciences*. Mahwah, NJ: Erlbaum.
Castro, A. J. (2010). Themes in the research on preservice teachers' views of cultural diversity: Implications for researching millennial preservice teachers. *Educational Researcher*, 39(3), 198-210.

Cochran-Smith, M. (1995). Color-blindness and basket weaving are not the answers: Confronting the dilemmas of race, culture and language diversity in teacher education. *American Education Research Journal, 32*(3), 493–522.
Cohen, J. (1988). *Statistical power analysis for the behavioral sciences* (2nd ed.). Hillsdale, NJ: Erlbaum.
Coleman, J. S. (1966). Equal schools or equal students? *The Public Interest, 1,* 70–75.
Curtis, D. D. (2004). Person misfit in attitude surveys: Influences, impacts, and implications. *International Education Journal, 5*(2), 125–143.
Du Bois, W. E. B. (1903). *The souls of black folk: Essays and sketches.* Chicago, IL: McClurg.
Delpit, L. (1995). *Other people's children: Cultural conflict in the classroom.* New York, NY: New Press.
Dimitrov, D., & Rumrill, P. (2003). Pretest-posttest designs and the measurement of change. *Work, 20,* 159–165.
Dugard, P., & Todman, J. (1995). Analysis of pre-test-post-test control group designs in educational research. *Educational Psychology, 15*(2), 181–199.
Garmon, M. A. (2004). Changing preservice teachers' attitudes/beliefs about diversity: What are the critical factors? *Journal of Teacher Education, 55*(3), 201–213.
Garmon, M. A. (2005). Six key factors for changing preservice teachers' attitudes/beliefs about diversity. *Educational Studies, 38*(3), 275–286.
Gay, L. R., Mills, G. E., & Airasian, P. (2006). Educational research: Competencies for analysis and application. Upper Saddle River, NJ: Pearson.
Georgia Southern University College of Education. (2006). *Conceptual framework.* Retrieved from http://coe.georgiasouthern.edu/pdfs/cfram.pdf.
González, N., Moll, L., & Amanti, C. (Eds.). (2005). *Funds of knowledge: Theorizing practices in households, communities, and classrooms.* Mahwah, NJ: Erlbaum.
Gorski, P. (2013). *Reaching and teaching students in poverty: Strategies for erasing the opportunity gap.* New York, NY: Teachers College Press.
Grant. C. (1977). *Multicultural education: Commitments, issues and applications.* Washington, DC: Association for Supervision and Curriculum Development.
Greene, M. (1995). *Releasing the imagination: Essays on education, the arts, and social change.* San Francisco, CA: Jossey-Bass.
Hilliard, A. G., III. (1974). Restructuring teacher education for multicultural imperatives. In W. A. Hunter (Ed.), *Multicultural education through competency based teacher education* (pp. 40-55). Washington, DC: American Association of Colleges for Teacher Education.
Klassen, F., & Gollnick, D. (1977). *Pluralism and the American teacher.* Washington, DC: American Association of Colleges for Teacher Education.
Koppelman, K. L., & Goodhart, R. L. (2005). *Understanding human differences: Multicultural education for a diverse America.* Boston, MA: Pearson.
Kress, T. (2012). Rethinking feminism: Towards a critical-feminist pedagogy for solidarity and social movement. In M. Pruyn, C. Malott, & P. Orelus (Eds.), *Paths to gender justice in education: Theories & practices.* Charlotte, NC: Information Age.
Kuhn, D., & Lao, J. (1996). Effects of evidence on attitudes: Is polarization the norm? *Psychological Science, 7*(2), 115–120.
Lake, R. L., & Rittschof, K. A. (2012). Looking deeper than the gradebook: Assessing cultural diversity attitudes among undergraduates. *Journal of the scholarship of teaching and learning, 12*(3), 142–164.
Linacre, J. M. (2011). *Winsteps® Rasch measurement computer program.* Beaverton, OR: Winsteps.
Martin, J. R. (2002). *Cultural miseducation: In search of a democratic solution.* New York, NY: Teachers College Press.

Menchaca, M. (1997). Early racist discourses: The roots of deficit thinking. In R. Valencia (Ed.), *The evolution of deficit thinking: Educational thought and practice* (pp. 13–40). Washington, DC: Falmer Press.

Messick, S. (1995). Validity of psychological assessment. *American Psychologist, 50*(9), 74–149.

Morris, S. B., & DeShon, R. P. (2002). Combining effect size estimates in meta-analysis with repeated measures and independent-groups designs. *Psychological Methods, 7*, 105–125.

Nieto, S. (1986). Equity in education: The case for bilingual education. *Bulletin of the Council on Interracial Books for Children, l7*(3 & 4), 4–8.

Nieto, S. (2000). Placing equity front and center: Some thoughts on transforming teacher education for a new century. *Journal of Teacher Education, 51*(3), 180–187.

Nieto, S., & Bode, P. (2008). *Affirming diversity: The socio-political context of multicultural education.* Boston, MA: Pearson.

Pearl, A. (1997). Cultural and accumulated environmental deficit models. In R. Valencia (Ed.), *The evolution of deficit thinking: Educational thought and practice* (pp. 132–159). London, England: Falmer Press.

Pollock, M. (2004). *Colormute: Race talk dilemmas in an American school.* Princeton, NJ: Princeton University Press.

Rasch, G. (1980). *Probabilistic models for some intelligence and attainment tests.* Chicago, IL: University of Chicago Press. (Original work published 1960.)

Reynolds, W., & Webber, J. (2004). Introduction. In W. Reynolds & J. Webber (Eds.), *Expanding curriculum theory* (pp. 1–18). Mahwah, NJ: Erlbaum.

Rittschof, K. A., & Lake, R. (2011). *Constructing measures of attitude change on diversity issues.* Paper at the Annual Meeting of the Association for Psychological Science, May 28, 2011, Washington, DC.

Schofield, J. (1997). Causes and consequences of the colorblind perspective. In J. Banks & C. M. Banks (Eds.), *Multicultural education: Issues and perspectives* (pp. 251–271). Needham Heights, MA: Allyn & Bacon.

Sleeter, C. (1995). White preserves students and multicultural education coursework. In J. Larkin & C. Sleeter (Eds.), *Developing multicultural teacher education curricula* (pp. 17–30). Albany: State University of New York Press.

Sleeter, C. E., & Grant, C. A. (2009). *Making choices for multicultural education: Five approaches to race, class and gender.* New York, NY: Wiley.

Smith, E. V., & Smith, R. M. (2004). *Introduction to Rasch measurement: Theory, models, and applications.* Maple Grove, MN: JAM Press.

Valencia, R., & Solorzano, D. (1997). Contemporary deficit thinking. In R. Valencia (Ed.), *The evolution of deficit thinking: Educational thought and practice* (pp. 160–210). Washington, DC: Falmer Press.

Valenzuela, A. (1999). *Subtractive schooling. U.S.-Mexican youth and the politics of caring.* Albany: State University of New York Press.

Wilson, T. D., Lindsey, S., & Schooler, T. Y. (2000). A model of dual attitudes. *Psychological Review, 107*(1), 101–126.

Woodson, C. (1933). *The miseducation of the Negro.* New York, NY: AMS Press.

Wright, B. D. (2003). Rack and stack: Time 1 vs. time 2. *Rasch Measurement Transactions, 17*(1), 905–906.

Wright, B. D., & Stone, M. H. (1979). *Best test design.* Chicago, IL: MESA Press

Zeichner, K. (1996). Educating teachers for cultural diversity. In K. Zeichner, S. Melnick, & M. Gomez (Eds.), *Current reforms in preservice teacher education* (pp. 133–175). New York, NY: Teachers College Press.

15 Building Student Self-Awareness of Learning to Enhance Diversity in the Sciences

Erin Peters-Burton and Giuseppina Kysar Mattietti

MANY MEMBER COUNTRIES of the Organisation for Economic Co-operation and Development have reported significant growth in their skilled workers in STEM, some surpassing the United States (National Science Foundation, 2014), which is an indication that the United States is doing a poor job encouraging and retaining young learners in the fields of STEM as compared to other countries around the globe.

To exacerbate this problem, of the few students who are pursuing STEM fields, there is a disproportionately low participation of African Americans, Native Americans, and Latinos. Although 33 percent of the school-age population is comprised of African Americans, Native Americans, and Latinos, only 11 percent of these minority groups become professionals in the STEM fields (Chubin, May, & Babco, 2005). Some of the most important precollegiate factors in completing a bachelor's degree, particularly in science, were found to be academic intensity in high school (Adelman, 2006) and level of mathematical proficiency (Astin & Astin, 1992). However, schools with students who are in the lowest socioeconomic status rarely offer mathematics above Algebra II (Adelman, 2006). The United States needs a more representative workforce, particularly in the STEM fields where innovations in technologies and medicine affect us all.

Recent reports indicate that not only is the United States falling behind in science proficiency in its K–12 education system, its international rankings tend to get worse as students mature. For example, in tests comparing achievement across students internationally, US students are relatively competitive in fourth grade but are below the fiftieth percentile in eighth-grade testing (National Center for Educational Statistics

[NCES], 2013), and there is a dearth of young people, particularly from diverse backgrounds, pursuing science as a career (President's Council of Advisors on Science and Technology, 2010). US students also possess relatively low levels of interest in science and exhibit deficiencies in various types of science practices, such as designing investigations to reliably collect data and then analyzing and using data to support logical conclusions (NCES, 2013). The dearth of typically underrepresented groups in STEM could be remedied by renovating educational experiences starting early in students' careers so that everyone has an opportunity to understand how science works and to pursue employment in the STEM fields.

Supportive educational environments have been positively linked to retention and persistence of students of color in STEM fields (Cole & Espinoza, 2008; Fries-Britt, Younger, & Hall, 2010; Hurtado, Cabrera, Lin, Arellano, & Espinosa, 2009). Tsui (2007) found in a review of the literature three factors that are effective strategies to increase diversity in STEM fields: bridge programs, mentoring, and exposure to research experiences. Although there are clearly a variety of contextual (e.g., quality of instruction, nature of feedback) and student variables (e.g., motivation, self-regulation) that may contribute to this perpetual pattern of science underachievement, researchers have increasingly turned their attention to the importance of building self-awareness of learning processes in students in the hopes that it will increase participation of students who consider themselves "not science-minded," particularly those students who are traditionally underrepresented in science. By making progress in student understanding of how science works as a field, we can also increase the number of those typically left out of the STEM pipeline.

Students who have a deep understanding of how science works as a discipline and how they personally learn science may be more able to make more logical decisions that are scientifically valid (Akerson & Abd-El-Khalick, 2003; Crawford, 2005). Although it is intuitive to think that just by conducting inquiry students will understand how scientists operate, there is a body of research demonstrating that the current ways that science is approached in classrooms, both in the K–12 system and at the college level, has been found to be less than effective in building foundational knowledge in science (Gess-Newsome, 2002; Khishfe & Abd-El-Khalick, 2002). Further, the teacher plays a pivotal role in designing class discussions in what science is, how scientists work, and how to be active learners in understanding the scientific enterprise (Bianchini & Colburn, 2000; Peters-Burton, 2015). A typical student is exposed to the content of science, not to the culture of science (Hogan, 1999), so it is important for teachers to provide the scaffolding that will illustrate how scientists think and operate. We feel that communicating the culture of science is essential in science education because knowing all the types of fish in the world doesn't make you a fisher. This is particularly important when engaging underrepresented students because they tend to not identify with scientists, who often do not look like them, and they do not feel a part of the community of science (Walls, 2012). Seventy percent of the current STEM workforce is white, and the second largest racial/ethnic group in the STEM fields is Asians (19%). Unfortunately, there are only 5 percent Latinos, slightly less than 5 percent African Americans, and 0.2 percent Native Americans that make up the STEM workforce (National Science Foundation, 2014). Since we do not yet employ many Native American, African American, and Latino STEM professionals, we must look to other ways to help students of color feel part of the STEM community.

Many students are being left out of pursuing further studies in science because the current system of science education values only students who learn via completion in an isolated rather than collaborative way (Tobias, 1990). The stereotype is that students who excel in science tend to be the ones who can conform to the institutional structure where the teacher is the sole source of knowledge (Freire, 1970). Through the idea of "education as the practice of freedom" (hooks, 1994), we explore tangible ways to break down that stereotype. Our research begins with the assumption that if teachers teach the ways science operates as a discipline, students will gain more power to construct their own scientific knowledge because they will understand the "rules" of knowledge validation (Duschl, 1990). Learning how scientific knowledge is constructed and being self-aware of one's own learning in science can help level the playing field so that students can do inquiry well (National Research Council, 1996; American Association for the Advancement of Science, 1993). In turn, the science classroom will be a more inclusive, positive environment rather than relying on isolated competition, which tends to marginalize rather than motivate students. In this chapter, we present an overview of the purpose, methods, and results of the research agendas that we have pursued over eight years that focus on helping students become self-aware of their learning in science and of how scientific knowledge is constructed. Many of these strategies have demonstrated the ability to help all students understand heuristics that STEM fields use to learn about the world and innovate products, thus creating opportunities for less-represented groups to gain numbers in the STEM professions.

In this chapter, we will give an overview of the constructs that have provided a gateway to engaging students in meaningful science learning, such as metacognition and self-regulated learning. Then we provide tangible interventions in these areas and educational research on their outcomes, suggesting ways to engage all students in meaningful scientific endeavors. We hope to demonstrate the value of doing Scholarship of Teaching and Learning in supporting all students in science. We begin the discussion of the interventions and outcomes by focusing on ways to support student self-awareness of learning. The next section in this chapter describes interventions that have worked well to support teacher pedagogical knowledge on science topics that help students to see how knowledge is generated in science, such as epistemic beliefs and argumentation structures. Presenting interventions focused on both students and teachers provides multiple fronts from which to address the imbalance of the backgrounds of STEM professionals as well as a foundation of knowledge that is necessary for all participating citizens in a democracy.

Building Self-Awareness of Learning Science

Some students enter science courses equipped with the cognitive skills to take on new challenges with confidence, adapt to new learning environments, and use feedback on their failures to reposition their learning strategies in a positive way in the future. However, many students tend to be passive learners who blame their failures on external, uncontrollable sources, such as "I'm just not good at science" or "Mathematics is too hard for me" or most destructively, "The teacher just doesn't like me." It is the latter students who tend to be from underrepresented groups in science, and although focused recruitment into the sciences is a start, there needs to be approaches for retaining these students (Cole & Espinoza, 2008). The following section discusses a variety of approaches that can assist teachers in helping learners of all ages become more aware of their learning, to be less afraid of the subject of science, and to adopt processes of learning that will result in successful academic achievement.

Metacognition

Metacognition consists of executive functions that control actions or the ability to recognize and evaluate thinking patterns (Weinert, 1987). In other words, metacognition is the ability to think about your thinking and consider the effectiveness of those processes (Brown, 1987). Metacognition is a requirement of self-awareness of learning and needs to be supported for students unskilled at this type of reflection. Active support of metacognition in educational settings can level the playing field for those underrepresented in science fields.

Metacognition has two factors: monitoring of cognition and control of cognition. Monitoring allows individuals to be aware of, observe, and reflect on cognitive processes (Schwartz & Perfect, 2002), whereas control makes up the conscious and unconscious decisions that are made based on the output of the monitoring process. An example of the implementation of metacognitive monitoring and control is seen when a student approaches the analysis of data. A learner who is metacognitively monitoring her approach considers processes of analysis that she has used in the past, both fruitful and nonproductive, that fit the type of data she has acquired. The decision she makes to use the fruitful approach, rather than the nonproductive approach to analysis, demonstrates that she has metacognitive control as well.

Empirical studies have shown that metacognitive monitoring and control processes can be taught to students and are not necessarily innate characteristics of learners. From our own experience, we notice that students are surprised that they can actually control how they learn because they have never heard of the concept previously. Teaching students about metacognitive strategies, such as prompting students to check their thinking (Peters & Kitsantas, 2010), and instruction on adaptive and flexible control strategies (Thiede & Dunlosky, 1999; Son & Schwartz, 2002) have improved academic learning. Magntorn and Hellden (2005) demonstrated that providing students with metacognitive cues helped them to recognize the importance of knowing a few key species in the study of ecology. Wetzstein and Hacker (2004) used question-based reflective verbalization to help students improve solution quality to a design problem. Metacognition can be taught explicitly, and teachers can take action to shift their students' thinking to be more scientifically oriented through metacognitive prompts. Teachers can develop metacognition in their students as a step toward students building a self-awareness of learning, which can result in students feeling less alienated and more engaged in science class. Students who previously felt marginalized from science can be involved in opportunities that were once closed off to them.

Self-Regulated Learning

Self-regulated learning is another mechanism to support student self-awareness of learning in science. Students who are self-regulated are metacognitively, motivationally, and behaviorally active participants in their own learning processes (Zimmerman, 1989). Self-regulated learning is also a process that can be instructed and does not need to be an innate characteristic of learners (Zimmerman, 2000). Although self-regulated learning is an internal property, teachers can assist students to become independent learners by modeling how they themselves are self-regulating their learning (Hadwin & Oshige, 2011). Naïve self-regulators, who attribute their failures to ability limitations, seldom use strategic learning processes and rely on trial-and-error experiences to implement new methods of learning (Costa, Calderia, Gallastegui, & Otero, 2000). Skillful self-regulators attribute negatively evaluated outcomes mainly to strategy use, learning method, or insufficient practice. Teachers can help learners progress from naïve to skillful self-regulated learners through modeling and providing supported opportunities for students to practice their skills to be independent learners. When students become independent learners, they no longer need to depend on teachers to give them information. Rather, they are free to explore and learn about the world around them in a way that is personally enriching.

Learners who are typically disenfranchised from science do not attempt to engage in learning science and attribute their failures to their own internal limitations. Of course, all students can learn science, and therefore teachers need to engage in alternative methods of instruction in order to capture the students who believe they are not "science-minded." Consider a student who lacks engagement in eighth-grade science class. This student is uninterested, most likely because he cannot get a foothold in learning the subject. He tends to fail the tests, which further discourages him from trying to learn in science. If his science teacher could scaffold learning strategies for him, such as focusing on one or two key skills before progressing on to the others instead of trying to learn about all of the science process skills necessary to complete a laboratory report, this student can experience small successes, which can bolster his confidence to learn. Little by little, the student can take more risks in his learning without experiencing crushing defeats with each evaluation he receives. As the student learns more strategies for learning science, he adds to his portfolio of successes, gradually learning more and becoming a more independent learner. There must be a tipping point of success when this student begins to feel more accepted in the community and builds an identity as a science learner. Self-regulated learning is the foundation for supporting students who need to learn how to learn, and sadly, the students who need support in learning how to learn typically come from groups underrepresented in STEM fields.

Self-regulated learners enter three phases of a learning cycle: forethought, performance, and self-reflection (Zimmerman, 2000). The forethought phase sets the stage for action, such as analyzing tasks and setting process-oriented goals (e.g., student teachers are asked to organize the content they already know about the nature of science). The performance phase includes processes that occur during the action, such as implementation of the task and self-monitoring (e.g., student teachers are asked to write about their understanding of the nature of science). The self-reflection phase refers to the processes that occur after the performance efforts that influence a person's response to the action (e.g., student teachers compare their understandings of the nature of science against pieces written about the subject or instructor feedback). Because learners continue to cycle through the self-regulation feedback loops, they have more sophisticated forethought, performance, and self-reflection. Although self-regulatory processes are internally driven, they can be encouraged by mentors or an appropriately constructed learning environment (Zimmerman, 2000), thus allowing for effective incorporation of how science is performed in a directed way. Teachers, particularly those serving Native American, African American, and Latino students, should model self-regulated learning strategies in science to give all students the ability to effectively learn on their own outside of school.

Within each of the three phases there are variables that further explain how the self-regulation cycle works. Table 15.1 explains the subprocesses that occur in each phase. Productive and successful learners have positively oriented subprocess strategies that lead to improved learning with each cycle. Unsuccessful learners have negatively oriented subprocess strategies that cause a downward spiral of misinformed learning strategies and decreased learning outcomes.

Table 15.1. Phases, subprocesses and definitions of subprocesses in Self-Regulated Learning Theory.

Phase	Subprocess	Definition of subprocess
Forethought	Goal setting	Ability to make benchmark decisions to progress learning (Locke & Latham, 2002)
	Strategic planning	Methods chosen to meet the benchmarks set during goal setting (Zimmerman & Martinez-Pons, 1990)
	Self-efficacy	Personal belief about one's ability to accomplish a task (Bandura, 1986)
	Task interest	How much the learner values the task (Deci, 1975)
	Goal orientation	Continuum of values for performing the task, ranging from appearing successful to mastering the learning (Ames, 1992)
Performance	Attention focusing	Ability to pay attention to factors leading to the goal of learning and avoiding distractions (Corno, 1993)
	Self-instruction	Steps to proceed through learning task (Schunk, 1982)
	Metacognitive monitoring	Awareness of learning strategies and how well they work to achieve goal (Flavell, 1987)
Self-Reflection	Self-evaluation	Comparison of performance to an exemplary performance (Zimmerman, 2000)
	Attribution	Crediting reasons for the outcome of the self-evaluation (Zimmerman & Martinez-Pons, 1990)
	Self-reaction	How the learner feels and behaves, either positively or negatively, to the self-evaluation (Zimmerman & Kitsantas, 1997)
	Adaptivity	Ability to find new strategies for those that didn't work and maintain the ones that did (Zimmerman & Martinez-Pons, 1990)

Studies Addressing Self-Awareness of Learning in Science

The authors of this chapter have conducted various studies, across a variety of learner populations, that are anchored in innovative approaches to engage people who believe they are not "science-minded" as well as studies on people who are traditionally effective learners. The studies reveal a variety of ways to help learners become aware of their learning processes, leading students who feel excluded in science classes to become more aware of the scientific enterprise and how scientific knowledge is generated, which is a step toward including a diverse population in the scientific community.

Metacognitive Prompts to Develop Nature of Science Knowledge

Awareness of how learners think and act on the evaluation of their thinking is a critical tool for the development of knowledge and skills and is particularly important for students who have had poor educational experiences in the past. Developing pedagogy for student understanding of the nature of science is of particular interest in the field of science education and has been a focus in educational standards for the past fifty years (American Association for the Advancement of Science, 1993; National Research Council, 1996; Achieve, 2013). An understanding of scientific epistemology and how it relates to content knowledge is especially important for young learners as they begin to consider career and college in their future, so promoting student metacognition in their science class is foundational to future success. Students can unintentionally cut off opportunities to future STEM careers or college majors by not progressing in mathematics or in science classes. For example, if a student graduates high school without taking a mathematics class at the level of precalculus or higher, she or he may not be admitted to a highly regarded college or, at best, will need to take additional bridge courses before beginning undergraduate studies. Bluntly put, this is a social justice issue because, in part, STEM careers tend to be more stable and offer higher salaries than many non-STEM careers.

In this study, we focused on how a metacognitive prompting intervention in science (MPI-S) affected eighth-grade student content knowledge and nature of science knowledge (Peters & Kitsantas, 2010). The study featured a quasiexperimental design wherein students in a comparison group ($n = 114$) learned about electricity and magnetism through guided inquiry and students in the treatment group ($n = 132$) had the same learning environment with added supports of metacognitive prompts. Both groups had the same amount of time on task, and during the time when the treatment group used the MPI-S system, the comparison group studied additional content knowledge.

The MPI-S consisted of four coaching elements focused on aspects of the nature of science that were embedded into the guided inquiry curriculum and were related to the content the students were learning. The first element modeled the aspect of the nature of science. For example, for learning about how scientists use empirical evidence to support claims, the first element of MPI-S modeled an exemplary set of observations and the teacher explained why they were scientific observations. The second element supported students in their implementation of the aspect of the nature of science with a checklist of the critical features of the implementation. For example, students were asked to make observations about permanent magnets and then check their observations against a checklist that included statements such as "my observation has no inferences" and "I used standard measurements rather than subjective ones, such as 'big' or 'small.'" The third element of MPI-S used a checklist including only the key features, which faded support, and supplied questions to students about how they were being scientific. For example, a question about empirical evidence would ask the student, "How do you know that you will be able to understand your data table three or four months from now?" The fourth element coached students to be self-regulated in their thinking by asking them questions such as "How have you acted like a scientist in this lab?" Students engaged in four modules over an eight-week period that studied permanent magnets, static electricity, current electricity, and electromagnetism.

Outcomes

Students in the treatment group significantly outperformed students in the comparison group on tests of both nature of science knowledge and content knowledge. Although students in the comparison group spent more time learning and studying the content of electricity and magnetism, they learned less than the group of students who were coached in their metacognitive strategies. Promoting an understanding of the nature of science seemed to give the students agency in learning and provided a rationale for why they were studying the content. In other words, the students were given access to how scientists think, felt a part of the community, and learned more content. When asked about the MPI-S prompts, students explained that they knew that science was different from other subjects in school, but they couldn't put their finger on how it was different. They reported that the prompts gave them a tangible way to see how science was different. Students in the treatment group stated, "I knew I had to do something special in science, but I didn't know what until the prompts told me" and "Now that I think about it, the modules make me think really like a scientist. Asking questions to think beyond what we've been doing." Students articulated their new understanding of how science works as a discipline by stating, "Thinking like a scientist requires lots of details, seeing things in a lot of different ways" and "When you see something over and over, you will expect a similar thing to happen again." The students in the comparison group talked about science as if other people do science (scientists) and they are consumers of the information. However, the students in the treatment group discussed science as if they were producers of science and thus felt that they were part of the community.

Building an awareness of how one thinks or has metacognition has been shown to improve content knowledge and knowledge about scientific epistemologies. However, in examining the statements of the students in the study, there seems to be more than academic improvement. A close examination of student actions and interactions in a course is vital to designing tools that can build a diverse STEM workforce and STEM-literate citizens. Students who didn't feel comfortable learning science demonstrated sophisticated scientific understanding and actions. For example, Ted (pseudonym) mentioned, "When I first started the modules, I would go back to change my answer to make it more detailed."

Making his observations more detailed is a sophisticated scientific endeavor and a unique behavior for eighth-grade students, who tend to get the work done and not look back. Similarly, Karen (pseudonym) stated, "When you get a conclusion, you *want* to support it with your data." Here she shows her value of acting like a scientist and her desire to be accurate. This study demonstrates that even students who do not consider themselves science-minded want to have strong evidence and arguments, but they might not have the skills to do so. Giving students metacognitive skills, particularly those focused on how scientists think and act, provides opportunities for students to engage in the discipline in the same ways that experts do. When students have an understanding of the mores of the field, they embrace learning, and, as demonstrated here, students from many different backgrounds can be excited by science and fully engage in scientific endeavors. More students engaging in scientific endeavors will yield more diversity in the STEM fields.

Calibrating Self-Efficacy and Content Knowledge of Geosciences

This case study addressed the approach to science in large-enrollment undergraduate general education courses. Our study focused on the introductory geology classes, traditionally chosen by the self-identified nonscience students as the easiest of the courses that fulfills the science requirement. Because most of these students felt they were not "science-minded," we believed that studying their learning patterns was particularly helpful in building a diverse science-literate student population and addressing social justice issues. The undergraduate geology population is large (well over five hundred students per academic year) and demographically very diverse (large ethnic variety, age of students ranges from freshmen to seniors). Students' attitudes toward the geosciences range from those who are very eager to learn about Earth (very few students, mostly the science majors or those who had positive experiences with science in their earlier schooling or in informal educational settings like museums or parks) to those who would prefer to ignore science altogether (the majority of students). In conversation with students enrolled in the class, it seemed that most expected to memorize the material in order to learn, and only a few students realized the opportunity for a rich cognitive experience. Geology is a synthetic discipline that relies on the development of a variety of complex thinking skills. Although memorization is necessary to build foundational knowledge in geosciences as well as in other sciences, it is only the first step in understanding the discipline of science. Because of the diversity of backgrounds, attitudes, and expectations, geology courses are fertile grounds for investigating how awareness of learning through examination of self-efficacy can promote the paradigm shift to an understanding of science for all.

We next discuss the results of our case study about one of the skills needed in the discipline: integrating spatial information and diachronic thinking, which is needed to reconstruct the geologic history of an area. We designed an exercise to have a low discipline-specific content but a high cognitive value to evaluate the students' ability to reason scientifically. The discipline content was about application of the stratigraphic principles of superposition, lateral continuity and unconformity, and the procedure of correlation. These core concepts are used simultaneously to sequence events of the geologic past, where time is measured by changes in the rocks. The exercise required students to explain with both a diagram and a short answer why and where the principles were applied. Students also had to rate their level of confidence in each answer provided. The exercise was constructed to "see" the students' reasoning and the level of confidence that they associated with it.

Outcomes

We found that students were more self-confident about responses they gave to the open-ended questions than they were with questions involving interpretation of diagrams. The students answered diagram-related questions correctly but felt less confident about their answer than about their written responses. Conversely, the students got the written answers wrong but felt highly confident about their answers.

An unexpected pattern emerged: the incorrect answers mainly involved listing isolated concepts rather than the identification of interactions among concepts. This indicates that students did not think about finding more depth to their answer. This type of behavior could have been fostered by the high-stakes testing environment, where science questions come in a multiple-choice format, forcing one single answer possibly provided instantaneously. Students who come from this environment need help building their confidence so that they are not only aware of opportunities for concept connections but are successful and confident in their attempts at synthesizing material. This is further evidence that building student self-awareness of learning should be undertaken early in an educational career in order to help all students forward their knowledge and skills.

A second outcome to this study indicated that the undergraduate students showed lower self-confidence in answering questions containing symbolism. Difficulties with symbolic language are similar to "math anxiety," which is historically related to self-efficacy of students in learning science. It is common to hear students comment about choosing geology because "there is no math" (so they think, as evidenced by the ubiquitous name for the geosciences course, "rocks for jocks") or say that they would have liked to study science but then "there is math." These results indicate that there is a need to model scientific reasoning for the students and to provide many opportunities for them to practice giving complex explanations and using more symbolism (Peters-Burton & Mattietti, 2011). Students who have more confidence in their science learning tend to pursue more risks and push themselves further cognitively (Bandura, 1986). More confident students can result in higher achievement for all, opening doors for students typically underrepresented in STEM fields.

Finally, with this study students became aware of self-efficacy as learning to detect areas in need of improvement. As a follow-up to the exercise, students were encouraged to revise their understanding of the material covered by the incorrect answers to which they gave high confidence. We were surprised by the results and demonstrated the need for increased Scholarship of Teaching and Learning, particularly in science instruction since it could be valuable for creating a diverse STEM-literate citizenry. The focus shifted from providing the correct answer to making sure there was a correct understanding of the topic by applying the knowledge to a simple problem-solving exercise. This shift in attitude is key to changing the relationship of students to science and to addressing the social justice issue of a lack of diversity in STEM fields. Science thrives on seeking questions for which there are not yet answers. Students of science should be comfortable with acknowledging uncertainties and, ultimately, liberating themselves from the fear of the unknown. Students understand that a scientist venturing in the uncharted territory of discovery must self-regulate to proceed with confidence, especially when developing new models, theories, and connections across theories. The paradigm shift from presenting science as an "amount of knowledge" to science as a "way of knowledge" is needed to develop diverse thinking in the science area from people of diverse backgrounds. Science is a work in progress to understand the world, and when students begin to see that there is no need for an exceptional memory or fast reaction rate to provide the answers, they may consider themselves science-minded after all.

Visualizing Subject Matter with Concept Maps

There is a general trend in undergraduate and graduate science teaching that promotes the use of visualization as the ultimate learning tool. Image-processing software affords stunning visualization and opportunities for immediate interaction with the material. Unfortunately, curriculum involving visualization can be misleading because it appears to engage a high cognitive level but is often limited to recall and application. This low expectation of cognition drove our scholarship in the area of visualization because we wanted to create enriched learning experiences for all students, demonstrating the value in learning science. In our study, we retooled visualization by asking students to generate visualizations in concept mapping rather than administering visualizations (Mattietti & Peters-Burton, 2015). We adopted concept mapping because it is an instrument of metavisualization (Gobert & Clement, 1999), which is the ability to elaborate the perception of the physical world as personal experience and to apply it to creative problem-solving. Concept mapping is an open-ended activity that allows students to design their own forms of presentation, making connections among discipline-specific concepts and increasing the cognitive load to analysis and above. The success of concept maps as an education tool has been demonstrated and is widely accepted as part of the meaningful learning paradigm (Ausubel, 2000) and as one of the best practices in the Scholarship of Teaching and Learning (Angelo & Cross, 1993).

Our study was based on several years of practicing concept mapping with students in introductory geology classes. Understanding that these students come from diverse backgrounds, we adopted concept mapping as a bridge from traditional science learning to more meaningful representations of science concepts. Concept mapping was introduced to the students not just as a study technique but most importantly as a metavisualization tool. Many students seemed to be startled at the idea that the learning process could be more effective and ultimately rewarding. Students expressed surprise that we put more importance on how they thought rather than what they thought.

We encouraged students to avoid using preformatted concept-mapping charts readily available in software packages because we wanted their maps to be as open-ended as possible and as much as possible a visual representation of their own knowledge and how it is organized. Our study was based on 159 maps produced by a very diverse student population by age, ethnicity, and social status; male and female students were present in about the same percentage. Most students found the exercise more challenging than they thought it would be, not because they could not recall concepts but because they were asked to meaningfully link them.

Outcomes

Because we were interested in the usefulness of concept mapping in bridging the gap between students who were "science-minded" and those who were not, our analysis of the maps focused on the hierarchy of concepts and the type and value of the links. All students could easily list/recall concepts, and most recognized some sort of hierarchical role, but there was a significant range in the complexity of the hierarchy of concepts, from a simple list of concepts (like a string of beads) to multiple clusters of ranking concepts. Some students applied well-known hierarchical structures, such as ones they had seen from the rock cycle diagram in the textbook. This strategy not only relinquished them from having to organize the concepts themselves but also caused them to misinterpret the map as a challenge to fit in as much writing in as small an area as possible. The students' concept organization allowed us to see how students organized their own knowledge and to support them with an initial intervention focused on explaining that there are ranks in concepts and how organization helps us retain growing amounts of knowledge. We felt that this addressed a social justice issue because concept mapping is open to all skills and levels, regardless of amount of background knowledge, and with a little training all students could be metacognitive about some aspect of their knowledge.

A noteworthy aspect of some maps was the "tangled" links, lines connecting concepts but also intersecting other lines/links. This demonstrated that the student perceived the deeply interrelated nature of knowledge. These maps provided material for rich discussion with the students who were interested in having their concept maps analyzed.

After receiving feedback for their maps, all students seem to more easily grasp the need for ranking and linking knowledge in order to manage the knowledge better. All students who followed up with the instructor about their map showed significant score improvement, and their second map showed an increase in complexity. A few students engaged with the exercise by personalizing the map with sketches and decorative elements that indicated some sort of affective engagement with the effort of mapping their knowledge.

Additionally, the maps offered a rare opportunity for the instructor to identify the presence of misconceptions and to "show" the student exactly where they nest within the learning framework of the map. Misconceptions are not about the incorrect understanding of the definition but in the connection of concepts not correctly ranked. In a concept map, a misconception always triggers a weak or wrong link. It is difficult to address misconceptions based on answers from a typical multiple-choice exam, but concept maps create opportunities for conversations between instructor and student about what really matters in the building of discipline knowledge (rather than just giving a wrong definition, of which they can be aware without instructor input).

A case study from the work we have done with concept maps is a particularly poignant illustration of the life-changing effects of achieving ownership of learning. Sheila (pseudonym) was a self-declared "nonscience person," an older student of color with two children, she initially struggled with the idea of the concept map, and like many other students, she preferred to rely on memory cards for exam preparation. Eventually she started to make concept maps for each class, asking for instructor feedback. Sheila wrote that she wanted to create "something that captures all of the different interactions and processes of water with rocks." This is a sophisticated statement demonstrating that this student has progressed from retaining a lower cognitive level of knowledge (which caused her a great deal of anxiety about forgetting something in performance assessments) to having the motivation to investigate the material in a way that is more personal and engaging. Sheila's transformation is a clear indication of a student engaged with sciences at a personal level, achieved by becoming self-aware of her learning. As a bonus, Sheila's test scores increased significantly over time.

It is nearly impossible to have an entirely "wrong" concept map; this gives students the opportunity to show what they know rather than being penalized in a deficit model for wrong choices. Concept mapping also creates possibilities for a more constructivist learning environment in which students experience and overcome challenging tasks, gaining confidence to embark on more complex challenges, which is a fundamental attitude when one is learning in the sciences.

Self-Regulated Learning of the Nature of Science

We felt that studying student self-awareness of learning was a start in revealing ways to help level the playing field in STEM learning. However, we noticed that we need to address this early in a student's school career. Therefore, we took our Scholarship of

Teaching and Learning into the arena of preservice science teacher instruction and investigated how we might be able to create more equitable classrooms in science in the K–12 setting. As the memorization of information becomes less relevant and the ability to understand what a reliable resource is and how disciplines validate knowledge becomes the "coin of the realm," learning how to think scientifically becomes an ever more important skill for an informed citizenry. A true democracy has citizens who can fully participate by understanding issues rationally. Therefore, science teachers in the K–12 setting must be equipped to teach students about the nature of science. In this study, the self-regulated learning strategies of graduate students studying to obtain their teaching license were examined to determine effective approaches to teach this difficult-to-understand topic, the epistemic underpinnings of the scientific discipline. In order to be inclusive, teacher educators should have evidence that they are developing teachers who can engage all students, not just the ones who are typically successful in science. Studying the candidate teachers' self-regulated learning processes gives a real-time look at learning processes, so that teacher educators can intervene before the new teachers enter the K–12 classroom. To begin building a more diverse STEM-literate citizenry and encourage more diversity in STEM careers, we need to create a critical mass of teachers who can support student self-awareness of learning.

Methods

Microanalysis of self-regulated learning (or SRL microanalysis) is a process that codes and analyzes specific self-regulated learning variables while the learner is participating in a specific task (Cleary, 2011). In this case, the learners were participating in a graduate-level class that focused on two learning tasks: personal learning of the nature of science and how the scientific discipline operates, and how to teach the nature of science to secondary students in a formal classroom. SRL microanalysis features individualized assessment protocols, strategic administration of context-specific questions during a particular learning event, and records of verbatim participant responses (Perry & Winne, 2006). Having individualized assessments helps increase the likelihood that responses are free from social influences, and the one-on-one nature of the assessment exposes the thinking of the individual (Winne & Jamieson-Noel, 2002). Questions in an SRL microanalysis must be simple and brief and target a specific subprocess, such as task interest or goal setting (Cleary, 2011). SRL microanalysis protocols were designed for all of the subprocesses listed in table 15.1 for forethought, performance, and self-evaluation. Questions on the protocol were a mixture of open-ended questions and rating scales.

The participants in this study were sixteen graduate students who were career switchers and had an average of 9.7 years of work experience. The preservice teachers involved in the fifteen-week nature of science course had a range of experience in the field of science from three years to fifteen years and varied in STEM content disciplines. The participants were evenly divided between men and women and were predominantly white (with one Asian). Five of the scientists were earth scientists, seven were biologists, three were chemists, and one was a physicist. We felt that examining the teaching practices of scientists who want to become teachers and then informing the instruction of these candidate teachers based on the results was an effective way to help a large number of public school students from all walks of life become more engaged in their own learning and ultimately feel part of the STEM community.

Two learning tasks were identified (learning about the nature of science and teaching about the nature of science), and the microanalysis questions were asked temporally around the learning tasks. The forethought questions were asked before the learning task, the performance questions were asked during the learning task, and the self-reflection questions were asked after the learners received feedback on their performance of the task.

Outcomes

At the beginning of the course, the candidates' self-efficacy was low, and although the teachers found the subject valuable to understand, they had concerns about the philosophical nature of the course. The initial goals candidates set for learning the nature of science were incongruent with the goals of the course. That is, the candidates set goals that focused on their future students' learning, not their own. The goals set by the candidates were also vague and difficult to measure, such as "I want to understand the nature of science in this course." Fortunately, because the microanalysis questions are administered during the learning phases, the professor had the information about how the candidates were learning, was able to intervene, and realigned the goal setting of the candidates to focus on their own learning of the nature of science. The next cycle of goal setting by the candidates was improved, and the goals were aligned with the goals of the course and were measurable. The candidates used the improved goals to metacognitively monitor their learning outcomes, which led to high satisfaction with their learning for the second task and improved how they attributed their successes and failures[o]. In the first cycle, the candidates often attributed their learning to innate ability, but in the second cycle, the candidates attributed their learning to their processes. The questions in the microanalysis along with instructor feedback helped the candidates to be more aware of their learning processes, which also helped them to act on their failures in a timely fashion.

The use of SRL microanalysis helped to illuminate the candidates' learning processes for both the instructor and the candidate. When both parties were aware of their learning processes, improved learning occurred because the candidate could change his or her process to use strategies that were better suited to academic achievement. SRL microanalysis was a worthy tool to ensure teacher candidates could adequately understand and teach scientific epistemologies to their students.

This is important because understanding the science epistemologies has helped students who do not feel as though they are science-minded to not only appreciate science more but to learn more science (Peters & Kitsantas, 2010). Not only did the SRL microanalysis help learners understand how to learn more effectively, it also provided a model that these teacher candidates can use to help struggling students identify their learning processes and to offer guidance for more effective techniques. This demonstration of the Scholarship of Teaching and Learning is also powerful because this study engaged graduate students, who have a solid understanding of how to be successful in a school setting. Even though the candidates were adept at schooling, they improved their learning processes when they understood more about self-regulated learning. One can extrapolate the improvement of learning to students who are not as engaged in schooling, such as in the study with the eighth-grade students using metacognitive prompts. The use of SRL microanalysis holds promise for helping people who do not feel as though they are science-minded to engage meaningfully in understanding the science discipline, which can further help them to feel part of the community of science consumers. The undergraduates taking the easiest science classes to fulfill the school requirement are a perfect population for this type of engagement, since for most of them, the undergraduate science class is the very last time they will have any formal education in the sciences while their lives will unfold in a society of science consumers.

Self-Regulated Learning of Argumentation in Science

Developing preservice teachers into educators who can address social justice issues is important, but it is equally important to help in-service teachers learn these techniques. In this study, the same SRL microanalysis technique as used in the previous study was used in a professional development setting with in-service teachers who were given two learning tasks: (a) learning how to use argumentation to communicate scientific research and (b) teaching argumentation to their secondary students (Peters-Burton, 2015). Argumentation is a particularly fruitful area to study because in studying the key elements of argumentation, the ways science knowledge are constructed are broken down into understandable chunks. Developing argumentation skills allows students to identify the logic and links between evidence and claim that are the backbone of scientific knowledge. Explicitly teaching argumentation may be a key mechanism for encouraging students from underrepresented groups in science and who are not interested in science to attempt to unpack scientific claims, building agency for science learning. The participants in this two-week intensive professional development consisted of twelve teachers of grades nine to twelve from rural counties. Less than 70 percent of the students in these rural counties passed the state science exam, indicating a need for research into the educational settings provided to these students.

The teachers in the professional development experience were tested on their argumentation knowledge and self-regulation knowledge using an essay-format assessment before and after the experience. Additionally, two learning tasks were identified for measurement of self-regulated learning cycles: evaluating arguments and constructing arguments. Teachers' SRL processes were measured before, during, and after each learning task using the microanalysis interview process described in the previous study.

Outcomes

Teachers demonstrated a great deal of growth in their understanding of argumentation, which bodes well for future student instruction, but less progress in their understanding of self-regulated learning. However, teachers improved their self-regulated learning processes from the first cycle of learning to the second cycle of learning. Participating in the reporting of the self-regulated learning processes may have helped them do their own reflective thinking but may not have supported the declarative understanding of self-regulated learning.

Argumentation Knowledge

In terms of the change in knowledge of argumentation, it was noted on the pretests that the teachers initially confused argumentation with experimentation. They stated that one can only make an argument when the investigation in science was a controlled, randomized trial. They were unable to analyze the argument presented and were only able to identify the variables. They did not report any knowledge of the connections between claims, evidence, and reasoning. However, teachers did connect data acquisition with the evidence needed for arguments. In the posttest, teachers demonstrated a change in their ability to analyze arguments and were able to identify all three key pieces of an argument: claims, evidence, and reasoning. They were also able to build evaluation and construction of arguments into lesson plans using data related to scientific phenomena.

Self-Regulated Learning Knowledge

Teachers entered the professional development experience appreciating the value of SRL for their students, but they were also aware that they did not know what SRL involved for their own learning or for their teaching. They felt there was not enough time to teach both the content that was mandated to teach and SRL, so although they valued it, they logistically did not have strategies to fit SRL into their curriculum. After the professional development, teachers' positions remained the same for all of the categories measured. They had limited knowledge of SRL but reported that they had high self-efficacy for modeling their own SRL for students during lessons. They retained their high value for SRL for students but continued to report that there was a lack of time to explicitly teach it during class.

SRL MICROANALYSIS FOR EVALUATING ARGUMENTS

The first learning task in the professional development was evaluating arguments. The variables measured in the forethought phase demonstrated a variety of levels of sophistication of SRL with regard to the learning task. Overall the teachers' goals and strategic planning were either missing entirely or were not congruent with the goals of the professional development. That is, the teachers set goals to make their class fun or engaging, while the goal of the professional development experience was to increase their own knowledge of argumentation. Teacher-reported interest in the experience was low, although they had a high value for the topic. This may also be explained in the teachers' perceptions that there wasn't enough time to teach SRL, so they could value it but think that they couldn't realistically teach it. During the performance phase, the teachers did not seek help in their learning, and they did not self-monitor their understandings. This, not surprisingly, led to a low satisfaction for learning in the self-reflection phase, and some teachers neglected to even self-evaluate their performance, avoiding any evaluation.

SRL MICROANALYSIS FOR EVALUATING ARGUMENTS

In the second cycle of SRL microanalysis, teachers had higher interest and self-efficacy for constructing arguments and about the same task value. They demonstrated more help-seeking behaviors, checking with outside sources when needing additional instruction. They did more self-monitoring, but it was not from an exemplary source, so there was still room for improvement in the performance phase. Teachers did have a more robust self-reflection phase and rated their satisfaction with learning as very high. They showed how they evaluated their performance on the creation of lesson plans, which was not aligned with the goals of the professional development but showed that the teachers no longer avoided evaluation.

Outcomes

The most prominent lesson learned from this study is that contextual factors greatly influence adult learners. In this study, the teachers maintained the perception that they did not have time to teach SRL to their students. Even though they thought SRL processes were important for learners, they could not envision how to put it into practice given their time constraints. Therefore, they did not spend their efforts on learning about the characteristics of SRL to teach to their students. This is unfortunate because the lack of time is noted extensively as a barrier for teacher change (Brownell & Tanner, 2012) and needs to be addressed in the future. If teachers are not going to support students' SRL processes no matter the reason, that is a social justice issue. Preventing instruction on self-awareness of learning perpetuates the barriers for underrepresented students in STEM. We cannot continue to educate students in science with traditional methods because we will continue to have a lack of diversity in STEM as well as allowing only those privileged to be innately aware of their own learning to succeed in science. Teachers need to give students the skills to be aware of the learning opportunities before them.

Another lesson learned was that the SRL instruction increased the teachers' processes but not their declarative knowledge about SRL. Perhaps the teachers limited their efforts because of their perception of the logistics of teaching SRL to their students, but at least the teachers were able to improve their own processes. Follow-up studies on teachers' attitudes about teaching SRL in the class after they learn about SRL may shed some more light on how to convince teachers that spending time teaching SRL in the class is an investment with great payoff later in the year.

The SRL instruction and SRL microanalysis measures supported teacher learning about argumentation. This demonstrates that learning about SRL gives learners opportunities to improve their learning and to be more proactive in their learning strategies. Building an awareness of SRL was an investment that will continue to generate opportunities for learning in the future. This is another case where the SRL microanalysis was an effective tool for "keeping an eye" on learner metacognition and cognitive processes so that they could learn how to learn.

Synthesis of Findings

The findings of these studies can be coalesced into self-awareness priorities and how those constructs will ultimately impact social justice by providing more opportunities to see alternative perspectives and learn the "rules" of knowledge validation in science. As a result, students develop a sense of agency and the belief that anything is possible because they can learn independently in any situation. When students who are underrepresented experience a broader opportunity structure, they gain cognitive capital, resulting in prosperous career avenues such as those in STEM fields. Continued study of teaching and learning in science across K–12 settings and in college is necessary to understand how we can change science instruction to include all students and to promote students who have been traditionally underrepresented. Self-awareness of learning can be the keystone for student understanding of how science disciplines operate and for identifying with the way scientists, technologists, mathematicians, and engineers work. Student self-awareness of learning is a transferrable skill that builds confidence in STEM learning so that students are free to pursue any field of interest without facing barriers due to lack of educational experience.

Priority 1: Motivation

No teacher can force a student to be motivated. Since motivation is internal, teachers can create environments where they can encourage reticent students through situational motivation. This type of motivation can be triggered by learning environments that are designed to have students understand the "rules" of the discipline and where students can navigate learning tasks with success. When teachers teach explicitly about how learning opens doors and demonstrate this in situational motivation, it ultimately encourages personal motivation. A self-awareness of successful strategies for learning, particularly in a field that is perceived to be unapproachable, such as science, can produce motivation to seek challenging learning opportunities.

Priority 2: Metacognition

Foundational to being self-aware of learning processes is an ability to both monitor thinking and control behaviors to keep strategies that work well and change strategies that do not work well. When students are aware of what they know and what they don't yet know, they are empowered to take learning into their own hands and become active learners. Instructors can help students be more metacognitive by purposefully modeling the ways they think in the field and by embedding prompts for students to move from a naïve orientation to a more expert one. Perhaps the biggest outcome of developing student metacognition is learners' independence in learning, which affords them the opportunity to be lifelong learners, continuously enriching their lives.

Priority 3: Self-Regulated Learning

Being a self-regulated learner is akin to having unlimited resources to learn. Self-regulated learners possess skills to build their knowledge meaningfully and the ability to change when they are not meeting their goals. A precursor to being a self-regulated learner is metacognition. If one cannot be aware of one's strategies, it is difficult to monitor and evaluate them. The theory behind self-regulated learning goes beyond metacognition to include affective features of learning, such as self-efficacy and goal orientation. Although self-regulated learning is a more complicated set of skills to teach than just metacognition, it is more inclusive of all learning processes and therefore a more powerful tool to give students. Teachers again have a large role in mentoring self-regulated learners by modeling and asking questions about students' processes before, during, and after they learn. Not only will the conversation between teachers and students about self-regulated learning processes help teachers support students in productive learning habits, it will also help students gradually become more aware of their learning.

Priority 4: Visualization

Since we are encouraging self-awareness of learning in a science context, visualization is a skill that is extremely useful across the sciences. Learning how scientists visualize the knowledge (through connections in concept mapping) opens opportunities for students to analyze their environment and increase identity and agency because they learn to think like geoscientists, or any other practitioner in another scientific discipline. In the same way that research experiences are supportive for those currently underrepresented in STEM fields, focusing on the ways scientists see the world can bridge the gap between nonscience-minded students and those who embrace science. Even those students who are not interested in pursuing a career in STEM will learn to appreciate a logical and systematic way of interpreting the world around them.

When students see that they can be successful at learning in all different contexts and subject matter, they become empowered to set goals, monitor their progress, and achieve their goals, reflecting on what worked and what didn't for the next time they face a similar challenge. In addition to the factors for encouraging people from underrepresented groups into STEM fields found by Tsui (2007)—bridge programs, mentoring, and exposure to research experiences—we hope to add building an awareness of learning science to this powerful list. Education is the practice of freedom because it is a democratic arena that builds one's knowledge and skills, which in turn opens opportunities and affords intelligent choices. However, education can only truly be a practice of freedom when all students have the ability to understand their own learning processes and are able to adapt when necessary.

ERIN PETERS-BURTON is Donna R. and David E. Sterling Endowed Professor in Science Education at George Mason University. Her research involves measuring and developing student scientific epistemologies and engaging underrepresented students in STEM education.

GIUSEPPINA KYSAR MATTIETTI is Assistant Professor in the Department of Atmospheric, Oceanic and Earth Sciences at George Mason University. She has previously worked as a teacher of math and science in high school and as a junior researcher at the National Institute of Geophysics, Rome, Italy.

References

Achieve. (2013). *Next generation science standards*. Retrieved from http://www.nextgenscience.org/.
Adelman, C. (2006). *The toolbox revisited: Paths to degree completion from high school through college*. Washington, DC: US Department of Education.
Akerson, V. L., & Abd-El-Khalick, F. (2003). Teaching elements of nature of science: A yearlong case study of a fourth-grade teacher. *Journal of Research in Science Teaching, 40*, 1025–1049.
American Association for the Advancement of Science. (1993). *Benchmarks for scientific literacy*. New York, NY: Oxford University Press.
Ames, C. (1992). Achievement goals and classroom motivational climate. In J. Meece & D. Schunk (Eds.), *Students' perceptions in the classroom* (pp. 327–348). Hillsdale, NJ: Erlbaum.
Angelo, T. A., & Cross, K. P. (1993). *Classroom assessment techniques: A handbook for college teachers* (2nd ed.). San Francisco, CA: Jossey-Bass.
Astin, A. W., & Astin, H. S. (1992). *Undergraduate science education: The impact of different college environments on the educational pipeline in the sciences*. Los Angeles: University of California, Graduate School of Education, Higher Education Research Institute.

Ausubel, D. P. (2000). *The acquisition and retention of knowledge: A cognitive view.* Dordrecht, The Netherlands: Kluwer Academic.

Bandura, A. (1986). *Social foundations of thought and action: A social cognitive theory.* Englewood Cliffs, NJ: Prentice-Hall.

Bianchini, J. A., & Colburn, A. (2000). Teaching the nature of science through inquiry to prospective elementary teachers: A tale of two researchers. *Journal of Research in Science Teaching, 37,* 177–209.

Brown, A. (1987). Metacognition, executive control, self-regulation, and other more mysterious mechanisms. In F. E. Weinert & R. H. Kluwe (Eds.), *Metacognition, motivation and understanding.* Hillsdale, NJ: Erlbaum.

Brownell, S. E., & Tanner, K. D. (2012). Barriers to faculty pedagogical change: Lack of training, time, incentives, and . . . tensions with professional identity? *Life Sciences Education, 11,* 339–346.

Chubin, D. E., May, G. S., and Babco, E. (2005). Diversifying the engineering workforce. *Journal of Engineering Education, 94*(1), 73–86.

Cleary, T. J. (2011). Shifting towards self-regulation microanalytic assessment: Historical overview, essential features, and implications for research and practice. In B. J. Zimmerman & D. H. Schunk (Eds.), *Handbook of self-regulation of learning and performance* (pp. 329–345). Abingdon, England: Routledge.

Cole, D., & Espinoza, A. (2008). Examining the academic success of Latino students in science technology engineering and mathematics (STEM) majors. *Journal of College Student Development, 49*(4), 285–300.

Corno, L. (1993). The best-laid plans: Modern conceptions of volition and educational research. *Educational Researcher, 22*(2), 14–22.

Costa, J., Calderia, H., Gallastegui, J. R., & Otero, J. (2000). An analysis of question asking on scientific texts explaining natural phenomena. *Journal of Research in Science Teaching, 37,* 602–614.

Crawford, T. (2005). What counts as knowing: Constructing a communicative repertoire for student demonstration of knowledge in science. *Journal of Research in Science Teaching, 42,* 139–165.

Deci, E. L. (1975). *Intrinsic motivation.* New York, NY: Plenum.

Duschl, R. A. (1990). *Restructuring science education: The importance of theories and their development.* New York, NY: Teachers College Press.

Flavell, J. H. (1987). Speculations about the nature and development of metacognition. In F. E. Weinert & R. H. Kluwe (Eds.), *Metacognition, motivation and understanding.* Hillsdale, NJ: Erlbaum.

Freire, P. (1970). *Pedagogy of the oppressed.* New York, NY: Continuum.

Fries-Britt, S., Younger, T., & Hall, W. (2010). Underrepresented minorities in physics: How perceptions of race and campus climate affect student outcomes. In T. E. Dancy (Ed.), *Managing diversity: (Re)visioning equity on college campuses* (pp. 181–198). New York, NY: Peter Lang.

Gess-Newsome, J. (2002). The use and impact of explicit instruction about the nature of science and science inquiry in an elementary science methods course. *Science & Education, 11,* 55–67.

Gobert, J., & Clement, J. (1999). Effects of student-generated diagrams versus student-generated summaries on conceptual understanding of causal and dynamic knowledge in plate tectonics. *Journal of Research in Science Teaching, 36*(1), 39–53.

Hadwin, A. F., & Oshige, M. (2011). Self-regulation, co-regulation, and socially-shared regulation: Exploring perspectives of social in self-regulated learning theory. *Teachers College Record, 113*(2), 240–264.

Hogan, K. (1999). Relating students' personal frameworks for science learning to their cognition in collaborative contexts. *Science Education, 83,* 1–32.

hooks, b. (1994). *Teaching to transgress: Education as the practice of freedom.* New York, NY: Taylor & Francis.

Hurtado, S., Cabrera, N. L., Lin, M. H., Arellano, L., & Espinosa, L. L. (2009). Diversifying science: Underrepresented student experiences in structured research programs. *Research in Higher Education, 50*(2), 189–214.

Khishfe, R., & Abd-El-Khalick, F. (2002). Influence of explicit and reflective versus implicit inquiry-oriented instruction on sixth graders' views of nature of science. *Journal of Research in Science Teaching, 39*, 551–578.

Locke, E. A., & Latham, G. P. (2002). Building a practically useful theory of goal setting and task motivation: A 35-year odyssey. *American Psychologist, 57*, 705–717.

Magntorn, O., & Hellden, G. (2005). Student-teachers' ability to read nature: Reflections on their learning in ecology. *International Journal of Science Education, 27*, 1229–1254.

Mattietti, G. K., & Peters-Burton, E. E. (2015). Student-centered visualization in general education introductory geoscience classes. In K. D. Finson & J. E. Pederson (Eds.), *Application of visual data in K-16 science classrooms* (pp. 333–355). Charlotte, NC: Information Age.

National Center for Educational Statistics. (2013). *The nation's report card*. Retrieved from http://nces.ed.gov/nationsreportcard.

National Research Council. (1996). *National science education standards*. Washington, DC: National Academies Press.

National Science Foundation. (2014). *STEM education data: Science and engineering indicators*. Retrieved from https://www.nsf.gov/nsb/sei/edTool/.

Perry, N. E., & Winne, P. H. (2006). Learning from learning kits: gStudy traces of students' self-regulated engagements with computerized content. *Educational Psychology Review, 18*, 211–228.

Peters-Burton, E. E., & Mattietti, G. K. (2011). Cognition and self-efficacy of stratigraphy and geologic time: Implications for improving undergraduate student performance in geological reasoning. *Journal of Geoscience Education, 59*, 163–174. doi:10.5408/1.3605042

Peters-Burton, E. E. (2015). The relationship of goal setting and teacher learning in professional development settings. In B. Higgins (Ed.), *Goal setting and personal development: Teachers' perspectives, behavioral strategies and impact on performance* (pp. 15–33). Hauppauge, NY: Nova.

Peters, E. E., & Kitsantas, A. (2010). The effect of nature of science metacognitive prompts on science students' content and nature of science knowledge, metacognition, and self-regulatory efficacy. *School Science and Mathematics, 110*, 382–396. doi:10.1111/j.1949-8594.2010.00050.x

President's Council of Advisors on Science and Technology. (2010). *Prepare and inspire: K–12 education in science, technology, engineering, and math (STEM) for America's future*. Washington, DC: Author.

Schunk, D. H. (1982). Effects of effort attributional feedback on children's perceived self-efficacy and achievement. *Journal of Educational Psychology, 74*, 548–556.

Schwartz, B. L., & Perfect, T. J. (2002). Introduction: Toward an applied metacognition. In T. J. Perfect & B. L. Schwartz (Eds.), *Applied metacognition* (pp. 1–11). Cambridge, England: Cambridge University Press.

Son, L. K., & Schwartz, B. L. (2002). The relation between metacognitive monitoring and control. In T. J. Perfect & B. L. Schwartz (Eds.), *Applied metacognition* (pp. 15–38). Cambridge, England: Cambridge University Press.

Thiede, K. W., & Dunlosky, J. (1999). Toward a general model of self-regulated study: An analysis of selection of items for study and self-paced study time. *Journal of Experimental Psychology: Learning, Memory, and Cognition, 25*, 1024–1037.

Tobias, S. (1990). They're not dumb, they're different. A new "tier of talent" for science. *Change, 22*, 11–30.

Tsui, L. (2007). Effective strategies to increase diversity in STEM fields: A review of research literature. *The Journal of Negro Education, 76*(4), 555–581.

Walls, L. (2012). Third grade African American students' views of the nature of science. *Journal of Research in Science Teaching, 49*(1), 1–37.

Weinert, F. E. (1987). Introduction and overview: Metacognition and motivation as determinants of effective learning and understanding. In F. E. Weinert & R. H. Kluwe (Eds.), *Metacognition, motivation and understanding,* (pp. 1–16). Hillsdale, NJ: Erlbaum.

Wetzstein, A., & Hacker, W. (2004). Reflective verbalization improves solutions: The effects of question-based reflection in design problem solving. *Applied Cognitive Psychology, 18,* 145–156.

Winne, P. H., & Jamieson-Noel, D. L. (2002). Exploring students' calibration of self-reports about study tactics and achievement. *Contemporary Educational Psychology, 27,* 551–572.

Zimmerman, B. J. (1989). A social cognitive view of self-regulated academic learning. *Journal of Educational Psychology, 81*(3), 329–339.

Zimmerman, B. J. (2000). Attaining self-regulation: A social cognitive perspective. In M. Boekaerts, P. R. Pintrich, & M. Zeidner (Eds.), *Handbook of self-regulation* (pp. 13–39). San Diego, CA: Academic.

Zimmerman, B. J., & Kitsantas, A. (1997). Developmental phases in self-regulation: Shifting from process to outcome goals. *Journal of Educational Psychology, 89,* 29–36.

Zimmerman, B. J., & Martinez-Pons, M. (1990). Student differences in self-regulated learning. *Journal of Educational Psychology, 82,* 51–59.

V.
Applied Classroom Practices and Social Justice

16 Reimagining the Student Evaluation: Using Democratic Frameworks in College Teaching and Learning

Phillis George

STUDENT EVALUATIONS ARE among the most widely accepted and common assessments for teaching (Boyer, 1990, 1996). Yet they rarely provide substantive feedback on ways to enhance teaching and learning (Hutchings, Huber, & Ciccone, 2011). This conceptual chapter seeks to address the issue by focusing its lens on the student evaluation and reimagining it through a unique framework that delineates critical strengths, weaknesses, opportunities, and threats (SWOT) to improve teaching and learning. The goal is to reenvision the student evaluation as more fluid and consistent, mutually beneficial and empowering for students and instructors, and seamlessly integrated into the fabric of the course. A tailored SWOT analysis is provided to outline instructional and/or course design (a) strengths that aid learning, (b) weaknesses that inhibit learning and inquiry, (c) opportunities for instructional and/or course improvement, and (d) threats to learning. The SWOT analysis is intended to serve as an effective and efficient democratizing tool. Specifically, it is meant to promote a decentralized and shared framework for students and instructors with hopes that they will continually assess and evaluate the quality of teaching and learning taking place while simultaneously taking ownership of quality improvement and maximization efforts.

A Review of the SWOT Analysis

Many may find the intentional pairing of the student evaluation and SWOT analysis an unconventional and rather curious combination. While uncommon in academic settings, the SWOT analysis is considered commonplace in other corporate and organizational settings. It is frequently used as an analytic and strategic planning tool to improve corporate efficiencies and overall effectiveness. Many credit the origins of the SWOT analysis to Albert S. Humphrey. Although initially trained as a chemical engineer, Humphrey (1926–2005) was widely known as an American corporate and management consultant whose specializations included cultural change and organizational development. While working at the Stanford Research Institute (now SRI International), Humphrey oversaw an extensive research project from 1960 to 1970 designed to explore and analyze organizational failures of Fortune 500 companies and to create effective and sustainable change strategies that improved corporate planning and management (Humphrey, 2005). As Humphrey described in a paper published in the December 2005 edition of the *SRI Alumni Association Newsletter*, corporate planning and restructuring served as the true foci of his research at that time:

> Corporate planning struck first at Du Pont in 1949, and by 1960 every Fortune 500 company had a Corporate Planner. But nearly all of these companies felt that Corporate Planning, aka Long Range Planning, was not working. They knew that managing change was difficult and often resulted in questionable compromises.
>
> From 1960 through 1969, we interviewed some 1100 organizations. A 250-item questionnaire was designed and completed by over 5,000 executives. Seven key findings led to the conclusion that the Chief Executive should be the Chief Planner and that his immediate functional directors should be the planning team. (pp. 7–8)

Although Humphrey's research focused on long-range planning or corporate planning, it prompted corporations to document inefficiencies and efficiencies by analyzing satisfactory, opportunistic, faulty, and threatening (SOFT) practices (Humphrey, 2005). SOFT analysis (as it was termed) was a precursor to the SWOT analysis, and the corresponding framework was one in which satisfactory practices were associated with being good in the present, whereas opportunistic practices were deemed good for the future. Conversely, faulty practices were associated with being bad in the present, and threatening practices were deemed bad for the future. Humphrey's SOFT analysis was modified during a long-range planning seminar in Zurich, Switzerland, in 1964. British delegates Lyndall Urwick and John Leslie Orr, founders of the management consultancy Urick Orr and Partners, introduced the concept of the SWOT analysis by changing the F in faults to W to signify organizational weaknesses (Brech, Thomson, & Wilson, 2010; Morrison, 2012).

As a result, Humphrey's SOFT analysis evolved to what is now generally considered the SWOT analysis. The basic SWOT framework differs slightly from the SOFT analysis because of the emphasis on key strengths (previously referenced as satisfactory practices), weaknesses, opportunities, and threats to organizational optimization. The SWOT analysis is commonly presented using a two-by-two matrix, which was introduced in 1982 by Heinz Weihrich (Morrison, 2012). The matrix is generally termed the SWOT matrix (see table 16.1).

Weihrich's SWOT matrix served as a critical tool for advancing Urwick and Orr's SWOT analysis (and ultimately Humphrey's SOFT analysis), as it streamlined the analytic framework, thereby increasing the relative ease with which others (i.e., beyond the corporate realm) could access and employ the SWOT analysis for their organizations and affiliate missions. This includes higher education and its core mission of teaching.

Teaching and Learning in Higher Education

Quality teaching (and learning) is a long-stated organizational goal in higher education (Barr & Tagg, 1995; Bok, 2006; Boyer, 1990, 1996). Colleges and universities of all types and sizes (i.e., public or private, two or four year, minority serving, graduate and professional degree granting, etc.) have employed a variety of pedagogies to encourage student learning and engagement (e.g., assessment, engaged pedagogy, teaching with data, and quantitative reasoning) (Gurung, Chick, & Haynie, 2009; Hutchings, Huber, & Ciccone, 2011; Kuh, 2008). As a collective (and with varying degrees of success), these pedagogies have shaped the twenty-first-century higher education landscape into one that is more amenable and susceptible to instructional change strategies. In the midst of this change, active learning has emerged as a signature pedagogy. Active learning can best be described as "a process whereby students engage in activities, such as reading, writing, discussion, or problem-solving, that promote analysis, synthesis, and evaluation of class content" (University of Michigan, 2015). Active learning strategies generally include (but are not limited to) peer learning, collaborative learning, cooperative learning, project-based learning, problem-solving, and simulations (Barkley, 2009; Bonwell & Eison, 1991; Mabrouk, 2007).

From a theoretical perspective, active learning originates from the constructivist school of thought, which posits that student learners construct and build their own understanding of content based on prior knowledge (Fosnot, 2005; Steffe & Gale, 1995). At its core, the constructivist paradigm is considered cognitive, metacognitive, evolving, and affective in nature and scope (Brooks & Brooks, 2001; Pelech & Pieper, 2010). Within the confines of the paradigm, the mere acknowledgement of a priori knowledge is extremely critical because it is a rightful rejection of tabula rasa (i.e., an assertion that students are blank slates). In essence, it is a strong and unequivocal affirmation that students are not void of relevant knowledge. Further, it is an explicit acceptance that a priori knowledge can be used to build and construct new and more complex funds of knowledge. These very simple yet profound acts of affirmation and acceptance coupled with the act of continuous knowledge construction are essential components of active learning. When students' prior learning and experiences are authentically acknowledged as valuable and applicable, they inevitably feel emboldened. Further, when given intentional opportunities, students become more engaged and take more ownership of the learning experience. These preferred outcomes of enhanced engagement and learning are primary across disciplines and span institutional types.

In addition to constructivist theory, it is important to note other contributing theories (i.e., relevancy and contextualization) that have helped and continue to shape the pedagogy of active learning. These theories fiercely promote and defend the idea that at all times "learning should be relevant and situated within a meaningful context" (Cambridge International Examinations, 2015). Historically, noted scholars and philosophers of the likes of Jean-Jacques Rousseau (1712–1778), John Dewey (1859–1952), and Maria Montessori (1870–1952) all advocated for the use of applied, real-world learning to stimulate students' understanding as well as their appreciation of exposed content.

The aforementioned theories combined with knowledge construction help ground the macro discussion of active learning and its direct (not to mention long-term) contributions to quality teaching (and learning)—for which the inherent emphasis is student engagement. As a collective, these theories give primacy to analytic, synthesis, and evaluative skills that promote understanding, growth, and mastery of thematic content. Furthermore (and perhaps most notably), they give impetus to an emerging teaching and learning framework that promotes learning as an applied and structured meaning-making process. From an organizational change perspective, the utilitarian goal of the framework is to illicit continuous and unmitigated opportunities for deep learning within the college classroom. At its core, the emergent framework equates deep learning with quality learning and presupposes both are manifestations of quality teaching. The framework also posits active learning as a transformational pedagogy that leads to quality teaching.

An Emergent and Democratic Framework for Teaching and Learning

Having established constructivism, relevancy, and context as a multifaceted, theoretical gateway to quality teaching, it is equally important to establish a conceptual foundation that clearly outlines and links critical change elements required for quality teaching and learning to take place. Active learning is one such element, and direct application is another. When these elements work in concert for a prolonged period, their shared and core nuclei become readily apparent within the emergent framework.

Active teaching requires some relinquishing of power by instructors to students, and applied learning demands that students increase ownership of the learning experience. The resulting dynamic is one in which democratic learning and/or student engagement becomes the strong, unalterable, and conceptual base on which quality teaching and learning are predicated. Restated, democracy is the conceptual core or nucleus. In so being, it serves as a key strategy when seeking to engage students and to incite deep, meaningful, continuous, and applied learning. As conceptual complements to the core, the terms "stakeholder" and "reciprocity" and/or "mutuality" emerge as equal contributors.

INSTRUCTORS   STUDENTS

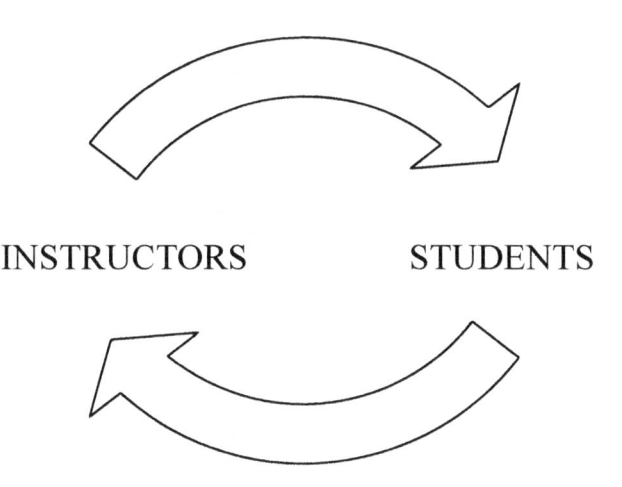

FIGURE 16.1.

In keeping with the works of Dewey (2000, 2012), democracy is broadly defined as an organizational system of governance in which all members or stakeholders are involved in making key management and strategic planning decisions. Contrary to one of Humphrey's suggestions stemming from his research with SRI International in the 1960s, the role of chief planner (i.e., the instructor) is expanded within the current framework to include all planning agents (i.e., the instructor and students). Doing so makes for a more democratic (and arguably more effective) instructional framework that acknowledges one simple yet undeniable truth: Students and instructors serve as coeducators and therefore key and equal stakeholders in the college classroom. As such, they engage in mutually beneficial and reciprocal exchanges of teaching and learning (figure 16.1), and they are both responsible for inciting deep as well as quality teaching and learning.

In keeping with the previous discussion of constructivism and related theories, the current framework emphasizes the term "coeducators" because of the inherent assumption that students are not void of prior knowledge. In fact, the knowledge they possess (however vast or limited) is deemed relevant and applicable and can, therefore, enhance the quality of teaching and learning taking place. The assumption applies to all types of classrooms (i.e., vocational, technical, undergraduate, graduate, professional, and continuing education) and teaching environments (i.e., face to face, online, and blended). Conceptually, what emerges is a democratic classroom that accesses and uses existing reservoirs of student knowledge or a priori knowledge while promoting student ownership of learning and encouraging the inevitable development of a posteriori knowledge (i.e., knowledge derived from learning taking place within the college classroom). With enhanced ownership comes increased accountability. As students actively and equitably contribute to exchanges of teaching and learning, they

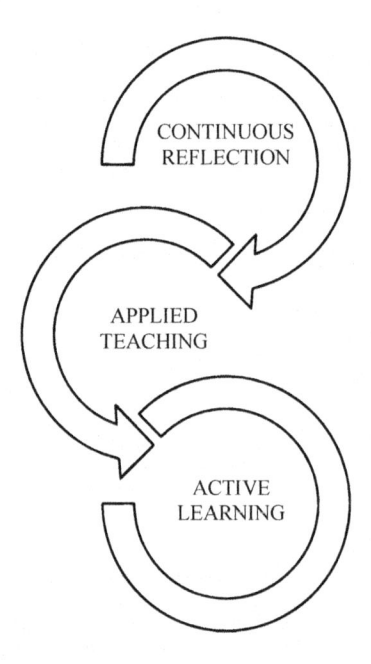

FIGURE 16.2.

take ownership of the quality (or lack thereof) and share in the action-oriented and meaning-making processes of learning—processes that should always and without hesitation include opportunities for critical reflection.

Reflective responsiveness is another active and necessary component of the emergent framework, as it heightens the levels of accountability concerning quality teaching and learning among students and instructors. Reflection may seem oddly placed in this conceptual framework, but it cannot and should not be understated. If democracy is the conceptual core or nucleus, then reflection is the active change agent. Through an active learning lens, reflection becomes an explosive catalyst for creating reflective student learners who use applied knowledge to enhance their understanding of thematic content and therefore the development of a posteriori knowledge. In essence, quality teaching and learning are both catalyzed by continuous reflection (figure 16.2). In the absence of reflective catalysis, the democratic classroom and instructional framework are rendered obsolete.

It is assumed that within a democratic classroom, active learning cannot transpire without quality teaching. Further, neither of the critical stakeholders is excluded from the iterative process of reflection. Instructors and students are both responsible for engaging in continuous reflection about the quality of teaching and learning taking place along with effective change strategies for improvement. As a result of these individual and collective actions, reflection is then seamlessly integrated into the core fabric of the democratic classroom.

Democratic Teaching and Learning with SWOT Analyses

The democratic framework for teaching and learning is without question a sharp contrast to more conventional instructional frameworks within higher education. Traditionally, instructors are the presumed subject-matter experts, and they play a singular and dominant role in the selection and delivery of course content (Saroyan & Amundsen, 2004). The democratic classroom effectively rejects this notion and embraces the idea of democratized inclusiveness in which all stakeholders (i.e., instructors and students) play an equally important and contributing role in the learning process.

When contemplating the notion of democratized inclusiveness, it is important to note Urwick and Orr's 1964 SWOT analysis serves as a unique instructional tool in this regard. Originally purposed for strategic management and long-range planning within the corporate realm, the SWOT analysis has immediate and direct applicability to course management and instructional improvement efforts (i.e., short and long term), especially within a democratic classroom. The signature two-by-two matrix offers a visual display and analytic frame that supports active teaching and learning via focused and continuous reflection on course strengths, weaknesses, opportunities, and threats. The following SWOT matrix along with its guiding questions (tables 16.2 and 16.3) jointly serve as a demonstrative, evaluative tool that is purposed for predetermined points during the semester (i.e., midsemester and end of semester), thus matching internal factors with external factors to improve course planning and implementation. Instructors and students are encouraged to employ the SWOT matrix as an applied and reflective tool to promote mutually beneficial and reciprocal exchanges of ideas that facilitate and/or enhance learning comprehension, course organization, and instructional design and delivery.

Within the matrix, internal factors are design attributes of the course (i.e., face to face, online, blended, cohort, noncohort, thematic content, textbooks, course schedule, etc.), and external factors are instructional attributes of the learning environment (i.e., employed pedagogy, classroom dynamics, diversity, learning styles, etc.). The positive components of

Table 16.1. The SWOT Matrix.

	POSITIVE	NEGATIVE
INTERNAL	STRENGTHS	WEAKNESSES
EXTERNAL	OPPORTUNITIES	THREATS

The SWOT Matrix matches internal factors (i.e., strengths and weaknesses) with external factors (i.e., opportunities and threats) to develop strategies that improve organizational planning and management. Internal factors are attributes of the organization, and external factors are attributes of the environment. The positive components of the matrix (i.e., strengths and opportunities) help organizations achieve their primary objective. The negative components (i.e., weaknesses and threats) are harmful to organizations and prohibit the realization of stated goals and objectives.

Table 16.2. Mid-Semester & End-of-Semester Course Evaluation.

	POSITIVE	NEGATIVE
INTERNAL	Course STRENGTHS	Course WEAKNESSES
EXTERNAL	OPPORTUNITIES for Course Improvement	THREATS to Student Learning

The SWOT Matrix is an alternative and more democratic, evaluation tool.

Table 16.3. Guiding Questions for Mid-Semester & End-of-Semester Course Evaluations.

	POSITIVE	NEGATIVE
INTERNAL	What are / were the course **STRENGTHS**? How did they enhance my learning, progress, and/or engagement? What helped me to be effective?	What are / were the course **WEAKNESSES**? How did they hinder my learning, progress, and/or engagement? What hindered my effectiveness?
EXTERNAL	Are / were there **OPPORTUNITIES** (i.e., potential or missed) to make the course more effective and to maximize my learning, progress, and / or engagement?	Are / were there **THREATS** that prohibited my learning and success? What stifled my learning, progress, and / or engagement?

The guiding questions are a supplement to the SWOT Matrix and help focus the reflective analysis on improvement areas in order to develop and implement short and long range, instructional change strategies.

the matrix (i.e., strengths and opportunities) help achieve the primary objective of deep and quality student learning. The negative components (i.e., weaknesses and threats) are harmful and prohibit the realization of the stated learning goals and objectives.

Discussion and Implications for Democratic Stakeholders

The SWOT matrix is a novel addition to critical and complex processes of assessing teaching and learning. Thus far (when describing the matrix), the term "tool" has been consistently used to invoke a sense of conceptual utility. The goal of any organization or structured unit that employs the matrix as an analytic, evaluative, or assessment tool is to promote change and sustained improvement. Within the corporate realm, the matrix is used quite extensively in short- and long-range planning and organizational management efforts (Johnson, Whittington, Angwin, Regner, & Scholes, 2014). Within higher education, the matrix can and should be used in a similar fashion to promote organizational change that leads to quality teaching and (by extension) deeper learning, understanding, and knowledge transfer.

Mindfulness concerning the SWOT matrix and its core utilitarian function is imperative, as the matrix is not a stand-alone tool but rather part of a much more extensive evaluative process intended to gauge true levels of student engagement and learning. In essence, the matrix can and should complement other learning assessment tools (e.g., reflective journals, portfolios, etc.). When using the matrix effectively, healthy by-products emerge, such as relevancy and contextualization, not to mention democratized inclusiveness, reciprocity, and mutuality among stakeholders (i.e., concerning the learning exchange). The aforementioned are unique and key components of college classrooms that uphold democracy as a chief learning principle. All learning stakeholders (i.e., instructors and students) are active contributors to this democratized dynamism. As they engage in the process, they elevate the role of the SWOT matrix from instructional assessment to democratic engagement, thereby promoting shared and reflective decision-making regarding course design and implementation.

The enclosed references to democracy and its learning derivatives (i.e., democratized inclusiveness and dynamism) are purposive. The SWOT matrix is a single tool that can be used at defined points during the academic semester, but the effective use of democracy as an instructional practice and learning principle has reverberating potential that extends beyond the formal course and well into a student's academic major or program of study. If faculty and instructors are strategically intentional in developing discipline-specific curricula and assessments that rely on more democratic frameworks (i.e., frameworks that acknowledge students and instructors as costakeholders and equal contributors to the learning process), then democratic teaching, student engagement, and learning can inherently become part of the academic core instead of the periphery. Faculty support and buy-in is needed, but once obtained, democratic frameworks and their operative tools (e.g., SWOT analyses) can become the academic norm instead of the noted exception.

Consider the latter a paradigm shift rather than a seismic overhaul of the current learning assessment and student engagement landscape. The current learning paradigm in higher education adheres to a very simple rationale. All student learners should show mastery and proficiency (i.e., relating to the academic course, discipline, or program of study) using prescribed learning styles and tools within prescribed learning environments. Usually, the referenced prescriptions are made by the disciplinary or program faculty and attending instructors. This is essentially termed "academic socialization" (Kolb, 1981). Although socialization is a resulting inevitability of program matriculation and degree completion (namely because of defined and program-specific learning outcomes), such marshaling invariably denies students with contrasting learning styles and learning environmental preferences of opportunities to fully engage in critical reflections and substantive analyses of thematic content.

As higher education seeks to accommodate a growing and more diverse student population (i.e., diverse in thought, experiences, abilities, and expectations), these socialized tendencies and socializing processes become highly problematic in the twenty-first century. In efforts to be more inclusive and responsive to the learning needs and preferences of diverse student stakeholders, swift and strategic actions are required—the least of which is the adoption and integration of evaluative and democratic engagement tools like the SWOT matrix into courses to assist with short- and long-range planning and improvement. If focusing on the very heights of strategic change and improvement, a total paradigm shift in learning and assessment is needed. The emergent paradigm must then be firmly rooted in the core theories and concepts of constructivism, relevancy, mutuality, reciprocity, and (perhaps most important) democratized inclusiveness.

Conclusion and Opportunities for Further Analysis

By virtue of the academic enterprise, teaching and learning are perennial goals within higher education. Teaching is in fact the primary means by which students are prepared to enter and make meaningful contributions to the twenty-first-century global workforce (Altbach, Gumport, & Berdahl, 2011). Although elevated in status in this regard (i.e., workforce training, development, and preparation), the tripartite mission of higher education is actually one of teaching, research, and service (Boyer, 1990, 1996). Research typically dominates the academic agenda primarily because of the ability to garner monies from public and private sectors. In an age of dwindling state and federal financial support, research increasingly plays a prominent role on the global higher education stage. Teaching and service usually fall in a distant second and third place within the academic enterprise. While service has always occurred in myriad forms (i.e., committee service at the institutional, school/college, departmental/program, and professional levels), the accepted methodologies of teaching have been severely restricted in instructional form and function along with approved evaluative and assessment tools.

Traditionally, college teaching has been evaluated via a combination of (a) peer observations conducted annually or biannually during a nine-month academic term (excluding summers and intercessions) and (b) course evaluations completed anonymously and usually electronically by students upon completion of a given course. Annual faculty activity reports encourage documentation of discernible improvements to instructional design and delivery—which often means (but is not limited to) the integration of diverse technologies into existing and preferred teaching strategies. Faculty incentives to deviate (even slightly) from these very dominant and pervasive evaluative methods have been virtually nonexistent. In fact, such deviation and exploratory risk taking have historically been punitive (i.e., particularly for nontenured faculty members) because of the unknown yield or instructional gains and what many perceive as an inordinate investment of time.

Seemingly (and arguably troublingly), viable and sustainable alternatives to the evaluation and assessment of college teaching (and by extension student learning) fall beyond the purview of "the 'academic rationalist conception' [which] is concerned chiefly with passing on the established [instructional] traditions . . . usually in the form of the established intellectual disciplines [and teaching and assessment methodologies]" (Vallance, 1985, p. 205). The enclosed framework and corresponding SWOT matrix are hereby presented as an emergent and critically responsive alternative. By virtue of their democratic design, the framework and matrix intentionally serve as a joint and counterrationalist narrative and assessment lens for the evaluation of college teaching and learning at individual course, programmatic, and institutional levels.

From an organizational management and change perspective, the aforementioned sense of counterrationalism is boldly posited as efficacious, healthy, and required in order to holistically and substantively respond to the learning needs and desires of an increasingly diverse collegiate body. Individually and collectively, the framework and matrix offer a much-needed and alternate academic rationalist conception of learning and assessment in the twenty-first century—one that accepts and promotes the use of democratic instructional strategies and active engagement tools to incite deep and quality learning. To clarify, the use of democratic frameworks and their affiliate tools (e.g., the SWOT matrix) refers to a single counterrationalist conception of learning and assessment. Additional counterrationalist conceptualizations are needed to (a) establish critical mass, (b) affirm their short- and long-term instructional utility, and (c) move the public opinion pendulum so that premiums are placed on alternate frameworks and they, in turn, can become the norm (i.e., the new and improved academic rationalist conception of teaching and learning in the twenty-first century).

PHILLIS GEORGE is Assistant Professor of Higher Education at the University of Mississippi. She specializes in higher education curriculum design, college teaching and learning, and service learning.

References

Altbach, P. G., Gumport, P. J., & Berdahl, R. O. (Eds.). (2011). *American higher education in the twenty-first century: Social, political and economic challenges* (3rd ed.). Baltimore, MD: Johns Hopkins University Press.
Barkley, E. F. (2009). *Student engagement techniques: A handbook for college faculty*. San Francisco, CA: Jossey-Bass.
Barr, R. B., & Tagg, J. (1995). From teaching to learning: A new paradigm in undergraduate education. *Change, 27*(6), 13–25. doi:10.1080/00091383.1995.10544672
Bok, D. (2006). *Our underachieving colleges: A candid look at how much students learn and why they should be learning more*. Princeton, NJ: Princeton University Press.

Bonwell, C. C., & Eison, J. A. (1991). *Active learning: Creating excitement in the classroom*. (ASHE-ERIC Higher Education Report No. 1). Washington, DC: George Washington University Clearinghouse on Higher Education.

Boyer, E. L. (1990). *Scholarship reconsidered: Priorities of the professoriate*. Princeton, NJ: Carnegie Foundation for the Advancement of Teaching.

Boyer, E. L. (1996). From scholarship reconsidered to scholarship assessed. *Quest, 48*(2), 129–139. doi:10.10 80/00336297.1996.10484184

Brech, E., Thomson, A., & Wilson, J. F. (2010). *Lyndall Urick, management pioneer: A biography*. Oxford, England: Oxford University Press. doi:10.1093/acprof:oso/9780199541966.001.0001

Brooks, J. G., & Brooks, M. G. (2001). *In search of understanding: The case for constructivist classrooms* (2nd ed.). Upper Saddle River, NJ: Prentice-Hall.

Cambridge International Examinations. (2015). *Active learning*. Retrieved from http://www.cie.org.uk/images/271174-active-learning.pdf.

Dewey, J. (2000). *Liberalism and social action: Great books in philosophy*. Amherst, NY: Prometheus Books.

Dewey, J., & Rogers, M. L. (2012). *The public and its problems: An essay in political inquiry*. University Park: Pennsylvania State University Press.

Fortune. (2015). *Fortune 500 2015*. Retrieved from http://fortune.com/fortune500/.

Fosnot, C. T. (Ed.). (2005). *Constructivism: Theory, perspective, and practice* (2nd ed.). New York: Teachers College Press.

Gurung, R., Chick, N. L., & Haynie, A. (2009). *Exploring signature pedagogies: Approaches to teaching disciplinary habits of mind*. Sterling, VA: Stylus.

Humphrey, A. S. (2005, December). SWOT analysis for management consulting. *SRI Alumni Association Newsletter*, 7–8. Retrieved from https://www.sri.com/sites/default/files/brochures/dec-05.pdf.

Hutchings, P., Huber, M. T., & Ciccone, A. (2011). *The scholarship of teaching and learning reconsidered: Institutional integration and impact*. San Francisco, CA: Jossey-Bass.

Johnson, G., Whittington, R., Angwin, D., Regner, P., & Scholes, K. (2014). *Exploring strategies: Text and cases* (10th rev. ed.). Harlow, England: Pearson Education.

Kolb, D. A. (1981). Disciplinary inquiry norms and student learning styles: Diverse pathways for growth. In A. Chickering (Ed.), *The modern American college* (pp. 232–255). San Francisco, CA: Jossey-Bass.

Kuh, G. (2008). *High-impact educational practices: What they are, who has access to them, and why they matter*. Washington, DC: Association of American Colleges and Universities.

Mabrouk, P. A. (2007). *Active learning: Models from the analytic sciences*. Washington, DC: American Chemistry Society. doi:10.1021/bk-2007-0970

Morrison, M. (2012, July 28). Re: History of the SWOT analysis [Online forum comment]. Retrieved from https://rapidbi.com/history-of-the-swot-analysis/#.VoCmNcArJaE.

Pelech, J., & Pieper, G. (2010). *Comprehensive handbook of constructivist teaching: From theory to practice*. Charlotte, NC: Information Age.

Saroyan, A., & Amundsen, C. (2004). *Rethinking teaching in higher education: From a course design workshop to a faculty development framework*. Sterling, VA: Stylus.

SRI International. (n.d.). *About SRI International*. Retrieved from https://www.sri.com/about.

Steffe, L. P., & Gale, J. (Eds.). (1995). *Constructivism in education*. Hillsdale, NJ: Erlbaum.

University of Michigan, Center for Research on Teaching and Learning. (2015). *Active learning*. Retrieved from http://www.crlt.umich.edu/tstrategies/tsal.

Vallance, E. (1985). Ways of knowing and curricular conceptions: Implications for program planning. In E. W. Eisner (Ed.), *Learning and teaching the ways of knowing* (84th Yearbook of the National Society for the Study of Education, Part II, pp. 199–217). Chicago, IL: University of Chicago Press.

17 Minding the Brain: Three Dimensions of Cognition in Social Justice Curriculum

Dan Glisczinski

"Dad! Dad! Check this out! This book is soooo good," insisted my seventeen-year-old, Flannery, who was engrossed in Malala Yousafzai's biography. "Dad, you have to read it! It's about this Pakistani girl my age who survived being shot by the Taliban just for going to school, and she's now leading an international movement for universal girls' education. She's completely amazing."

"Hmmm, sounds interesting, peach," I responded, mostly still distracted by my tasks at hand. "Tell me more about it when I get home. Gotta run." And I was out the door. On my way to school, I brainstormed pertinent metaphors that my students and I might consider in our study of how neurons fire together and wire together based on environmental stimuli. Disappointingly, I remained too preoccupied with my own curriculum designs to realize that school was already in session in my own home. My daughter was trying to introduce me to a remarkable social justice and education movement. And I mostly missed it.

By the time I returned home that evening, Flannery was at play practice, and so in the ritual of dinner, dishes, and homework, I went to sleep without asking her to tell me more about Nobel Peace Prize laureate Malala Yousafzai's story.

If meaningful learning deepens us by adding dimension to our awareness, relationship, and decision-making, my daughter's thinking about Malala Yousafzai had become multidimensional. Mine had not yet taken much shape.

Michael Posner's research on this very topic—paying attention—earned him President Obama's 2009 National Science Award. Posner's research informs us that attentive learning requires activity in three separate brain networks dedicated to (1) alerting, (2) orienting, and (3) executive cognition (Posner & Keele, 1968; Posner, 1981,

1994; Posner & Rothbart, 2005). The first network observes, the second associates, and the third constructs informed decision-making. These three separate networks function independently yet interconnectively. And together, they are the physiology from which all attention and dimension in learning develop.

Purpose

This essay invites scholars of teaching and learning to consider the roles that neuroscientific research on the brain's (1) alerting, (2) orienting, and (3) executive thinking networks play in structuring three-dimensional social justice curriculum. On a literal level, this chapter examines Yousafzai's work in relationship to the research on how neurons fire and wire to construct three cognitive networks dedicated to progressively advanced dimensions of awareness in education. On a figurative level, this discussion of the three dimensions of attentional networks is offered as a heuristic for visualizing and constructing a social justice curriculum that is concordant with research on how the human brain meaningfully—perhaps even transformatively—alerts, orients, and engages in executive thinking in the context of social justice education.

Learning's First Dimension: Alerting

Learning from My Experience

Sometimes social justice curriculum comes to us when we're least expecting it. That was my experience last week, as darkness fell earlier and I watched the season's first snowflakes cling to my office window. The snow reminded me of a season I love, which reminded me of the high-altitude film *Everest* I've been meaning to see. I checked our independent theater's listings for the stormy story that chronicled the epic Mount Everest climbing catastrophe from a couple decades back. I've been fascinated by the written accounts of those stories for going on twenty years. But no such luck, *Everest* had already moved on.

But what I discovered in the theater's listings was far from disappointing. Instead of seeing the familiar Everest story, I was treated to something novel and inviting; the theater was showing *He Named Me Malala*, the documentary about Malala Yousafzai's remarkable campaign for universal girls' and women's education. This is the movie version of the book Flannery was trying to tell me about months earlier. Yousafzai, not yet twenty years old, is the youngest-ever Nobel Peace Prize winner and the protagonist for one of the most important social justice movements of which I've become aware.

In the same way that a theater's illuminated and flashing marquee lights draw the eyes of passersby to consider the featured titles, the human brain's alerting network receives and transmits salient stimuli to adjacent meaning-associating neurons.

My alerting network was engaged, and I wanted to learn more.

Research Reminds Us

In a typical twenty-four hours, individuals are subject to tens of thousands of environmental stimuli, so the brain's millions of sensory neurons have adapted to be selective about which stimuli merit alerting. Those stimuli that succeed in alerting the human brain then prompt neurons to fire and wire in the right dorsolateral prefrontal cortex and the anterior cingulate cortex and stimulate frontal as well as parietal activity (Bush, Luu, & Posner, 2000; Medina, 2008; Zmigrod, Colzato, & Hommel, 2014).

The more frequently and successfully the alerting network is meaningfully aroused, the more robustly these neurons fire and wire together, constructing durable, highly efficient, well-myelinated axon pathways for electrical impulses to travel (Coyle, 2009; Doidge, 2007; Medina, 2008).

In a sense, a brain thus shaped by experience develops into a social justice mind. Its alerting network becomes active, perceptive, and robust in its attention to balances and imbalances of social justice. This is due to the brain's remarkable neuroplasticity—or the ability to grow, repurpose, and prune its form and function based on life experiences (Siegel, 2010; Sousa, 2011; Sylwester, 2005).

Scholarship of Teaching and Learning (SoTL) Social Justice Curriculum Implications

What then might such network-shaping experiences include? In the case of studying Malala Yousafzai's social justice movement for universal access to quality education for girls in Central Asia, this may sound like listening to her (2014) Nobel lecture. It might look like a viewing of a segment of Davis Guggenheim's (2015) documentary film *He Named Me Malala*. Or it might sound like a chapter read aloud from her (2013) book *I Am Malala: The Girl Who Stood Up for Education and Was Shot by the Taliban*. And, of course, it may combine or supersede these examples.

The essential takeaway of the brain's alerting dimension is that this network of neurons, axons, synapses, and dendrites is the essential first dimension of learning. Without it, no attention is captured, no networks become enriched by experience, and the second dimension—known as orienting—neither fires nor wires.

Learning's Second Dimension: Orienting

Learning from My Experience

As is typically the case with my own sleepy synapses, it takes repeated stimuli to alert my attentional networks. Yet, after being alerted to Malala Yousafzai's story—first by Flannery and then by the theater's digital marquee—my orienting network urged me to learn more.

So I checked the show times. Nope. Same time as Greta's middle-school saxophone concert. Then I googled Malala. The top hit: Malala Yousafzai's Nobel lecture.

I immediately watched. And listened. And watched again. And listened again. Here's how she began:

> Education is one of the blessings of life—and one of its necessities. That has been my experience during the seventeen years of my life. In my paradise home, Swat, I always loved learning and discovering new things. I remember when my friends and I would decorate our hands with henna on special occasions. And instead of drawing flowers and patterns, we would paint our hands with mathematical formulas and equations.
>
> We had a thirst for education; we had a thirst for education because our future was right there in that classroom. We would sit and learn and read together. We loved to wear neat and tidy school uniforms and we would sit there with big dreams in our eyes. We wanted to make our parents proud and prove that we could also excel in our studies and achieve those goals, which some people think only boys can.
>
> But things did not remain the same. When I was in Swat, which was a place of tourism and beauty, [it] suddenly changed into a place of terrorism. I was just ten when more than four hundred schools were destroyed. Women were flogged. People were killed. And our beautiful dreams turned into nightmares.
>
> Education went from being a right to being a crime. Girls were stopped from going to school. When my world suddenly changed, my priorities changed too. I had two options. One was to remain silent and wait to be killed. And the second was to speak up and then be killed. I chose the second one. I chose to speak up. (Yousafzai, 2014)

The Nobel laureate's prescience was remarkable. My attention was captivated. Something was taking place that I had to engage.

The Research on Orienting

Research indicates that after my alerting network was jump-started, my brain's orienting network—the second dimension of learning—was surging with electrical impulses relayed between the frontal eye fields, the temporoparietal lobe, and the pulvinar and superior colliculus (Medina, 2008; Petersen & Posner, 2012; Sara & Bouret, 2012). I was attempting to situate my perception to the context of Yousafzai's story. My social justice mind was active in seeking relationship and positionality between my existing synaptic schema and these powerful possibilities. Now all I needed was more guides from all sides.

SoTL Social Justice Curriculum Implications

Mindful that the engaged and positively problematized mind is poised for inquiry, the scholarly teachers and learners inside us will scaffold curriculum rich in exploration of relevant history, present, and possibility. Questions at this point in a curriculum learning cycle are poignant, as they enable learners' temporal brain regions to develop associations between prior learning and new stimuli (Glisczinski, 2011; Zull, 2002, 2011). These connections between one's existing schema and new stimuli play powerfully on intrinsic motivations to orient long-held meaning schemes and emerging perspectives.

What then might such experiences include? In the case of studying Yousafzai's social justice movement for universal access to quality education for girls and women in Central Asia, this may sound like brainstorming our associations of resonance and dissonance with Yousafzai's words. In what ways do we orient or associate our existing interests, cares, and values with Yousafzai's endeavors? Interacting in small groups of peers will enable modest risk and enable sociocognitive development—by orienting our own personal as well as our peers' collective associations in relationship to social justice opportunities. Such opportunities to explore emotionally competent stimuli in safe and collaborative environments are more powerful than forced, cold cognition, as emotional associations release positive neurotransmitters that construct powerful memories (Glisczinski, 2015; Immordino-Yang & Faeth, 2010; Medina, 2008; Willis, 2010).

Scaffolding active learning in the orienting dimension of cognition is pedagogically and andragogically essential for connecting our alerting network with our executive decision-making network. In the absence of such mindful learning, research suggests that little long-term learning—something on the order of 15 to 20 percent—results (Mazur & Redish, 2015; Medina, 2008).

Engaging the brain's orienting network of neurons, axons, synapses, and dendrites is essential in adding dimension to learning. Without it, minimal executive decision-making is procured, and the alerting network's marquee draws a disappointing audience for even the most profound of social justice opportunities.

The Brain's Executive Dimension

Learning from My Experience

Alerted by the mental marquee, invited in by the mind's orienting usher, I had arrived at the critical-thinking dimension that takes place in the brain's executive network. I turned pages of *I Am Malala*. My thoughts accelerated like meteorites as I viewed *He Named Me Malala*. And as happens when studying the examples of history's greatest exemplars, I, like many, decided that it would be unconscionable to not take action. Yousafzai provides such a dignified, compelling, and admirable example that my decision-making mind has concluded that I, we, must join in this work.

Skillfully, director Davis Guggenheim—of the Academy Award–winning *An Inconvenient Truth, Waiting for Superman, It Might Get Loud,* and related documentaries—designed smart curriculum by not only alerting and orienting audiences to recognize and better understand the beauty and tragedy that coexist in the world but by also sending audiences out of the theater ready to take committed, thoughtful action. As our executive decision-making networks analyze these inconvenient truths of widespread social and environmental injustice, we arrive at the conclusion that it is morally and intellectually unacceptable to wait for Superman to save the day.

So what was it about Yousafzai's words that so lit up my mind? My mind was loud with internal discourse. I had to sort things out.

Research Reminds Us

Research on the executive dimension of human attention identifies a network of problem-solving neurons connecting the basal ganglia and the prefrontal cortex. This network serves as the brain's planning, reasoning, and decision-making center (Petersen & Posner, 2012; Posner, 1994; Posner & Rothbart, 2005). The prefrontal cortex monitors the alerting and orienting networks and then makes executive decisions. It is analogous to the function of a book editor or a movie director that observes, interprets, and makes judgment calls to optimize meaning making and minimize minutia.

As follows from the principle of neuroplasticity, the brain that regularly engages in alerting, orienting, and executive decision-making develops dedicated, highly effective neuronal networks that enable subsequent similar cognition to take place at greater speed, with greater acuity and less effort (Begley, 2008; Doidge, 2007; Restak, 2009). In this sense, the brain that practices executive problem-solving in matters of social justice becomes an increasingly adept social justice mind.

This executive dimension of learning is, to our knowledge, perhaps one of the primary distinguishing factors of the human mind. With this neocortical function comes an important opportunity to direct our considerable thinking power to something greater than the pursuit of our own personal needs. In a broader sense, it is our executive network that enables us to analyze the greater good in working toward an ecology of human and cultural homeostasis. This might otherwise be understood as our collective moral and intellectual imperative to engage in social justice action.

SoTL Social Justice Curriculum Implications

So as researchers remind us that our brains are culturally modified by our life events—meaning our experiences reorganize our neuronal schema (Doidge, 2007; Draganski, 2004; Fisher & Heikkinen, 2010), scholars of teaching and learning seek out ways to help us connect our enduring values with executive thinking and action opportunities.

My own history of growing up with sisters as well as my experience of raising daughters has positioned me to be alerted, oriented, and engaged in critical thinking about educational equity for girls and women. Hence my own culturally modified mind drew me in to Malala Yousafzai's story. Similarly, my fascination in reading Mortenson's *Three Cups of Tea* (2007) and *Stones into Schools* (2009) have led me to respect and support the Central Asia Institute, which builds relationships and schools in remote communities in Afghanistan and Pakistan. The successes as well as struggles of these movements indeed provide me with mental models for ways that I can take informed action to increase social justice in education. As a result, I am alerted, oriented, and engaged in my role in advancing the good work of education as a social justice right and responsibility.

The SoTL social justice implications that follow from Posner's research indicate that constructing curriculum that students experience to be alerting is the starting point for three-dimensional learning. Secondly, providing associative, reflective, orienting activities invites student learning to move beyond noticing and into the more elaborative encoding of orienting, identifying with, and feeling compelled to further think critically on their relationship with the social justice topic. Finally, using one's prefrontal cortex to analyze various perspectives and action opportunities is the uniquely human mental operation that solidifies cognitive connections and neuronal networks that will guide socially just behavior. Such activities will range from discussions, debates, and position papers to other active learning pedagogies that invite neurons to fire together and wire together.

Conclusion

"Dad! Dad! Check this out! This book is soooo good," insisted my seventeen-year-old, Flannery, who was engrossed in Malala Yousafzai's biography. "Dad, you have to read it!" Indeed, Flannery was right. I must, if I am to engage in that fully human developmental continuum of learning about social justice exemplars and the lessons they teach us. Indeed, social justice education is all around us. It comes from the invitations of our children, our students, our peers, and our elders.

Thankfully, we as scholars of teaching and learning benefit from participating as cocontributors to that larger inquiry that seeks insights into the scientific evidence and artful application of life's curriculum. In this case, decades of research on the human attention system suggest an educative heuristic for alerting, orienting, and executive cognition. And as a starting point, we together consider activating these neuronal networks in pursuit of understanding Malala Yousafzai's remarkable contributions to social justice.

This discussion is humbly offered as a dialogue toward more fully understanding how patterns of human brain function might provide curricular insights into constructing multidimensional social justice education for a more educated, equitable, and peaceable humanity.

DAN GLISCZINSKI is Associate Professor in the Department of Education at the University of Minnesota Duluth. His research interests include the Scholarship of Teaching and Learning with emphasis on the neuro-education dynamics of perspective transformation.

References

Begley, S. (2008). *Train your mind, change your brain*. New York, NY: Ballantine.
Bush, G., Luu, P., & Posner, M. (2000). Cognitive and emotional influences in anterior cingulate cortex. *Trends in Cognitive Sciences, 4*(6), 215–222.
Chilcott, M. (Producer), & Guggenheim, D. (Director). (2011). *Waiting for Superman* [Motion Picture]. United States: Paramount.
Coyle, D. (2009). *The talent code: Greatness isn't born. It's grown*. New York, NY: Bantam.
Doidge, N. (2007). *The brain that changes itself: Stories of personal triumph from the frontiers of brain science*. New York, NY: Penguin.
Draganski, B. (2004). Neuroplasticity: Changes in grey matter induced by training. *Nature, 427*(6972), 311–312.
Fisher, K. W., & Heikkinen, K. (2010). The future of educational neuroscience. In D. Sousa (Ed.), *Mind, brain, and education: Neuroscience implications for the classroom* (pp. 248–269). Bloomington, IN: Solution Tree/Leading Edge.
Glisczinski, D. J. (2011). Lighting up the mind: Transforming learning through the applied scholarship of cognitive neuroscience. *The International Journal of Scholarship of Teaching and Learning, 5*(1), 1–11.
Glisczinski, D. J. (2015). Transforming our perspectives: Tattoos, the hippocampus, and premise reflection. *Journal of Transformative Learning, 3*(1), 22–27.
Immordino-Yang, M., & Faeth, M. (2010). The role of emotion and skilled intuition in learning. In D. Sousa (Ed.), *Mind, brain, and education: Neuroscience implications for the classroom* (pp. 67–83). Bloomington, IN: Solution Tree/Leading Edge.
Mazur, E., & Redish, J. (2015). Don't lecture me. *American Radioworks*. Retrieved from http://americanradioworks.publicradio.org/features/tomorrows-college/lectures/
Medina, J. (2008). *Brain rules: 12 principles for surviving and thriving at work, home, and school*. Seattle, WA: Pear Press.
Mortenson, G. (2009). *Stones into schools: Promoting peace with books, not bombs in Afghanistan and Pakistan*. New York, NY: Penguin.
Mortenson, G., & Relin, D. (2007). *Three cups of tea: One man's mission to provide peace—one school at a time*. New York, NY: Penguin.
Petersen, S., & Posner, M. (2012). The attention system of the human brain: 20 years after. *Annual Review of Neuroscience, 35*, 73–89.
Posner, M. (1981). Cognition and neural systems. *Cognition, 10*, 261–266.
Posner, M. (1994). Local and distributed processes in attentional orienting. *Behavioral and Brain Sciences, 17*(1), 78–79.
Posner, M. (2010). Neuroimaging tools and the evolution of educational neuroscience. In D. Sousa (Ed.), *Mind, brain, and education: Neuroscience implications for the classroom* (pp. 27–43). Bloomington, IN: Solution Tree/Leading Edge.
Posner, M., & Keele, S. (1968). On the genesis of abstract ideas. *Journal of Experimental Psychology, 77*, 353–363.
Posner, M., & Rothbart, M. (2005). Influencing brain networks: Implications for education. *Trends in Cognitive Sciences, 9*(3), 99–103.
Restak, R. (2009). *Think smart: A neuroscientist's prescription for improving your brain's performance*. New York, NY: Riverhead.
Sara, S., & Bouret, S. (2012). Orienting and reorienting: The locus coeruleus mediates cognition through arousal. *Neuron, 76*(1), 130–141.

Siegel, D. (2010). *Mindsight: The new science of personal transformation.* New York, NY: Bantam.

Sousa, D. (2010). *Mind, brain, and education: Neuroscience implications for the classroom.* Bloomington, IN: Solution Tree/Leading Edge.

Sousa, D. (2011). *How the brain learns.* Thousand Oaks, CA (pp.45–66). Corwin.

Sylwester, R. (2005). *How to explain a brain: An educator's handbook of brain terms and cognitive processes.* Thousand Oaks, CA: Corwin.

Willis, J. (2010). The current impact of neuroscience on teaching and learning. In D. Sousa (Ed.), *Mind, brain, and education: Neuroscience implications for the classroom* (pp. 45–66). Bloomington, IN: Solution Tree/Leading Edge.

Yousafzai, M. (2013). *I am Malala: The girl who stood up for education and was shot by the Taliban.* London, England: Orion.

Yousafzai, M. (2014). *Nobel lecture.* Retrieved from http://www.nobelprize.org/nobel_prizes/peace/laureates/2014/yousafzai-lecture_en.html.

Zmigrod, S., Colzato, L., & Hommel, B. (2014). Evidence for a role of the right dorsolateral prefrontal cortex in controlling stimulus-response integration: a trans cranial direct current stimulation (tDCS) study. *Brain Stimuli, 7*(4), 516–520.

Zull, J. (2002). *The art of changing the brain: Enriching the practice of teaching by exploring the biology of learning.* Sterling, VA: Stylus.

Zull, J. (2011). *From brain to mind: Using neuroscience to guide change in education.* Sterling, VA: Stylus.

18 Using Applied Learning to Engage with Social Justice: Lessons Learned from an Online Graduate Course in Social Justice

James M. DeVita

My philosophy of social justice includes (a) learning about the experiences and development of marginalized/targeted populations, (b) reflection about our own identities and privileges, and (c) a commitment to engage in work that attempts to improve the climate for those populations on campus and in society. This philosophy frames my teaching, particularly in Social Justice Topics in Education, a required course in the Higher Education Concentration of the Master's Degree in Education at the University of North Carolina in Wilmington (UNCW). The primary required project in the course asks students to engage with both of these social justice components. The goal of this project is to ensure that students have personal experiences that connect and ground theory with practical applications of social justice work. The hybrid format of the course provided a unique opportunity to encourage students to develop projects that were uniquely tailored to their personal and professional interests as well as their physical location. The use of online reflections to frame small-group discussions helped create a sense of community among students that helped with honest, open conversations on difficult topics.

Indeed, student reflections collected as part of the assessment process demonstrate several positive outcomes that support the transformative potential of applied learning in social justice education. Among those discussed below are (a) an appreciation for being challenged, (b) a desire to continue learning about social justice, and (c) enhanced outcomes from applied work with marginalized populations. This chapter is focused on lessons learned from the assessment of student learning and development in a graduate-level course on issues of diversity and social justice. In addition to describing the elements of the course and the ways in which applied learning was integrated into the course activities, this chapter includes a discussion of student outcomes and implications for instruction.

EDL 558: Social Justice Topics in Education

EDL 558: Social Justice Topics in Education is a master's-level course in the Department of Educational Leadership that is focused on the examination of topics related to privilege, marginalization, and social justice work in education. Readings, discussions, and activities focus on theoretical foundations that frame social justice work and practical implications for multiple stakeholder groups. The applied learning activities that are the focus of this chapter were initially developed under the support of a pedagogy grant funded by Exploring Transformative Education through Applied Learning (ETEAL) at the University of North Carolina-Wilmington (UNCW) (see http://www.uncw.edu/ETEAL/). The pedagogy grant provided me with a doctoral student who assisted in the development of applied activity guidelines, critical reflections, and assessment tools that were first implemented in the course in summer 2013.

EDL 558 is one of seven required core courses in UNCW's higher education concentration of the master's of education degree. However, the course is offered broadly, and graduate students from other UNCW degree programs and North Carolina universities have also completed the course. I have taught this course four times at UNCW: three times as an online course in summer session (five weeks) and once as a hybrid course during spring semester (fifteen weeks, five face-to-face meetings). Most students are current and aspiring administrators in higher education leadership and student affairs and represent a range of social identities (race/ethnicity, gender, age, ability, sexual orientation, etc.). The course is also offered as an elective in the College Teaching Certificate offered by the Department of Educational Leadership at UNCW.

Integration of Applied Learning Activities

As previously stated, my philosophy of social justice includes (a) learning about the experiences and development of marginalized/targeted populations, (b) reflection about our own identities and privileges, and (c) a commitment to engage in work that attempts to improve the climate for those populations on campus and in society. The use of applied learning activities allows me to require students to engage *with* the identities they study while learning about them through scholarship and online resources. Simply put, I see the requirement of applied activities as the means by which students become personally connected to what they are studying. The applied activities also allow me to address each of the learning goals for the course described above by framing the course activities with best practices of applied learning (ETEAL) and social justice.

ETEAL Framework

Because this project received funding support from ETEAL, a number of high-impact applied learning practices guide the applied learning activities in this course. ETEAL's model emphasizes four student learning outcomes: (a) articulating a clear intention for each learning activity, (b) applying knowledge from past and current course work, (c) critically reflecting on the experience as a whole, and (d) evaluating the impact this experience has on the student individually and will have on the community and discipline (see http://www.uncw.edu/eteal/). Course activities and assignments were designed to address the four student learning outcomes of ETEAL.

The development of the ETEAL framework was guided, in part, by the high-impact educational practices (HIEP) identified by the American Association of Colleges and Universities (AAC&U)—all of which related to the principles of applied learning in ETEAL. Researchers have identified positive relationships among HIEPs; students' self-reported personal, professional, and general gains; and exposure to "deep learning" experiences (Kuh & O'Donnell, 2013). Thus, I used three of the HIEPs identified by the AAC&U report in my preparation for EDL 558: (a) Diversity/Global Learning, (b) Service Learning, Community-Based Learning, and (c) Learning Communities (Kuh & O'Donnell, 2013). Course content is focused on issues of diversity and social justice (Diversity/Global Learning); the applied learning activities in the course are processed through critical reflections where issues in real-world application are compared to topics in course readings (Service Learning, Community-Based Learning); and small groups are used to support reflection and development among peers (Learning Communities) (Kuh & O'Donnell, 2013).

Social Justice Frameworks

One goal of the course is to encourage students to develop a passion for engaging in social justice work. Frameworks that have examined the development of social justice allies in higher education also help to shape the course and provide support for the implementation of applied learning activities. Conceptual frameworks about the development of social justice allies share several characteristics, notably the need for allies to acknowledge their own privilege and to be willing to participate in actions that can bring about change (Bishop, 2002; Broido, 2000; Edwards, 2006; Reason & Davis, 2005). Action is an important component in each framework of social justice ally development. Bishop (2002), Broido (2000), and Edwards (2006) also emphasized the role that emotions and personal relationships play in an ally's commitment to act on behalf of marginalized individuals. Personal experiences are important motivators for encouraging allies to engage in social justice work (Broido, 2000; Edwards, 2006). Thus, the applied learning activities that aligned with the HIEPs discussed above also need to provide students with exposure to the voices of the marginalized populations they sought to learn about. The integration of applied learning activities into a course on social justice provides students with exposure to personal experiences while also requiring them to engage in active learning.

Course Structure and Activities

Learning Modules

I organized the course into five learning modules that require participation in activities related to students' social justice projects and participation in an online video discussion board. Over the course of the semester, students identify and participate in five to ten (depending on the semester) interactive activities where they engage with members of the marginalized population they have chosen as the focus of their social justice project (SJP). Each student must complete an individual project and participate in a small-group video discussion board where they examine connections across course readings and engagement in their SJP. In addition to an initial reflection video post regarding the readings and module activities, students review their colleagues' posts and provide a follow-up response, also in a video format.

The course's first module includes two reflection activities that were designed to prepare students for engagement in course activities. The first reflection asks students to consider the challenges and opportunities associated with the SJP and how the project will enhance their personal and professional development (intention). The second reflection requires students to record and share a video where they discuss how they identify in multiple categories (race, ethnicity, gender, sexual orientation, etc.) and how those identities shape their work as professionals (critical reflection). Students are encouraged to select aspects of their identities they discussed as salient in these two reflections. Since identity salience is connected to engagement and development (Callero, 1985; Santee & Jackson, 1979), the focus on salient aspects of identity was intended to provide a more personal and meaningful connection to the topic explored in their SJP.

Applied Learning Activities

Students are required to complete numerous learning activities associated with their SJP, and through these I expose students to the population selected as the focus of their project. Student learning activities include reviewing TED Talks and other online resources (YouTube videos, webinars), visiting a museum or art exhibit, volunteering at a facility or event, attending a performance or play, participating in a peaceful protest or demonstration (e.g., #BlackLivesMatter), interviewing students or administrators, reviewing scholarship about their selected group, and touring campus from the perspective of another identity group. I also require a brief learning activity report (LAR) for each completed learning activity that details their learning activities and reflections about their attitudes and experiences while participating in the SJP. The LAR allows me to track the students' engagement in applied learning activities to ensure they have completed a diverse set of learning experiences that will provide them with meaningful exposure to their selected group.

The final project in the course is an alternative format presentation (e.g., video, website, art display, visual representation, poetry, or performance) that encourages students to be creative and innovative in their approach, to honor the voices and depictions of their participants/population, and to use technology. The alternative format presentation is intended to celebrate other forms of representing knowledge that more appropriately reflect the experiences of marginalized populations. Students have used unique formats for these projects, including a children's book, blog, play, video diary, and comic strip, among others.

Differentiation of Instruction

I require students to frame their social justice project as an exploration of intersecting identities from aspects that are meaningful to them yet different from how they identity (e.g., a white heterosexual may study black lesbian identities). Since students also select their learning activities, I designed the course for differentiated instruction for each student, thereby honoring and modeling alternative ways of learning and representing knowledge. Additionally, the online format of the course provides a unique opportunity to encourage students to develop projects that are uniquely tailored to their personal and professional interests as well as their physical location. Several students were located at internships throughout the United States during their enrollment in the last course, which exposed them to communities beyond those with which they would normally engage. One student was interning in Australia and was able to participate in a project connected to her local context.

Assessment of Student Learning

In order to avoid overtaxing students, course evaluation methods (i.e., assignments) are aligned with assessment strategies whenever possible. For example, module reflection videos are used as a primary assessment product to evaluate student learning. A pre-post design questionnaire with several open-ended questions is also required of all students in the course. Completion of the questionnaire is included in the course participation grade, and the post questionnaire includes a self-evaluation score that students assign to themselves (5 percent of overall grade). At the conclusion of every ETEAL course, student reflections are examined for evidence of intentionality, application of past and current course work to a problem or challenge, critical reflection, and evaluations of impact. The results of this assessment not only help UNCW evaluate the effectiveness of HIEPs but also provide individual instructors with detailed feedback about how they can improve their own practices. The discussion of lessons learned below is drawn from the assessment results from all four iterations of the course.

Lessons Learned: Student Perspectives

Students expressed a great deal of uncertainty at the start of the course. In the intention reflections completed during the first two modules, students identified concerns about the time they would need to commit to the SJP and discomfort with populations with which they were not familiar; however, by the end of the course, students expressed (a) an appreciation for being challenged, (b) growth and development through reflection, (c) a desire to continue learning more about social justice, and (d) enhanced outcomes from applied work with marginalized populations.

Challenge

Students consistently commented that the SJP challenged them to think critically about both the communities with whom they engaged and their own identities. One student simply said, "Thank you for pushing me and making me grow outside my comfort zone." Another student elaborated on her experience in the course and how it challenged her to grow: "I learned more about my individual power and privilege and how I myself have the responsibility not to waste opportunities like these to be a part of the change I have spoken about in previous modules. Quality not quantity was focused on and a more serious look at the topic was allowed because of the intimate group of players. I am even more hopeful in the possibility of real justice because the kids involved in my project are our future." Students expressed a level of gratitude for being pushed to step outside of their comfort zones to engage in applied learning activities within the course. This challenged students at times but provided meaningful opportunities for growth and a deeper appreciation of issues of diversity and social justice.

Reflection

The integration of reflection, particularly within small learning groups, was critical to students' learning and development and the creation of community. One student commented: "I think the biggest thing that has changed since this course is my knowledge and understanding of equity, diversity and inclusion. This course has forced me to think 'outside the box' and has challenged my previous opinion. It was very helpful to hear the responses of my classmates especially through video which I thought had a personal touch." Another student noted the value of reflections in the online course format: "I really enjoyed having the opportunity to write the learning activities to reflect on what I learned—it's not often that you get to have that kind of critical reflection. I was not looking forward to having to post YouTube videos at first, but I actually found it to be very beneficial to not only share opinions but to also get that engagement that you miss out on with an online course." Reflection was acknowledged as a tool for learning in the course. Video reflections were occasionally a source of frustration for students who were less skilled with technology early in the course; however, once that skill was mastered, most students appreciated the ability to engage with each other using video responses because of the personal connection.

Social Justice Action

Several students have commented on their engagement as a starting point for future learning and work with social justice topics, which was often attributed to the meaningful connections made through applied activities. One student noted: "I enjoyed the freedom to research a topic of my choice and present it in a fun creative way as I saw fit." The opportunity to explore a personalized topic provided students with a meaningful experience that was both personally and professionally impactful. One student noted in his reflection, "I can't even express here how thankful I am for the experience with the social justice project. I tried my best to put it into words in my report, but I'm so glad I have these final projects to share and use in both my personal and professional environments." The ability to apply what was learned in the SJP into professional contexts demonstrated students' depth of reflection and critical thinking. One student's enthusiasm about her work on the project exemplifies a commitment to future work: "The social justice project helped to bring the readings and discussions to life! I found that I enjoy being engaged with marginalized populations and look forward to working with other populations in the future! These experiences have shaped me and have now become a part of my new identity as a professional in the higher education field." The direct relationship between applied learning experiences and the students' development is evident.

Enhanced Learning

The applied learning activities integrated into the course were essential to students' development in working with diverse student populations (one of the goals of the course). One student discussed the effects of her engagement with LGBTQ populations during her SJP and associated applied learning experiences, a population with whom she had never worked before:

> Some of the things that I have learned during the course of this class have been a better definition of what social justice is and how we as professionals can better help serve marginalized populations. I have also become much more comfortable around LGBTQ persons. When I first started going to the LGBTQIA office at the start of the session, I was somewhat uncomfortable going in there because I was thinking that people would think that I was an LGBTQ person. I found that the more I went in and talked to people the more comfortable I became and by the time I finally got to interview [the LGBTQIA coordinator], I no longer had any kind of apprehension about going in and out. I also had a chance to visit a LGBTQ friendly church, which I normally would never have gone to but once I got there the people that I met were so kind and welcoming that they changed my paradigm of what a

church is supposed to be. Speaking to the ladies at the [community] center opened my eyes to the fact that bi-sexual women are far more victimized than either lesbian or straight females.

Another student spoke in depth about her exposure to individuals with physical disabilities. Her experience evoked powerful emotions that are represented in her reflection:

> I learned that having an abled body is a privilege. I learned that normal for everyone is different. I learned that we must really push ourselves beyond what we think is possible to grow more than we thought possible. The children in the class I volunteered in were a mix of abled body children and disabled bodied children with varying degrees of ability. Normal varied depending on what their body and mind would allow them to do. There were some children there that simply did not possess the ability to feed themselves and the possibility that they ever will is very bleak. There were children that have learned to walk in the last year and are still falling down every few steps but push themselves off the ground to keep going because of MS. There are other children who will never walk. Expectations are relative and yet there must be some to keep the children progressing. Growth is hard but worth it. I realize I need to relax and enjoy my own process of growing and becoming, I am too hard on myself sometimes. I am thankful for the experience with these children.

While not every student provided a reflection that mirrored the depth of those above, I was consistently impressed by the connections students made between their experiences in the SJP and their personal development. Student reflections confirmed an alignment with the expected outcomes of HIEPs previously discussed. Additionally, the core concepts of philosophies of social justice were also expressed in student reflections and demonstrate potential commitments to social justice work in the future.

Lessons Learned: Instructor Perspective

There are two lessons that I take away from including an applied learning element in this course: (a) to be comfortable with uncertainty, and (b) to encourage students to be creative despite their hesitations to do so (and yours). Although I provided guidelines and rubrics for students, each student worked independently on his/her/hir project in the course. Online video reflections and LARs allowed me to regularly check in with students to provide support and address questions or concerns, but the process also required trust that they were engaging in the ways they described. Because students were allowed to tailor both the focus and timeline for completing their work in the course, there was a lot of uncertainty about their engagement.

However, I found that my trust in the process has been rewarded each semester. Not only have students engaged in meaningful work, the creative projects shared as final representations of learning have been powerful and thoughtfully designed to honor the voices of their identity groups. That trust was difficult to grapple with in some instances. For example, students enrolled in the course and participating in the SJP, which was the central applied learning component, were located not only in other parts of North Carolina but in other parts of the world. One student was in Australia during the course—follow-up on specific learning activities with these students was virtually impossible. Yet my comfort with that uncertainty provided some really powerful learning opportunities that would not have been possible if this course was taught in person only—and only for students in the local area—and that encouraged students to engage in work within the context in which they were located at the time. Physical distance from students, particularly when examining topics that can be difficult and emotional, produced uncertainty for me as the instructor but also provided unique learning opportunities for students. One student discussed this in his final reflection: "This social just[ice] project was meaningful for me because the majority of the work I did for it took place in my home county. I learned a lot of valuable information and wish I could share it with education administrators in the county to try and make a change for the students and their perceptions of college." Without trust in the students and their engagement, I would not have been able to provide the meaningful learning experiences afforded from this applied experience.

The SJP also empowered students to take ownership over their work and to use art and technology to represent their learning. Students learned about social justice from direct engagement with marginalized populations and then represented learning in ways that honor the voices of those populations. One student noted the value of the creative approach: "I chose to write a poem because in doing so, it put me out of my comfort zone and challenged me in an even greater way." The creative, nontraditional approach allowed students to directly engage with their participants; one student stated, "The Social Justice Project enabled me to take what our readings provided and experience first hand experiences of a marginalized group."

Conclusion

The integration of applied learning in my graduate-level social justice course presented some challenges but provided many more opportunities for enhanced learning and development. Some students were challenged by the course format, which required a new approach to learning and engagement; however, by the end of the course most students agreed with what one student said in his final reflection: "This class is helpful and is a breath of fresh air from the typical boring lecture class." While feedback like this is encouraging, it was often a challenge to support students who resisted the applied approach to learning about social justice. I've come to really appreciate the ability to provide students with an experience that meets them at their level of professional and personal development. While challenging to manage and trust the students to do what they should be doing in their applied learning activities, the SJP and format within an online/hybrid course allowed them to tailor something that was unique to their interests and experiences and was actionable within their current setting—regardless of where that was located.

JAMES M. DEVITA is Assistant Professor of Educational Leadership and Program Coordinator for the MEd in Higher Education at the University of North Carolina-Wilmington. He currently teaches both master's- and doctoral-level courses that focus on student learning and development, social justice topics in education, and research methods.

References

Bishop, A. (2002). *Becoming an ally: Breaking the cycle of oppression in people*. London, England: Zed Books.
Broido, E. M. (2000). The development of social justice allies during college: A phenomenological investigation. *Journal of College Student Development, 41*(1), 3–18.
Callero, P. L. (1985). Role-identity salience. *Social Psychology Quarterly, 48*(3), 203–215.
Edwards, K. E. (2006). Aspiring social justice ally identity development: A conceptual model. *NASPA Journal, 43*(4), 39–60.
Kuh, G.D., & O'Donnell, K. (2013). *Ensuring quality & taking high-impact practices to scale*. Washington, DC: AAC&U. Retrieved from http://www.aacu.org/resources/high-impact-practices
Reason, R. D., & Davis, T. L. (2005). Antecedents, precursors, and concurrent concepts in the development of social justice attitudes and actions. In R. D. Reason, E. M. Broido, T. L. Davis, & N. J. Evans (Eds.), *Special issue: Developing social justice allies [New Directions for Student Services, 110]* (pp. 5–15). San Francisco, CA: Jossey-Bass.
Santee, R. T., & Jackson, S. E. (1979). Commitment to self-identification: A sociopsychological approach to personality. *Human Relations, 32*(2), 141–158.

SoTL: Next Steps Toward Social Justice

Delores D. Liston and Regina Rahimi

As we have stated throughout, the aims of this volume ultimately reside in an interest to encourage transformative education for students and teachers through the practice of SoTL. Our work demonstrates interest in recognizing that the work of teaching and learning ought to represent the idea that we are communities of learners (Huber & Hutchings, 2005), and the relationships among us are critical to the experiences of classroom practice (hooks, 1994, 2003; Freire, 1998, 1970/2006; Palmer, 2004). In seeking to examine relationships, it is necessary to recognize and appreciate the diverse perspectives that teachers and students bring to form this praxis. As stated in the introduction, this volume seeks to "solidify the foundation of social justice as fundamental to SoTL" and to "explicate and highlight the interlocking frameworks of SoTL."

As we noted in the introduction, SoTL has already made great strides in revolutionizing teaching practices in higher education through encouraging faculty to integrate scholarship and teaching. This step has gone a long way toward releasing the tension that faculty feel as they are pulled between their teaching duties and scholarship requirements. Through SoTL, teaching is enhanced while generating publications to satisfy requirements for promotion. But relieving this tension between scholarship and teaching in a "publish or perish" environment is not the sole revolution that SoTL promotes. SoTL, by redirecting attention to the scholarly aspects of both teaching and learning, simultaneously enacts an even more profound and dual revolution: transforming teachers and learners into *scholars* and thereby opening the door to the potential of SoTL to support education as transformation toward a more just society.

This text provides an opportunity to examine critical and transformative pedagogy from the perspective of our own classrooms in institutions of higher education.

Broadly examined across a number of disciplines, this text has explored practices that have helped students and faculty benefit from the examination of teaching and learning. Through examining diverse views and uses of SoTL, the authors in this volume have demonstrated provocative ways to improve conditions for communities of learners and honor the values of social justice.

The authors in this volume have shared incredible examples of their own classroom practices, self-reflections, and impact on social justice issues. Included are SoTL practices from the disciplines of sociology, nursing, education, health, anthropology, biology, and chemistry, among others, demonstrating that SoTL can prove meaningful for any content area.

As the authors in this volume have shared, as we examine our classroom practices, we can (and, we argue, ought to) examine how those practices help us all become more aware of community, more interested in our role as members within the community, and more appreciative of the diverse perspectives members of the community provide. Underscoring all of the chapters in this volume is the concept that we as scholars, through the study of our teaching and learning, can have a meaningful impact on all members of the community, including those of us who have been marginalized and underrepresented. The authors in this volume have in their own classrooms worked toward examining their practice with the goals of social responsibility and, in many cases, civic engagement.

The authors in this volume have reminded us that SoTL can address issues of inequality through raising awareness of classroom practices that may overtly or more subtly contribute to oppressive hegemony through the pedagogy offered in the class (Atkinson and Grether; Benton Lee and Kayongo-Male; Ross and Stevenson; Garno and Bennett). Through this volume, we are reminded that even our student evaluation instruments carry biases, and these can be examined to elevate practice, not just in the microenvironment of the classroom but in the larger campus community, and can ultimately generate greater equity throughout the profession of teaching (Atkinson and Grether; Lake and Rittschof). We are also reminded in this volume that teachers have roles as mentors and peers and those can be hugely significant as *agents of change* for marginalized groups (Benton Lee and Kayongo-Male). This text has presented multiple examples of the use of counternarratives or counterstories as a practice to disrupt harmful grand narratives that serve to hinder social justice (Farver and Dunn; Ross and Stevenson). The authors in this volume remind us that SoTL is a mechanism for the recognition of social and cultural capital within any and all disciplines of study.

We are also asked to consider the importance of self-reflection in the work of SoTL. Numerous chapters in this book touch on the importance of the relationship between student and teacher and how self-reflection can transform relationships and ideas. Relying on the canonical works of Freire, hooks, Palmer, and others, these authors have woven together theory and practice to provide powerful examples of transformative education (Moeller, Moeller, and Filler; Ross and Stevenson; Vaccaro, Chartelain, Croft, D'Aloisio, Hoyt, and Stevens).

Additionally, in fields of professional preparation, SoTL provides an opportunity for teachers and students to examine their professional dispositions on diversity and begin to develop conceptual frameworks for social justice within their professional lives, highlighting ways social justice consciousness can be integrated into professional values. Glisczinski has shared efforts in examining neuroscientific research and the ways in which cultural experiences impact the brain. Peters-Burton and Kysar-Mattietti examine how classroom practices can influence who chooses what fields of study and how we can work to address underrepresented populations. DeVita has shown how social justice issues and applied work with marginalized populations can be created and examined through online contexts.

The authors in this volume (e.g., especially Moeller, Moeller, and Filler; Meaney, Zimmermann, Martinez-Ramos, Lu, and McDonald; Garoutte) provide a number of transformative projects that involve civic engagement through service learning, community-based learning, asset-based community development, and study abroad. In a variety of fields, these practices have enormous impact on the learning experiences of both teachers and students, and the authors in this volume have articulated very well how these practices serve as the very definition of transformative education. Reminding us of the foundational principles of SoTL, that teaching and learning are public activities based on the principles of community, the authors have provided superb examples of how academic knowledge and the needs of the community can be connected. We are reminded by the authors that it is important to not only teach social justice but to engage in acts that support it. Willermet, Mueller, and Alm provide us with examples in which interdisciplinary study between social science and "hard" science can have a profound impact on teachers, learners, and community. Moeller, Moeller, and Filler; Meaney, Zimmermann, Martinez-Ramos, Lu, and McDonald; and Garoutte describe community-based programs that engage SoTL in projects where communities and learners come together to enhance the lives of those living in the community. Through examining their own cultural and social locations and through recognizing the importance of gaining the trust of the community, authors in this volume share their experiences with successful study-abroad programs and the way their work has served as a transformative experience for the community of learners. In short, this volume demonstrates how SoTL's threefold emphasis on (1) the integration of teaching and learning to make scholars, (2) the public nature of education generating discussion and involvement in scholarship, and (3) the recognition of the commons as central to establishing a community among scholars, produces and sustains an environment fertile with potential for transforming schooling from an "ivory tower" focused on solitary and individualistic advancement into communities of scholars invested in cooperatively advancing knowledge in order to make the world a better place for everyone.

This volume, with its truly diverse examples of SoTL and the potential for supporting social justice, is a reminder that we *do* have a responsibility to our community, our students, and ourselves to examine our work as it relates to the creation of a better world. They constitute samples of the potential of SoTL as a vehicle to authorize and legitimize scholarship with the intent of building greater social justice.

Nonetheless, to date, the work regarding SoTL and social justice remains limited. As we are reminded by the literature reviews presented in the first chapter of this volume, there is much that can be added to this work, and we hope to encourage others to continue to use SoTL as a vehicle for producing and sustaining social equality. Boldly stated, one intention of this volume is to bring attention to the fact that *every* discipline, when revolutionized through SoTL, can be used to generate and sustain a more socially just world.

The next steps anticipated by this volume include increasing understanding of how social justice initiatives in disciplines *not* included in this exemplary volume may be linked with SoTL as well as strengthening commitments to social justice within SoTL and various disciplines. This volume deliberately remained open to various interpretations of social justice. Next steps include expanding both the breadth and depth initiated in this dialogue. Future research may begin by broadening perspectives through including a greater variety of disciplines in the discourse, encouraging interdisciplinary research and discourse, and advancing international and global perspectives.

The primary disciplines represented in this volume are education, service learning, nursing and health, neuroscience, and interdisciplinary perspectives in anthropology, biology, and chemistry. Our hope is that future endeavors will be inspired from this volume, linking SoTL and social justice with arts-based disciplines, business and technology, social sciences, and other liberal arts disciplines. We believe SoTL is uniquely situated to support vigorous scholarship uniting disciplinary perspectives in the task of advancing knowledge, thus sustaining a commitment to social justice.

Greater depth may also be attained through vigorous interrogation of the assumptions and concepts related to SoTL and social justice, including application of values as well as engaging in complex analysis of social conflict and maintaining dialogue during contentious debates. The chapters in this volume initiated dialogue in SoTL, addressing a wide variety of contexts, including explorations of applied learning, civic engagement, asset-based development, and even student evaluations. The authors of these chapters explored diversity and postulated ways for teachers and learners to be change agents through developing self-awareness, critical reflection, and counternarratives. Fertile ground has been exposed for further development in these (and other) contexts, and future research may build on the concepts introduced here to clarify procedures and enable their application on a broader scale (interdisciplinary and internationally).

The field of SoTL is uniquely situated to keep teachers and learners simultaneously mindful of the micro and macro perspectives needed to advance knowledge and social justice. As teachers, SoTL reminds us to remain focused on the details of our learning environments (objectives and learning outcomes) as well as the ultimate purpose of conveying these details to our students (so that they may live meaningful lives) and promulgating our successes (and failures) in these endeavors through publications so that this experience will endure and enrich the explorations of others as they also pursue meaningful lives.

We maintain that the chapters in this volume unlock SoTL's potential to generate and sustain movements toward social justice. This volume establishes a strong foundation and constitutes our call to action to *all* scholars, for future SoTL work in *all* disciplines to grow the commons as locations where students not only learn the language of their fields but also come to view themselves as scholars committed to enhancing knowledge and understanding within and across disciplines in order to fulfill the promise of creating more socially just societies and communities.

References

Freire, P. (2006). *Pedagogy of the oppressed.* New York, NY: Continuum Press. (Original work published 1970.)

Freire, P. (1998). *Pedagogy of freedom: Ethics, democracy and civic courage.* Lanham, MD: Rowman & Littlefield.

hooks, b. (1994). *Teaching to transgress: Education as the practice of freedom.* New York, NY: Routledge.

hooks, b. (2003). *Teaching community: A pedagogy of hope.* New York, NY: Routledge.

Huber, M. T., & Hutchings, P. (2005). Surveying the scholarship of teaching and learning. In M. T. Huber & P. Hutchings (Eds.), *The advancement of learning: Building the teaching commons.* San Francisco, CA: Jossey-Bass.

Palmer, P. J. (2004). *A hidden wholeness: The journey toward an undivided life.* San Francisco, CA: Jossey-Bass.

Index

accountability, xiii, xvi, xxi, 51, 59, 86, 132, 301–302
activism, 120, 124, 126, 133–134, 136, 139, 165–166, 169–170, 237
activist, 51, 60, 124, 126–127, 138, 179; activist model, 53, 56–57
Adams, Maurianne, 3, 189, 235
advocacy, 53, 64, 78, 124, 126–127, 133–134, 137–138, 165, 210, 242, 267
agency, xxiii, 26, 51–53, 55, 58–59, 61–64, 66, 68–69, 102, 118
Asset-Based Community Development (ABCD), xxiv, 144–151, 153, 154–159, 330
asset mapping, 144–145, 148–149, 153–158
assets-based model, 56–57
attitude change, 244, 246, 255, 258, 266
awareness, 19, 153–155, 209–210, 253, 266; critical, 119; cultural, 237; faculty, xxv, 209; global, 211; historical, 19; self, xxv, 18, 244, 271–274, 276, 280, 283–284, 288–290, 331; social, 145, 153, 155, 158–159

Bandura, Albert, 98–99, 276, 280
Bell, Derrick, 179
best practices, xxiii, 11, 13, 17, 77, 132, 147, 281, 319
black feminist thought, xvii–xviii, xxvii, 193–194, 206, 239
Bourdieu, Pierre, 55, 65–66, 70
Boyer, Ernest, xii, xiv, xxvii, 17, 30, 46, 82, 96, 178, 188, 287, 299, 306, 308
bridging capital 53, 55, 64
Brookfield, Stephen D., 189–193, 196–197, 200, 202, 229–231, 233, 237–238
built environment, 107–111, 114–116

campus climate, 210, 214–215, 220
change agent, 53–54, 56, 58, 60, 62, 64, 65, 69, 86, 136, 302

change agent theory, 51
change in school relationship structures model, 56, 58
civic engagement, xxiii–xxiv, 10, 13, 99, 117, 121–129, 134, 139–140, 329–331
Cochran-Smith, Marilyn, 56–57, 77–78, 87, 93, 118, 205
Collins, Patricia Hill, xvii–xviii, 193–194, 229–233, 238
commons, xii–xvi, xx–xxi, 46, 79, 91, 205, 230, 330, 332
community, xiii, 8, 36, 94, 118; based community research (CBCR), 116; based learning (CBL), 85, 143–145, 147, 153, 157, 159–160, 320, 330; based participatory research (CBPR), 98–99, 101, 108; cultural wealth, 58, 66; of learners, xiii, xv, 242, 330
concept-map, 152, 165, 282–283
consensus, 36, 83, 124, 225
constructed environment, 99
constructivism, xvii, 300–301, 306; constructivist, 126, 283, 299–300
cooperation, 85, 144, 162, 168
counterstories, xxiv, 54, 73, 177–180, 183–184, 186–187, 329
critical pedagogy, xiv, 15–20, 56, 67, 126, 134, 164, 192–193, 202–208, 304; consciousness, xxi, 66, 89, 194, 196; literacy, 196; race feminism, xvii, 205; race theory (CRT), xvii, 54, 69; service learning (CSL), xxiv, 99; theory, xvii–xviii, xxiii, 193; thinking, 16, 137, 195, 200, 324
cultural values, 17, 20, 41, 63–64, 80, 100, 185, 192–195, 213, 314; background, 195, 201; capital, 53, 55, 66, 329; change, xvi, xxi, 165–166, 298; cross-cultural, 82, 84, 219; differences, 86, 88, 93; diversity, 78, 185,

333

241; immersion, 94; sensitivity, xxi, 211; wealth, 243
culturally relevant pedagogy, xx, 192
culturally responsive pedagogy (CRP), xix, xx
culturally responsive teaching, 77, 95, 134, 190–192
culturally subtractive schools, 52, 59
Cummins, Jim, 51, 58, 67–68, 119

deconstructionism, xvii–xviii
deficiency model, 146
Delpit, Lisa, 195, 199
democracy, xix, 8, 85, 273, 284, 300–302, 305
deontology, 4–5
detracking, 53, 67
Dewey, John, 89–90, 300–301
dialogue, 19, 28–29, 59, 66, 80, 82, 86, 93, 193, 218, 267, 315, 331
distributive justice, 3
diversity, xv–xvi, 19, 51, 70, 159, 178, 207–222, 241–247, 319–320, 330; committee, 209–210, 212–218; course, 80, 138, 203–204, 241, 249, 256, 259–261; cultural, 78, 185, 241; ethnic, 51, 146; issues, 209–211, 217–219, 227, 241, 246, 251, 255, 257, 262; in STEM, 271, 279, 281, 284, 289
dominant ideology, 53–54, 69, 233

empathy, 11–12, 120, 263
empowerment, xx, xxiv, 29, 51, 53, 66, 145, 148, 155
endorsement difficulty, 251–253, 269
entrenchment, 262–263
equal opportunity, 5, 69, 233
essentializing, xviii–xix
ethics of care, 6, 8, 12–13
exclusion, 149, 182, 233, 245

feminism, xvii–xviii, xxiii, 37
feminist, 6, 37, 194, 262
Freire, Paulo, xix, xxv, 51, 56, 66–68, 89, 92–93, 136, 164, 179, 192–193, 195–196, 229–230, 238, 272, 328–329

Gay, Geneva, xix, xx, 192, 195, 203
Gilligan, Carol, 6
Gilpin, Lorraine, xii–xiv, xxi, 78, 80, 90–91, 189

Giroux, Henry, 51, 67, 193
Greene, Maxine, 162, 165, 243, 267
grounded theory, 102, 120

hegemonic agents, 53, 62
heterosexual, 35, 40, 41, 230, 234–236, 322
homosexual, 244–245, 247, 250–251, 252–254, 261, 263
hooks, bell, xiv, xix, xx, xvii, 164–165, 178, 229, 238, 272, 328–329
Huber, Mary, xii–xv, 46, 178–179, 297, 299, 328
Hutchings, Pat, xii, xv–xvi, 3, 37, 46, 178, 187, 297, 299, 328

inclusion, xiv, 41, 51, 149, 198, 209, 211, 213, 221, 239, 323
inequity, xvii, 9, 25–26, 43, 164, 231, 234
interdisciplinary, xxi, 10, 163, 165–166, 210, 330–331
interpersonal relationships, 91
intersectionality, xviii, xix, 41, 180, 236, 239

Ladson-Billings, Gloria, xix–xx, 164, 179, 192, 194–197, 202–204
LGBTQ+, 210, 212, 244, 264, 324; gay, 40, 242–243, 254; lesbian, 40, 44, 225, 242–243, 322, 325
likert scale, 247, 249
Liston, Delores, xii–xiv, 78, 80, 90–91, 189, 228, 231, 235

marginalization, 194, 229, 234, 319
marginalized populations, xxvi, 37, 40–41, 145, 194, 214, 220, 318, 322–324, 326, 329, 330; groups, 194, 196, 214, 329; students, 54, 66
matrix of domination, 229–230, 232–233, 237–238
McKinney, Kathleen, xii, 36
metacognition, 272–274, 277–278, 289–290
microaggressions, 212, 214–215, 225
minority teachers, 50–52, 54–55, 62, 66, 70
model minority, 184–185
multicultural differences, xxi
multicultural education, 60, 242, 241, 247
multiculturalism, xxv, 241

narrative inquiry, 77, 97
narratives, 54, 69, 109, 127, 237; counter/competing, 54, 60; dominant/grand/master, xvii, 178–179, 187, 329; life history narratives, 11, 243; personal, 109–110, 127, 186, 190, 237, 243, 261; student, 100
Nieto, Sonia, 196, 242, 261

oppression, xviii, 5–9, 12, 29, 58, 66, 132, 164, 178–180, 193–194, 229–230, 233–234

Palmer, Parker, xix, 68, 328–329
participatory photo mapping (PPM), 108, 114, 116
partnership, 79, 82–87, 113, 123, 136–138
pedagogy, xii–xiii, 51, 125, 178–179, 190, 219, 242, 299–300; critical, xiv, xvii, 67, 72, 126, 140, 164, 171–172, 192–193; of discomfort, 8–9; feminist, 229; of the Oppressed, xix–xxi
personal relationships, 92, 320
philosophy, xvii, xxvi, 83, 149, 211, 318–319
postmodernism, xvii, 172
praxis, xii–xxi, 77, 82, 93–94, 140–141, 196, 267, 328
pretest-posttest, 157, 245–260
principle based ethics, 4–6
privilege, xviii, 35, 54, 69, 144, 159, 177–182, 229–235, 319–320; epistemic, xviii–xx

racism, 8, 19–20, 22–23, 28, 30, 54, 66, 179, 186–188, 233–234, 237
Rahimi, Regina, xxvi, 228, 231, 235
Rasch, 245, 248–249, 250, 260–261, 265, 267–269
reflection, 175, 302
resistance, 59, 148, 160, 165, 180, 204, 207, 230–231, 260
responsibility and accountability, xxi, 132

self-reflexivity, 53
service learning, xxii, 10–11, 77–80, 94–99, 139–140, 307, 320, 330
sexism, 234, 253, 262, 266sharing, xv–xvi, 3, 12, 82, 86, 90, 94, 118, 163, 229

Shulman, Lee, xvi, xviii, xx, 164–165, 228
snowball sampling, 103
social awareness, 145, 153, 155, 158–159
social change, 51, 60–61, 66–67, 71, 78, 88, 99, 120, 143, 152, 158–161, 235, 268
social cognitive theory (SCT), 98, 112, 114, 282
social imagination, 243
social justice education, xxiv, xxv, 14, 60, 178, 189–190, 192, 204, 228–230, 232, 234–235, 237, 239–240, 310, 315, 318
social location, xx, 35–36, 53–55, 62, 63, 69
social reconstructionism, 53, 56
social responsibility, 7, 10, 14, 117, 121–123, 125–131, 136, 139, 329
social systems, 6, 145
standards, 4, 15, 20, 39, 59, 78, 86, 200, 277
stereotypes, 48, 78, 143, 159, 177–178, 183–185, 225–226, 253, 255, 262
sustainability, 87, 94, 143, 146–147, 151–151, 163, 168, 171, 245, 263, 298, 307

teachers of minorities, xxiii, 50–51, 53, 55, 57, 59, 61, 61–65, 67, 69–71, 73
theoretical framework, 18, 55, 104, 216, 243
transformation, xii–xxix, 9, 36–37, 52–53, 63, 71–72, 88, 112, 180, 189, 191–193, 209, 235, 283, 300, 328
transformative education, xiv, xix, 13–14, 50, 52, 70–72, 96, 318–319, 328, 330
transgressive education, xiv, xix, xx, 229

Utilitarianism, 4–5, 12

Valenzuela, Angela, 52–53, 59, 242
validity, 39, 140, 149, 247–248, 260, 267, 269
Villegas, Ana Maria, 56–57, 59, 68, 77–78, 87, 118
virtue ethics, 4

wicked problems, 162–163, 165–166, 170–172

Yosso, Tara J., 54, 58, 66, 69, 179, 220